MW00658334

Stories That Need to Be Told 2020

Howard Isaac Williams
"Stuck On a Stranded Dog"
(p. 129

# Stories That Need to be Told 2020

Edited by

Jennifer Top

TULIPTREE
PUBLISHING, LLC

Cañon City, Colorado
ISBN: 978-1-7349690-2-3



The works in this volume, as in the Stories That Need to Be Told contest, were not segregated by category or genre; therefore, the stories may be fiction or nonfiction. As such the publisher makes no claims as to accuracy, and any similarities to true events are considered coincidence.

www.tuliptreepub.com

# Contents

GRAND PRIZE WINNER

# Red Bluff

## Michael Pearce

"I'M A MAN WHO LIVES BY A CODE," HE TELLS ME. "YOU ARE MY blood, and I couldn't look you in the eye if I didn't follow my own sacred creed. That's why I did what I did, and that's why I sit here in front of you with no remorse." We're looking at each other through two-inch-thick glass and talking on phones.

The last time we talked was six months ago, when Dad stayed at my place. He was all humble when he first showed up, asking if he could crash on the couch for a couple nights. I said nobody "crashes" anymore, not since, like, the seventies, but sure, he was welcome. The place had felt lonely since Karen left, and I hadn't been around Dad for more than an hour at a time since I was thirteen and he came up from Mexico for the Fourth of July. I didn't even mind cooking dinner for us, or letting him borrow a few twenties and lots of cigarettes. But Dad likes to hang out in bars with other drunks, and then he invites people over to drink some more and play cards and sleep on the floor. I came home one morning, after spending a heartbreaking night with Karen (she called it a "minor relapse" and told me not to call her anymore) and found Dad and a redhead with freckles and faded tattoos on her shoulders in my bed. The mattress stunk of urine (from which of them I don't know), and Dad got all miffed that I'd walked into my own bedroom and stumbled on them there. Then it turned out that one of his so-called buddies had made off with my old Martin D-18 that was hanging on the living room wall.

Now he sits there in his orange overalls and looks at me with snot-yellow eyes that radiate compassion and a compromised liver.

He speaks with calm, quiet concern, like he's a priest and I've come to confess. "Clarence," he says, "if you're worried about the guitar, I know how to get it back. I know where that dingleberry lives. I will retrieve it from him, dead or alive."

"You're not retrieving anything from anybody. You can't go where that dingleberry lives. You cannot leave this place."

"I'm here because I'm a man of my word. And if I say I will hunt down the weasel who stole your guitar, that means it will happen, period."

"Fuck the guitar, Dad," I say. "I mean, take the strings off it, stick your dick in the sound hole, and fuck it. Do you have a clue why you're here?"

He flashes his patronizing, asymmetrical smile and tells me to calm down.

"You're here because you shot somebody." He looks down at his fat, calloused fingers with their horn-like dirty nails and shrugs, just slightly. "And do you know who you shot?"

He gets this resolute, serious look on his face, his eyes narrowing and the sun-damaged, zit-scarred skin around his mouth scrunching up. "It was a matter of honor," he says. "Honor—it still counts for something, don't it?"

The person he shot to make good on his personal system of honor was my mother. Whom he hadn't seen in twelve years. Mom was in the hospital for surgery and radiation for the tumors in her lung, which made her a pretty easy target. A resident was in her room giving her a shot of Vicodin for the pain when Dad walked in, but he paid no notice to the resident. He walked right up to Mom and said, nervously, "Hello, Ariana, it's been a while, hasn't it." Then he unloaded a bullet into her chest and another into her head and walked out fast. Somebody saw him ride out of the parking lot on a '98 Yamaha Fazer, and somebody else found the crime weapon, a Glock 17 pistol, in the stairwell. They didn't find Dad for another two weeks.

* * *

SINCE MOM WAS ALREADY in the hospital when Dad opened fire on her, they instantly moved her into the ice-cold trauma surgery room and somehow kept her alive and stable. She was unconscious and her prognosis was somewhere deep in the realm of Forget It, but she was alive. The nurses on Mom's floor all know me, and Brandi called me at the house in Rancho Cordova where I was installing a security system and a safe for a shady rich guy named Frank Jankowski. "Clarence, it's about Ariana—some crazy motherfucker walked in and shot her."

I went straight over to Mercy General and sat with Mom in the recovery room. She looked about as dead as a live person can look. It didn't occur to me that the "crazy motherfucker" who shot her was, well, *my* crazy motherfucker. Then Darcy Gilchrist, the resident who eye-witnessed the whole thing, came into the room with two cops and started recounting all that had gone down, with a detailed description of the killer, and it hit me like a falling redwood. I mean, how many seventy-two-year-old men have a tattoo of Madonna on their neck?

An hour or so later Ellen arrived from Chico. I began filling her in on what had happened, but I guess I got a little hysterical because of Mom's condition but also because I was afraid that the killer must be Dad, yet I knew, I thought I knew, that Dad would never do something like that. Ellen is nothing if not calm and cool, and she had me start from the beginning and go over what I knew, and then she shrugged and said, "Yeah, it's gotta be Dad." She held Mom's hand and started talking to her, but Mom just lay there like a fresh corpse with her arms all bruisy from all the needles for all the shit they'd been pumping in and out of her over the past month.

I got a call from Chub, my assistant, and stepped out into the hall to direct him on the safe installation, which was not going well. The safe needed to be bolted into concrete in a retaining wall in Frank's basement. Chub's got this crunchy voice, achieved through decades of cigars and boilermakers, that in person sounds colorful, like an old country singer, but on the phone it sounds like a horse walking on broken glass. So, it took me a minute to decipher that he'd managed to scratch up the mahogany wainscoting that covers the retaining wall, and couldn't get the safe to inset flush with the wall, which was necessary so that it could be covered up with a golf trophy plaque to hide it from burglars and whatnot—"whatnot" including the law and Frank's wife Rita.

When I came back into the room Ellen had her iPad out and was sitting there next to Mom playing online poker. Half the professors at Chico State wear khaki pants and sweater vests or long dresses with colorful scarves; my sister belongs to the other half, who wear jeans and black leather jackets but still manage to look like dorky intellectuals. It's easy to tell when Ellen's playing online poker because (A) she's addicted and does it a lot, and (B) she starts talking to her opponents—who can't hear her—in very colorful language, like, "Why you little cunt-sniffing dwarf, you want me to think you have another diamond down there, don't you," or "Well guess what happens now, pizza face: I'm gonna cut off your penis and feed it to my goldfish." You had to hope that Mom really was for sure unconscious, because Ellen has no self-restraint when she's kicking men's asses online.

In the late afternoon a bald, sunburned head poked in from the hall and asked if it was okay to enter. I shrugged, and in walks this world-weary news guy with a gray goatee followed by a tiny woman holding a great big video camera. NewsGuy started asking us about the crime. I told him we didn't want to talk, but Ellen ignored me and answered his questions, and pretty soon I was chiming in too. The guy had seen the police report and knew Dad was the prime suspect, so we just filled in a little about our parents' marriage and divorce. We explained that we rarely heard from Dad, and that he very likely didn't have a place of residence. Then Ellen started holding forth about how the shooting was a metaphor for the way marriage has enslaved and maimed women, historically speaking—but NewsGuy told VideoLady to cut before Ellen had even gotten warmed up. VideoLady shot him a nasty scowl and stomped out of the room without a word. She wore silver boots.

* * *

I SAT THERE, IN the ongoing vigil of waiting for Mom to wake up from her coma, reading. Ellen teaches math and philosophy, and strange problems of epistemology fascinate her. So, when she was about to head back to Chico, she handed me this book, written by a colleague of hers. The book—or at least the first chapter—was about how we could all be zombies or robots, without any will or consciousness, and still eat and work and mate and even talk to each other and the world would look exactly the same. At the end of chapter 1 the author concluded that consciousness is not only unnecessary, it may actually be an illusion. For some reason that made me laugh out loud, and once I started laughing I kind of lost it and kept laughing and laughing until Mom suddenly spoke up.

"Oh, shut up!"

I looked over at her. Her eyes were still closed, but her face had a nasty frown on it.

"Mom, it's me—Clarence."

"I know who it is. You can't keep a girlfriend long enough to settle down and give me a grandchild, but you can sit there next to a murdered woman and laugh like there is no tomorrow. Well for some of us there is no tomorrow, so put that in your pipe and smoke it. Speaking of which, are you high on something, is that why you're so giggly?"

"Of course not, Mom, I—"

"Well then pull yourself together and start taking life a little more seriously. You were not put on this earth to live for the pleasure of the moment. You should be raising a family and going to church and . . . and . . ." She kind of trailed off, and then put her hand over her bandaged head and looked to be in serious pain.

"Mama!" I took her other hand and held it. "Should I call the nurse?"

She opened her eyes and breathed an impatient sigh. "And what about your sister and that Adonis gigolo of hers. Too selfish and full of themselves to have children. Life's just a big party for me me me, that's all that matters, isn't it?"

I didn't quite know what to say. First off, Mom never talked like that before. I mean, we knew that she wanted grandchildren, but she wouldn't have had a tirade about it. And she wouldn't have spoken so unkindly of Ellen and Danny. Also, the manner of her speech was disconcerting. The words came out very fast and kind of sloppy, like she was picking up handfuls of them and throwing them at the wall to watch them splatter. Even stranger was her accent. Mom is Dominican and speaks flawless English with an elegant Spanish lilt. But somehow her speech had shifted to a peculiar cadence that, if I'd had to put a name on it, I would have called Irish. I thought, maybe she is some sort of robot zombie, and now she's been reprogrammed to be a cranky Irish lady. The doctors said the bullet in her head went into her frontal lobe and damaged it in a way that the executive function there can't communicate with her emotional centers. Ellen's book tells about a guy a hundred and fifty years ago who had an iron rod blast through his head. He survived—in fact he never even passed out—but a bunch of his frontal lobe was blown out and his personality changed big-time. Mom still seemed mostly like Mom, only maybe a less inhibited, Irish-ish version of herself.

While I was pondering all of this, she lapsed back into a coma. A doctor came by and said it was a good sign that she'd spoken with some coherence and awareness. I went back to Ellen's book.

THE COPS FOUND DAD camping in the Yolla Bolly Wilderness Area up on the Eel River. He'd ridden his motorcycle in from the trailhead and set up a two-man tent there on the middle fork of the Eel. The only reason he was discovered is that he was bathing naked in a river eddy, and this annoyed a group of young women who were camping just downstream. Then they saw the motorcycle parked next to his tent, and that really ticked them off. When they hiked back out to the trailhead they complained to a ranger. The ranger, three sheriff's deputies from Red Bluff, and a couple state police ambushed Dad in the tent at dawn. He surrendered without a struggle.

It was on the news: Dad getting out of the police car in Red Bluff and being escorted into the station. At some point NewsGuy managed to get his microphone in Dad's face, and Dad started carrying on about how he had every right to walk naked in God's wilderness and those girls wouldn't have complained if it'd been Brad Pitt or Leonardo DiWhatever prancing around in their birthday suit. You could hear an off-camera cop telling Dad that being charged with going naked was the least of his worries, and then you saw Dad's face get very serious, and sad, and suddenly he looked like an old man.

THE DAY NEWSGUY INTERVIEWED us, Channel 7 ran it on the evening news. The video showed close-ups of Ellen and me talking about Dad, with cutaways to Mom's inert, sagging face. Somehow it captured the oddness and discord of our family, and it made me cringe. Over the next week or so there was more coverage of the event, including some of VideoLady's footage on the national news, as well as a couple articles in the paper. Then they lost interest, which was okay with me. When Dad was arrested there was another mini media flurry for a couple days, then nothing.

Now there's a new story out. It seems Dad's been talking. He claims that he shot Mom as an act of mercy, because of her grave illness. At first nobody paid attention to a crazy guy giving a bad excuse for shooting an innocent person he hadn't even talked to in over a decade. But then Aunt Jasmine, Dad's sister, told somebody she remembered hearing Mom and Dad say something years ago about an agreement they'd made to not let each other suffer unnecessarily. Somehow NewsGuy got wind of this and went and interviewed Jasmine and then went to Red Bluff and talked to Dad, who said he and Mom had a written pact that if one of them was dying of some awful disease, the other would put them out of their misery. This threw a new angle on the case, and more media jumped on it. Legal scholars and clergy and then politicians weighed in on the morality of euthanasia, and the whole thing got bumped up to network news again. Mom is still in a coma and unavailable for comment.

* * *

THE NEXT TIME MOM woke up she thought she was in Santo Domingo. It was a hot day in Sacramento and the hospital air conditioning was misbehaving, and she started stirring around in her bed and pushing the covers off, and then she thought that my sister Ellen was her own mother, and she looked at her and said, "Mami, please, let's go over to the Malecón and buy cashews and sugarcane." She said it in Spanish; then, later, in a mixture of Spanish and English. But since everyone around her was speaking English she ended up speaking English, but still insisting she was in Santo Domingo, which is where she grew up. Her Spanish accent was the thickest I've ever heard it—no hint of Irish.

Her mouth was dry and sticky, which made it hard to talk. We offered her water, but she had trouble drinking it. Brandi, the nurse who had called me when Mom was shot, happened to be in there and said patients often have trouble drinking water. She went and got some ice, and showed us how to chip it into little pieces that Mom could suck on. Mom seemed to like that.

Though her chest had a bullet and a thicket of tumors in it, she was breathing okay, and once she managed to wet her mouth with melted ice she spoke with real force and some of her old authority, though much of what she said was a bit strange. At first she was requesting fried *plátinos* and cut sugarcane from the Haitian vendors on the Santo Domingo boardwalk. Next thing she was talking about how her uncle's brother-in-law had disappeared and she was sure Trujillo had killed him. Trujillo, the Dominican dictator, died in 1961, when Mom was nine. She went on about disparate pieces of her past—the nuns at the grammar school she went to, the match factory where her father was foreman, her friend Luisa's famous pranks. Much of it was hard to follow, but she kept coming back to food. The doctor said she could nibble small bits of things. She'd been asking for Dominican comfort food, but when we gave her bites of *plátino* and yuca, she said they tasted like shit and spat them out. She did eat a few small chunks from the mango I brought. Mostly she sucked on ice chips.

* * *

ALL THE HUBBUB AROUND Mom and Dad is like jet fuel to Ellen's intellectual preoccupations. There's the question of the ethics of mercy killing, the stuff they talk about on TV: When is it okay to put a suffering person out of their misery? If a person is already dying, albeit badly, shouldn't you just try to alleviate the pain and let nature run its course? Is there a threshold of suffering that makes mercy killing an act of grace? If two people make a contract, each to put the other out of their misery, should that count for anything?

We're sitting on opposite sides of Mom's bed. Ellen says she's more interested in deeper philosophical questions about free will. If Mom is talking oddly and not acting like herself because of a brain injury, has she lost some of the ability to freely choose her actions? What if she went out and robbed a 7-Eleven or strangled a baby—should she be held fully responsible for what she did? I don't think Mom's personality has changed all that much. Neither does Ellen, but she likes to ponder such questions, maybe because they're difficult and you can get students to argue on and on about them, which is a good thing on a slow day in Philosophy 101. But she says these issues relate to the current situation: maybe when Mom and Dad made their contract, they wanted it to be ironclad because later, when one of them was sick and suffering, their brain would be too scrambled to make a good decision.

Ellen is here more than I am because she's only teaching Tuesdays and Thursdays this semester and has time on her hands. I get over here whenever I can, like when I'm pretty sure Chub can handle the work alone for a couple hours—we're securitizing an electronics warehouse now, though yesterday we had to go back to Frank Jankowski's place to reinforce his basement door. Sometimes Ellen and I overlap and keep vigil together. Which often means that Ellen holds forth about philosophical questions related to death and dying. Danny, her boyfriend, says she lives too much inside her head. They met when Danny took her Intro to Philosophy class. He dropped out of the class—he didn't know it would be so dry and logical. He expected more Eastern thought, more Buddhism. Danny's a tennis pro.

I always thought I was as smart as Ellen, but now she gets paid to think about deep epistemological questions and I sell and install security systems. I still like to think I'm as smart as her, but maybe in a different way. I mean, I can beat her at online poker, or offline poker for that matter. I quit college because I couldn't stand the kind of thinking that she revels in. I always felt silly talking about hypothetical shit that doesn't happen. To me that's like floating in some parallel universe where there's nothing you can smell or touch and no way to know if your answers are right in any useful sense. Most of my time at college felt confusing and unreal, like a dream. I prefer results you can rap your knuckles on, like a safe that fits flush in discreet mahogany wall paneling where you can hang a golf plaque over it so some wealthy crook doesn't have to worry about the law or his wife finding all the cash and white powder and compromising photos and foreign bank account numbers he's squirreling away.

AMONG THE FEW THINGS Dad had with him when he was arrested was a key to a storage room he rents in Lemon Hill, outside of Sacramento. He's had it for years, and sometimes he's even camped in there for short spells, until the manager boots him out. He has all his fishing gear there, along with an immaculate antique Indian motorcycle that he claims he could sell on eBay for a hundred thousand dollars, several old tube TVs, a couch, a table, a rusted steel file cabinet from the 1930s, a suit for job interviews that never happen, the mounted head of an elk that he claims to have shot even though the engraving plate says otherwise, a butcher's band saw, a 1973 Dodge Slant-6 engine, and piles and piles of junk, some of it in boxes, some of it in piles and piles. Since Dad hasn't had a real address for years, he gave the storage people mine, and they got in touch with me when the rent was three months overdue.

I told the Red Bluff police about the storage unit, and asked for the key. They gave it to me but said I couldn't go there without the Sacramento police, who would want to come search the place. So, I drove out there yesterday morning and met up with two Sac cops who went through Dad's stuff in a haphazard sort of way. I mean come on, they already had what they needed to convict him. I guess they were looking for a note or something that might show premeditation or some evil motive, like an insurance policy on Mom. All they found were a couple ounces of ancient marijuana and some prescription pills, long expired, whose name none of us recognized.

After they left I went and paid the manager what Dad owed him, plus another three months' rent. Then I walked back over to the storage room and poked around through the old man's junk. Eventually I flopped down on the couch with a magazine called *Hog Huntin'* and read an article about shooting wild boars from a helicopter with a crossbow. It wasn't as fun as the book about people being zombies with no consciousness, but it took my mind off the miserable mess that is my family, at least for a little while. I could hear the guy next door watching a Raiders game on TV, cheering and groaning as though he was with a bunch of buddies. It occurred to me that I had seen several of the storage units with their aluminum garage doors rolled up and a single guy in each one, sitting on a couch or easy chair and holding a beer in front of a TV plugged into the overhead light socket, no doubt enjoying a respite from family life.

IT WAS OVER MY objections that Ellen told Mom who it was tried to kill her. We were standing at the foot of Mom's hospital bed. Mom's face looked limp, almost viscous, like most of the muscles and bones had walked off during the night, and gravity had taken over. Her head was tilted to the right side, and her lips, once full and sensuous and expressive, sagged down toward the bed, with a string of drool stretching from the corner of her mouth to a puddle on the sheet. Even her nose was in gravity's thrall, drooping down the right side of her face. "She struggles just to stay conscious," I said to Ellen. "She's fighting pain, disease, death. When she is conscious, she's drugged to a near-stupor. She doesn't need any confusing or stressful information."

Ellen's eyes danced upward as she spoke in that cool, all-knowing tone that must sound like the voice of God, or at least Aristotle or Descartes, to her students. "We have no right to withhold information from her. She's a thinking, feeling adult with the right to be the agent of her own destiny."

"Please, Ellen, it can't do her any good to tell her right now. She has no memory of the event, and that's a good thing."

"What's all the noise about?" Mom's face had somehow pulled itself together and was once again cranking out fairly normal speech. "What do you have to say to me?"

So, Ellen told her everything. Mom just stared at her, and her face got droopy again, and I thought she was going to melt back into a coma. Until she spoke up.

"Oscar Wolf walked in here and pointed a gun at me and pulled the trigger."

"Yes, Mom."

"Holy shit." I thought I heard some of that Irish lilt in her voice.

"One of the bullets entered the front of your brain. That's the injury we're most worried about. It's not clear how much damage it did."

"It made a hole in my head. I would call that severe damage."

"We're wondering how much it changed you—altered who you are."

"That's ridiculous. I am me."

Ellen shrugged, and our dad's lopsided smile crossed her face. "We don't really know. Your emotions, your thought processes, they seem different."

"You stop that," Mom said. She raised her voice. "Don't say these things to me." She began to weep, quietly, and I felt sad to see her that way, and angry at Ellen.

"That's enough of this for now," I said. "Mom, you're still you, and we're going to help you get better. Right, Ellen?"

Ellen's eyes looked upward again, and she spoke slowly. "We're all changing from moment to moment. The idea that any person is some sort of coherent, immutable soul is an illusion. A brain injury just makes for a more obvious disjunction from one point in time to the OUCH!" The OUCH was me kicking Ellen's shin.

There was silence, and then Mom spoke. "I'm not sure about anything anymore. Oscar Wolf tried to kill me."

Ellen nodded. "He says it was meant to be a mercy killing."

Mom just stared at Ellen, who for some reason fell silent. So, I jumped in. "He said that you and he had a pact, Mom. An agreement that, if one of you got terminally ill, the other would kill the dying, suffering one. Out of compassion and love."

There was a short pause as our words coalesced into meaning in Mom's head. Then Mom burst into laughter, a creepy alien laughter that didn't sound like her, and for a minute it seemed like she might not stop, like she couldn't stop. But she did. She composed herself, and then she spoke up loud and clear. "That man always was a psycho. That's why I divorced his sorry *culo.*"

ELLEN BROUGHT DANNY TO the hospital for a visit. She had that stiff, aloof, defensive look that she gets when she's with him. Danny was Danny—tanned, creased face, tight tank top with deltoids and biceps on display, sweatpants, running shoes—only he had an extra glow in his eyes, like he was about to play in an important tennis match. He walked right up to Mom and started talking fast. He told her that, even in cases of serious physical impairment, the greatest obstacles to recovery are psychological and spiritual. That deep inside her is an awesome competitor who can accomplish tasks she's never dreamed of. He said he can get her standing and even walking in a matter of weeks. In addition to being a tennis pro, Danny's a personal trainer.

Mom gave Danny an exasperated look, then stared imploringly at Ellen. Ellen shrugged, then turned her head and sort of hid behind her long dark hair. I figured she'd already tried to head Danny off.

"The body always knows where it's at, and it always knows where it needs to go," Danny said. "Let's see what yours is up to. Can you move your foot?"

"Of course I can, and I don't need an underwear model to get me to do it." But she did it, wiggled her foot and her toes at the same time. That seemed to please her.

"What about your hand. Starting with each finger, then the whole hand . . . Good. Now raise and flex the arm." Mom did all right with the fingers and hand, but her arm was weak.

"Grab my wrist, Ariana."

She shook her head. "No, thank you."

"You need some motivation. Get the fire burning. Say 'I want to get well.'"

"I want all dummies out of my room."

"That's good, focus your anger." He put his face a little too close to hers. "Now move your whole arm, Ariana. In fact, take a swing at me. Go on, slap my face." Mom moved her hand wanly in a slow swipe across Danny's face, pushing it more than hitting it. "Good! Nice work, Ariana. Take another shot at me. Come on, you saucy lady, a good hard slap."

Mom shook her head. "Heck, no. You want more of that, you pay me for it, *pervertido*."

"That's the stuff. You've still got plenty of fire, Ariana. You're gonna be fine, I'm sure of it. We'll have you walking in a month. I gotta get back to the gym." He made a vigorous, fist-pumping gesture to all of us and trotted out the door.

Mom smiled serenely at Ellen and spoke in a voice full of loving kindness. "Sweetiepie, promise me you won't let that *pendejo* back in here."

She looked around the room and took a deep, noisy breath. "I got something to tell you two. Come close." We did. "You know all that stuff about me and Oscar having a pact, pledging to put each other out of our misery in the event of a prolonged, agonizing illness? It's true. He wrote up two copies, and we signed them. I threw mine away after we split up." She giggled slightly. "The poor idiot was trying to do the right thing when he murdered me." Her voice relaxed to a shaky hum, and she slid into a deep sleep.

* * *

I MADE THE MISTAKE of mentioning Dad's storage unit to Ellen, and now she wants to go through his things. "It's a kind of research project," she said. "Urban archeology. You can learn a lot about a person's life and times just by going through their possessions. I call it the Semiotics of Stuff." But we both know that she wants to find Mom and Dad's death contract. I guess I'm starting to believe that the thing actually existed, though I don't fully trust Mom or Dad's testimony on that score. Regardless, it seems highly unlikely it would turn up in that storage room, and for some reason it bugs me to think of Ellen snooping around in a sanctuary where men go to escape women and children. But I have a key duplicator in my truck so it was easy to knock out a copy for her.

I GOT A CALL from Rita Jankowski, wife of Frank, the guy with the secret safe in the retaining wall in the basement. Frank didn't want her to know about the safe, so we'd only worked on it on Tuesday and Friday afternoons when she went to the gym or the nail salon. When she was around, we had our hands full with the larger security system, which was elaborate—an indoor alarm with motion detection plus an outdoor system with an electric fence, a gate alarm, and video surveillance everywhere.

Well, she found the safe. She didn't understand why there was a golf plaque on the wall, and then she didn't understand why it was held in place with eight tamper-resistant pentalobe screws. So, she investigated, which means she had her cousin, a detective with the Stockton police, come and check things out. He popped off the plaque with a crowbar, and they saw the sticker with my company name on the front of the safe. Rita called me and then put her cousin on the phone. He introduced himself as Sergeant Ronnie Doile and asked for the combination to the safe. I said I couldn't divulge it to a stranger on the phone, that I was bound by contract. He said, "Then get your contract-bound ass over here pronto or it will be in deep shit."

On the way over I called Frank and told him what was up. His voice got shrill and nasty as he told me not to give them the combination. But when I got there Sergeant Ronnie said that the house and anything bolted to it was community property that Rita had a right to and that Frank was suspected of criminal activity and I better open it for them—he used the word pronto again, which coming from his mouth sounded like "fuck you." So, I opened it. Sergeant Ronnie pulled out stacks of hundred-dollar bills and records of offshore bank accounts and some flash drives and what he estimated to be half a million worth of pharmaceutical cocaine, enough to put Frank away for a while. Then Rita said to Sergeant Ronnie, "You gotta arrest this Clarence Wolf too, for accessory to the crime and for defrauding me, the deceived wife."

I began to feel a little sick, and I probably sounded like a guilty teenager when I told them I had no knowledge of Frank's activities and was just doing a standard installation. Rita started thumping my chest with her finger and calling me a slimy accomplice and other nastier names. But Sergeant Ronnie, bless his heart, stepped between us. He told me I could go, but would need to go downtown later and make a statement to the Sacramento cops. As I was on my way out Rita said, "You haven't heard the end of this, Mr. Fat Slob Security Expert."

THE DA SHOWED UP at the hospital. He was asking Mom about the shooting and jotting notes on the screen of an electronic pad. Mom told him that she and Dad did indeed have a pact, and, therefore, she had decided that he should be given a lesser charge. The DA gently told her that he would take that into consideration in his decision. Mom said that she was the victim and she had made her decision. The DA, a handsome, square-jawed guy named McGregor who talked like he was running for governor, smiled kindly and said that, legally speaking, the crime was against the state, not her.

Mom threw him a withering sneer. "I am just a ditsy *dominicana*, so somebody explain this to me. The state got shot? The state has a bullet sitting inside its brain and gets twitches in its fingers, and its legs won't do what it asks them to do? The state has a bag of yellow wee-wee hanging at its bedside?" She went on like that for a while, and it occurred to me that she might have been a good lawyer herself.

The DA wrote some more notes on his pad, told Mom that her input was very important, and left.

ELLEN AND DANNY NEARLY broke up. Mom doesn't like having Danny around, and she definitely doesn't want him giving her advice or touching her. Danny says he's a professional at physical rehab, and he should take the lead in this matter. According to Ellen they had their worst fight ever, and she ended up telling him he couldn't visit Mom at all. So, he told her it was over—if he couldn't see Mom that meant they no longer had a real relationship.

Eventually they worked out a compromise. Sometimes he'll show up with Ellen, but he just parks himself quietly by the bed. When the nurse brings in a bucket of ice cubes, Danny's job is to produce little pieces for Mom to suck on. The ice pick has a pink handle with a little picture of a penguin on it, and it's kind of fun watching Danny with this intent look on his face making precise punching motions, knocking out chips that he collects in a Styrofoam cup and hands to Mom. Mom looks at Danny appreciatively as she puts one ice chip after another on her tongue—she can go for hours chain-sucking ice chips. She'll blow through a cup in fifteen, twenty minutes, so Danny keeps stabbing away at the cubes, and everyone is happy.

I'm happy that Mom is recovering, more or less, and that a tiny chunk of ice can bring such peace to her face. I suppose I'm happy that Ellen and Danny worked things out. I'm unhappy that Rita Jankowski is suing me for helping her husband deceive and defraud her, even though DA McGregor refuses to press any charges against me for installing a secret safe in the Jankowski basement. Rita says my actions caused her financial harm and emotional pain, and she even listed poor old Chub, who rents a room in a crummy downtown hotel at $150 a week, as a defendant in the suit. My lawyer says don't worry, but I have to pay him $425 an hour to tell me not to worry, which seems at cross purposes. Frank is out on bail, living in his uncle's guest house.

I needed to talk to someone about all my woes. I still don't have a new girlfriend, so I called Karen. I hadn't talked to her since the time I'd spent the night with her while Dad was shtupping some bladder-challenged bimbo in my bed. Karen had called our encounter a romantic relapse, and had made it clear that the relationship was over for good. So, now I told her that I just needed her to lend me a sympathetic ear. I heard muffled voices, and then she told me that she was with somebody and could I call her back tomorrow.

DAD'S LAWYER, A PUBLIC defender assigned to him by the state, just called. He wants to go for an insanity plea, but Dad refuses. Dad says he's sane and did what he did out of love and duty, and if they want to give him the chair for being honorable and compassionate, then so be it. The PD, who has no sense of humor and talks like an accountant, said that he told Dad a plea of diminished capacity is his best bet. That's when Dad fired him.

He wants me to go persuade Dad that he needs a proper defense. But the last time I visited the old man we ended up yelling at each other, and I realized how much I hate him for being such a selfish asshole. On the drive home I decided that Mom is right, we're all selfish assholes, me, Ellen, Dad—Mom's the only one who has truly sacrificed for others, and she's the one in a hospital bed full of cancer and bullets and tubes and wires.

BELIEVE IT OR NOT, my sister the philosopher-archeologist found it. The "contract," or rather a letter with something like the contract in it. It was stuck in a bible in a stack of books in Dad's storage unit. Ellen spent hour upon hour going through chaotic piles of junk and papers and odd artifacts like a box of antique Heddon fishing lures and a set of Marples woodcarving tools. She seemed to enjoy the process, but she was looking for that letter, and over time became less interested in all the curiosities she was turning up and cataloguing in her notebook (though I guarantee she'll get three or four articles in obscure academic journals out of it all). The letter was carefully folded and placed at the first page of the Song of Solomon. It had been written by hand—Dad's distinctive printed scrawl—and signed by both Mom and Dad. It went on for three pages, but here's the pertinent part:

> *Our love knows no borders, not the border of time, nor of marriage even, nor of life itself. Our love lives on its own little island somewhere way out in the Pacific where there's lots of sharks and hurricanes and a mass of garbage the size of Connecticut, but it will survive all these dangers and more, and come out smelling like a fresh cup of coffee. And it is in the spirit of our love and devotion that we make this pledge, to wit:*
>
> *At such time as one of us is in a terminal state of illness or unbearable pain or unable to perform basic bodily functions, the other able-bodied one of us will put the unable-bodied one out of their misery in the most quick and painless manner, i.e., a firearm.*

HERE I AM AGAIN, sitting across from Dad, talking through glass. I tell him that things are looking up. That Ellen found the letter. He just nods, shrugs—like this was the natural order of things. "It should help your case, Pop. There's some public sentiment on your side. The time might be right to cut a deal."

"A deal? I'll make a deal on some righteous Humboldt weed. I don't go bargaining my principles."

"You can stand by your principles, and get a lighter sentence in the process."

"I'll see what the PD says. But Oscar Wolf doesn't compromise his principles, not for no Mister Charlie or anybody else."

I want to reach through the glass and rip his eyes out. "Right, Dad. Just think about it. Okay?"

He shrugs again. "I'm still tracking down that guitar of yours. Very close to a retrieval."

MOM HAS MOVED TO a convalescent home and is cruising around in an electric wheelchair—she even uses a walker a few times every day for ten-minute workouts. She cruised into the TV room and watched McGregor the DA announce that he's agreed to a lighter sentence for Dad. This put her in a strange emotional state—it was hard to tell if she was happy or upset. When she talked about it, her syntax got funny, as though she hadn't been speaking flawless English most of her life. She wasn't making much sense, which of course worried me. There were tears in her eyes, and I honestly couldn't figure out if they were tears of relief for Dad or rage at what he'd done to her.

Dad was transferred from Red Bluff to the Mule Creek State Prison, southeast of Sacramento, where he'll serve out the rest of the sentence. He seems okay there, though he claims he'd rather be in Folsom, where Johnny Cash played, or San Quentin, where Merle Haggard did time.

I GOT A CALL from Karen. It was nine in the evening and I was just sinking into my La-Z-Boy recliner with a beer and a cop show—it must have been the Channel 7 cop show where the big tall policewoman who was abused as a child goes around kicking the shit out of rapists. Karen said she felt a romantic relapse coming on and that she missed my bedroom.

This was upsetting. I'd begun to feel like I was moving on, but just hearing her voice made my heart ache and then my dick began stirring in its cocoon and I got this feeling of powerlessness and also great sadness. When I didn't respond directly to her brazen hint, she asked if she could come over, and I said yeah. "Just for a night," she said. "I just want to hold you for a while. We both know we don't belong together."

"Right," I said.

Then her tone shifted. "I shouldn't do this. It's not healthy. We need to move on. . . I don't know what to do. What should I do?"

"You want me to beg you to come over? I'm not going to beg you. I miss you. I even ache for you. But you called me. Figure out what you want."

"I have to think about it. Don't expect anything. If I show up, fine, if not, that's just how it's going to be." She hung up.

I went back to my cop show. Big Tall Policewoman had some child molester face down on his own front lawn with his hands cuffed behind his back and his neighbors watching in disbelief. A half hour later I heard a quiet knock. I flipped off the TV and dimmed the light on the way to the door.

The guy standing there was slim and tallish, but with a body that seemed to bend in three directions, like a plant that had never been able to figure out where the sun was, and maybe didn't get enough water either. "You Clarence?" I nodded. He held up an old guitar. "This is yours. You should take it."

I looked at it. "Where did that come from?"

"I'm the guy that took it. So here."

I stared at the guitar. It was old, but it didn't look like mine. "I don't think—"

"Just take it, dude." He said it like he was trying hard to be assertive. Then his voice went up a third and sounded younger and truly scared. "Please. You should take it."

I didn't know what else to do, so I took the guitar.

He breathed a deep, quiet sigh. "And tell Oscar and that Bernard dude that we're good now, nobody owes anybody anything, nobody needs to go around flexing their shit in anybody's space. You can do that?"

"I'll tell Oscar you brought this back to me."

He nodded, then turned and walked away. His twisted spine gave his body a kind of syncopated rhythm as he walked, like a hipster musician in a bad movie.

I sat down with the guitar, which clearly wasn't my old Martin D-18. It looked Mexican, with Aztec-like figures in the rosette and the binding, and probably wasn't worth a tenth of what he got for the Martin.

But when I strummed it, it was in tune, and had a rich, sustained sound and pretty good action and intonation on the neck. I sat there for at least an hour, fingerpicking old Mance Lipscomb songs and thinking about Dad, or at least trying to figure out what to think about him. He gets out of prison next Friday.

Karen never showed up.

THEY LET DAD OUT this morning. He'd been talking to NewsGuy, and they staged a media event where NewsGuy and VideoLady followed him over to the convalescent home. The media event was them and a bored-looking guy from the Bee, plus a young woman fresh out of journalism school sent by Reuters.

Mom was in her wheelchair when Dad showed up. He appeared in the doorway and stood there squinting at her, looking almost timid. At first she didn't seem to recognize him. But he smiled his lopsided smile and said, quietly and not without charm, "Hello, Ariana. It's been a long while," which was pretty much what he'd said right before he shot her. We'd prepared Mom for the visit, telling her several times he was on his way, but now she just stared blankly. When she finally recognized him, she looked a little scared, or maybe confused. He just stood there, not quite knowing what to do.

Suddenly Mom beamed and held out her arms. "Come on, you big idiot, give me some *azúcar*!" Dad, still smiling, took a couple unsure steps, hesitated, then trotted over, stooped down, and gave Mom a big bear hug. I was sitting on the bed just behind Mom, and I watched Dad as he embraced her. It seemed like half a lifetime's worry and suffering drained from his face in seconds as he closed his eyes and rested his head on her shoulder.

Mom wrapped her arms around him, and now Dad's face filled with emotion and a quiet moan came from his lips. He pulled back so he could look into Mom's eyes, and he stared at her with something like bewildered admiration. He started to stand up, but his knees buckled, and then he started walking, which made him look like Groucho Marx. Mom stretched out her arm and pointed at him in an accusing gesture. "Now there's an act of mercy!" she shouted. "Put you out of your own damn misery, Oscar Wolf!"

Dad stared at her with that puzzled look. He reached over his shoulder and down his back, then slid his arm around his ribs and tried to reach up. In the process he turned sideways, and I got a glimpse of the pink handle of the ice pick at the center of his back. He took a couple more wobbly steps away from Mom, then slipped down into a sitting position. NewsGuy put down his notepad and went over to Dad, crouching and supporting him with his arm. The Reuters lady stepped outside the door and called for help. Dad relaxed a little, and looked back at Mom, who gave him her most haughty, aristocratic look, with her lips pursed and her eyebrows raised. They continued to stare at one another, and then Dad let out something like a weak laugh. I can't say exactly why I just sat there through all this—but it felt like I was watching from a great distance as something like fate unraveled. VideoLady was shooting the whole thing.

A nurse appeared in the doorway, then yelled down the hall for someone to get an ambulance over from Mercy General. She went quickly to a rollaway cabinet across from the bed and pulled a scissors out of a drawer. NewsGuy got out of her way as she bent over Dad and started cutting away at his shirt until his back was bare with just the ice pick handle sticking out. She spoke soothingly to Dad as she checked out the ice pick, which seemed to be going right through his spine. She tried to get him to lie on his side, but he resisted.

Dad exhaled with a slight wheeze, and some red saliva dripped from the corner of his mouth. "Oh, lordy, just take me back out to the Eel River, set me down in the shade, and let me die at the bosom of Mother Nature."

Mom was leaning forward in her wheelchair, intently watching the commotion she had caused. She pointed at Dad for the second time. "Nobody is dying today, Oscar. That's too easy. They will patch you up in no time, and you will live out your days in misery like the rest of us."

Dad shrugged. "Maybe so. But sooner or later I will die, and so will you. And I fully intend to get back up to the Eel before that happens." He managed to wiggle free of the nurse's grip, and struggled into an upright, kneeling position. "Ariana Ariza Quintana, I invite you to come with me as my traveling companion and paramour."

Now Mom laughed with abandon, shaking so hard that I couldn't tell how much was the laughter and how much was her body's helpless frailty. "Oscar Wolf, if your craziness and your stupidity had a boxing match, I don't know who would win."

"So, what's your answer, Ariana?"

Mom looked thoughtful for a moment, and her voice became softer, almost coy. "You cannot be serious, Oscar."

"I just made you an offer, and I am a man of my word." The old, crooked grin elbowed its way onto his face. "You want me to put it in writing?"

MERIT WINNER: LOVE

# Bruised

## Ron L. Dowell

BEFORE EVERYTHING COLLAPSED AND MAMA STILL ALIVE, AS A little kid, I thought the world a safe place where someone would always take care of me.

One day Mama spelled out my job.

Our monthly picnic took her, Tyquan, and me to South Central Los Angeles—SoLA we call our piece of the city—on the Metro Blue Line to the 103rd/Watts Towers platform. Two blocks later, we ate greasy chicken beneath a cloudless sky. White sunlight flashed through leaves, our blankets spread under the sharp eucalyptus smell. Behind and over us towered seventeen sky-high interconnected sculptures Sabato Rodia, an Italian immigrant, had checkered with small colored pieces of broken glass, seashells, tile, ceramic scraps, and metal made with simple tile setter's tools over thirty-one years. Tour guides reminded visitors of Rodia's words, motivating words, *I'm going to do something,* words I breathed deep like smog. Time passed slowly, and bees sucked nectar from small silvery leaved flowers growing barely above the grass. Tyquan crapped himself climbing the tower rungs, and I was content to let him stink until Mama's stare. My chest tightened, and from habit, I cleaned his shitty butt.

Pretty soon, she started the big sister stuff.

Her well-shaped lips were like Lauryn Hill's smile. "It's just you two, Trina, and you must love him, help him get through," she'd say, her scarf unable to hide bruises on her dark brown chin, neck, and shoulders. "That'll be your job, your responsibility," she said as if she could foretell something terrible. Her words stuck to me like the cement Rodia used to bond the Watts Towers without bolts, rivets, or welds. Then she emphasized, "Try to avoid *niggashit* too, you hear?" She rubbed her wrists. "Just because the trap's set, you don't have to step on it."

Whenever I argued, her backhand found me, or at home, she'd have me pick an outside tree branch, a *switch* she called it, which she lashed across my naked legs.

Tyquan age seven, and me, fourteen, and almost her height when I finally rebelled. "But why's Tyquan my job? How's it on me to worry about *him*? I've changed his diapers since he was a baby—*he's* your kid."

"You smelling your piss?" Mama said glaring. Her tone I understood and whimpered into the backyard, and pulled a switch I thought might not sting. "You can do better, Trina."

A few months later, Marcus, Tyquan's daddy, my son-of-a-bitch stepfather, murdered Mama and then took his own wretched life in a sleazy Whittier motel.

The church pew strained my ass next to Dupree, the social worker. Tyquan sat next to her.

Throat scratchy, I studied the key lock on the closed pink casket and overheard Miss Dupree describe Mama's face as riddled. A week later, Dupree made me attend Marcus's funeral. She said he had mental problems, depression, as if to excuse his murderous niggashit. His open casket smelled like death, the small bullet hole to his forehead hardly visible. I hated him, but Mama was right. I must protect Tyquan.

But Children's Services separated Tyquan and me, cast us astray in the shit crazy world of county services, where I learned of all the county offices and their supposed function.

I've searched for two years, and no one will help me. *Talk to your director*, they'd say, but no one took the time to listen simply, always, *maybe later*.

I must find Tyquan, and nothing else matters. I'm going to do something.

* * *

AT SIXTEEN, I'M NEW to Lost Souls Group Home in East Compton, my third stop in two years. The other homes say I'm angry, resistant, ever ready to fight, and they claim I need pills——*you have trouble listening and following instructions, and attention deficiency,* the psychiatrist says.

Yeah, right, but the Adderall she prescribes combined with blunts and Olde English 800 malt liquor, eight-ball we call it, and other drugs I've learned to like make me feel safe, protected, sane. Except for Hattie Melrose, our adult live-in group home staff, almost everyone I know takes pills, drinks alcohol, or smokes something. Dope is like air. I deserve to feel safe and should not knuckle under bullshit. That's what Mama taught.

Hattie's a good listener for an adult who doesn't treat me as a pain in the ass. I convince her to help me find where Tyquan lives. She discovers he stays with a Watts woman named Starkãna Wilkerson. I skip school, push in earphones, block out crap like the nasty bastard wearing a faded Laker T-shirt sitting across the aisle on the crowded Metro Blue Line train. His hand thrusts jerking himself, and his lips pull tight against his yellow teeth when he utters, "Hey, Nubian Queen."

Heads spin when I say, "Stop it, pervert," but nobody says or does a thing.

He winks a droopy eye and says, "Yeah, I know. It's stupid, right?" I cringe, turn away, and scrutinize a frenzy of shapes and colors, three tall spires, and Watts Towers' skeleton-like gazebo as we approach the platform. Clouds form, dulling the glass and scrap metal pocked fretwork assemblage. Suppose Tyquan doesn't live with Starkãna Wilkerson or even in Watts?

Flower sprays, empty liquor bottles, and stuffed animal death memorials rise in clusters along the Metro route before I arrive at the 103rd/Watts Towers platform. A mile east leans Starkãna's clapboard shack where my brother supposedly lives.

Under a tree on the opposite corner, I crouch between the shells of two cars that smell like cat litter, on jacks, and no tires. I spy Starkãna's house, its missing roof shingles, and a saggy chain-link fence.

Across a dirt driveway, a river of crack zombies flood to the base of a concrete stoop. Two women perch above the rise as if to orchestrate confusion below. Leashed to a stake, a steel gray pitbull with thick thighs and a brown smudge behind his stubby nose chases his tail and barks to awaken the dead.

The puny woman's big feet straddle the stoop edge. She wears mirror aviator sunglasses and surveys all directions at once. "Shaadup, Buster," she says, but the dog ignores her command. A belt knife glints underneath her sun-yellow camisole, SOS scrawled across her flat chest in blackletter.

Her skin is sorrel-colored, she has wavy, purplish shoulder-length hair, and what looks like a green sofa throw wraps around her waist down to flip flops the size of snowshoes. Sweat drips down my back. One of those women is Starkãna. I pray it's not her. She looks nutty. But of course, my prayers aren't answered.

"Whaddup, Starkãna, whoop whoop woo you in the pocket?" one visitor among a small group hollers, and the purple-haired woman scans him. The man squints at Buster before he enters the driveway.

"Come on up. My dog won't bite. Buster's had his shots." She nods from on high. "You got a dime. I got time."

The other, a blonde white girl, her widely spaced cornrows show scalp. Her tits lumped over the back of the metal folding chair, which her significant butt pressures. She wears a red plaid Pendleton shirt, oversized even on her fat ass, faded blue jeans, creases sharp enough to cut, and white tennis shoes. She looks like a pig in an American flag. The zombies say blah blah blah, gobbledygook I can't make out, swap something with flag woman, and scurry away.

Sweating, I pinch away my blue/gray uniform, my CHS T-shirt, and beige Dickies. I swagger to the stoop, face to face with Starkãna. The Killaz Life tattoo stretches when she twists her turkey neck, her missing teeth. Buster barks as if he's losing his mind.

"Ahem," I clear my throat, fake a low tone. "What you got?" I crane my neck, search for evidence, any proof of Tyquan's presence.

Starkãna eyes me up. She makes short, jerky movements. "For schoolgirls, a piece of chronic for one dollar, a tab of Ritalin for same." Her dry monotone and pouty lips unnerve me. "No crack or meth for schoolkids. Fucks 'em up, make 'em crazy." She adjusts her SOS top. "I'll throw in a Save Our Sons bodice for five bucks more."

"Chronic, Rit only, thanks." I pull two balled George Washingtons from my pocket—my lunch money—and push them to her, but she brushes me off and nods to the fat flag who's checking me as if I'm po-po.

"Hook her up, Bec," Starkãna says to flag woman.

"Where you from?" asks Bec, her voice deep, steely. She's surly and intimidating. Bec looks meaner up close than she did from a distance, like an Anderson Silva opponent who's taken one too many face strikes. I quiver inside and hope it doesn't show.

"Compton."

"You're a ways from home, Nappy Locks," she says, mouth twisted.

She ogles my unprocessed hair. Oh. Is this about turf? *Niggashit* Mama said. I need her to stop now.

"I don't remember you asking my name," I force words.

Her blue eyes pierce me like needles. Buster bares his teeth. *Grrrr*, foam drips from his mouth. I probably look pretty shitfaced.

"Hush," Bec says. Buster whimpers and curls next to the stake, resting his big head on clumsy paws. Her mouth corners turn up slightly but show no teeth. "Happy liftoff," she says and hands me a small clear plastic bag containing a brush of weed. She then reaches into her pocket, forks a prescription bottle, and pours one white tablet into her fat grimy hand. "That'll twist ya."

I take a risk. "Is Tyquan home?" I ask. The silence makes me queasy.

"Who wants to know?" Starkãna says.

I'm chewing fingernails in my reflection off her sunglasses. "Tyquan plays with my little sister sometimes."

Starkãna regards Bec, who side-long looks me and hunches her shoulders.

"No, he at school," Starkãna finally says. "Move on, get on back to school." Then, in a maternal tone, she says, "Get your education."

This dump of a place where Tyquan lives don't feel right, the crazy dog, makes my group home look like a Beverly Hills estate I've seen on the internet.

I skulk to the Blue Line station, stuff Starkãna's weed into a Swisher Sweets cigar, fire the blunt to get my head straight, but pot doesn't slow my racing heart nearly enough.

What does Tyquan look like now? I have to know.

THE NEXT DAY I'M back in Watts before the last bell rings, King Elementary, the school nearest Starkãna's shed. Heat flushes me, just recalling the two women I'd seen controlling the porch and clutching money, the dope fiends, the scary dog. Maybe I'll borrow a classmate's gun, do a run-by, steal away Tyquan. Nonsense. I could hurt him by mistake or wound an innocent crackhead if there is such a thing given the hell crackheads cause the community. Plus, I don't know how to shoot. I'm going to do something. I'll find him first.

The bell rings, gates burst open, and kids flood past me like raging water. The flood turns to a trickle, and a security guard closes one of two entrances. I check my watch. Is King the right school?

He's last, but Tyquan bounces toward me wearing a red hoodie. He's much taller now, but the hitch in his run is a dead giveaway. There was never anything physically wrong with Tyquan. I believe he imitated Marcus's swag, the slight delay, and twist in his hip, the way he'd hitch his shoulder, causing his right arm to rise and move forward, graceful, like someone in control, cool even under pressure. Looking back, I think motherfuckin' Marcus was just crazy. My insides vibrate.

Crouched behind a palm tree, I await the right moment, leap into his path. "Tyquan!" My skin tingles. He ducks and covers his head as if under attack. His backpack thumps the grass. Eyes full, he double-takes.

"Trina?" he gasps, then jumps into my outstretched arms. His face blurs through my tears. We face each other, sit cross-legged, knees touching, and in short order, we revisit what's happened in the last two years. Whoa, he's so frail and undersized, like starving Somaliland children on charity commercials, flies covering their bugged eyes. My throat's scratchy.

"Are you hungry, Lil' Brother?"

*Pop, pop, pop,* gunshots sound nearby. Tyquan jerks his paper-bag brown face, he's a shade darker than me, and we jump up. That's when I notice a black welt below his eye. Police sirens wail past the corner. My shoulders tighten.

"That bruise—did you fight today?" He recoils when I brush the eye bruise with my thumb.

We're poised to run opposite the gunshots when a kid taller than Tyquan bully bumps between us, a red bandana tied to his bony arm. He holds up black school uniform pants hung halfway down his ass, butt crack exposed. He couldn't run from bullets or nothing else if his life depended on it, but he has an attitude.

"Whaddup." He nods. "I got chronic." Tyquan ignores him. The kid struts to another curbside death memorial, a clump of candles surrounding a red baseball cap. A brown stuffed teddy bear and a sympathy card fastened to a makeshift cross read RIP Lil' Renzo. Real G.

"Are you in a clique?" I ask.

"Naw." He shrugs. "Everybody wears red."

"Gangsters wear a lot of red—I'm just sayin'." My neighborhood wears blue colors. It's dumb since pink is my favorite color, more *niggashit* as Mama would say, fighting over stuff we don't own, so we all wear colors of our hoods even if we don't bang, which most don't. We feel safe in numbers, though, almost like family.

I hug him again. "What's your new home like?"

"Starkãna has friends over," he says. "They smell like smoke." He lowers his head.

"Smoke?"

"Yeah, they smoke pipes. Pops when they suck. Like Daddy

used to do. The whole house stinks." I flinch. "I bag empty liquor bottles, aluminum cans she recycles," he says.

Hmmm. "Sounds like crack cocaine." My breath quickens. "And eight-ball." Marcus fouled the air, smoking tobacco, blunts, crack, and whatever else could maintain a spark. He'd chug Olde English forties, nut-up, punch our mother, and then beat us for helping her.

"Makes me sick—so I go to my bedroom, try 'n' sleep."

The wiry kid passes again, slow, holds his pants. He frowns at Tyquan. "Whaddup, my nigga—I got sticky icky buds?"

Oh shit. Those are fighting words in our house. Mama insisted we were never niggers or niggas, which means we struggle often.

"Back up before I bomb on your ass," I say, chest to chest, and shove the kid to the dirt. "Bompton in the house." I use a gang name from my hood, a gang to which I don't belong.

The kid tries to stand; Tyquan kicks and leaves a single sneaker print on the taller boy's butt. It's two against one. The boy scowls, throws up Blood's finger signs, hunkers away. "I'll be back," he says and disappears into a Jacaranda thicket scattered along the train tracks, scented lavender leaves in full bloom. I spread my fingers and fan myself.

"Bring your mama," Tyquan shouts. "We'll kick her ass too."

"I saw Starkãna yesterday," I say. "Does she have you on Ritalin?"

"Once she did," he says. "I started banging my head on the television." He looks confused. "My brain said it didn't want to be in my body anymore."

"She don't put her hands on you, does she?"

Tyquan pauses. And studies Lil' Renzo's memorial.

"Becca came yapping—snatched the cover—I bumped her chest." Another long pause, Tyquan clutches his knuckles, his gaze locks into the curb gutter, the teddy bear, Lil' Renzo's dried blood. "She had a cigarette in her mouth." My stomach knots.

Becca must be Bec. "Why was she in your bedroom?" I lean forward.

"Then she burned me—burned my pee-pee—whipped me with a clothes hanger too."

"Oh—hell naw." Pangs of fire gnaw inside me.

Gingerly Tyquan peels back the sleeve of his hoodie. "Becca put my hand, my arm on the kitchen burner," he says. Scabbed over burn marks form an X on his forearm. "I screamed, but Starkãna wouldn't help me—just niggashit." He juts his chin. "I'm good, though—didn't let the white girl see me cry. Starkãna's a bitch."

Mama once said white people took the worst part of themselves, invented niggers and niggas, flipped the script, and fed the scraps to black people long ago, keeping for themselves the best of everything. People like Starkãna eat niggerness like they eat Popeye's Fried Chicken. Traitors like Judas Iscariot, Mama told us.

My head drops. My brother's sturdy, but he's just a kid. Math isn't my favorite subject; I get by. I like history. History taught me how adults plus alcohol and other drugs, plus children equal abuse. Abuse and neglect are the stories of my group home roomies. It's our story. A bitter taste forms in my throat.

I want revenge, but most of all, I want Tyquan safe. If I snatch him now—then what? I need a plan, a way to save him before Starkãna kills him. I must do something, something big like the Watts Towers.

I give him my cell number and make him promise to call if anything else happens.

He'd be with those twisted bitches another night. Hollowness sets my chest.

BACK HOME IN BED, I swig eight-ball stashed in my backpack, wash down Adderall and Ritalin, scarf Flamin' Hot Cheetos, toss one way turn another, woozy, and watch the ceiling fan spin. If I close my eyes long enough, maybe I'll fall asleep, but they pop back open and Mama's sweet pie face, riddled like shredded paper, turns long, hard-bitten. Her lips move a heartbeat before her words, *and you must love him, help him get through.* My body fights an urge to run outdoors. *Try to avoid niggashit too,* she said.

*Whaddup nigga, whaddup nigga, whaddup nigga,* the skinny kid's words bounce between my ears. My mother once told us niggers and niggas are the same things, bucket crabs pulling each other, unable or unwilling to love and help one another rise. She had said keep your body clean inside and out, bathe, wash your hands, don't drink too much alcohol, or take harmful drugs. She joked of a Deniggerlator, a room with revolving doors to prevent drafts. And a machine, like an MRI, some of her people could pass through. Beneficiaries crowd the snaking lines; white people who made niggers for the good ole US of A. A Deniggerlator to recreate Americans like magic, cure hard heart diseases, PTSS, and mental cancers so many needed. The inventor would make billions because some people will repeat pain several times, exorcising their *niggashit.*

Mama always laughed about the Deniggerlator. Maybe she wasn't joking. Something I can't touch lives inside my mother's wisdom, an extra weight I don't want. Can I avoid the traps—do better?

The rotating fan can't cool or stop me from thinking about Starkãna and how she allows Becca to abuse Tyquan.

I'll get Hattie's help.

I sniff morning's fried bacon, coffee, and follow Hattie's singing—*Through many dangers, toils, and snares, I have already come. 'Tis Grace hath brought me safe thus far, and grace will lead me home.* She hovers over the stove. I'm in first and hug her waist.

Hattie gazes from her cup and smiles. She wears a flowered headscarf, a white chef's jacket, and has smooth brown sugar skin.

Across the tiny table, I face her. "I saw Tyquan yesterday. I never would've found him without you. Thank you for getting his location."

"You're welcome, sweetie," Hattie says, honey-voiced. She blows her steaming coffee. "How is he?"

"Not good. My brother's foster mama is a crackhead bitch," I say, hoping she'll grab keys, rush the door, start the van, peel rubber to Watts, and rescue Tyquan. Instead, she places her palms on the table as if she's having a manicure. "Starkãna and her people are hurting Tyquan—and I need your help again."

She squirms. "Tyquan's your brother and all, but maybe you should let go, Trina," she says. "Let the Children's Service Department handle Wilkerson."

"What do you mean *let go*?" I say. My voice rises. "My brother's in big trouble. Children's Service don't do shit but get people killed." I pound the table, spill Hattie's coffee, and blindside her. "Group home staff ain't shit either." Immediately my knees weaken, having said such a fucked up thing to someone like Hattie.

"You need to step back, little lady, chill out." Her eyes narrow. "Have you taken your medicine?" She pushes the coffee cup to the middle of the table and takes several deep breaths. Then the furrows between her eyebrows disappear. "Hey, I understand. I was abused and lived in foster homes as a child too. Hell, I even lost my two children to the system—from stupid shit I did." Her tone is sharp. "This job . . . My PO is helping me get them back."

Blah blah blah. Hattie's understanding, but I'm not hearing what she has to say. "I could kick Starkãna's ass." My hands burn hot, sliding atop my school uniform pants. "Will you call Children's Service and report Starkãna for me? They'll listen to you."

Hattie hesitates, but I can't change her mind. She shakes her head slowly. My eyelids get all gummy.

"No, Trina," she says. "I risked my job telling you where Tyquan lived. You even ditched school. And with your grades, you should double up on books, especially math." She collects the coffee cup, stands, steps to the sink, and turns her back. "I'm out, girlfriend."

Blam! I slap and shove and the table screeches. "Screw it. I'll figure it out myself." My head aches, hand hurts, a wave of cold hits me.

I fuss to my bedroom, flick the ceiling fan highspeed, lift the window, push a cassette, a guy's rapping about drinking gin and smoking chronic. I fire a blunt as the music suggests.

Shit—Adderall, marijuana, Hattie's pissed and won't help me. It'd be my fault if Becca kills Tyquan. Sheesh, what drama. Maybe I need a clearer head to think things through, a plan to save Tyquan.

The ceiling fan turns round and round. The situation strains my brain way too much.

Maybe I can do better—dodge the *niggashit* trap. But how?

I HAVE NO RESCUE plan, not Hattie, and not armed kidnapping. I'm lethargic, my mind tormented like devils congregating at a Baptist church. Get a grip, I tell myself. I must get Tyquan nearer to me before it's too late.

Fuck it. I'll make Children's Service do their job, investigate Starkãna and Becca.

I rake aside spare change and candy wrappers littering the greasy shared desk and flip *Hip-Hop* magazine pages. The Children's Service hotline number delivers a recorded menu list, a droll voice sounding miles away: *If you are calling to report a missing child, call your local police department.*

Maybe we can live together in the same foster home. *If you wish to apply to become a foster parent, press one; to report suspected child abuse, stay on the line.*

I hear a click, and music on hold grates me an hour before another click.

"CSD, this is Gina speaking, please give me your name and tell me how can I help you today?" She sounds friendly. Yes, I got this.

"My name is Trina, Trina Thomas—that crackhead bitch Starkãna abuses my brother at her shack near the Watts Towers—you've heard of the Towers, the little dude who built them. She sells drugs, zombies, flag-bitch-Becca, a crazy-assed dog, Buster, looks like he has rabies, foaming at the mouth, always barking—"

"Okay, let's slow down a little, Trina. Are you at the house you're calling about?"

"No, ma'am."

She asks me the essentials: Tyquan's full name, our ages, where I live, where he lives, annoying stuff that doesn't matter as much as the fact wicked Watts witches torture my little brother.

"Are you in temporary placement, a group home? What medications do you take?"

"A group home, ma'am," I say. A leaf blower whines, and a mower engine rumbles outdoors. I hardly hear Gina as I pace, struggling to control my tone. "But this ain't about me. Starkãna and her friends hurt Tyquan, beat him with wire." I tell Gina about the stove burns and drug use. "They're killing him."

"Did you see any of these things occur?"

"No, ma'am, but he told me. I saw his black eye."

"When was that?"

"The day before yesterday. I went to his school, King Elementary in Watts—"

"What school do you attend when you go?"

"Compton High."

"Un-huh, please hold, Miss Thomas." Music on hold. Several minutes later, Gina returns. "Compton High School is several miles away from King Elementary, another district. Shouldn't you have been in school?"

"Ahh . . . yes, ma'am—"

"You ditched? Schools don't get paid when you don't attend." Doubt hardens her voice. "So, let me get this straight. You say you saw a bruise on your brother—"

I interrupt the bitch. "Yeah, but what about his burn scabs?"

Her tone sharpens. "At his school in Watts, when you should be in school, Compton High, yourself, correct?"

"Why you keep asking me about me?" I say. "Starkãna hurts Tyquan—just go and see yourself," I shout, lips pressing the cell phone. "Go right now." Begging makes my throat sore.

"Calm down, young lady. I'd like to help you here, but you must not raise your voice at me."

"How can I calm down when skanky Starkãna and her friends are killing my brother?" My belly feels the heat. "What're you gonna do, wait till they murder him?"

"Hold, Miss Thomas." Stupid music on hold again rattles my ears. I slam the *Hip-Hop* magazine to the floor. "Okay, Miss Thomas. I spoke with my supervisor. We looked into your allegations, and, I shouldn't tell you confidential information, but I assure you—" I hear Gina swallow. "Our workers and their police team have visited Starkãna Wilkerson's home several times and found the environment satisfactory."

"Your workers are either blind or lazy. Didn't they see Tyquan's bruises?"

"The children in the house showed no visible signs of abuse and seemed to be adjusting well in the home—the complaints were unfounded."

If only I could reach through the phone and squeeze Gina's neck.

"Did you go to the right house? Her name is Starkãna, a scraggy bitch with missing teeth—a friend named Becca, a crazy dog named Buster."

"Sometimes, Miss Thomas," Gina says, "we have situations where siblings manipulate, scheme to reunite into the same household. That's what you sound like to us." Sickness in my stomach rises to my throat. "How did you find where Tyquan lived?"

"This is bullshit!" I say, my shirt soaked in sweat. "If you assholes won't help me, I'll fix it myself."

"Suit yourself. Know we'll post a truant alert and notify your school district," Gina says. "Is there anything else we can help you with, Miss Thomas, before I screen out your call?"

I slam the phone shut, curse Gina for her terrible service, *niggashit*, my body so tense. I relight the blunt, suck eight-ball, and lay back watching the fan blades turn.

I'M STILL PRETTY FUCKED in a dream sleep when Tyquan calls sobbing.

"Becca hit me in the face with a telephone book," Tyquan says. Grrrrr, Buster goes mad in the background. "She sicced Buster on me—said I stole her money—Buster bit my leg." I wobble and sit on the side of my bed. "Starkãna said she'd kill me if I tell the school nurse."

Pull yourself together, girl. I have to if I'm to save Tyquan. "Tomorrow morning, we're riding the Blue Line, to the county office," he says, his voice trails, "to fill my prescription."

I press my hands together and pray. County offices, some people go for *niggashit*, like Starkãna, when they run office to office, hustling money. They'll loud-talk and jack the overworked county workers and even customers waiting for aid review. She'll front Tyquan and say she needs assistance, and refill his Ritalin prescription for her to sell.

"Can't you come and get me now?" he asks.

Woozy, my mind says maybe, but the body says no. "We'll see. Let's wrap you with a bow for now, okay?" What if I rode to Watts, grabbed my brother, and ran away to safety? But where is such a place? We'd already been there if I had a clue.

"We'll meet there tomorrow." I strain for answers. "Act like you don't know me, okay?"

No medicine, weed, or alcohol for me in the morning. *I'm going to do something.* I'll watch the fan spin and deniggerlate tonight.

RAIN FALLS THE NEXT morning, a rarity in summertime SoLA. The drops cool my arms and oh, the sweet, musty smell of rain meeting the hot concrete 103rd/Watts Towers Blue Line platform. My disguise, a goldilocks wig and dark Ray-Ban sunglasses, blends perfectly, even making me look a bit older. I'm careful and must avoid school police bounty hunters. I'll save my brother—snatch him away from Starkãna, cut her fucking throat—if she's not with Becca and if Tyquan's not dead.

The canopy covering the platform protects riders from the warm rain. The bench underneath already packed, so I mosey just beyond into the misting rain, a fluttery, empty feeling pits my stomach, the butcher knife handle in my waistband pressing against me concealed under my LA Sparks team jersey. The serrated steel blade hungry for Starkãna's Killaz Life neck tat. I'll use the weapon if needed, but not because I have it. Mama had said because vehicles drive fast, they aren't licensed to operate foolishly. I wait and wait. Could I have already missed them? A woman wearing a blue Metro Line uniform checks passenger tickets. My legs feel restless, and I sweat. She saunters by and down the platform.

My head jerks to a commotion at the platform base. Starkãna's dragging a limping Tyquan by his burned arm, casting him every which way like a marionette.

Her hand cupped, she says, "Save Our Sons tees and camisoles for sale. I'm styling one." She wears tight fake designer jeans, a blinding pink camisole, SOS scrawled across her puny chest, flittering back and forth she's like a scared bird, flip flops, clack, clack, clack, each hoofbeat slapping hard against concrete. She stops and yelps, "You can buy the shirt off my back." She taps a card once on the transit access pass machine and whisks them both past the turnstile. The combined stink of crack cocaine, beer, and weed hover over her like a cloud when she passes and nudges away two women under the canopy.

I maneuver next to Starkãna. I lean behind her, using an index finger over my lips to shish Tyquan, who twists opposite her.

"What's up?" I say. Starkãna turns, and we lock eyes.

"Oh, feels sticky out, but I'm good," Starkãna says. She looks me over, and her shaded eyes rest on my school Dickies. "Do I know you?"

I wipe sweaty hands on my pants and nod. Starkãna looks smaller than she did towering over the porch, even fragile. We're about the same height. Her eyes are red; pupils dilated, lips blistered and cracked having pressed hot pipes against them, skin pulled tight against her bony face, jowls sucked in resembling a walker on *The Walking Dead.*

"You got anything to smoke?" she says. She doesn't recognize me. Suddenly she turns away, drags Tyquan past the STAY BEHIND THE YELLOW LINE strip to the platform edge, my mouth falls open. She leans over a SUICIDE CRISIS LINE sign, shades her eyes, and gawks up the tracks toward downtown LA. "We can hit-a-lick after I make a run to the county building."

She's a nervous rat, a bucket crab doing her part to keep Watts tormented. I must say something to this nut, but what? Mama's advice slips from my lips. "You might try the Deniggerlator."

Instantly Starkãna's vacant expression turns furious. "What? Try what? You callin' me a nigga? Bitch, you don't know me."

I look away from her, study spires on the Towers, the intricate fretwork at Starkãna's back.

"I'll throw your ass on them tracks," she says. "Nah mean?"

"My bad, miss—no disrespect." I show both palms.

Starkãna turns to Tyquan. "Nigga, tie your shoe," she says to him. His face flushes, both eyes are puffy and dark. He winces, but dirty gauze and duct tape covering his hand won't allow his fingers to flex. I slant away and feel for the knife handle. I picture my blade plunging, riddling her neck. Starkãna squats. She pushes the strap of her fake Coach purse stuffed with shirts and ties Tyquan's shoe. "Don't let me find you poisoned Buster last night." She looms beneath the no-smoking sign, whips out a lighter and cigarette, fidgets, and then lights a Newport. "He had his shots—was a good watchdog," she says, blowing smoke into Tyquan's face.

"I didn't," Tyquan says, his lips forming a little smirk.

Starkãna drags and inhales deep her nicotine, turns, grins baring rotted teeth, and puffs smoke in my face.

My eyes grow hot and tear up, and I summon the softest voice I can muster.

"What happened to the boy's arm?"

"Oh, that. School accident—he's on the football team," Starkãna says. "The doctor said to give it some air. He'll be all right."

"Football—air?" I repeat, crowding Starkãna's personal space. She doesn't budge. "What about his black eyes?"

She whips purplish hair. "What's it to you, bitch? Huh? All up in my business." She adjusts her camisole, an S covering each of her tiny tits, shoulders still her head rolls side to side. "Back off, biaatch, unless you want a scrum."

I shrug, lower my eyes onto Tyquan, and swallow. I'll scruffle maybe, *niggashit,* but not on her terms. Tyquan stares straight ahead in her grasp.

The train whines slow and stops—passengers in front board. Starkãna elbows people and cusses louder than ever to no one in particular. My legs are restless.

Timing precisely, I grip the knife handle in my left hand and step just ahead. As Starkãna inches forward, I slam my right elbow across the bridge of her nose. Her head jerks back, sunglasses cracking against her face. She releases Tyquan, stumbles backward onto her back. Splat! Her head bounces off the concrete. SOS shirts fly everywhere. Tyquan snatches away and stomps the middle O of her pink camisole.

Starkãna's mouth flies open. "Oh—what the fuck . . ."

Tyquan's shivering. I grab his hand. PLEASE STEP INSIDE. THE DOORS ARE ABOUT TO CLOSE, says the canopy speaker voice. Two steps later, we are on the train.

Outside the window, a bloodied Starkãna gathers herself on the platform and spasms in the soft rain, weak. Shards of broken sunglasses lodge in her left eye. No one helps her. Some train passengers clutch SOS shirts.

Starkãna mouths, "You mothafuckas," one hand pressing her bleeding eye, her fist waving wild in the air, the Killaz Life tattoo has swollen on her neck. The Blue Line rumbles north. Slats of sunshine pierce the clouds and rainbows form above the Watts Towers, majestic behind Starkãna's emaciated frame. She appears smaller and smaller.

I pull Tyquan's shaking body close. It's a start. For sure, I did something big, but I'll do better, pass again through the Deniggerlator to exorcise niggashit, love him, help him get through. Keep him away from what we'd left on the platform.

Different won't be easy.

"I got you, Lil' Brother." Tyquan snuggles up closer to me. "I. Love. You."

# My Life of Crime

Jim Gish

My name is Harold Weems, and I think that this is what you might call a cautionary tale about bad decisions and bad luck. If somebody decides to make a Movie of the Week out of it, I would not be surprised. This story is all true, and it is a shame and a disgrace I am not proud of, this story of my life of crime.

I guess I might never have entered a life of crime if it hadn't been for Bitsy Jean's fibromyalgia. She was assistant night manager at the Clugg Dairy Queen and pretty much on the fast track when the fibromyalgia bubbled up in her blood, pain all over her body, in every joint and bone. She took so many sick days off that Dilbert Homart, the owner, fired her and told her she needed to get on disability. Then the man who came to examine her was an old boyfriend who sneered at her maliciously and stamped "Not Disabled" because, according to Bitsy Jean, she had once said unkind things about his manhood when he tried to show it to her in the dark upper balcony of the Starplex Theatres at the mall.

Anyway, the long and the short of it was that Bitsy Jean did not get disability, and she commenced to have migraines. Fibromyalgia all morning and afternoon and migraines at night, and finally, all she did was sit out on the back deck, drinking vodka and taking Valium and using my .22 pistol to shoot at possums and raccoons that came out of the city dump and tried to get into our garbage cans. She once swore she shot a coyote, but I never found the carcass and I figured that was one of her heavy vodka days. Since it made her a little happier that she had bagged a coyote, I just told her that I dragged it down and threw it into the river, but that did not even make her happy because she had decided she wanted it stuffed and mounted.

Even then, after Bitsy Jean lost her job at the Dairy Queen, we might have been able to scrape by if I had not been fired from my job as the high school history teacher over at Shadetree Consolidated. I had put in five years and gotten good reviews from my principal, but then little Madonna Yates, that little dark-haired cheerleader with the purple contacts, talked me into signing her out of study hall as my sixth-period aide during my planning period. That went okay since I was too busy to talk to her much, but then Tommy Hargrove, the quarterback on the football team, broke up with her on a Sunday night in October. The next day she was in my room, moping around and smearing her mascara, when I made the mistake of asking if she wanted to talk about it. In the process of talking, she started crying and came over to lean her head on my shoulder, and I put my arms around her to console her. That might have been all right, but in the process of consoling, she started kissing me and then stuck her tongue down my throat like she was plumbing for my tonsils, and five minutes later while my left hand continued to pat her back, my right hand began consoling her perky little breasts.

She didn't seem to mind the consoling at the time, but then she said she went home and prayed about it, and Jesus told her that she needed to tell her mother, which I think was a big mistake. Her mother was a Pentecostal woman who was twice divorced, which turned her into a man-hater, and she called her uncle Trot Gibson on the school board. The next day was full of surprises. One minute I was giving a quiz to the sophomores on Roosevelt and the trustbusters, and the next minute, I was cleaning out my desk and walking humiliated through the halls toward my Escort, wondering how a man could get into so much trouble by trying to be a Good Samaritan.

For a few days I stayed home with Bitsy Jean and drank vodka and shot at the raccoons, but I could tell she missed having me gone. She told me I was holding the gun wrong, and then she complained that a half gallon of White Tavern vodka normally lasted her nearly a week, but now it was gone in three days. I was just trying to numb myself and adjust to my new circumstances, talking on the phone three or four times a day to my mother, who cried and screamed and told me that the devil moves in mysterious ways. I said it was true, although I never thought that Madonna Yates and her breasts were very mysterious. It was just something that happened in the heat of the moment, and it might have just been water over the dam in a few days if Madonna and Jesus had not decided that telling her mother was a good idea.

But things were what they were, and I was stuck out on that redwood deck with Bitsy Jean, who said, "When I married Eddie Redmon, he was the quarterback and I was the football queen. I thought that was all the marriage I would ever need. Then he turned into a brain-damaged retard, so I latched onto you and your education and a solid future. Now I've got a me a child molester who has one nut and no job."

Bitsy Jean had never let me forget that I was born with one testicle. On the nights when my passions waned before her own, she sometimes muttered unkind things about my single dangling appendage and suggested that if I was a real man, I might just grow me another one or maybe go to Denmark or Sweden and have an operation.

As to that remark about her other marriage, Bitsy Jean married Eddie Redmon in June of '89 after she graduated, but he lost a finger that summer in the sawmill, and they gave him a five-thousand-dollar settlement.

He promptly went out and bought himself a used Harley, and three days later, he missed a curve out by the mall and ran head-on into the cement wall of Tilburn's IGA. He was never right after that, and when Bitsy Jean questioned him, he didn't know the states and capitals or any of the apostles. One night at her parents' house, right in the middle of her father's birthday party, Harold took a dump in the kitty litter box and then tried to call people in to witness it like it was something he was proud of. That was the last straw for Bitsy Jean who divorced him and said good riddance. We met at a Methodist skating party and got married a year later with stars in our eyes, and then came the fibromyalgia and then the migraines and then Madonna Yates's breasts. It was pretty much downhill after that first year of great beginnings.

I knew that I had to get off that deck with Bitsy Jean before I started shooting phantom coyotes, too, and so I talked to my cousin Dawky Reese, who got me on at Pentplast, a plastic factory out near the interstate, and so we finally had a steady paycheck coming in. It was touch and go with the school board and the sheriff's department there for a while that I might be designated a sexual predator, but finally, me and my lawyer Troy Jo Starks went into a private meeting with Judge Leo Draper. We showed him a picture of Madonna Yates in her cheerleader outfit, and he nearly spit out his false teeth.

"This is the child whose bosoms you manipulated," he said to me.

I said that I had done exactly that thing as much as I regretted it. Judge Draper shook his head and leaned back in his chair.

"You just rest easy, son," he said. "I think losing your job was a fit punishment."

We started to leave, but he insisted that he be able to keep the picture of Madonna as evidence in case somebody wanted to refile charges. When we left, he was studying that picture like he might have to take a quiz on it later on.

Well, having said all of that, I come to my own entry into a life of crime. Without any income from Bitsy Jean, and my paltry seven dollars per hour at Pentplast, we were falling behind fast. We were at least four months behind on rent, and Norman Cutright said he wanted to see some of that rent money by Friday "else we would be tossed out post haste with an eviction note pinned to our clothing" is how he put it.

I thought his language was a little overly dramatic, but I understood the portent of it. I suggested that Bitsy Jean might quit drinking vodka and try to find a job. She suggested that for a one-nutted child molester, I had a lot of nerve, demanding things of a cripple who was in constant pain. I started to point out that she was not crippled, nor was she even technically disabled, but it did not seem like the time to bring that up. So, I got me another part-time job as a security guard at Haven Rest, a retirement home for old people outside of Shade Tree. Even then, we were not flourishing, and that was when Bitsy Jean came up with an idea for me to steal Social Security checks.

"Look, Harold," she said, punctuating the air in front of my face, "you can steal these checks and drive off somewhere like Owensboro to cash them. Tell them it's for your mama or your old Aunt Celia. Go to a different bank every time and maybe wear a mustache for a disguise. The old people will report their checks stolen, and the government will send them a new one. This is a plan that God give to me because he knows that we are people in need, and he feels bad about giving me fibromyalgia and giving me a husband who cannot control his one-nutted sex impulses."

The holy trinity was busy that winter, what with Jesus deciding Madonna Yates should tell her mother and now God deciding that I should steal Social Security checks. I guess that made as much sense as counting sparrows falling or wiping out entire tribes because Onan spilled his seed upon the ground.

But I knew we were in desperate straits, and knowing that all our bills were coming due, I reluctantly agreed, although I pointed out that I would not look good in a mustache.

I have to admit, I was surprised how well it worked for a while. I was the night guard for a retirement complex with seven hundred old people, seventy-five and older. I was careful to take a random check here or there, always wearing gloves and normally at about three thirty a.m. when old people are not likely to come wandering down to ask why I am looking in mailboxes. The government did its part by sending the checks right at the end of the month. Sure enough, I cashed old lady Darlene Sims's check at a branch bank in Henderson where a fat girl with cat-eye glasses did no more than make me sign a false name. I chose Archibald Cox, and she stamped that check as quick as you could say Watergate. She would have known better if she had been in my history class, but I was glad she had not been since she looked like one of those girls who might cheat. I always hated a cheater.

That worked for three months, and then I had a near thing over in Brumly when I tried to cash Mr. Howard Arthur's check for eleven hundred dollars. The woman was calling the constable when I said I needed to go to the bathroom and slipped out a side door and hightailed it down a bunch of alleys and out of town. I was so scared by the time I got home that I hyperventilated and Bitsy Jean had to give me a juice glass full of vodka and a Valium, a sacrifice that she was not happy with.

I was pretty sure that my life of crime might be over because my nerves just were not made for close calls like I had in Brumly, but Bitsy Jean's doctor bills started piling up, and I was having to spend half of my days arguing with creditors and fat boys named Lonny who came to try to take my TV.

"Harold Weems," Bitsy said one night after we had sweated ourselves out in desperate lovemaking, "we need a quick infusion of cash, about two thousand dollars. If you ain't up to any more Social Security shenanigans, you need to come up with an idea of some kind unless you know next week's lottery numbers, and I know that you don't because you never knowed them before."

I told her that I would put my brain to it, but what I really did was to get up and sit at the TV and watch John Wayne kill a lot of Indians while I killed about six inches of White Tavern vodka and wondered if that big beam in my uncle's barn would support a rope and a skinny man with one nut.

I woke up the next morning with a headache, and I was seriously thinking of just going down to jump in the river where I hoped to become some kind of big fish that sat at the bottom of the river and ate plankton or whatever the hell they ate and never worried about paying off the Sears charge card.

Bitsy Jean got up and never multiplied a word about the serious dent I made in her plastic half gallon of vodka. She fixed me a cup of coffee and sat down across from me.

"I got a plan, Harold," she said, her squinty little eyes nearly lost in the rolls of fat that had collected all over her face since she fell in love with vodka and Reese's Peanut Butter Cups.

I have to admit I did not like the sound of that, but I drank my coffee and nodded for her to go ahead, although I had pretty much made up my mind about me being in the river sometime in the next day or two, no matter what.

"Parker's Liquor Store is out there on South 41 in Henderson," she said. "I know because my gay cousin Maurice worked there before he went off to Indianapolis and became a male stripper at a place called Boys Town. Every Friday night, Tommy Parker brings in ten thousand dollars because the boys from Whirlpool stop there on their way home and cash their checks and buy beer and whiskey for the weekend. If you was to be there, Harold, on a Friday night about ten o'clock with a ski mask and this old .22, you could make enough money in five minutes to pay off all our bills and have enough left over for us to spend a weekend at Dollywood."

She sat back, pretty pleased with her criminal mind, and I sighed deeply, thinking that if nearly getting caught cashing a Social Security check gave me a panic attack, that robbing a liquor store might just pop a geyser in my head just as quick as you could say "Jack Robinson." My family had a history of strokes, and since I had nearly made up my mind to drown, I might at least die in the course of putting my wife back on firm financial footing.

I knew in my heart that I should tell Bitsy Jean no, that what I needed to do more than anything was to leave Bitsy Jean, move back in with my mother, go to the Baptist church, and throw myself on the altar and ask God to cleanse me of my sins. That would have been the logical thing to do, the right thing to do, but it just had too much common sense about it, plus by then, I was partaking with some regularity of White Tavern vodka and any of the Valium that was left lying around. So, like the fool I had turned out to be, I said yes.

On a Friday night, about 8:50, I drove over to Henderson and scoped out the liquor store. I'd stopped there several times as a teenager and bought beer or half pints of whiskey. I knew it was next to the park, and my plan was to leave my car in the park next to that pavilion where they have teenage dances on Friday night.

Nobody would notice one more junky car, and I could sneak through the woods, do the deed, and make it back to my car and drive home with lots of money. It would not make Bitsy Jean happy, but it might keep her off my back another month or two or until I got up the nerve to drown myself.

Everything went pretty well, I thought. I parked my Escort near the back of the lot, and I could hear some rap music playing inside, and lots of girls that looked like Madonna Yates were parading around in the parking lot, drinking beer and talking dirty.

I sneaked through the woods with that .22 stuck down in the deep pocket of an old navy overcoat I bought at the Goodwill. I waited until the parking lot was empty and scrambled across the street and came in with my ski mask pulled down.

The person behind the counter was an old black man who looked at me and then looked at the gun.

"You take that whole fucking cash register if you want it," he said casually as though he was giving me advice on stocks to buy. "I get paid five dollars an hour, and I ain't aimin' to die for no five dollars an hour."

I kept a close eye on him as I slid behind the counter.

Just then the door opened, and in walked one of my nineteen-year-old cousins from Shade Tree. His name was Robert Ellis, but everybody called him Snippy because he was full of energy and always being a smart-ass.

The black man looked up at Snippy and said, "Get the hell out of here. I told you before that you ain't old enough to buy beer."

Snippy needed the beer to cut his meth high. He took crystal meth most of the day, and he needed beer to slow him down long enough to fall into a coma and build up his energy for the next day.

"You ain't behind the counter," Snippy said. "That man with the ski mask is."

He walked right up there where I was stealing the money and asked for a twelve-pack of Pabst Blue Ribbon. I sold it to him and told him that I didn't have any change.

"How is your mama doing?" he asked me. "I mean since you got fired for having sex with that cheerleader."

I told him that Mama was a little depressed.

Snippy nodded. "Yeah, my mama ain't very happy with me either."

Then he gave the black man the finger and walked out.

"He gets drunk and has a wreck, his blood will be on your hands," the black man said and went back to reading his book by Danielle Steele.

I took all the money I could find and put it in a Kroger's sack. I waved the gun at him and started to say something, but he put a finger up.

"I done let you rob the place," he said. "Don't you go insulting me by acting like you're some punk-ass mobster. You just some ugly white boy who wants to buy a bunch of pot or impress a girl who's going to treat you like shit and take all that money and leave you anyway."

I backed out of the liquor store, feeling like I ought to be more triumphant. But then I had to scuttle across the street and into the trees. I made a straight line for my car, but I tripped on a root and hurt my ankle. I was hobbling bad when I got to the parking lot, just in time to see my cousin Snippy driving away in my car.

My first thought was to call the police, but my second thought was that my first thought was really idiotic, considering I had a Kroger's sack full of money I robbed from a liquor store. Finally, I called a taxi and paid over a hundred dollars to have him take me back to Clugg.

When I got home, Bitsy looked into that sack and hugged me to her, then pulled me down on the bed and gave herself freely. When we were finished, she sat up and pinched my nipple.

"Go to the liquor store and get me some vodka. I feel like celebrating."

That was when I told her that Snippy had stolen my car.

"How did you get home?"

"I took a taxi," I said.

"Then take a taxi downtown to a liquor store before it closes. It is nearly midnight."

I called a taxi and he dropped me off at a hole-in-the-wall liquor store called Red's.

Just as I pulled out a wad of money to pay for the half gallon of vodka, Snippy came in the back door with a ski mask on, waving his gun. The first thing he took was my wad of cash, and then he emptied the cash register.

"You stole my car," I said as he backed toward the door.

"You can have it," Snippy said, throwing me the keys. "It is a piece of shit anyways."

So, I took the vodka and drove home to Bitsy Jean and reported that I had the car back, but Snippy had robbed me of three hundred dollars. We both sat down and had a few shots, and then she got up and went into the bedroom. Twenty minutes later, while I watched Blondie sing "Heart of Glass," Bitsy Jean came out of the bedroom with her suitcase.

"I got all that money in it, Harold. I deserve it for having to put up with you and your one nut. Snippy is picking me up in a minute. We're going to live in Tijuana and drink tequila all day. If my mother calls, tell her that I went to look for work in Louisville and I will call her in a week or two. If your mother calls, tell her she is the worst mother-in-law I ever had."

Then she walked out the door. I drank the rest of that half gallon of vodka over the rest of the weekend, floating in and out of consciousness. Then Monday morning, I walked home to my mother's house and moved back into my old room. Wednesday night I went to church with her, and when I heard the Lord calling my name, I did not hesitate to go down that aisle and fling myself down on the altar and surrender my all to his goodness and mercy.

I had made a big mess of things following my own willful impulses. When I was singing and dancing and hugging people in the aftermath of my conversion, Madonna Yates came up and hugged me. Even in the midst of my spiritual rapture, I was careful to hug her in a gingerly manner guaranteed to show the purity of my intentions.

"Oh, I know what you're doing," she said. "You're still worried about touching my boobies. Well, I have got over that completely. You are now just another soldier in the army of God, and we have got to stick together and love one another."

She offered to drive me home, and then she detoured through the park. She pulled into an old access road, and we prayed together for a long time, holding hands and asking for God's guidance.

"If you come back next Wednesday, I think we get to handle rattlesnakes," she said joyfully.

I said I thought that sounded like something I might rather watch for a while before I jumped into it full throttle.

"When you have got faith, everything is possible," she told me. Then she jumped into my lap and started kissing me and making deep moaning noises. Three weeks later, we were engaged. A month later, her uncle got me my job back at the high school.

So, everything has pretty much come full circle.

Bitsy Jean and Snippy got drunk and stoned and ran off into the Rio Grande and drowned in about three feet of water. I went to the funeral and cried a little, but Madonna held my hand and told me to be strong.

I am back to teaching Roosevelt and the trustbusters. I quit drinking vodka for Madonna and Jesus. My mother now proudly talks about her son the teacher again, and I have tried to stay on the straight and narrow.

Like that song says, I think this has been a lesson for us all.

# Muzzles

Doug Marrin

"MUZZLES! . . . MUZZLES! . . . MUH-ZELLES!"

On a warm afternoon in 1972, I stood in the rutted truck yard of a duck farm calling for my best friend. At twelve years of age, I had absolutely no inkling of the frightening world that I was about to enter. That day terminated my childhood, my innocence, and my self-confidence.

"Muzzles! . . . Muh-zelles!"

The more I called, the more the beagle's name took on an eerie, forlorn yowl, as if I were part hound myself. It broke the silence of that Sunday afternoon and echoed through the surrounding farmyard and woods. Where is she?

"Muhh-zellles! . . . Muhhhh-zellllles!"

Reining Muzzles in from her exploits was one of my weekend chores on the duck farm. The large truck yard in which I stood was a forty-yard open square, providing enough room for the trucks, tractors, trailers, and other big equipment to park and maneuver when called into action. The ground was a jumble of dusty ridges from the churning action of the big tires in mud. The surrounding buildings—garage, workshop, feed coop, old horse barn, and of course the hatchery itself—created a natural amphitheater. Here, in my Redwing work boots, jeans, and shirttails flapping in the breeze, I yelled out, a one-boy show in this rural theater in the round.

"MUHH . . . ZELLES!" I took a breath in between syllables for more volume.

Muzzles was nowhere to be seen. I was irritated, but not surprised. When Muzzles fastened her nose to the hunt, it was an addiction that sacrificed all other cares and concerns. Her sense of smell was the door to adventure, coloring the world in brilliant hues. Asking my little beagle to return home was insisting she return to a dreary black and white existence.

Stopping to catch my breath and settle my rising temper, I locked my hands on my hips and surveyed the yard; Dad was talking nearby with one of the farmhands, "Chick" Vandenberg. (His nickname had nothing to do with his job in poultry. As a toddler learning to talk, his younger sister pronounced "Dick" as "Chick." The name stuck.) Dad was leaning on a rake looking up and listening to the younger man, who rested his sinewy forearms on the white fence separating our lot from the hatchery.

I grew up in Holland, Michigan, on C&D Duck Farm. Instead of planting seeds and raising crops, this farm collected eggs and hatched ducks. The main chore was the daily collection of eggs from the flocks housed in the different coops. The duck eggs would be then stored in the hatchery's cooler until placed in the incubators. Baby ducks hatched twenty-eight days later. They were immediately boxed and shipped off to Wisconsin. Upon arrival, the baby chicks would live a pampered life for six weeks before having their throats slit, at which time they would be dressed for market.

The duck farm was by no means a small enterprise. The primary operation, where we lived, was home to some 20,000 ducks. The hatchery was roughly the size of two barns. Three-quarters of the ducks were divided evenly among three large coops, where they laid their eggs in nesting stalls. The remaining 5,000 roamed outdoors on an open range, for a rotational rest period from laying. A second farm housed flocks totaling 30,000. In addition to these two nuclear farms, Dad contracted with independent farms to house a flock or two and deliver eggs to the hatchery. The end result was 28,000 baby ducks ready to ship to Wisconsin every day, Monday through Friday.

Working C&D Duck Farm was hard and dirty. A rough and durable crew kept it running. Somebody supervised the whole operation so it would make money for the owners. That somebody was my father. At five foot three, what he lacked in stature he made up for in toughness and intimidation. More than once I witnessed Dad go toe-to-toe with a worker, looking up at them through his thick black-rimmed glasses, his balding head bobbing in sharp rhythm to his words. On a few occasions, I had been on the receiving end of that raw strength, with more occasions coming in my teen years. These encounters could leave me feeling nauseous.

In addition to the rote responsibilities of purchasing feed, bedding, rotating flocks, and repairing equipment, the operation faced the constant threat of disease, either to the ducks or the eggs. Bacteria thrived in the ubiquitous duck manure, and if the wrong microorganisms found their way onto the farm, they could quickly spread through the flocks and their ova.

Four-legged threats were also constantly on the prowl. Coyotes, raccoons, foxes, and even a stray dog now and then gorged themselves on an all-you-can-eat duck and egg buffet. Should an animal get caught in the act, the sentence was swift and brutal: death by gunshot. The farmworkers would often go out hunting in an attempt to thin the population of predators, a practice I took up in my teen years, although I never killed anything. I just liked telling people how I fearlessly held the predatorial appetite of nature at bay.

The farm attracted the best of the best when it came to workers—men and women of noble character who exemplified a commendable work ethic. Dad had high praise for these folks. "You know," he sometimes said to me while pointing at one of the workers, "that guy always shows up and keeps his mouth shut, never complains." Not raised in the art of emotional expression, this was how Dad, a hard man, gushed.

As if to balance the fine character of some of the crew, the farm also drew the worst kind of humans—drunks, addicts, thieves, cheats—who were irresponsible, undependable, and required constant checking to maintain the quality of their work. Always careful with his language around me, Dad would often describe them to me in his gravelly voice as "not having a brain in their head." Once I overheard him describe one worker as "a piece of shit." Dad always got right to the point.

Dad and I never spent time together just having fun. Instead, he drafted me to help him with repairs around the house or hatchery. I held a flashlight while he worked on some electrical or plumbing issue. Clever and self-reliant when it came to fixing things, my father made frequent trips to Van Wieren Hardware Store and let me tag along. He rewarded me with a pack of Chuckles out of the deal. Our real fun, however, always involved the family. Some of my favorite memories were loading up the car for a trip out to Cal's near Lake Macatawa for a soft-serve ice cream cone. An even better treat was a hard-pack cone at Mills House of Flavors in downtown Holland.

Sports provided some common ground for my father and me. Dad was a big fan of major league baseball. The Detroit Tigers were his team. When the season was on, so was the television or radio, for every game. I grew up listening to the games and to Dad talking about the players. One particularly memorable exception to our baseball fanaticism, however, was the first of three championship fights between Muhammad Ali and Smokin' Joe Frazier. Dubbed the Fight of the Century, it was held at Madison Square Garden in 1971, when both Ali and Frazier were undefeated and the undisputed champions in their respective leagues. I was excited. Dad was excited. Game night came. Mom popped the popcorn and then left the room announcing, "I don't see how you fellas can watch such a thing," which turned the event into an even more appealing forbidden fruit. My father and I were both rooting for Smokin' Joe. The night was truly memorable, just Dad and me, talking smack at Ali through the TV screen and having fun. He let me stay up late, until the end, because the two gladiators lasted all fifteen rounds. Frazier won by unanimous decision. We were elated.

But back to the truck yard. When Dad and Chick noticed me, the two stopped their conversation to turn and stare, probably wondering at the sudden silence. Embarrassed at having been caught gawking, I turned away and resumed attacking the afternoon's peace.

"Muhhh-zellles!"

The beagle is a scent hound, a species that hunts by smell rather than sight. Somewhere far back in history, beagles were developed primarily for hunting rabbits. Thanks to their extraordinary sense of smell, beagles are also the primary breed used as detection dogs for contraband food items in luggage coming into the United States or bedbugs in hotels. During the 1950s, the scenting abilities of various dog breeds were tested by putting a mouse in a one-acre field. The dogs were timed as they hunted the rodent. The beagles found it in less than a minute. Fox terriers needed fifteen minutes. Scottish terriers couldn't find it at all.

Now, I was on the hunt for my beagle. I always let Muzzles out of her pen on weekends to stretch her legs unsupervised on the eighty-acre farm, on Dad's advice. "Hunting dogs don't want to be cooped up." After a few hours, I always called her home. Sometimes she came right back. Most of the time she took her time, but she always returned. This time, however, she wasn't ambling toward me with her familiar flapping ears, despite the rising tone in my voice. My irritation faded, replaced by a small black bullet of concern. Where is she?

ON ANOTHER QUIET SUNDAY afternoon, forty-eight years later, I am writing at my desk when a sudden screech of tires on pavement pierces the pleasant spring air wafting through the open window. My fingers freeze on the keyboard mid-word. I wait for the crash. Instead, the sharp, crunching thunks of a rolling vehicle are followed by a metallic impact. An unnatural silence follows, as if the birds, bugs, and trees are holding their breath.

Without hesitation, I grab my mobile phone and dial 911. Five rings. Am I interrupting lunch?

"Nine one one. Where is your emergency?" The voice hits my ear like a saw striking a nail. Where did they find her?

"I live on Joy Road in Dexter." An image of Dad talking to me in the old truck yard comes to mind, and I get right to the point, like he did that afternoon in 1972. "I heard a loud screeching of tires and a crash. Near Potts Drive."

I expect questions. Is anybody hurt? How many people are involved? Instead, I get silence. I wait, careful not to fall into nervous chatter. This is my first experience calling 911, but, thanks to decades of television shows, I expected more urgency. Meanwhile, I imagine people bleeding and slumped over a dashboard.

Confused by the silence, I offer a clear directive. "I did not witness the crash, but judging by the sound, somebody needs to get out here." But the operator has joined the birds and bugs in their preternatural quiet. I hear no breathing, no talking on another phone line or clacking of computer keys. I conclude that we have lost our connection.

But we haven't.

"Okay. I'll send someone out." She actually does sound annoyed. I hang up and listen for sirens. A Huron Valley ambulance station is two hundred yards down the road. More silence. Where are they?

I will go to the accident scene—but I do not want to be first to arrive. However, what I want doesn't matter. Something, or someone, inside of me kicks me out of my chair. For a split moment, not even a nanosecond, the memory of Dad talking to Chick Vandenberg at a white fence flashes through my thoughts like distant lightning at night, the portent of a terrible storm. The thought is gone as quickly as it arrives, but not before leaving that familiar black bullet of worry in my thoughts once again.

Psychologists coined the phrase "awake mental replay" to describe the ripple-like burst of neurological activity in the brain's hippocampus that consolidates information from short-term memory into long-term memory. These sudden flashes of memory are not random. The brain is drawing upon encoded information from the past in order to instruct us through the future. Triggered by emotion, the brain is processing what to expect, based on what it has experienced. In my case, my brain has identified similarities between that Sunday afternoon in 1972 and this Sunday afternoon. Because I have been in this situation before, I know what to expect. *Brace yourself.*

The hippocampus is the brain's filing cabinet for episodic memories. The hippocampus feeds information to the prefrontal cortex, which exerts executive control over a person. If people were computers, the prefrontal cortex would be the operating system and the hippocampus the storage files. The prefrontal cortex gives expression, in the form of thoughts and decisionmaking, to what the hippocampus has stored. The two collaborate to create reality.

When the prefrontal cortex confronts a potentially threatening situation, such as approaching a rollover car accident, it calls upon the hippocampus to provide stored data that relate to the situation—as counsel, to forecast a response and form a decision. Flashes of memory literally create visions for the future. Laurence Gonzales, in his book *Deep Survival,* calls this process "remembering the future."

The relationship between your memory and present thought, your hippocampus and prefrontal cortex, can be compared to a car traveling down a highway. Your hippocampus serves as the tires picking up pebbles of memories along the road of life, only to drop them at some point farther along your way, maybe when you hit a bump. Not every stone is picked up by the tires. When considering the innumerable life experiences we have (pebbles), remarkably few make the journey with us.

As I slowly drive toward the tragedy, I am in two worlds at once—felt/insentient and emotion/indifferent—in both my past and present. The former overshadows the latter. At the speed of crackling synapses, my hippocampus recalls the devastating afternoon in 1972, when my beagle wouldn't come home. I am also two people at once, a twelve-year-old boy and a grown man. The boy from the duck farm has stepped out of a hidden world I thought long gone, warning me to brace myself for what lies ahead.

MY FIFTH BIRTHDAY WAS also on a Sunday. Lunch was over, the dishes cleared; dessert plates sprinkled with crumbs of red velvet cake were scattered around the table. The real excitement was about to begin. Mom, Dad, my sister Sandy (who is six years older than I am), and my brother Larry (seventeen years older) came bearing their presents.

Sandy's gift came first. I clearly recall her freckled and smiling face framed by chestnut hair. I can't remember what she gave, but I'm sure it was nice. My parents gave me their gifts next. I don't remember what they were, either, because of what followed.

Until that moment, I had barely noticed Larry leaving the room. Probably out doing chores. But I definitely noticed when he reappeared, carrying a big cardboard box used to transport dozens of duck eggs at a time.

"You've got one more present," Mom pointed out. Her eyes danced like sunlight through leaves behind her black horned-rim glasses. She straightened a stray lock of her gray hair.

Larry set the box on the floor and said, "Open 'er up!"

My older brother has always been my hero, especially during my childhood years, when kids search for approval and role models to imitate. And imitate Larry I did—the way he cuffed his jeans at the bottom, how he rolled the sleeves of his shirt, how he talked, and what he said. At about this time, he taught me to say "apple grunt." It was the funniest thing I'd ever heard. I spent the rest of the day making up sentences to use "apple grunt" and then laughing at the sound of my own voice. Mom finally put a halt to my annoying behavior by threatening to wash my mouth out with soap. The threat of soap didn't stop me from giggling at the thought, or whispering "apple grunt" to myself. The danger made that more appealing. And now, getting a present from him was an absolute thrill.

I slid off the kitchen chair, bent over the box, and lifted the lid. Inside, a bundle of black, brown, and white jumped and pawed at the side of the box, trying to get to me. Larry's two hunting beagles, Pat and Duke, had produced a litter of four puppies. My brother's intention was to sell them, I knew, though he let me play with them "until then." I looked up at Larry, not quite sure why he would bring a puppy into the house.

"She's all yours, Buckshot." That was the nickname Dad and Larry gave me.

My breath still catches at the memory. I picked up my new baby beagle and held her to my chest. She licked my chin. I understood then what people meant when they said their heart could burst—the joy inside is stretching the seams of the person on the outside.

"Thank you." It was a feeble response compared to the happiness I felt.

Mom began clearing the dessert dishes. Dad went to watch TV, where he would take his Sunday afternoon nap.

"What are you going to name her?" Sandy asked.

This was a big decision, and I gave it serious thought. A burger drive-in on the south side of Holland called Muzzy's always represented a treat; on rare occasions we went there for a hamburger, fries, and root beer, and I loved the place. Like "apple grunt," the name was fun to say.

"Muzzy's," I said.

"You can't call her that," Sandy objected. "That's where we eat. You can't name a dog after a place we eat."

I thought again. The puppy was still squirming and licking my face. If I couldn't use Muzzy's, then perhaps something like Muzzy's.

"Muzzles," I said.

"Muzzles?"

"Yup, Muzzles."

Larry built an addition next to the pen where Muzzles's parents Pat and Duke lived, and my little beagle spent her nights there. But her days were spent with me, as I played with friends and roamed the farm, which offered countless adventures. An old abandoned incubator left to rot in a field was a ship battling sharks, pirates, and storms on raging seas. The old decrepit horse barn was our castle teeming with gremlins, ghosts, and monsters. The woods and fields, however, were our world within a world. Out there, among the stabbing calls of blue jays and the clack of flitting grasshoppers, our real adventures began. Together, Muzzles and I tracked ferocious beasts with long ears and fluffy tails. We discovered strangely twisted sticks and countless mysteries underneath rotting logs. I loved the outdoors, my head in the clouds and my thoughts on the breeze—and I still do. Muzzles, too, found her place and purpose there, as a hunter roaming the farm with her nose to the ground and visions of wild game in her head.

Three years after Muzzles joined our family, we moved off the farm and into a large subdivision full of houses and kids. Dad still ran the duck farm, but my world dramatically changed. I found new friends, many friends, and with the larger gang came bigger and constant adventures. Adjacent to the subdivision, behind our house, were expansive tracts of white pine interspersed with meadows. On any given day, when we were not in school, you might find anywhere from two to twelve of us darting through the pines and fields, playing war with stick rifles and pine cone grenades thrown from brush pile forts. And we careened through the trails and trees riding our bikes but competing in a wild motorcycle race. We played football and softball and hung out at each other's house on rainy days, watching reruns of *Gilligan's Island* or *Scooby Doo*. We were a mob of adolescents with many arms, legs, mouths, and missing teeth—but only one half-developed brain.

As I grew closer to my friends, I spent less time with Muzzles. Instead of roaming a farm sniffing out game, she spent long hours chained in the backyard to her doghouse. I sometimes let her come along when I was out and about with my friends, but she became a liability when her own adolescent independence led her in other directions, running off on her own, nose to the ground, in search of her own adventures. Not everyone in the neighborhood appreciated a dog in their yard, and some neighbors complained. As a result, I kept her chained for days on end. Looking back, I deeply regret keeping my free-spirited beagle shackled while I enjoyed the freedom of the woods and fields.

This is not to say we didn't have any memorable moments. One evening several neighboring families spontaneously gathered in our backyard, the adults busy chatting about uninteresting stuff and my friends and I messing around, wrestling, playing tag, and insulting each other—the usual activities that made living in a neighborhood so enjoyable for growing boys.

"Look!" shouted one of the kids, pointing past the fence at the woods.

The adults stopped talking. We stopped messing around. Everybody turned to look. Muzzles wriggled under the bottom rail of the fence into our yard, dragging something along with her mouth.

"What does she have?" one of the moms asked no one in particular.

It looked like an old rag. Please don't let it be a dead animal. It was neither.

"OH MY GOD!" whooped one of the other moms. The men exploded into laughs and the kids all started yelling and screeching like the monkey house at John Ball Park Zoo.

Muzzles was dragging a pair of soiled cotton briefs. And by soiled, I mean fully loaded and still glistening. Grass, twigs, and leaves were stuck to the sodden mass. I joined my friends in fits of laughter and rude comments.

"Go get that from her!" my mother snapped. Ever prim, ever proper in the public eye, she was mortified.

I broke away from the group with a couple friends and ran to grab my dog. She dodged me. Another kid lunged, and she dodged him as well. More kids joined in the fun. A hilarious game of keep-away ensued, us against Muzzles, which no doubt entertained the adults—except for my red-faced mother.

Another time, Muzzles drew a crowd when she broke the tranquility of yet another peaceful Sunday afternoon by romancing the neighbor's poodle in our front yard. The streets were quiet and deserted until Muzzles and her beau staged a romantic rendezvous on the grass. Kids suddenly appeared out of nowhere, once again whooping and hollering the play-by-play like Ernie Harwell for the Detroit Tigers. Once again, Mom was beside herself.

I BELIEVE WE LIVE in two worlds—the world we see and the world we feel, the prefrontal cortex and the hippocampus. The world we feel (hippocampus) interprets the world we see (prefrontal cortex), and provides context and meaning, offering advice on the proper response.

In reality, the world is neither harsh nor comforting. It is indifferent. The world happens—the laws of nature, relational transactions, and the inexplicable—as it always has and always will. It is our emotions that give these events significance. A circumstance is defined by how we feel about it. The world is a monochrome sketch waiting for colors to be applied, and we all have our own ideas about appropriate colors. Each of us carries our own individualized palette in the form of memories, which are touchstones of emotion used to interpret the outside world.

Our inner world is created during the formative years of childhood and adolescence, when our acrylics are placed on the palette, and we learn how to paint the canvas of our life. As with any artist, instruction is needed to develop our skill in understanding our subjects and how to express them adequately and appropriately. We need to be taught how the world works and what our responses should be. Without a hand on our shoulder to guide us, we could be left standing in a dirty truck yard, crying and abandoned, with our colors a disappointing mixed mess of gray.

Back in my adulthood, driving the short distance in the direction of Potts Drive, I spot a group of bystanders gathered on a lawn looking across the road.

This is in the world I see (prefrontal cortex), but it has no meaning—until the world I feel (hippocampus) replays the scene in which I am a boy standing alone at the duck farm with Dad and Chick talking a short distance away, bystanders to an unfolding tragedy. The flashback of something familiar explains the unknown. It tells me what to expect. The world is no longer indifferent. It is menacing. I know how to feel. I am frightened. I am remembering the future.

I believe inside every person lives another person, an interloper, intrusive and controlling, a schemer who bullies his way into our happy lives at the most importune times. This creature has the mind of a child, a younger version frozen in time, a recalcitrant ghost petulantly insisting its messy and undeveloped paintings are the current reality.

* * *

THE SPRING I TURNED twelve, we left the subdivision and moved back to the duck farm, this time into the owner's old house, which was larger and had a swimming pool. Muzzles's home, too, was upgraded to a large run connected to a shed on the back of the garage. We did not resume our old ways of roaming the woods and fields. I was older and more mobile, visiting friends and pursuing other interests. Muzzles was also older, so she was allowed to explore the farm on her own. I called her in at the end of the day, and she always came. As we drifted apart, I gave my beagle less and less thought until I almost lost her.

That spring, a hard and unseasonably cold rain fell one day and into the night. I raced out to shut the flap to Muzzles's run. Otherwise, invariably she would bark through the night at every rustling leaf, calling bird, or chirping cricket. I made sure her shed was dry and warm in the cold, wet night. The straw had that musty farm smell I have always loved. On a miserable night such as this, I imagined how inviting this warm, dry shelter would be for a beagle. But Muzzles was not in her shed. She must be out in the run.

"Muzzles!" I barked over the sound of the rain on the roof and trees.

She didn't come. What was she doing out there?

I called again, even louder, but with no response. I was perplexed. She hadn't been out of her pen because of the weather. The run was dog-proof, thanks to its wire fencing, so she couldn't escape. Cursing was new for me, and I practiced a few words now knowing I would have to go outdoors into the storm and get her. Hatless, I was already drenched. I walked out of the shed and into the rain, clambered over the gate into the run. Calling her name, I circled the pen. The dark made it difficult to see, the rain even more so. I discovered Muzzles curled up nose to haunches under a torrent of ice-cold water gushing out of a broken downspout from the roof of the garage beside the run.

"Muzzles!"

She didn't move, as if frozen stiff. I dropped to my knees on the cold, wet ground and put my hand on her head. She lifted it a bit and put it down. I was scared. I scooped her up in my arms, fumbled to open the gate, and rushed her indoors.

Mom helped me make a bed for Muzzles in the laundry room. My dog shivered and shook, barely responsive. I had to repeat the story of where I found her several times to Mom and Dad. They couldn't understand why a dog with cozy shelter just yards away would lie under a gushing downpour of cold water. It puzzled me too. I sat next to her, softly stroking her head. Please don't die.

I asked Mom and Dad if Muzzles was going to die. They didn't know. All sorts of memories, precious episodes from my boyhood poured in like the storm outside. The two of us exploring woods and fields. Muzzles loping along, ears flapping. A puppy scrambling to get out of an empty egg case and into my lap. "What are you going to name her?"

Thankfully, Muzzles recovered, and life went on pretty much as it had before, except now I had an inkling that Muzzles was more than just a dog. She seemed a part of me somehow. And after seven years, the dog still had a few surprises.

One evening she surprised me by returning from her hunt covered in green and greasy duck shit. I was shocked. I did not yet know dogs, especially hunting dogs, would sometimes roll in animal scat. While I was thoroughly disgusted, oddly, my little dog seemed happy, even ecstatic, with tail wagging, eyes bulging, and tongue lolling.

"Sometimes dogs will do that," Dad said when I told him about it.

"Why?"

"That's just what dogs do." Dad's explanations were always short and to the point. I considered what he had said. An epiphany occurred and I realized Muzzles was an animal with animal instincts. Up until now, I always thought of her more as a person.

I had another startling glimpse of my dog's animal side when I caught her behind the hatchery eating rotten eggs. A dozen or so fifty-five-gallon steel drums were kept outside and out of sight where rotten and unused eggs were discarded along with dead ducks. The smell was horrendous, especially after a few days in the hot summer sun. Simply driving past the barrels on the way out to the coops was enough for the odor to sink its talons into you and not let go without a good scrubbing.

The eggs often spill when being dumped into the barrels behind the hatchery. When I found Muzzles with her muzzle deep inside a small pile of putrefying black and green egg innards chewing shell and all, I was disgusted. What the heck? My beagle was eating perhaps the worst substance known to mankind . . . and enjoying it. I took a deep breath, held it, scurried the few yards to my dog, and dragged her by the collar away from the disgusting mess.

This happened a few times. I began to question the personification that I so endearingly attached to my beagle. I slowly became convinced that Muzzles was more dog than person. I began to suspect that, after all these years, I didn't really know my little dog at all. She seemed to have a secret life with strange animal cravings and desires.

"Muh-zellles . . . Muh-zellles! . . . MUH-ZELLLES!" I resumed my hollering, slowly pirouetting like a rotating air siren.

But Dad, not Muzzles, came to me. He was only a few inches taller than I was, but would always be an imposing figure to me, even long after I shot past him in height. I expected him to gruffly tell me to "knock it off and stop disturbing the neighbors" with all my yelling. He didn't. Also, expecting to see the familiar irritated boss expression on Dad's face, I was surprised at the softness I glimpsed in his features. I looked over to the fence and Chick was gone.

"Chick said there was a dog in the ducks earlier today," Dad said with typical lack of preamble. An animal "in the ducks" was farm code for "killing the ducks."

Raccoons, foxes, and stray dogs were a constant nuisance to the flocks, which were easy pickings for an easy meal. It wasn't uncommon for the farmhands to come across a bloody and partially devoured duck carcass when doing chores. I often found half-eaten kills while I was out wandering the farm. I sensed bad news coming. Did a larger dog attack my beagle? Muzzles was no fighter. A vision of Muzzles lying bloody and partially devoured flashed through my thoughts. Was she hurt? Was Dad telling me to go out and find Muzzles?

"Chick shot it," Dad said bluntly.

Large flocks make loud noises when a predator is in the pen chasing them. Five thousand terrified quacking ducks can easily be heard from a substantial distance. The noise invariably alerts the attention of the farmhands, who shoot to protect the ducks and their livelihood. I was relieved to hear the intruder had been shot, or, as one former Vietnam vet on the farm expressed it: "The threat has been neutralized." I looked past Dad, hoping to see Muzzles trotting home with ears flapping.

"It was Muzzles."

My mind went blank, as if sucker punched. I was confused. I couldn't have heard right! No, not Muzzles! Why would Dad say that? Dad quietly nodded as if reading my thoughts. I must have stopped breathing because moments later I sucked in a big, quavering gasp. Two great cascades sprung from my eyes. I looked away from Dad and down at the dirt, where my tears hit like stones. I opened my mouth wide, to quiet my sobs. I hated crying in front of Dad, but I couldn't contain the unimaginable aguish.

Dad stood in front of me, helpless to comfort, but trying to be caring. The problem was that he just wasn't a soft person. His own father was a drunk and his mom was mean. What parents don't give to their kids when they're growing up, the kids won't have as adults. I don't hold this against Dad. He took care of us far better than his own parents had taken care of him.

"He didn't know it was your dog until he walked up to it," Dad continued. "He didn't mean to shoot her."

A memory pushed its way to the forefront of my thoughts. A dog belonging to a neighboring family got into the ducks once and was shot in the rear leg by the owner's son with a .22 rifle. The cocker spaniel eventually healed, although its leg was forever stiff after that. The image of my beagle with a stiff hind leg was another punch to the gut. I knew how much Muzzles lived to run and hunt. How could she do that with a stiff leg?

But where was Muzzles now? She would be scared and need me. I remembered stroking her head in the laundry room.

"Where . . . is . . . she?" It is impossible to simultaneously bawl and speak. I was embarrassed by my halting speech.

"Chick took care of her."

Why is Chick taking care of her? She's my dog! A picture of Chick stroking her head in the laundry room came and went. But then, the full weight of what Dad was trying to tell me without actually saying the words outright hit me like Ali's best right hook.

"Is . . . ?" I couldn't say the words either. I wiped the running snot from my nose, took a big breath, and tried again.

"Is . . ." I forced myself to say it. "Is she dead?" I choked on a sob, terrified of Dad's answer.

Dad then told me in plain words what was impossible for me to believe. I learned that "shot your dog" was farm language for "killed your dog."

I stood in the middle of the truck yard blubbering, vision blurred and snot snuffling. My chest heaved. Great primordial sobs escaped my mouth refusing to be stifled. My arms gesticulated with no purpose. The sun was shining in a rich blue sky, but a great blackness closed in around me. I now knew what people meant when they said a heart could break. The person on the inside has burst and lay in tatters in an indifferent world, like a ruptured balloon on a busy street.

Dad was with me, but I was utterly alone. Dad didn't hug me or put a hand on my shoulder. He, too, was helpless as he watched his youngest son empty and wither.

"Once a dog gets a taste of blood, you can't keep them away," Dad said at last. "You would have to keep her penned up or on a leash. That's no life for a dog."

"But she wouldn't be dead," I rasped.

We live in two worlds, the world we see and the world we feel, each with its own language. The world we feel dictates the meaning of the world we see. We interpret our world through the lens of our emotions. What gives something meaning is not what it is, but how we feel about it. Dad was doing his best to speak into the world I feel with the language of logic and reason, an effort that often results in a mistranslation. I was living in the land of overwhelming sorrow and emotion.

I don't remember going back to the house, what Mom said or did, or anything that transpired the rest of the day. I don't remember how I broke the news to my friends. Nothing from those days immediately following my dog's death has ever replayed in my thoughts, a blank spot in my memory, files corrupted and unusable.

DECADES LATER, I PARK my Sierra on the shoulder of the road about thirty yards from the clutch of onlookers. Their attention is on the opposite side of the road. They are talking. One casts me a glance. Dad and Chick. I switch on the pickup's emergency flashers and wait. The wreck is out of sight behind some brush and saplings.

I am puzzled by the lack of urgency at the accident scene. Why isn't anybody doing anything to help? Why is everyone just waiting? Once again I am the twelve-year-old boy standing in the open truck yard calling a dog that will never come home, waiting. It must be too late. No first responders have arrived. This scene has an old familiar feel, and the boy inside me is screaming, "Don't go to the wreck!" I wait. I recall sobbing in front of Dad, embarrassed, and I am reminded of the many times I have fallen apart in a crisis. Where others take charge and fly into action, I freeze. I hate this about myself.

I am always waiting, waiting for someone else to help the people in the car, waiting for the EMTs to arrive, waiting for a dead dog to return from her hunt. For the sake of self-preservation, I stay in the truck to keep my world, the world I feel, from falling apart once again.

Psychologists call awake mental replay our past self guiding our present self in order to preserve the future self. Our younger, immature self, who inhabits the world we feel, is informing our present self living in the world we see, in order to prevent birth defects in the person we will become.

A fire truck arrives with flashing lights but no siren. Not a big fire engine, but a modified pickup in high-visibility yellow. Dexter Area Fire Department is painted in bold gold letters on the door. Instead of jumping out and dashing to the wreck, the driver remains inside, writing on what appears to be a clipboard. What the hell? Nobody moves. My anxiety rises. The gawkers watch the first responder. I watch the gawkers watch the fireman.

The first responder finally gets out of the truck, hitches up his pants, and grabs what looks like a toolbox. After opening it to look inside, he shuts it and saunters over to the crash, high-stepping through the ruined brush. Like Dad walking over to me with few tools in his emotional kit. The fireman disappears behind the trees. I let out a breath I hadn't realized I was holding. Bloody carcass of a dead duck. It must be a mess in that car.

The fireman reappears moments later with his toolbox. My heart drops like a stone to the earth. Muzzles isn't coming home, and neither are the occupants of that car. My hand freezes on the truck's door handle. I don't want to go to the scene. I don't want to hear what Dad has to say. The onlookers don't react. I cannot determine from their body language what the state of the wreck might be. Nobody is acting distraught. I get out of the Sierra and begin the death march to the gawkers.

As surreal as the entire scene is, it feels familiar. Dad and Chick talking at the fence. Calling Muzzles to come home. Screeching tires, crash, silence. A hard punch to the heart. Dad watching me break down. People moving in slow motion. My hippocampus is shooting buckshot at my prefrontal cortex as my mind frantically scrambles to make sense of what lies just ahead. The world I feel is a maelstrom of past and present. The twelve-year-old boy has lurched out of the past, counseling his adult self. This is the same boy who has haunted me my entire life, pulling back on my leash, holding me back, always scared, always nervous.

"What happened?" I ask the onlookers.

"It was Muzzles," Dad said. I brace myself.

"We didn't see it," said one woman. "We didn't even hear it."

Calling out to my beagle, unaware of her death.

I explained how I had heard it and heroically called 911.

"I did too," said another woman. "Twice."

"But they look like they're okay," said the first woman, directing my attention to the wreck.

What? The plot twists and my inner boy is confused. This isn't how the story ends.

Following her gesture and looking across Joy Road, broken saplings and flattened scrub mark the car's destructive swath. A white Volkswagen Passat lies on its side, driver's side down, against the tree that stopped its roll. The scene is a place of violence and destruction, chaos and death. But I am shocked when I see two people, a boy and a girl, incongruously sitting atop the car . . . waiting. In the next moment, however, my initial surprise is eclipsed by an even greater astonishment.

"Holy shit! That's my nephew!" I bark over my shoulder as I dash across the road.

My brother-in-law Patrick adopted Yevgeniy Alexeyevich Glazkov, or Zhenya (the Russian nickname for Yevgeniy), from Russia eighteen years earlier. Zhenya, or Z as I call him, was two years old at the time, living in an orphanage under the charge of chain-smoking, coffee-swilling attendants.

Patrick told me that Zhenya had set himself apart from the other kids in the orphanage. While the others cowered in corners and around the legs of the workers, Z continued moving around the room, playing. And then, he fearlessly walked up to Patrick, offering him a toy so the two of them could play together. A beagle puppy in a cardboard box scrambling to get out. Curiosity and spunk have been Z's defining hallmarks his entire life.

I didn't have much to do with Z during his early years. He was smothered with attention from his dad, grandparents, aunts, uncles, and cousins. Although he lived next door to us with his father and grandparents, I kept my distance, not wanting to add to the cacophony of voices always clamoring for his attention. The ice broke for us when he was around age ten. I made him laugh, and our die was cast. We began our adventures together a few years later, although "adventure" may be too strong a word for the errands we ran on Saturdays. We enjoyed a few hours together riding around in my Honda Element with regular stops at Whole Foods to get, among other things, a box of brownie bites and Virgil's Black Cherry Soda.

"Are we going to get some 'verge' and 'bites'?" he would ask as we pulled into the parking lot, knowing full well I would. Our Saturday morning ritual developed our own private code.

"Heck, yes, we are," I would say and Z would laugh, not because it was particularly funny, but because he was happy.

Music was another interest we shared. I'm drawn to the shredding guitar styles of hard rock groups such as Greta Van Fleet, Arctic Monkeys, AC/DC, and my all-time favorite, Tool. At first, Z gravitated in my direction with musical tastes, but like a beagle puppy getting more independent, he developed his own preferences. He was quickly drawn to rap's smooth, sub-bass range, where the bass notes would rattle the car and resonate in your chest. I played him my songs. Z played me his.

Through adolescence, Z's pervasive curiosity drove deep conversations about life, growing up, and relationships. He listened closely to what I had to say, making me feel smart and respected. Z would sometimes repeat my advice back to me weeks later, impressing me that he remembered and seemed to take it to heart. But all puppies grow up, and Z was no exception. Middle school turned into high school, which led to community college. As the currents of life carry us each in our own direction, we've drifted from each other a bit. We don't see each other as much, but we're still close. Our conversations turned from teenage interests to life plans. And he became the instigator of time together as often as I did.

"Do you want to grab some lunch?" twenty-year-old Z texted me.

"Sure. When and where?"

Over a burger at the Dexter Pub, we catch up. I tell him about my world, my writing, and the grandkids. Z tells me about finishing school debt free, managing a Taco Bell restaurant, and plans to transition into an automotive career. I listen, proud of the man he has become. I tell him so.

Atop the ruined Passat, Zhenya's head is bowed. It breaks my heart to see him like this. His arm is around the girl. I presume this is his new girlfriend. I've heard about her, but we have not yet met. The Volkswagen is not his car, so I also presume it is hers or her parents'. She is sobbing. Z is motionless and doesn't react to my approach.

"Zhenya," I say. Perched on the rear wheel of the Passat, he looks down at me.

"Uncle Doug." His face is red and puffy. He is dazed, and I'm guessing shocked, looking like hell on a day when nothing will burn.

"Are you okay?" It's a stupid question, but I don't know what else to say.

He jabbers. "Yeah. I think so anyway. We rolled the car. I'm just . . . I don't know . . . I feel like I'm about to—" He stops abruptly and his face contorts. He's about to burst into tears. A twelve-year-old standing in a dirty truck yard has just been told his beagle has been shot.

"That's okay—look at me—that's okay," I say, stretching my hand up toward him as if to lay it on his shoulder. "You've just been through a hell of a thing, and that's how you're supposed to feel."

He doesn't respond but holds my gaze, me looking up, him looking down. Dad wordlessly watching me come apart. But here is where I break ranks with my past. I shut the twelve-year-old boy I was out of the situation. Unlike my father on that terrible day on the farm, I'm not silent. I'm not a helpless onlooker. I don't know what to do, but I will do something, I resolve. I will not abandon Zhenya.

"Listen," I continue, not even sure of what I would say next. "Think about just one thing right now: everyone is all right. Don't let that go." I didn't know if that was the right thing to say, but it was what I was thinking.

"Everybody is all right," he repeats.

"That's right. Everybody is all right."

Z turns to the girl. "You hear that? Everybody is all right." There's a momentary pause in her weeping. She nods her head and resumes crying.

"Have you met Nyah?" Z asks me.

It's a strange time to ask that question, given the circumstances, but when we are overwhelmed, we autopilot to the familiar things of life, such as introducing your new girlfriend to your uncle.

"Not yet." How close her name sounds to *nyet*, the Russian word for no. I can think of a joke or two I'll save for another time.

"Uncle Doug, this is Nyah. Nyah, this is Uncle Doug."

"Hi, Nyah," I say. "This is a heck of a way to meet."

Nyah gives me a grimace, which I accept as a smile. Her hands are shaking. Zhenya is trying to comfort her.

"Hey, you two, look at me," I say. They don't. "Look at me!" I'm careful not to sound angry but commanding enough to gain their attention. "I want you to breathe. C'mon. Breathe with me . . . in . . . out . . . in . . . out. Everybody is all right."

Zhenya breathes with me. Nyah doesn't.

"C'mon. Keep it going." Z does and it appears to help.

A DAFD fire engine arrives, along with two Huron Valley ambulances. Responders are moving about, and this is reassuring. Two Huron Valley EMTs are soon at my side. One asks me questions. I'm not paying attention, but somehow answer anyway. The other paramedic extends a telescoping ladder and leans it against the undercarriage of the Passat. Nyah climbs down first, with strong hands guiding her steps. Z comes down and grimaces in pain. When asked, he says the pain comes from his lower back. They are led to separate ambulances.

I'm left alone next to the ruined car. Rutted truck yard. A sheriff's deputy is speaking with a woman and a girl I presume is her daughter. They cast furtive glances toward the wreck. Dad and Chick talking about a terrible thing. Thinking they might have witnessed the accident, I walk over to hear what they're saying.

"Tailgating . . . passed . . . hill." I snatch wisps of conversation above the running truck engines.

"Wait, did you say they were tailgating?" I interrupt.

The trio pause their conversation and look at me.

"Excuse me, who are you?" asks the deputy.

"I'm his uncle," I say, pointing my thumb over my shoulder at Zhenya's ambulance.

"Okay," he says, folding his hands down in front of him as if about to pray, still holding the pad and pencil. He nods to the women, giving them permission to answer me.

"They were tailgating us," says the mother, pointing at the ruined Passat. "We were already going fifty miles per hour. My daughter was driving." She turns her pointer finger to the younger woman. "When we came over the hill, they passed us on a double yellow."

I shake my head in disapproval, a fake commiseration. I am secretly elated Z is all right.

"When they came back into the lane, the car was weaving back and forth and then it flipped," says the daughter.

"Jesus," I mutter in a disapproving tone that I don't feel, and then louder, "Who was driving?"

The two looked at each other and then back at me. "The girl," says the mother.

I nod and step away. Z didn't cause this. Complicit I'm sure, but not directly at fault. I am relieved, but feel guilty at the relief. I resume my position with the gawkers, but not my conversation. A few moments later, the deputy seeks me out.

"Do you know if his parents are on their way?"

Patrick! In the entire hullabaloo, I had forgotten to call Zhenya's father.

"No. I've completely forgotten to call Zhenya's dad," I say. "I'll do that right now."

I do.

Since he lives next door to us, Patrick is also a short distance from the crash. I feel sorry for him as he arrives, walking into his son's chaos without a clue. A dog was in the ducks today. I introduce him to the deputy, who takes him to the ambulance where Z lies on a stretcher. Z's face contorts once again. This time he bursts into tears as his dad climbs in next to him. The medics determine that Nyah is unhurt, and they release her. The deputy asks her to sit in his SUV as he completes his report. I anticipate a reckless driving citation, court appearance, and loss of license. In the end, however, all she receives is a ticket for passing on a yellow line. The verdict seems paltry, considering she almost killed my nephew.

Z leaves in the ambulance for the nearest hospital. Patrick follows in his car. The deputy will see Nyah gets home. Somebody tells me a flatbed truck is on its way to gather up the wrecked Volkswagen. I'm left standing alone in the road. The show is over.

An hour later, back home, I tell my wife Tracy what happened. After the mechanical comments such as "That was a close call" and "I'm glad no one was hurt," she asks me, "Are you okay?"

Her question startles me. "Yes, I'm fine."

She repeats the question several times throughout the rest of the day. I dismissively give the same response, but I can tell she doesn't believe me. I want her to stop asking.

I wasn't fine. Tracy's question provokes a hurtful memory. The weight of what had almost happened perches like a heavy weight on my chest. I had almost lost Zhenya. Shot is code for killed. Accident is code for killed. Thinking about what might have happened hurts, but I can't stop replaying the accident scene with the flashing lights and crumpled Passat. Muzzles! Zhenya!

The old recorded memories, however, have taken an alternate route. The playbacks of Zhenya's accident scene introduced a new and unexpected file into my hippocampus. I was gratified and surprised at my ability to provide Z with comfort and strength, qualities my own father had not been able to give me when the canvas of my twelve-year-old world ruptured, qualities I didn't realize I possessed. Somewhere along the road of life, I have picked up a strength that was withheld as a child. Or, perhaps I simply did not know how strong I was until strength was my only option. Maybe that is true for all of us.

I have always been suspicious of the inside man lurking within me, that nagging voice of self-doubt. I've considered him to be conniving, with a keen desire to undermine the man I have wanted to become. However, I know this intruder's fatal flaw—memories are reconstructed files that bear little resemblance to the actual facts, no matter how real they feel. My memories as an inconsolable twelve-year-old boy have no doubt been altered over the years. I know now that this adolescent worldview that I've carried along does not equate to the grown man incapable of facing tragedy.

The interloper from the world we feel, the world of altered memories, is always younger, less wise, less mature, and scrambles fact into fiction. Why would a grown man accept the advice of a twelve-year-old? Lewis Carroll describes it beautifully through the words of Alice: *I could tell you my adventures—beginning from this morning . . . but it's no use going back to yesterday, because I was a different person then.*

AT SOME POINT, I don't know when exactly (a week? weeks?) after Muzzles's murder, I finally ventured into her shed. The water had evaporated in her brown plastic water bowl leaving a patina of dried film. Dry Purina Dog Chow filled the other bowl, as if expecting her imminent return back from a hunt. A half-full bag of her food still sat on the shelf. I stooped and ran my fingers through the straw where she slept. Memories closed around me like a cocoon, warm and safe. I felt a draft and saw that the wooden flap that led out to the run was still open. Standing up and taking a step, I unhooked the latch and closed it for the last time.

The years passed, and my interests led me farther and farther from farm activities. But on occasion, I would walk out to the old truck yard to get the tractor and wagon for hauling leaves and brush out of our yard. On my way, I passed the old dog run, noting its weeds growing taller and its wire fence sagging a little more each time. And then, memories of Muzzles crackled and flashed once again as I recalled my beloved dog standing there with her muzzle pointed to the sky, yowling in excitement at the thought that I might be coming for her and away we would go on another exciting quest. For a moment, a fleeting moment, I once again became that boy fetching his puppy so they could go explore a big world full of happy wonders.

Memories can hurt, but they can also heal.

Over the years, I've tried to remember my last adventure with Muzzles. Here, my hippocampus fails me. No doubt we would have been roaming the woods, meadows, and beyond certain that thrilling exploits awaited us just ahead of Muzzles's sniffing nose. But this I do know: one day we went out to play for the last time, neither of us having a clue.

THE DAY AFTER THE accident, I'm at my desk writing once again when my phone rings. The screen reads Zhenya.

I immediately answer. "Hey, man, how are you doing today?"

"Oh, I'm fine." And he does sound fine. "They sent me to a specialist who wanted to charge me three hundred bucks for a back brace."

"Holy crap," I say.

"Yeah. I'm like 'screw that.' I'll go buy one at Meijer for fifty bucks."

After a pause, he continues.

"Listen, the reason I called was to tell you how much it meant to me having you there."

Bawling and wiping snot while Dad stands there watching me, trying to comfort me by telling me why my beagle was doomed and better off dead.

"I was scared shitless and didn't know what to do," he continues. "Suddenly you're there, and I'm like, 'Uncle Doug is here. Everything will be okay.' That meant a lot to me."

Another pause, mine this time. And then I confess something I never thought I'd hear myself say. "I'm really glad I was there."

I mean it. But I cannot utter another word, in case I transform into that blubbering twelve-year-old boy who will always be with me. I refuse to look weak in front of my nephew.

And I no longer look weak in my own adult eyes.

# Scales

Mario René Padilla

*What I propose to narrate . . . is extremely difficult. I must render clear something that is almost obliterated. With stiff contaminated fingers I must touch the invisible.*

—*Clarice Lispector,* The Hour of the Star

AS A YOUNG BOY, WHAT I UNDERSTOOD—WHAT I CARRIED INSIDE my head like a piece of shrapnel—was the vague idea that my father survived the Second World War playing saxophone.

I'd heard the story several times, at family reunions, dinner parties with out-of-town guests, sometimes in the middle of the night when he'd stumble in from the garage carrying his saxophone case, pieces of the narrative pouring from his mouth like liquor—how Marcelino Quijones saved himself by winning a chair in the last military dance band at Camp Roberts.

"The ones not chosen had to trade their axes for M-1 rifles," he'd lament. "Imagine, being shipped off like cattle to some hell-hole in the Pacific."

My father jobbed nights on sax, flute, and clarinet, playing with different bands in supper clubs and dance halls, the names I've forgotten. At some point, he tried instructing children on reeds at a music store, but he burnt out on tone-deaf kids and had to walk away. Mornings he'd sleep in late. But every afternoon, scales climbed up the basement stairs from his twelve-by-eighteen-foot studio space—partitioned off from my mother's hair dryers and salon chairs where she bootlegged perms and cheap cuts to keep my sister Rosalie and me in Catholic school. Arriving home from school, I'd hear the regiment of humorless notes and remind myself he's alive because of scales—practice made him better than everybody else. Simple as that.

One mid-November afternoon, biking home, the air turning cold and leaves falling hard, I thought to ask my father why he never played songs, or wrote one of his own, like Ritchie Valens, whose "La Bamba" was the rage at the time. "He's Mexican too," I wanted to say, "and he's got a hit record. Why not you?"

But entering the house, I felt intimidated by the regimen of saxophone scales sounding in the basement—his perfect pitch, technical precision, the ascending notes in exact cadence—B C# D# E F# G# A# B—rising steady till peaking at the eighth, then descending at the same even pace—A# G# F# E D C# B—then shifting up a half step, ascending—C D E F—and so on, tirelessly. And the damn thing was, with my own perfect pitch, which the choir director said I had, I always knew what key he was in.

"Alex, change out of your school clothes and come have some soup," my mother called.

"Yes, ma'am." Italian mothers demanded respect. Didn't use "sir" with my father though—don't know why.

Every afternoon around two o'clock, with her last customer out the door, my mother gave up residency of the basement to my father—like the changing of the guard. And no matter how tired she was, something was always cooking in the kitchen when I got home.

In my bedroom, I put Ritchie Valens's "La Bamba" on the changer, hoping "para bailar la bamba" would drown out the scales marching lockstep up the stairwell, unstoppable, like Mickey's magical brooms in *Fantasia*. In 1958, I felt some pride being the only kid in St. Leo's, probably all of Ohio, who knew Ritchie Valens was Mexican—his real name, Ricardo Valenzuela. My father told me this did-you-know information handing me the Del-Fi 45 in its brown paper case, punctuating it with "and don't you forget it." I played the record constantly, switching to "Donna" on the flip side whenever I felt sad about girls in class who ignored me because I was so short, dark, and foreign looking. Listening to Ritchie, I imagined myself a taller, more handsome, light-skinned version of myself, singing "La Bamba" before the sixth-grade class in his gray jacket, the one he wore on *Bandstand.* In those three minutes of my daydream, it was my hit record, as I basked in the admiration of screaming classmates—no longer the dark gypsy-looking kid on the outside of another party I wasn't invited to.

"Alex, please turn that record down. Dad's rehearsing," my mother insisted.

"Yes, ma'am."

Changing out of my school uniform, navy pants and a white collared shirt, I found Mother Kathleen's detention slip in my torn shirt pocket, which a parent (meaning my mother) had to sign. I thought about the fight as I slipped on a pair of jeans and a white T-shirt. A couple of hillbilly kids in seventh decided they didn't like me. They commented every chance they got on my dark skin, my size, "Speedy Gonzalez" they called me, along with "dago" and "spic." I'd get pissed and say something back, then one or both would wrestle me to the ground (not without a struggle, I might add). The nuns never saw who started it, so when they arrived, they just grabbed whoever was in the mix and we'd spend the rest of lunch period washing chalkboards and banging out erasers. The hillbillies, Mitchell and Dirk, would be in there with me, and we'd glare at each other in silence—which we were sworn to keep in the name of Christ, or else we'd have to go into the cloak room and stand before a life-sized poster of the devil.

Stuffing the note in my jeans pocket, I headed for the kitchen, hesitating at the basement door—the underground world of music and hair spray. But disturbing my father in the middle of rehearsal was as safe as stopping a leopard mid-stride, especially on a day after he stumbled in at 2 a.m., bumping into furniture, mumbling, "Goddamned miserable musicians in this goddamned miserable cow town. *Coño,* how the hell did I end up in Ohio for Christ's sake! Man, I should be in New York. Nobody knows mambo here, none of 'em. New York goddammit . . . give 'em something they never heard before." And he would have too, as I understand it now, like Tito Puente, whose records he played to teach me congas and timbales. But then, or so the story goes, he ran into my mother singing club gigs in Detroit—it was all my mother's fault, you see, her southern Italian beauty stopped him mid-stride. Years later, Rosalie told me she put pillows over her head when Dad came home drunk. But I never did. I listened. Lying in the vibrating darkness, I listened, waiting for my mother's glass-shattering shouts and ultimatums to push through the walls of my room, like a battering ram. Just another night listening myself back to sleep.

In the copper-laden kitchen, heartbeat of the house, I felt comforted—safe from scales. It had distinct aromas that, to this day, take me home. And as I think about it now, nothing has ever matched her chicken soup made from boiled chicken breasts, garlic, basil, and onions, or her stracciatella made with Swiss chard, egg, and parmesan, or her escarole sautéed in olive oil, not to mention her gnocchi and other homemade pastas. Kids with Italian mothers always ate different from other kids in school, and after sleeping over at a friend's house, who I think was Polish or German, I thanked God I didn't have to eat his mother's sauerkraut and potatoes every Sunday night.

"So, how was school?"

"It was okay," plopping down in my chair at the dining table.

"Just okay?" I knew she saw the bruise on my face, but didn't mention it.

"We practiced Christmas carols in choir. That was fun." Then, I got it off my chest. "Mom, why does Dad always have to play scales? Why can't he play a song once in a while, like the ones they play on the radio?"

Approaching the table with the steaming tureen of stracciatella and placing it down, she said, "Your father plays plenty of songs every night on the job. And don't you have something more important to say to me? I got a call from Mother Kathleen today."

"Oh, that." She ladled out soup as I said grace and crossed myself. "I was gonna tell you." I pulled out the note and handed it to her.

"She said you got into another fight today, third one this year. Regardless of what you think, Mother Kathleen likes you. She suspects these boys are provoking you, but you won't tell her what's going on, so there's nothing she can do. When she catches you fighting she has to do something, because it's not the example she wants being set by one of St. Leo's altar boys." Then, with her stock tone of reprimand, she added, "It's serious this time, Alex. You may not get to serve mass this Sunday. She wants us to come tomorrow for a conference."

I didn't know it then, but my mother was a woman, not just a mother like the other kids' mothers. She knew the world outside of Columbus, Ohio, the nature of men—knew many of them during the war, witnessed lots of fights over her affections, as she sang and tapped her way across the states in her skimpy, spangled costumes, performing in USO shows before rowdy lovesick troops. Mostly, she knew musicians, many who were captivated by her dark-haired beauty, who fingered (*clammed*, my father quipped, 'cause their eyes weren't on the music) through her patriotic show tunes sung to anxious men on their way to war.

"Your father and I work hard, Alex. We don't have time to make trips to school because you can't ignore these jerks and just walk away."

"I'll walk away the next time. I promise."

"You think I don't know what's going on. Believe me, I know." She cradled my chin with her hand that smelled of oregano, turned my head left and right to inspect the bruise. "I know you can take care of yourself. But if you don't stop getting into it with these boys, they're going to ruin things for you with Monsignor."

Stop getting into it? *No fucking way* is what I wanted to say, but then my mother's triple-layer leather strap used for sharpening razors would have jumped off the wall hook right into her hand. "Mom, I try, but they step in front of me and say stuff."

"What stuff?"

"Like . . . dago, nigger-wop, and spic, stuff like that."

I could tell this pissed her off. I saw her jaw clench, frustrated she couldn't have those little piss ants in verbal range for just a few minutes. Like when she was traveling on a bus in Texas between USO shows, and a ten-gallon hat complained to the bus driver that

Indians weren't allowed on the bus. He assumed my dark Neapolitan mother with her long black braided hair was a Comanche. One of the women in her singing group, who she remained friends with after the war, went on and on at dinner one night, how "Anna gave that man a tongue lashing that was epic." That was the word she used, "epic," while my mother just smiled and kept on eating, refusing to elaborate.

"You have to tell this to Mother Kathleen," she insisted, walking back to the sink.

Jesus! I was already the little dark kid at school, now she wanted me to add snitch to the list? "Okay," I said, knowing I had a day to mull it over.

"I'm just tired, Alex." She fell quiet, staring out the kitchen window. I glanced out too. Gray clouds were piling up in the sky over my mother's purple and red plastic flowers in vases before a statue of the Virgin Mary. Leaves were floating down all around the cold mother of Christ, leaves I'd have to rake.

"As for your father," she resumed, "you should be glad he practices. He gets jobs because he's the best. But to be the best, you have to practice." Then, scrubbing the soup pot like she wanted the metal to come off, she lowered her voice. "Especially when you're a perfectionist."

"But playing a song won't stop him from being—"

"Your father's under a lot of stress," she cut in sharply—seeming more like the one stressed. "His last accident was a doozy. Cost us a pretty penny, with lawyers' fees and court fines. People got hurt, Alex." About to say more, she stopped herself. I stayed quiet, knowing more would be coming. "The judge hit him hard this time." I waited to see what hard meant while she rinsed the pot. "They took his license away and . . . on top of everything else, one of the clubs he plays in isn't hiring big bands anymore. Everyone wants rock and roll bands these days. He may have to go back out on the road. His nerves are frayed, and you know how he gets when that happens. The damn business is killing him."

Killing him! I knew what she meant about how he gets, but killing him? What the hell?

After drying the pot, she hung it on the rack. "Your dad has something he needs to tell you." Then, as if from a long way off, she added, "It's something that will take him away for a few months."

"What is it?"

"I think he should be the one to tell you. Now go down and let him know there's stracciatella, if he wants some."

Yep, he's going on the road again, I thought. Just like he did a few years back. I pushed open the basement door and shouted, "Hey, Dad, Mom says there's stracciatella if you want any!" But the steady, stubborn barrage of syncopated notes kept sounding. So, I raised my voice. "Hey, Dad, soup's ready!"

In mid-scale the notes stopped. With irritation in his voice, he said, "I'll be there in a minute." Then he resumed his B flat scale without missing a note. It was never just a minute.

Now, I loved my father, don't get me wrong, even though his drinking hurt me in ways I'm still dealing with. The shame I felt but kept to myself when he got drunk at parties or family reunions. The family's secret that wasn't a secret at all. But going on ten, what bothered me most was he wasn't famous, like other musicians on TV, playing their hit songs before applauding audiences. But I think I also felt some resentment too because he didn't look like everyone else's father—he was short, dark, and foreign looking. Plus, he gave me a name no one could pronounce, leaving me everyone's mark. "Hey, Key-joan's-ass." But he was the best sax man in town, probably the smartest too—and with only an eighth-grade education in Mexico. I mean, he could spit out history and geography facts from memory without ever consulting an encyclopedia. How Benito Mussolini was named after Benito Juarez, the Zapotecan who defeated the French, or how the name Gonzalez derived from Gunderzahl, a name left around by the Visigoths or Ostrogoths or some such Goths who conquered Spain in the third century. And math questions he solved without a calculator. I just assumed fathers knew all that stuff, that everyone's father did. Well, they didn't. Only later did I learn that he taught himself by reading—probably as tirelessly as he practiced scales. When I later formed my first rock band, a former musician turned manager who scheduled bands for dances at Buckeye Lake told me, "I hired you because of your dad. Man, that cat could really blow. He was a strange one though. On breaks, the band would hang out together outside, smoke a little weed, shoot the shit, but not your old man. No. Marcelino would go off somewhere and read . . . that is, when he wasn't speaking Spanish with the kitchen help, or hanging out at the bar knocking back drinks his admirers bought him because he was so damn good on that horn."

Slumping back into my chair, B flat scales still rising, I blurted out, "Mom, I know what I want for Christmas."

"Isn't it a bit early to be thinking about—"

"I want an electric guitar."

"Really?" Drying her hands more than she needed to, thinking. "Well, whatever it is, it can't be too expensive."

There it was again, Dad's drinking. His accidents always spoiled things for us, especially around the holidays. Now we had to count pennies at Christmas. But I had to have a guitar. The vision of me playing guitar on a stage, just like Ritchie, was what got me through the difficult days, when unhappiness piled on, like Mitchell and Dirk, my parents' heated arguments, my isolation, seeing my father's head bandaged and bloody, him lying on a hospital gurney at the emergency room when we picked him up, the silence on the ride home, another car hooked and towed heading for the junkyard, waiting fearfully for it to happen again—because it always happened again.

"You want anything else to eat, son?"

"No, ma'am. I think I'll ask the neighbors if I can rake their leaves or shovel their driveways for money."

"I think that's a great idea, son."

"That way I can pitch in for Christmas gifts."

She looked sad. "I don't want you worrying about that, Alex. We'll be all right."

My mother knew just how to handle me. But she didn't know how to help me survive in a boy's world. She could do nothing to replace a father who slept in every day, practiced afternoons, helped me with homework when I asked, then left right after supper to play a job. She understood, though, perhaps even more than my father, my burning dreams for fame and recognition winging me toward heights of invention—too close to the sun at times—all the pretending, standing on the bed with a broom as if I were on stage playing a guitar. She herself was never allowed to forget that she left Columbus at sixteen singing and tapping her way across the country to California to become a star. She took the stage name Nina Marie to conceal her activities from her strict Italian father, an immigrant laborer who made a living with a shovel in his hands. He never accepted her defiance, or her invitations to watch her perform when she headlined in Chicago. And he definitely didn't approve of her musician friends she hung out with after the war, especially the Spanish-speaking saxophone player who found her singing in Detroit and married her a few months later in a Kentucky courthouse two months pregnant. "*Mannaggia li sette ciucci*," was my grandfather's curse—all of them, just a bunch of asses.

Scales finally stopped, and I felt that piece of shrapnel in my head again, how scales helped him survive the war. Yes, he was a man of discipline—except when it came to drinking—the part we had to deal with. Others saw only the intelligent, talented, funny man, who knew how to tell a joke. Now, when my father laughed, you'd have to be a stone statue not to laugh with him. He'd flash his big smile, all white teeth and charisma, combined with his Mexican accent, and you were an instant fan (buying him another drink). But after his last car accident in September, I noticed he didn't joke around much anymore, and when he did laugh, it sounded less genuine, more force of habit.

Waiting anxiously for him to arrive to ask him about wanting a guitar, I thought of how, without his saxophone, he might have been just another World War II casualty. And though he rarely told the story sober, he told it something like this.

"When I got drafted in '41, I wasn't even a citizen. They sent me to Camp Roberts in Paso Robles, California, for my basic training. But while I was waiting to be assigned to a combat unit and shipped out, I heard a camp commander say he was looking for someone to blow 'Reveille' and 'Taps' on a bugle. Now, I'd never played that instrument before, but I told him I'd give it a try. I practiced that damned horn all day, and in the evening, I blew perfect 'Taps.' So, he assigned me to the 211th Special Services Corps as the bugle boy. I also was assigned to stock beer and other refreshments for camp shows and dances. But then, a musician friend who saw me handing out beer at a USO show said, 'Man, why the hell aren't you in the band?' I didn't have an answer. So, he convinced the band director to audition me. Immediately, I got reassigned to the dance band. And that was great for a while. But then the Japanese bombed Pearl Harbor, and music suddenly became a luxury. We were in it now. The camp commander was ordered to eliminate two of the three bands. Only the best musicians were to be kept to form one band. The musicians not selected would be transferred into combat units and shipped overseas. Jesus Christ, think about that."

At this point in the story, my father got dramatic. Holding up his fingers, he'd say, "Special Services reduced three bands down to one. Imagine. The warrant officer posted tryout lists. I'd never seen such fear in men's eyes. Fear spread through the corps like wildfire. It was awful. It created some hard feelings too, let me tell you. Most of us had already become friends, guys who'd jammed together, know what I mean? The real war, all the dying and killing, hell, that was someone else's war. We were musicians for Christ's sake! Point a gun and shoot somebody? Well, let me tell you how men can change. How fear and resentment can destroy friendships. I mean, you could feel it in the barracks, in the mess hall, during rehearsals for the prescheduled shows. We became suspicious of each other too: who had influence, gave bribes, were favorites, if race had anything to do with it. You'd hear guys practicing scales every free waking hour. So, out of fifteen or so saxophone players, only five were chosen. One by one, we were called in before the warrant officer. He'd place a piece of music on the stand, tell us to play it. Then have us run through some scales, and when we finished, he'd say, 'Thank you very much,' as if he'd just met us or something. Imagine!"

Around this point in the story, he'd bring up Johnny Lopez. "As long as I live, I'll never forget sitting up with Johnny that last night before he shipped out." Now my father always teared up a little talking about Johnny. And I remember that, for me, it was always his breaking voice, not Johnny's fate, that moved my emotions. "I was fifteen when I arrived in this country. Johnny and me played saxophone together in Kansas City, went on the road in Juan Rodrigo's band out of El Paso. He was a couple of years older, but we shared an apartment in Topeka and in Tucson for a while. I'm telling you, he was three times better than me. No one could ever figure out why he was transferred out of the band. Some said he was drunk at his audition, couldn't even see the notes. But I'd seen him play like that countless times. That wasn't it. Others say the warrant officer had it in for him, hated the way Johnny made fun of him, an officer assigned to supervise the band who couldn't play 'Twinkle, Twinkle, Little Star' on a toy piano."

Now that was the beer version. The whiskey version sounded more like this: "That goddamned warrant officer sent him to his death, that's what he did. The son of a bitch . . . couldn't play a toy piano to save his life. He got sent to the goddamned Philippines. *Carajo*! Right into battle. As long as I live, I'll never forget the look in his eyes that last night, packing his duffle bag, putting his sax in the case, his baby no one could ever touch, and flinging it on the pile of bags to be shipped out. The goddamned son-of-a-bitchin' warrant officer. Now there's a piece of luck for you."

As always, I'd listen. I'd watch his face get emotional listing the musician friends shipped out and killed in battle. I'd try to imagine my father as a young man in his army uniform, with thick black wavy hair, his handsome face appearing above a music stand with a sax between his lips, like in the black and white army band photos he kept in his basement studio in a department store shoe box, high up on a shelf. I'd bring them down from time to time when he was at work. One special one stuck out to me. It was marked basic training on the back. In this one, my father looked like a combat soldier, the ones I'd seen in war movies. He had on dirty fatigues, combat boots, and a camouflaged helmet. He was all stretched out in mud and dead leaves on hilly terrain, smiling his big professional smile for the camera, cradling an M-1 rifle in his arms, as if it were a sax.

I'd recognize some of the names on the backs of the photos, like Willy "Bones" Parker, the best trombone player he ever played with. Red Graham, a piano player, remembering how they both died at Normandy. There was Pete Vespi, a trumpet player, and a drummer named Max Watson, who were killed as well. I don't remember where though. "Good musicians, all of junk yard 'em," he'd dramatically conclude. "Guess I was just one of the lucky ones."

Lucky! No way. Luck had nothing to do with it, I'd silently protest. My father survived the Second World War because he made himself better than everybody else. Simple as that.

And as for the "luck" business, I never put any credence in it, especially since I'd determined, early on, that I was hopelessly unlucky. It was an absolute fact—I lost at everything that didn't require effort and action. Put me in a race and I left everyone in the dust. Put me in the Catholic League Bazaar drawing, the weekly school raffles, the Friday night bingo tables in the school cafeteria—nothing. For me, luck became linked with lazy, undisciplined, no-talent hillbillies like Mitchell, who couldn't find the rhythm to a water drip, but who won the school dance competition because he made the biggest fool out of himself. Somehow I sensed, even at ten years old, I was star material. It was in the genes, my father's talent on several instruments, my dark-haired, beautiful mother, the singer, as she appeared in her scrapbook 8x10s, with "Nina Marie" printed below the photo, pasted next to a yellowed newspaper clipping of her billings in night clubs in Chicago and Detroit. No, my fate would not be determined by luck. I was "born out of a trunk," as my mother always joked. Dance lessons age four, drum lessons beginning at eight. I sang solos in the school choir because I could actually sing on pitch. Becoming a rock and roll star I saw as my destiny—that is, as soon as I learned to play the guitar. And luck would have nothing to do with it.

Besides, luck is when opportunity meets preparation. The first time I'd heard this bit of wisdom was from Father Mike, a young visiting priest fresh out of the seminary. He was the first black priest assigned to St. Leo's, and I was always scheduled to serve his masses. During lunch sometimes, I'd go to the church rehearsal hall to do my homework (probably more to avoid Mitchell and Dirk). As usual, I ended up at the piano, teaching myself songs, practicing the scales my father had shown me, though I preferred plucking out "Heart and Soul" by ear.

"Son, why aren't you out in the yard playing football?" Father Mike asked me one afternoon, entering the hall after finishing his lunchtime confessions.

"I came here to do my homework, Father," I stammered.

"Oh yeah? Getting it done, are you?" I moved to get up. "Hold on. Slide over." He was a big man who perspired heavily. I slid over, noticing, as I always could, the smell of alcohol.

"Hey, do you know 'All I Have to Do Is Dream'?"

"A little bit." I lied—I knew the words by heart.

What happened then was unbelievable. Father Mike played and started singing—he could really sing—sang the song better than the Everly Brothers. He had a deep, soulful voice. I'd never met anyone in person who could sing just like they sing on the radio. Toward the end I joined in, and together, we were transported to wherever it is music takes you.

"You sing pretty good, young man," he said. I could tell he was somewhat impressed that I could carry a tune. "What's your name again?"

"Alex."

"You serve mass for me sometimes. Pretty good too. You in the choir, Alex?"

"Yes, Father. And Sister Aloysius picks me to sing solos all the time." Then I added proudly, "And if I'm lucky, I'm going to become a rock and roll star someday."

"Is that right?" he said, playing piano chords I later learned was a song called "Blue Moon." "Look here, Alex. I, too, wanted to become a singer at your age. It was my dream till I was, oh, about nineteen. I sang every day. And Sundays I performed in my mother's church. She was the organist. I even got a chance to front a band out of Tennessee after I graduated."

"You mean you've sung on stage?"

"Sure have. But just when the band was going on the road, I dropped out. Something else captured my heart and changed my calling. Yes, sir, and amen to that! You see, I made a choice between my ego and my soul."

"No offense, Father, but I think I'd prefer singing on stage than saying mass."

Father Mike chuckled. "Sure, sure, I know what you mean. Can't say that I blame ya. Now I can hear you've got a good voice, just needs a little work, that's all. And if you put in the time and effort, develop the gift God give ya, well, when your big break comes, you'll be ready. It's up to you, you know, because life is just that, a bunch of opportunities and choices. But listen here. Don't think that luck's got anything to do with it. You want to be a rock and roll star, then you just go out and do it. Prepare yourself, work hard, practice, and when you get your opportunity, you be ready to grab that big brass ring." And he reached out and grabbed at nothing in the air.

Just then, the bell rang. Getting up to leave, Father Mike stopped me. I looked at him as he pointed his finger at me, sweat dripping from his brow. "But, Alex, you stay away from the liquor. You hear?"

"Yes, Father." I grabbed my books and hustled out, as Father Mike turned back to the piano keys and began playing those chords again, only slower, a bit sad-like.

Entering the kitchen, my father had to squint his eyes—unaccustomed to the light.

"Alejito, *que tal mijo*?" he said, sitting down in his chair.

"*Bién.*" That was one of our little exchanges because he wanted me to know Spanish, though I knew more Italian really, living with Mom's people in the Italian section of town. It always bothered me when he called me Alejito. I wanted to be Alex. After all, Ricardo Valenzuela was Ritchie. And I definitely didn't want to be called Alejito, "little cute Alex."

My mother didn't look at him or say anything as she ladled soup into his bowl.

His face seemed puffy, with dark swollen bags under his eyes. He looked out the glass doors. "Changuito, looks like the leaves are coming down heavy now. Better start raking."

"Okay, Dad," still measuring when to mention the guitar.

"Where's Rosalie?"

"She's at cheerleading practice," my mother answered.

Unlike me, Rosalie loved school. She was one year older, lighter-skinned, popular with boys, always busy with friends, Girl Scout meetings, parties. She was the Annette Funicello of St. Leo's—sort of looked like her too.

"Anna, Hank can't pick me up tonight. You'll have to drop me off at the club. He said he could bring me home though."

"All right. But tell him right after the place closes." And she looked at him hard. He didn't look up from his soup. She was definitely annoyed having to drive him since he lost his license. "Did they find you a permanent sub yet?"

"They're working on it." Then he turned to me as he ate. "So, what's this about some trouble at school?"

I didn't want to talk about that. I wanted to talk about the guitar, not Mitchell and Dirk, with their rotten, yellow teeth, their "Hey boy, what are yous anyways, some kine-a spic or wop or somepin? Nah, Dirk, he just plain ol' niggah." Then they'd call me "kiss-ass" because I always volunteered to serve early morning mass and late-night stations of the cross. They resented how Monsignor chose me to lead religious processions. But I never asked to do it. Monsignor just assumed I wanted to be a priest. What other reason would a normal kid volunteer to come to church at the earliest and latest hours? But I loved the echoing sound of peace inside an empty church. The mystery of hundreds of flickering candles in the dark, where I could forget about the trouble at home or at school. Sunday mornings in the sacristy, putting on my black cassock and white surplice, anointed in the service of Christ, I felt special, believed that God was looking out for me. It was a relationship I depended on. Every night in bed, I prayed he'd grant me my three great wishes: first, that I wouldn't die; second, that my parents, sister, grandparents, and anyone close to me wouldn't die; and third, well that was a rotating wish, something particularly important I wanted at the time—a baseball mitt, a new 45. Now, it was a guitar. My grandmother, certain of my priestly calling, even took time away from her job sewing vestments for priests of the diocese to sew me a miniature set of vestments. I played priest in the basement serving mass before empty folding chairs. My parents' wooden bar served as my makeshift altar, a wine glass spray-painted gold for a chalice, a white poker chip for a host, and a fat telephone book, the altar missal in Latin.

Oh, there were moments, I suppose, when I half considered the idea of becoming a priest. I loved going into the rectory on errands for Monsignor Schwendeman, with its hushed, reverent atmosphere, the polished wood cabinets and floors, the long wooden dining table, books in the library, a life of study and reflection, a place without trouble. But mostly, I loved standing in front of the congregation during mass, the privileged one, lighting altar candles with the long brass wick rod, handling the censor, the responsibility of holding the brass plate under chins during communion. I felt admired as I recited the altar boy's responses in perfect Latin—everyone watching my performance, especially Lois Metzger, who usually sat in the front pew with her parents and who I usually daydreamed about. I'd tried sports but it was no use. I was fast, but too small for football, too short for basketball. Years later, I understood that the hours I'd spent serving mass, looking out at the congregation from the altar, all the mock piety, the costumed ceremonies were not in service to Christ, but satisfied a need for attention, for exhibition, for that exhilarating feeling I'd one day know as a performer on stage.

"I got an A on that history assignment you helped me with."

"That's good, *mijo*," he answered. But he wasn't going to let it go. "So, what happened?"

I began to fidget. Then my mother said, "All the clothes and toiletries you'll need are in your overnight bag. I'm going grocery shopping."

So, it was true. He was going out on the road again.

"Rags said I'm getting pretty good on the drums." Rags Anderson was a retired drummer who once worked with my father and was giving lessons.

"Yes, I can hear that. He's right. You've got natural rhythm, son."

"So, I'm thinking of learning another instrument, like maybe the guitar."

My father frowned. He was never thrilled about my focusing so much time on music. He'd help me when I asked, show me scales on the piano, teach me congas and timbales because Rags couldn't play those. But deep down, I knew he didn't want me to become a musician. I don't think he felt I had what it takes to be a real musician, someone like him, someone who could play seven different instruments professionally by the time he was twenty-five. He wanted me to read books and do my homework. It must have been sad when he realized the books he bought me never got read. Even so, my father was a reluctant accomplice—he could only purchase the finest instruments—he couldn't help himself. Like the Ludwig blue sparkle drum set with Ziljian cymbals and a Rogers snare he bought from a fellow musician and kept in his studio for me to learn on—when he wasn't around, of course.

"You didn't seem all that interested when you insisted on playing the drums."

"Well, I wasn't interested then. I wanted to make the beat. But I want to write songs, like the ones on the radio. The choir director said, to do that, I have to play piano or guitar, and you've been helping me with the piano. So, I'm asking for an electric guitar for Christmas."

"Yeah?" he said with a chuckle. "You think Santa's going to bring you that?"

"I'm hoping." Now I'd long ago stopped believing in Santa, but the family still played the game. Then I thought, a better strategy was to get him talking about why his first instrument was the sax. He loved telling that story. "Why did you pick the saxophone first?"

He thought for a moment. "Actually, I didn't. It was the instrument mi tio Gregorio bought me. I was about your age I think, and the band leader of our pueblo told my uncle he needed a saxophone player. That he'd pay four pesos a concert to anyone willing to learn how to play." He added, "You see, where I grew up, everyone had to work. We couldn't spend our afternoons listening to records and daydreaming."

I shifted. "You mean you got paid to play the sax when you were my age?"

"Not right away. While I was learning the instrument, I worked for Gregorio after school until he figured out I wasn't any good with horses. My whole family were *hacendados*, ranchers you'd call them here. But I was afraid of horses, hated the smell of cattle. Couldn't throw a rope to save my life. Ay, *Diós mio*," he chuckled. "But no one, I mean absolutely no one could handle a lasso like mi tio Gregorio. Hui, tio Goyo was a magician with a loop."

It was great seeing my father laugh again. And when he opened up, there was nothing to do but sit back and listen.

"When I was growing up in Guanajuato, I heard my father say that about his brother, Gregorio, that he was a magician. Now I thought he said musician—*mágico* and *músico* being similar-sounding words. Well, Goyo was definitely not a musician. He was rugged, loved to fight, and though he was short, he was powerful, had hands like sandpaper and the body of a bull. Rarely did you see Goyo without his rope. Man, he could twirl and curl the loop like nobody's business, working the rope until he jumped through as it spun around his waist. Now, your grandpa, Emeterio, my dad, he was different. He went his own way, ran a small convenience store and earned money at night playing guitar and singing in restaurants or in the zocalo. I often had to run the store for him in the morning because he worked late, you know, needed to sleep in. Well one day, I was sitting behind the counter, and Goyo, with his wide sombrero and colorful neckerchief, rode his big black horse right into the store, a space no bigger than an average horse stall. 'Marcelino,' he shouted, 'donde está Emeterio?' I had slid under the counter. 'In bed sleeping it off again, eh changuito?' he shouted, with his mischievous laugh. 'Don't be afraid, my horse won't bite you." His horse never acted skittish or disobeyed. "Oye! Tell Emeterio to send you out to the ranch so I can teach you about horses. Niño, you need to learn some real work instead of sitting around this place getting soft, selling tortillas and cigarettes to all the huevones playing dominoes.'"

I loved hearing the story of Gregorio riding his horse into the store. And I was fascinated that one of my ancestors was a cowboy who could twirl a rope like Will Rogers. But in another telling, my father said that, after watching a man play the saxophone in the plaza one Sunday, the sun gleaming off the shiny brass bell, the beautiful pearl keys, he asked Gregorio to buy him a saxophone, knowing his father could never afford it. He agreed to work off his debt doing chores at the ranch.

"But how did your uncle know you'd be able to play it?"

"He didn't." He ate a spoonful of soup. thought a moment, then smiled. "He was just damn certain I'd never make a living throwing a rope."

He stopped, and all I could hear was the clock ticking. "But he must have known you could play it to buy you such an expensive instrument."

"No, no. Goyo didn't know anything but horses. After I started going out to the ranch, he realized I'd never become a vaquero—it was embarrassing, the loop always twisted leaving my hand, while my cousins were already roping cattle. He had me cleaning out stalls and feeding the livestock. So, to help pass the time, I sang songs, mostly those I heard my father sing. That's why Goyo started calling me *pajarito*. At night after supper, he'd say, 'Pajarito, sing "Allá en el Rancho Grand,"' his favorite ranchera. So, one Posada, he rode up to our house on his horse with jangling silver spurs, chaps, and a wide sombrero carrying a black case for me, a dead chicken for my mother, and a bottle of tequila for my father. Inside the case was an old, beat-up tenor sax. A few keys were jammed, others had lost their tortoise shell inlays, and the bell had a large dent in it, but it shined and the reed was good. Although later I found out someone had shortened the neck, just sawed off a portion because they couldn't reach pitch with the standard length. Think about it! Because some numbskull couldn't reach pitch, I spent hours as a kid learning scales on a shortened neck, only to find out later, when I bought my Selmer, that I'd have to spend more countless hours learning how to play the instrument all over again at proper pitch." With that, my father grew silent, while eating a few spoonfuls of soup. "Goyo never got to see me play the instrument though. He died some months later when his horse stumbled and crushed his chest during a cattle roundup. They said he'd gotten himself tangled up in one of his notorious loops, a loop so large, he ended up roping the horns of a steer and the front legs of his horse at the same time, and they all went down together." My dad chuckled over the thought, then looked at me with a skeptical expression. "So, now you want to learn the guitar?"

"Yes."

"Tell me what happened at school."

I looked down at my empty plate. "There's these two hillbilly boys."

"Yeah."

"Mitchell and Dirk. They're seventh graders. They won't leave me alone."

"Why don't you go to Monsignor?"

"I can't do that. Even the guys I'm friends with would talk bad about me."

My dad nodded as if he understood—one boy to another.

Going to Monsignor wouldn't have done any good anyway—he was from the boys have to fight their own battles school of ecclesiastics, Bing Crosby in *The Bells of St. Mary's.*

"Yeah, I suppose," he said, glancing out the glass doors at the gray sky, the leaves falling in gusts of wind. "Everyone's got to fight their own battles, otherwise the solutions don't stick." Then he looked at me. "Listen, *mijo,* this may be hard for you to understand with that temper of yours, but if you really want these boys off your back you have to be smart—disciplined enough to act unaffected. Either that or you have to kick the living crap out of one of them. And I don't think you're ready to do that just yet.

Those cowards wouldn't let you do it anyway. The other one would jump you in a second. No, you look 'em straight in the eyes and smile. Confuse 'em. Don't act hurt or show anger because that's giving them what they want. And what they want is to screw things up for you at school." He hesitated, as if thinking of something else to say.

Now, what he said made sense. But I'd come to think I had more of Gregorio's *gallego* blood in me than Emeterio's, who I never got to meet since he died when I was three. All I know is, whenever Dad told the story of his family in Mexico, I always liked Gregorio best. I imagined myself dragging Mitchell and Dirk to the ground in a perfectly thrown loop from atop a big black horse.

"Listen, *changuito*, I'm going away for a while."

"Yeah. Mom mentioned something about you going on the road."

He looked at me. "She told you that?"

I nodded.

He looked out the sliding glass doors again, dead leaves piling up on the patio. "I'll be gone about three months." Hesitating, he decided, then continued. "Do your chores, take care of your mother and sister, and try to stay out of fights." Then he reached over and touched the back of my head. "*Más aguzado*, Alejito. More victories are won with brains than fists." Then he stood up, walked toward the glass doors. "Don't forget to rake the leaves."

I already knew what it was like to live without a father. The first time was when I was five. Mom quit show business and moved Rosalie and me from Detroit to her family in Columbus. We stayed at my grandparents' house until Mom finished beauty school and got a job in a hair salon. Then we got a house of our own. But my father didn't come with us. The story Rosalie and I got was that he was making too much money in Detroit for him to leave, Mom being in school and all. And I remember how strange it felt after about a year, when he finally came to live with us. Just when I'd gotten used to him not being in the house, I had to get used to him being around all over again. Then, two years later, he was gone, out on the road. Now, I had to get used to him being gone again.

The weeks running up to Christmas, it snowed a lot. With no school, I stayed busy shoveling neighbors' driveways, three bucks plus a quarter tip. I kept the money in a Nabisco tin, thinking, when I had enough, I'd give the money to my father to help buy the guitar. He called us on Christmas Eve. Said he missed us. Rosalie cried; my mother didn't. He sounded different, his voice thin and strained. When we hung up, my sister went to her room, Mom to the kitchen, and I sat near the Christmas tree to stare at the lights. I liked watching the patterns the twinkling lights made on the ceiling. For some reason, playing "La Bamba" didn't help. I went down into the basement—the first time since my father left. The space felt strange with him gone. I went to his music stand and turned on the light. It felt like a pulpit. I imagined my father standing there practicing his scales. I closed my eyes and could almost hear him. In fact, the studio space felt reverent, like the empty church feels when I'm the first one to arrive early in the morning.

I thought about the photos. Climbing up on the piano bench, I grabbed the shoe box, then sat down on the bench and began flipping through the faces—my father, young and healthy looking, smiling from behind a music stand, long before Mom, before Rosalie and me. His hair, black and wavy. Then, I found the one of him in fatigues and a combat helmet, cradling the rifle he never had to use. I placed it on the piano shelf, next to *Hanon: The Virtuoso Pianist.* I opened the book and began practicing the C scale my father taught me, lifting each finger, pressing down with even pressure C D E F G A B C, tucking the thumb under, then the declension at the same even pace: B A G F E D C, realizing that, in the effort and concentration, I'd forgotten I was sad. But the cinderblock basement walls started closing in. I felt claustrophobic or something, like I needed to get out—imagining it was just how people felt stuck in a jail cell. Years later, in a particularly difficult time in my life, I realized how life really is just a bunch of choices, and that, with some of them, we put ourselves in one cell or another, only to waste precious years having to find our way out. And as Father Mike told me, luck's got nothing to do with it.

Then I saw it.

In the corner, mostly hidden behind hanging clothes, was my father's saxophone case. I walked over, uncovered it, laid it down, pushed the snaps, and opened it. I stroked the shiny brass bell, pressed some keys. I lifted it halfway up and blew into the reed, but nothing but air came out—that beautiful, mysterious sound only he could make. Why was it here? I laid it back in the case, closed the snaps, covered it up with clothes again. I didn't want him to know I had messed with it. Then, I grabbed the photo off the piano shelf and took the stairs in twos.

"You hungry, Alex?" my mother asked from the kitchen.

"No."

"Pardon me?"

"I mean. No, ma'am. Sorry."

"What's wrong?"

"Nothing."

"What's that in your hand?"

"One of Dad's photos."

A hurt expression came across her face. "I think we need to talk about what's going on with Dad. But not tonight. It's Christmas Eve. Rosalie already opened a gift. Go look on your bed."

Arriving at my bedroom I saw it immediately. Lying across the bed was a slim black case with a big red bow. Fender was written on the side.

I put down the photo, undid the clasps, and lifted the lid. Inside was the prettiest blue electric Fender guitar in the world. Even today, so many guitars later, it remains my sentimental favorite. In the guitar strings was a note: *Alex, I'm a friend of your dad's. He asked me to pick out a guitar for you. He told me you want to play rock and roll. This Fender ought to do the trick. Call me Hi-3-8210 and I'll come and give you a few lessons. I've got a nice little amplifier you can use till you get your own. Hank*

Slowly, reverently, I lifted the guitar from the case, like taking out the consecrated chalice from its tabernacle. I was unsure just how to handle it. Sitting down on the bed, I put it across my knee and began strumming the strings with my thumb, just as I saw Ritchie do on *American Bandstand.* I didn't know what to do with my left hand. I pressed down on the strings, turned the knobs, stroked the smooth blue body.

"Is that what you wanted?" my mother said, appearing at the door.

"Oh, yes. It's exactly what I wanted. Thank you."

"Send your dad a letter and thank him. I'll give you the address tomorrow. I've got gnocchi in the kitchen when you're ready to eat."

"I'll be there in a minute." And I smiled, hearing my father say that from the basement.

Strumming the strings with a pick I found lying in the case, I was impressed that I could already make a cool sound. I immediately changed my third great wish from wanting a guitar to having my father home—down in the basement playing his scales.

On a cold, snowy morning in February, Ritchie was dead. Killed in a plane crash, my mother said. We watched the TV special news report, saying how the Big Bopper and Buddy Holly also died. It didn't seem real that Ritchie was gone. All that talent brought down by ice and snow. Then I heard the reporter say how unlucky Ritchie was because he was scheduled to ride the regular tour bus. But Buddy Holly didn't want to be cold, so he chose to charter an airplane. They reported that Ritchie had won the coin toss with Tommy Allsup for the last open seat in the plane. It was a flight Ritchie didn't have to take.

The first thing I thought was, *luck had nothing to do with it.*

MERIT WINNER: BONUS

# Wilful Damages

## Alan Whelan

IT'S THREE IN THE MORNING IN DENVER, AND EVERYTHING IS unnaturally black and bright, with the streetlights reflecting on the puddles on the bitumen; I'm keeping watch at the street end of an alleyway off Larimer Street in Five Points while my friend Paul throws a cat into a restaurant.

The cat's in a shoulder bag, calm and purring even though she was grabbed off the street and shoved into the bag just ten minutes ago. But there's a piece of premium steak in the bag and by now some of it's in the cat. Paul's down the end of the narrow alleyway I'm watching, at the back of the Moulin Rouge restaurant. There's a broken panel in the bottom left of the kitchen window, which hasn't been repaired because there are bars on the window anyway, and rain doesn't get in. Paul takes the steak off the cat and throws it through that hole onto the kitchen floor. The cat streaks in after it.

Paul shrugs at me and walks out of the alley. He's wearing stovepipe black jeans and a torn white T-shirt with a thin black tie. It was fashionable once. He's a telecommunications engineer when he's not strewing cats about, so he can dress how he likes. We walk back to my Subie. I'm already driving away when, a minute later, the burglar alarm goes off. It's a screamer. It goes up and down half an octave, and does it again and does it again. It won't stop until the owner's come out, talked to the plods, and turned it off.

But this story really starts a few weeks earlier. Paul's then girlfriend Jane lectured at the Denver State University's Department of Art on Naïve Criticism: The Demotic Response to Art. The course was about untrained people's ideas about art, which Jane pissed on from an enormous height, and . . . Oh look, I honestly don't care.

Anyway, we begin on the night of an after-work party at the Department of Art, because Nancy Anansi, of Male Perceptions of African Art, had just had her book published. Jane hated Nancy, who was born Ellie Hooper. Nancy's book was called *Women in the Spiderverse.*

Paul would normally have been with her, but he was working late that night, and Jane and I weren't close, back then. So, Jane, on her own in the department boardroom, drank the red wine of despond and ate the cheddar of jealousy. But I'm guessing that, just as I'm guessing about most of Jane's confrontation with Mackiewicz. I heard a version of it from Jane, but I wasn't there.

That night Radoslaw Mackiewicz took his painting, *The Naked City,* and went into Jane's office while she was in the department boardroom with her plastic wine cup, and he hung that painting, a spacious and unwieldy thing, behind her desk.

Back at the party he waited till Jane had finished her red, and brought her a glass of champagne. Mackiewicz had had minor fame once as a figure in late twentieth-century neo-Dadaism, but he was a charmless man whose few sexual successes had generally involved the supply of alcohol. When Jane thanked him, he nodded at her and said, "How many hours' discourse could you stand, d'ye think, on traditional drawings of spiders?"

Jane said, "Not many more, I'd say." She wasn't on her guard yet.

Mackiewicz stared at her. It occurred to her that he seemed a little intense. He said, "Your course would make a much better book. I could imagine people actually reading it for pleasure."

Jane looked at him, the ghost of a warning forming in her mind, but the flattery was still predominating. "Well, Rado, thank you."

Mackiewicz said, "Look, I made you something. It's importunate of me, but I put it in your office."

"Oh?" Now she was alarmed. But she wouldn't be far from her colleagues.

"Would you like to . . . ?"

Jane said, "Certainly," but now there was a harder, guarded edge to her voice. They went to her office. "Oh. Oh my god."

The painting was huge, about two meters square, mostly hyper-real scenes from around Denver: the blue mustang; the International Church of Cannabis; a plastic, bronze-painted statue made by a local artist of Warren Zevon on a stallion, waving a sword; the Room of Lost Things; the Cranmer Park Sundial; the Big Blue Bear; and Sloan's Lake. There was a sort of digital skin over this: it was computer art, and the pixels changed the paint below them from day to night, and back again. There was one image above that layer, in the bottom right corner: a realist naked woman who looked a little like Jane, and whose toes, face, breasts, and vulva faced the viewer. *The Naked City.* It was wit, d'ye see?

Jane took this in. Then she calmed. The woman would be taken from the internet, she guessed, because Mackiewicz was too tight to pay a model. The scenes around the woman were kitsch. She supposed they were intentionally so, but they were still kitsch. The night/day computer effect was clever, but it wasn't enough. As a work it was a failure; as a sexual overture, it was only sad. Jane was relieved. She could feel, if she wanted to, pity.

So, she said, "Oh, that's wonderful, Radoslaw," reverting to the more formal version of his name. "You want to . . . store it here?"

He looked at her, puzzled. "It's a gift. It's my gift! To you."

"Oh. I can't—"

"This is a beautiful city. And you are its most beautiful woman! It's homage, Jane, you must—"

Jane said the thing she thought would end this soonest. "Oh. Then, thank you, Radoslaw. I accept your very thoughtful gift."

Mackiewicz's eyes seemed to bulge. She was missing the point! "I want to say, your intellect is only one of your—"

Jane said firmly, "But though it's lovely, and very impressive, and I'm a bit overwhelmed, I've got to get back to the launch now. You should come too."

She went back to the boardroom and drank more red wine. Mackiewicz walked in little circles at the other end of the room, and then disappeared.

Jane walked with a colleague back to her car and drove back to her house on a little lane off Stout Street. It's a tiny house, with just two upstairs bedrooms. One of the bedrooms is Jane's, and the other was occupied by Gita Dhanial, who studied epidemiology at Denver State. I lived there too, downstairs in a little windowless room off the kitchen that the landlord called a bedroom. It was, or had been, a pantry.

Paul arrived about midnight. He had his own apartment on Market Street in Five Points, a once bohemian suburb rapidly gentrifying, but he stayed so often that he was a sort of nocturnal housemate. Jane didn't often sleep at his home; that's an indication of where the power lay. In bed, and postcoital, Jane told him about Mackiewicz's vast daub.

He said, "What on earth are you going to do with it?"

"I gave it to Gita. I bet she's never owned an original artwork. And Mackiewicz was a name, once."

"I heard he drank? I mean, too much?"

"Yeah. Hard-drinking Catholic mystic—he could get away with that in the 1990s. Fashionable. But the booze and the Virgin took root. Wouldn't let him go."

"Yeah. I've never met him. But what I've heard sounds weird."

"Yuh."

"Grief," said Paul. Then he thought of Gita. "Is it worth anything?"

Jane gave him a contemptuous look. "Of course not, it's garbage, even for Mackiewicz. Probably worth a couple of hundred for the signature, but that'd be it." Paul made a slightly disappointed sound. So, she added, "And that's now. His value's going down, not up. Were you thinking of buying it off her?"

They both knew Gita was in financial trouble. Gita's father Asim Dhanial was a progressive man, rich because he was a builder, who'd thought his daughter should get an overseas education. But Pakistan's military-religious revival was making life grim for progressive sorts, and Mr. Dhanial was in jail. So, there were no more checks from home, and she owed Denver State $3,000 in fees. When her deadline to pay ran out she would cease to be enrolled, and once she was no longer a student she was no longer complying with her visa. She'd be deported. Her job paid the rent and food and so on, but that was it. She couldn't save. Paying her fees had been her father's business.

Paul was wondering if the picture was worth enough to help Gita in any practical way. After two years with Jane he should have known better than to expect her to give away something of value. "Nah, just wondering."

They were on Jane's bed. It's a messy room, with an easel, a desk, art books, pictures, paints, paper, clothes all over the place. Jane was straddling Paul's leg. Jane was slender and very pale, her hair dyed chemical red and cut like a helmet. Paul had a muscular, even a knobby, body. He kept his hair shaved to a four-day growth and his beard to two days. Jane said, "She'll have to get a new job or something. Our own felicity we make or find."

Paul recognized her quoting voice for the line about felicity, though he couldn't place it. He replied, "For God's sake hold your tongue and let me love." He hoped she'd trace the slight hostility in tonight's line back to Donne, not him.

Jane claimed that the quotation swapping was one of their private games. Paul thought it was her game, not theirs, but he'd flip through his *Oxford Dictionary of Quotations* for an offering before he came over. He thought Jane was a bit demonstrative about being bookish. It was the first thing he'd found in her that he didn't like. Finding fault in her had shocked him, the first time he did it. She'd awed him when they first met.

Jane said, "Mmm, 'The Canonization,'" to show she recognized the line, and lowered her head to kiss him. A little later the bed-end began hitting the wall again, ringing through the house: Wap. Wap. Wappity-wap.

After the bed-end's culminating crash, they lay together for a while, without speaking. Then Jane said she was tired. She was still atop him. Paul reached to turn the light off and lay still, carefully dealing with itches from their dried sweat, and slowly removing his arm from under her.

He listened to the traffic until he fell asleep. Later still he woke up. Jane had slid off him, lying on her side with her back to him. He moved over to spoon her. She was crying. He held her tighter but didn't say anything. Eventually he fell asleep.

That was Jane and Paul's second to last night together.

"BURN IN HELL. YOU hypocrites, paying your taxes and obeying the law, hah! God laughs! For all your righteousness you will burn—" That's Warwick, standing on a seat in Writer Square. People were giving him plenty of room. I've got a soft spot for old Warwick.

Jane, Paul, Gita, and I were in Illegal Burger for chips and milkshakes. Gita was in her waitress outfit from Moulin Rouge Restaurant Français. It was a French maid thing—short, tight, black dress with a little frilly white apron. Her boss, Matt Dixon, used to pat her on the ass whenever she went past. Dixon was a prick, even as bosses go. He collected the tips and distributed them among his staff. It was obvious that he took about half of it. Gita was telling me she only gets paid to ten in the evening, but she never gets away till after eleven. But Dixon wouldn't pay her for the extra hour. It's a big, popular restaurant, not cheap, with a huge turnover. He could afford it.

"Fire a million times hotter than the hottest furnace on earth. The Lord provides spirit bodies that will not perish in the heat, so there is no escape from the pain. You shall feel pain a billion times greater than you can imagine, and your body will never be consumed—"

"Why don't you go to the union?" I said.

Gita looked doubtful. "It's temporary work. Casual. I'm not a member of any union. I don't think anyone there is. Do you really think they'd be able to do anything about it?"

"Yes, of course." Positivity Jane there. "That's what they're for, isn't it? Look, call them tomorrow, before you go to work."

"Burn in HELL. Unless you give up your transgressions and accept Jesus as your savior right now—"

Oh, Warwick's always outside, doing continuo. You've got his style, just take it for granted he's still shouting.

Gita tilted her head. "You think?"

"Go for it," Jane said.

Gita sighed.

Paul was being quiet. Paul, Jane, and I were going to the movies. A musical, supposed to be terrible, but directed by the Duffy brothers, so . . . Paul was in his neo-punk outfit as usual, Jane in a blue butterfly dress.

I was dressed stupid too. I had my hair in two rows of spikes, tartan trousers with chains and a bum-flap, and a green netting T-shirt, as worn by the Sex Pistols. Sometimes. The difference is that I knew I looked stupid—I'm in a theatrical costume while they were just wearing their clothes. They were both in their thirties, tugged at by gravity and too many events. Ah, sunflowers, weary of time, Jane would probably say.

I was at MSU Denver too, finishing an English degree. But I was taking, among other things, Naïve Criticism: The Demotic Response to Art. I knew things like Jane and Paul's conversation about Gita, and, I'm afraid, their sex life, because they told me. Paul liked me, partly because we both chose to dress from another age; that made me his younger self. While Jane had just started smanging me as well as Paul, so I got her side of the story too. Paul went off me a bit after he found out. I'm not being very likable, I know, but you don't have to worry. My name is Spike, and this story isn't about me.

There was a bit of a silence, or as much silence as you can get while Warwick's around. Gita said, "Well, I'd better get going. Matt's scummy if I'm late."

Paul and I watched her leave. Then Jane said, "We should move too. Film starts in ten minutes."

Paul finished his shake. "Yeah, this is true," he said. "We'd best get tickets, then."

Of course the film was crap. Jane sat in the middle, with a lover on each side. Only Jane and I knew that, of course.

JANE ENDED IT WITH Paul two nights later. Paul was lying over her, his weight politely on his elbows. A pool of his sweat had collected between her breasts. Paul was feeling pleasantly mindless self-satisfaction, playing with the moisture, blowing drops, rivulets, down toward her collarbones licking at her sweat, his tongue straying to the inner slopes of her breasts.

Jane looked at him suddenly. "I don't think we should do this anymore."

That woke him up. "What?" But he knew what she'd said.

"I don't think we should have sex anymore. See each other. As lovers, I mean. I think we should finish."

"Oh." Paul tilted his head to consider his reaction. He wasn't as upset as he might have expected. Nor as hurt. He considered protesting, asking why. He decided not to. He didn't like to be unintelligent in Jane's presence. Or pathetic. He said, instead, "Oh. All right. Okay. If that's what you want." He opened his mouth to say something else, but closed it when he realized he had no idea what it was.

"Oh, Paul." Jane grimaced, a harsh face he hadn't seen before. "That's it, that's why, I'm sorry, babe. I need more than this. We're not going anywhere. I just want something more . . . emotional, I think. I mean, it's been good, it just has to be over now for me, Paul."

But Jane had moved her sexual favor to me, and neither of us was emotional about the other. It was a polite lie, letting Paul save face. I think she was bored by Paul. He had a kind of sincerity that meant he'd never start certain games and made him slow to pick up on hers. He was what he seemed, and he was proud of that. Jane is not who she is.

Also, I was there, new, congenial, and convenient. We liked being a Younger Man and an Older Woman. We talked, laughed, and we had sex. Not emotionally.

Paul said, "I don't want to stop. I don't want to stop seeing you, or having sex with you." Their bodies were still touching, skin and skin. "But if it's what you . . . Anyway, it's your decision. I mean, I think it is. Are you sure? We can't, uh, change things?"

"No. Paul, I've been feeling wrong for a while, you must have known I haven't been, oh, you know, happy. I'm sorry, Paul, it's just . . ."

She looked about to cry, which put him on easier ground. "Oh shit, Jane, it'll be all right . . . I mean I'll be sad, but I'll live. I'll be okay. And we said we weren't . . . Will you be all right?" And so on. He liked being Good About It. It did him no good.

He admitted defeat then and lay beside her, on his back. They negotiated, dividing up their few jointly owned odds and ends, and agreeing not to slag each other off to their friends. Jane never mentioned me.

When they'd finished talking, Paul actually did feel sad, and closer to Jane than he had in months. "Hold me," Jane said, and he did.

And that was that.

THREE WEEKS LATER, PAUL went to a party with Jane. It was in Five Points, not far from Paul's. Paul and Jane still went to things together sometimes, though they'd go home separately. They had little in common now. Gita and I came along too, so it was a household expedition in Jane's car.

Paul hadn't seen me and Jane together before, though he'd guessed that we were on. But the sight of us together hurt him, though he knew better than to show it, me with my arm round Jane's waist, sort of negligent but under her shirt.

I caught Paul's eye watching me and I looked embarrassed. Paul smiled and saluted me: no problem, hey. But he slunk into the kitchen to avoid us. Gita was there, drinking juice and talking to a tall woman who had her hair gelled into rounded stalks so her head looked like a model of the Covid-19 virus. That woman was sitting on the bench so people had to reach round her to get at the bottles and cans in icy water in the kitchen sink. Paul found that someone had already stolen the bottle he'd brought, so he took a cup of port, grimacing.

Paul turned to the woman on the bench. Her name was Cathy. She knew people in the house he didn't know, she hated the party music, Italian hip-hop, that Paul quite liked, she didn't watch TV, and she liked jazz and live theater. She seemed interested in Paul, but when she got up to queue for the toilet he let her go. He talked to Gita instead.

He asked her how her work was. He didn't care, it was just a neutral topic. But it turned out that wasn't neutral. "Work. Fucking work. I don't have fucking work. I took your girl's advice; no, I'm sorry, she's not your girl anymore. Anyway, I called the fucking union. But here you have laws more backward than we have in Pakistan. The union woman couldn't even afford to go there to be laughed at. She called Dixon and got laughed at over the fucking phone." She was not a woman who had said "fucking" before, Paul guessed. "Then when I turned up to work he said I was a fucking troublemaker and ungrateful and I was fucking fired."

"Oh. Oh god, I'm sorry. Man's a pig."

"He is a fucking pig man. A dog man."

"Yeah. You should get revenge."

"Oh? And how do I do this?"

"I don't know. You could release cockroaches and rats into the dining area."

"Ah! I see! Or I could decapitate all the cats and leave them in the kitchen. And call the Health Department."

"Yes! I bet you anything you like he cheats on his taxes. You could report him to the tax office."

"I could call Mrs. Dixon, and tell her about the time he tried—"

"Oh, did he? Bastard." Cathy came back then and tried to get back into the conversation, got ignored and then bored. She drifted off somewhere.

Paul collected the port bottle and carried on talking with Gita. She drank some too. Like, she said, putting laxatives in his gateau. Like, Paul said, shutting his phones off so he couldn't take bookings.

And so on. Being nasty about people, even her ex-boss, was a new experience for Gita, and she seemed to feel she was being deliciously naughty.

Three cups of port in, Paul was thinking she was delicious any old way. Despite his occasional morning speculations when he'd seen her exiting the bathroom in her robe, Gita had never made much impression on him. Commitment to Jane was one reason. Also, Gita dressed conservatively, even by Paul's standards. That night she wore a respectable blue dress, but it looked good on her anyway, he decided. He watched her breasts with mildly drunken lechery, the deepening and relaxing of cleavage as she talked, her anger slowly turning into hilarity. The dress unbuttoned at the front.

About two in the morning Jane and I stumbled into the kitchen, arm in arm, drunk and silly. Jane announced we were going home.

Gita said she'd come too. She looked at Paul, meaning he should come with them.

Outside in the cold night air, we watched Jane try to get her key into her car door. It was pathetic. Paul intervened, ruling that we were all of us too messed up to drive. We should crash at his place on Market Street, which was only a few blocks away. It had a spare mattress and couches for everyone.

Jane and I had been sharing a bottle of vodka. Jane had had more of it than me, but we were both noisy drunk, I'm afraid. We shared the last inch on the way to Paul's, singing. Paul and Gita walked a disapproving distance behind us. Paul thought we were being wankers. He was right, but so what, you know? I turned to offer them vodka. There was Gita with her arm round Paul's waist, casual, as if she hadn't noticed it was there. So, I just leered at her. Young lovers, eh?

Paul's flat was upstairs in his tiny old house. He asked Jane and me to keep the noise down because other people lived there. Then he showed us through to his room. White walls, old-fashioned fireplace, futon bed, a lot of electronic gear.

He wanted to organize bedding for Jane and me. His idea, obviously, was to get Jane and me onto a mattress, then offer Gita half the bed. But Jane had already stripped and dived into bed. Force of habit, of course; it had always been her place before. So, I joined her. This gave Paul a strategic problem. He started to pull out a mattress from under the bed, for Gita. It wasn't big enough to be, self-evidently, bedding for two, so it looked like he was for the couch.

It was Jane who saved him. She was sitting up with me half on her, nuzzling her tits. I was showing signs of wear. But she said, "Fuck's sake, Paul, what are you doing? I didn't think you were that Victorian. There's plenty of room here, we can all just pile in together. I mean, come on."

Paul straightened up and looked blankly at Jane for a moment. Jane used to patronize him when they were together, of course, but he thought she'd waived the right when she'd dumped him. But he smiled, as if casually, and turned to Gita. "I think that's sensible. Is that okay?"

Gita also had to weigh it up for a few seconds. "Yes, of course." Paul went to get water, taking his time. Letting us work out our arrangements meant that he could work out his position in relation to Gita, and to us, when he got back.

When he came back the light was out. That was Gita, of course. Off with the shoes, dress, and pantyhose, and a scuttle under the covers. But the light out first. I was on the far side of the bed, nearest the wall, with Jane next to me, then Gita.

Jane had passed out, on her back, mouth open. I said, "Night, Paul," and put my head down. I was relieved Jane was out of action, because she'd probably have insisted that we had sex. Even I thought that would be antisocial. Instead I'd have to pretend to be asleep while Paul and Gita did their shy fumbling.

Paul put the water on the table, because we were bound to wake up thirsty. He undressed, leaving his underpants on, and read, from left to right, me, Jane, then Gita. So, he went to Gita's side of the bed. She turned to watch him and lifted the duvet. "You'd better come in, then." Her voice sounded constricted.

Paul didn't say anything. He wouldn't manage anything better than a croak unless he cleared his throat. His problem was that he still wasn't sure whether Gita was in his bed for convenience, like me and Jane, or socially, because she wanted to be in a bed with him. His cock had no ambiguity about her, though. She had to notice that.

He lifted the duvet a little farther to get in, getting a view of Gita's slip and sensible bra. She could go and buy bread and milk from the 7-Eleven wearing all that. But Paul rolled in beside her and pulled the covers over them both. Gita was warm, smelling of her own sweat and some sort of scent. They lay facing each other.

Gita touched his face, traced her fingers along his lips. She's in my bed socially, Paul decided, and put one arm under her shoulders to draw her close. They explored mouths. Gita wriggled, putting her hands on his shoulders, pressing her fingers into his skin. She broke contact with his mouth and kissed down along his neck. She looked at him, deciding. She sat up, pulling the slip over her head. Paul watched, thighs, panties coming into view, then her stomach, softly creased, then her breasts and shoulders. Leaning forward, she reached behind her to unclip her bra.

As Gita got the clasp free she lost her balance slightly and lurched forward. Jane stirred, opened her eyes as Gita let the bra fall. Jane met Paul's eyes for a second, still asleep, I think, then rolled over to face me. And the wall. Me, I'm still awake. Don't mind me.

Gita ducked back down under the covers. For a minute or two they kept still, until Gita cautiously reached over to stroke his stomach. Finally, when Paul was at a peak of frustration and impatience, she put her hand under his waist band and, if the change in his breathing meant anything, touched his penis.

Paul shifted, not disturbing the covers. He kissed her. Gita sighed, happily, but when he tried to push her panties down she took his hand again and looked over at Jane and me. Jane was actually asleep, and I had my eyes closed. I mean, what can you do?

"I'm sorry," she whispered. "I want to make love to you. But we really can't. Not now."

"Nnn," Paul conceded. "No, we can't. But I want you, I want to, I really want you, Gita." Gita mumbled something affirmative. She cuddled up to him when he lay back. He pulled her leg over his, but tried to relax, and detumesce.

Later, Paul told me, he had a dream. Paul and Jane were swimming together in a river near Walden. Their spot couldn't be seen from the road so they were naked. He'd swum up at her from the dark river bottom, then they'd embraced. Jane had slipped cold and hard against him, wrapped her legs around him. They headed for the riverbank and beached on the sand.

The dream was too intense and he woke up. Jane's face was beside him; she'd turned to him in her sleep. But Gita had given him this dream. She was under a heap of blankets, on her knees and elbows, licking him. He reached under her shoulders to hold her. She was soft; she filled his hands. She lifted her head, came up to kiss him. She said, "They're asleep. I want what you want. Yes?"

Paul checked the bedside clock. It was after four. I could have told him that. Gita had been tossing and turning, beside me, for the last hour. He whispered, "Come on," and got out of bed. Gita followed him out, shivering.

Paul pulled the mattress out from under the bed again, and dropped his spare duvet. Gita took a pillow and dropped it, then sat on it. She patted the space beside her, I assume for comedy. He lay down beside her and pulled the duvet over them. They squirmed and gripped under the tent, finally rolling over, Paul on top, while Gita looked up at him.

After a while I heard Gita say, "Slowly." She raised her knees so she was almost doubled up. Paul suddenly lurched away from her and waddled on his knees over to his bedside table. "Sorry. Damn. Damn," he said, and I heard the distinctive rip of a condom packet.

Jane used an IUD, so Paul must have stocked up on condoms since he became a single man. Gita said nothing, and closed her thighs round him, welcoming, as he returned. They rocked together. Gita grunted; Paul growled. They sounded happy: comforted. Paul got her name right at the crucial moment. Then Gita groaned and laughed in his ear—not something I've ever struck—tightening her legs around him and cracking a salvo from his spine.

They lay gasping side by side. Gita said, "Oh good, good. I'm glad."

"How blest am I in this discovering thee," said Paul, a leftover from Jane and the *Dictionary of Sodding Quotations*. She never pulled that on me, by the way. Gita made a "What?" noise, and he said, "You're completely wonderful," which went over better. They went back to nonverbal communication. After a long silent time I was slipping back into sleep. But Paul murmured, "We'd better get back to bed. It's getting cold."

"And you don't want Jane to know." Gita saw through him.

"True, I guess. Will you come and stay tomorrow?"

"Of course." No hesitation. Paul pushed the mattress under the bed, while Gita put her demure underwear back on and climbed clammily back.

That was how Gita and Paul started. Paul had a furious argument with Jane the next day.

JANE AND I LEFT early in the morning to get to her lecture. Gita was free till the afternoon, so when we left she was exploring Paul's kitchen and making coffee. Paul went to work at Phones 'n' Drones, where he was a technician. He said he was late. And fogged. He had trouble remembering names of things or making decisions. Nominal aphasia, that's called: hangover, stress, and the sudden acquisition of a new lover are all great for the nominal aphasia.

Jane visited Paul at six. Gita was due at eight. Paul let her in. No doubt warily. I heard Jane's what-a-bastard version later that night, and Paul's injured-innocent version a couple of days later. Jane leaned back against the windowsill. "So, what's going on?"

Paul sat on the bed. "How do you mean?"

"I mean you hitting on Gita. Last night."

Paul decided that Jane might have the right, as Gita's sort-of friend, to have this conversation. Still, he thought she was trespassing. "I didn't hit on Gita."

"You fucked her."

"We had sex. We decided we wanted to at about the same time. Like you were going to smush Spike, remember? Only you passed out."

"Paul, it isn't a good idea. I mean it, you should leave Gita alone."

"Yeah? Isn't that up to her? And me, for that matter?" Jane was ready to reply, but he continued. "Look, I don't know, you're concerned about Gita, that's fair enough. But she's not . . . She can make her own decisions. And I'm not pushing her or pressuring her into anything. Christ, you should know that."

"Yeah, I know, you'd make sure everything seemed to be her choice, nice guy, consenting adults, all the bullshit. Paul, that's just not the point. You don't know anything about Gita. She doesn't know anything about you. Or much about men or relationships. Or about America. You're going to hurt her. You're really going to mess her life up."

"Really? We're having sex. People have sex."

"Paul, Gita's really vulnerable at the moment. Her whole life's fucking up on her, and she's probably going to have to go back to Karachi. Things aren't so delightful there for independent women. Especially women who come back without a qualification. Especially women who've been fucking foreigners. She's not in a position to have a casual relationship at the moment. She needs too much; it wouldn't be casual to her. And you're not prepared to get involved in more than a casual relationship, are you?"

"Oh. Okay, I see that. I mean, I see what you're saying." She watched him think. "Jane, it's still her life and her decision. Not mine. Definitely not yours. I'm serious. I'm sorry, but that's how I see it."

Jane glared. "There's more to life than your cock, Paul. You should tell her not to come around. You're an irresponsible bastard if you don't."

"Ah hell, Jane. What do you think, Gita's an idiot, she can't think for herself? You're being arrogant."

Jane called him a stupid, selfish piece of shit and left. His door slammed and bounced. Jane and Paul weren't friends anymore.

Gita was punctual. Jane had raised doubts in him, and he was nervous with her. She wasn't nervous. She hugged him at the door, reestablishing contact.

She wasn't in love, but she was enjoying her experiment with sex. And while Paul talked to me about Jane, since we had her in common, he wouldn't talk about Gita, beyond the front door. So, the narration stops there. I heard a bit of what they talked about. I don't know what they did.

THE NEXT NIGHT PAUL was working late again, so Gita was home. She and Jane weren't speaking, that evening. Fortunately, Jane had to go to a function at the university because one of her colleagues was leaving. I stayed home to talk with Gita.

I made milky chai and we sat at the kitchen table. I'd still only lived in that house for a couple of months, and Gita was very reserved, though not, as I'd thought, shy. So, we hadn't had a heart-to-heart before. I said, "Sorry about Jane. She's worried about you, is all."

She smiled. "No, she isn't." I waited, but she didn't say more.

So, I said, "How's Paul?"

"Paul's fine. And he is worried about me. So am I. I don't want to go back to Karachi. But if I'm not a student, I lose my visa. And I haven't got enough money, now Papa's in jail, to keep being a student. As far as I can tell, I'm fucked."

It still seemed odd, hearing her use that word. I said, "What if we lent it to you? I mean, I don't really have any money. But Paul does."

"Yes, he's already offered. And by 'lend' he really means 'give.' But I can't take his money. I couldn't anyway, but especially I can't sleep with him and accept money from him."

I took a sip of the chai. "You know, that might be a little too scrupulous, just at the moment."

She banged her cup down. There was chai spillage. "No! It is not! Don't you even know what pride is?"

I said nothing. At last she calmed down. "You're weird, Spike. You care more than you pretend. I know that. I don't know why it's so important to you to pretend."

I didn't want to have that conversation. I said, "So, what happens?"

"I've got a while before my student status expires. Then Immigration comes to get me. I'm not going to run. I don't want to spend my life afraid of a knock on the door. Once I'm in Karachi I'll try to get to England. Or New Zealand, maybe."

I nodded. "I hope you stay, Gita. Don't know how, but I hope you can."

She smiled and thanked me. She talked, sadly, about her father, and her mother, living scared, alone with a few servants in the family home.

Then her phone beeped. Paul had texted: he'd just left work and he was double-parked outside. Would she like to Netflix and chill? She cheered up, suddenly giddily happy, and said goodbye. She ran down the stairs like she was Cinderella at the stroke of midnight.

I poured a little rum into my chai. Yeah, that worked too.

THE NEXT EVENING PAUL and I were back at Illegal Burgers. He raised his milkshake and said, "Cheers."

I said "cheers" back. We touched glasses together. We hadn't discussed the matter of me smanging Jane while she was, like, his girlfriend, maaan, and that meant we never would. I'd hoped we wouldn't have that conversation. That was true of a lot of conversations.

Paul had called me the following morning, after his scene with Jane, and the different, undisclosed, scene with Gita, and he'd asked me to meet him after he'd finished work.

Warwick was still outside, and he was talking about the unspeakable things homosexual lesbians, as opposed to some other, unspecified kind of lesbian, do to each other, and what, in turn, his god was going to do to them. The lesbians came across as nicer people than his god, no question. He had to dodge the occasional empty plastic drink bottle, but he was getting more attention than usual. It was the talking about lesbians that did it. He liked the extra attention. He'd probably talk about lesbians more often.

Actually it was Warwick who'd brought Jane and me together. We were at Illegals talking about art crit, but we were starting to say less and just look at each other. Appraising what we had here. Warwick had been outside giving people the straight dope about Satanism in popular music. Without quite using the n-word he ripped into "African jungle music." But when he singled out the name of James Brown I said, "That's it. 'Scuse me," to Jane and took my milkshake outside. Righteously.

I tapped Warwick on the shoulder, and when he turned around I poured it over his head. Jane followed me out and did the same. Mine was vanilla, hers was chocolate. Warwick stood there wild-eyed but sort of nonplussed, looking exactly as if someone had melted a chessboard over him.

A couple of the muscular Christians who hung around the square and sort of bounced for the evangelicals saw this and started moving in. I took Jane's arm because she hadn't noticed them, and we ran back into Illegals. We beat them by four yards, which was enough. They hesitated before going into licensed premises. Especially premises with bouncers. We dropped off our empty glasses and ran out the back door.

Then we ran to her car, got inside it, and fell about laughing. At Jane's flat we only got through the back door and closed it, then smushed each other, for the first time, on the carpet. Jane wouldn't have done that, any of it, with Paul.

So, Warwick, eh? As I said, I've got a soft spot for him.

Anyway, back in the present, in Illegals, Paul said, "You know Jane came to see me."

"Shout at you, by what she told me."

"Yeah, she got shouty. It built up fast. But I talked about it with Gita. She's very clear that she doesn't want to go home. Karachi's not going to be good, not without a degree, and not right now anyway."

"She said you offered to pay her fees."

"Yeah. It'd hurt a bit more than she knows, but I can get the money. But Gita was very clear that she won't take the money from a boyfriend. No matter what."

"Yeah. She said that too."

"Yeah. So, the Moulin Rouge is going to pay. I did a little spreadsheeting. If you take the time she worked there, and add up the unpaid hour every day, that bastard Dixon owes her at least six grand."

"That's not even taking into account the sexual harassment."

"Yeah. I think there was more of that than she's told us. And there's the wrongful dismissal. So, I want Dixon to put up the money. She reckons he makes more than six grand on a single night, over the weekend."

I raised my shake. "Oh, for sure. They're liable. For damages." We clinked shakes again and said, "Guilty," together. Jane would have pointed out that Dixon had, apart from the sexual harassment, probably committed a tort, not a crime. But she wasn't there. Instead we had an operatic moment: strong men reconciled by a noble cause.

Paul said that he could slow down their credit card connection, so they'd pressure their customers to pay by cash rather than card, if they could. They make an enormous amount of money at the weekend, Gita had told him.

"Oh? Does she know about this?"

"No. She was just telling me what a moron Dixon is. She says they can't bank their cash at the weekend, so they keep it in a small, perfectly portable safe until Monday. Even then, Matt keeps the combination on a piece of paper in his desk drawer. Which is good. But Gita doesn't know anything about what I want to do. You can't tell her, either."

"K. So, you're just going to walk in, right, with dark glasses and a handkerchief round your face?"

"Pantyhose and a Hawaiian shirt, but close. But they've got an alarm system. It picks up any movement inside the premises. Anything at all. Because of that they're not too worried about burglars. But I'm a technician. I can deal with that. And I will get Gita's money."

"Oh, Gita's money? Paul, I'm not a burglar. You're talking about rooms barred and painted pink, and long orange corridors, all concrete. You're in love, obviously, so good for you. But how deep do you expect me to get in this?"

"I just need someone to keep an eye out. If I have even a minute's warning, I can shut the kitchen door and be away over the roof before anyone reaches the restaurant. You'd be in your car, looking out. From a safe distance, Spike."

"Safe."

"You leave your phone at home. But if you see the plods, or Matt or anything bad, you'll have an RT and so will I. They have radio telephones in toy stores. They work for up to a kilometer and no one monitors them. You press the button to buzz me, and you drive off quietly. I can get out of that alley, easy. So, you're essential but safe. Well?"

So, of course, I was in. There was unspoken blackmail, that I owed him for smanging Jane while she was still his girlfriend. And even I knew that Gita was a good person and that bad things shouldn't happen to her. But mostly I was in because we made the first expedition that night, and he didn't let me get away to change my mind.

We went to his place first, because Gita wasn't going to come over that night. We had coffee and we talked about life with Jane, sex, films, great gigs I'd missed because I was too young, and so on, until it was time.

About two thirty he took a bag and a piece of steak and we went to Larimer Street. Paul and his steak had little trouble seducing one of the feline horde there. And that's where we came into this story, with Paul down an alleyway with a cat.

All the cat would have suffered was a headache from the alarm, and that not for long. It knew the way out. I dare say it thought the steak was worth it.

WE DID THE CAT thing four more times. Two days later, then three days later, then one day later, then two days later. The cats, it seemed, were never found. They made their own way out because of the noise, or they hid to be shooed out in the morning by one of the kitchen staff, who weren't going to tell Dixon that they'd let a cat into the kitchen and left it there overnight.

For these trials I stayed in the car, holding a yellow plastic RT. The fifth trial was the triumph. The mangy little starveling chased his steak across the floor. He glommed it. Nothing. Then he jumped around, trying to get at the hanging salamis. No invisible beams interrupted, no electronic arias. That's what Paul had meant when he said he was a technician. Throw enough cats at a sophisticated alarm system, and someone will get annoyed and turn it off.

There are people who can solve that sort of problem. It's just that they're in high demand and you have to wait. So, we came back on Sunday morning, three days after that trial. I stayed in the Subie while Paul repeated the cat test. The cat landed on its paws and walked around. Peacefully. Silently. Paul had a little more trouble getting in. The kitchen rear door had a strong, new, expensive Chubb lock. And a door that opened outward so that the hinges were on the outside. Paul used rust remover and oil on the hinge pins, knocking them up and out, opened the door from the hinge side, and slipped in, leaving the lock intact.

I sat with my head low, watching out. It was quiet, with all the night noises unnaturally clear. Torn posters flapping in the wind, unexplained bangs, the sex life of cats. It's nerve-racking, being an accessory. But nothing happened. A couple of cars went past, but they weren't cops and they weren't Mercs. Matt drove a Merc.

After about twenty minutes the RT beeped. I jumped. It was much louder than I expected, and I was more nervous. Paul was in the restaurant and feeling cocky. He asked, "How's it going out there?"

"Shut up, Paul. Get off the air."

"Relax, Spike. I told you these are toys. They don't carry far and no one's listening. I'm nearly done. I've got to make a mess so it doesn't look like I knew where the combination was. And I want to put the door back, to make it a bit puzzling. If you like, you can drive to 26th and Walnut Street in ten. I'll meet you."

"Oh, roger fucking wilco." But I waited and then started the engine. And as I was cruising up, he stepped out from an alcove across the road, with a bulge in his gabardine overcoat. He looked like he'd just ducked into the dark for a piss. He got in casually, and I drove away just enough over the speed limit not to be conspicuous. But I didn't relax until I turned onto Market Street.

I parked and we went up to his room, where we suppressed all our yeehaws and wah-heys, with regret. Paul's housemates didn't know what he'd been up to. It was best it stayed that way.

We rolled around on his bed in a celebratory, vaguely homoerotic way, then Paul got up and opened a bottle of Drambuie that he'd set aside for the occasion. No glasses, just the bottle. We exchanged swigs. It was an old house, and there was a fireplace in his bedroom. He lit it, as if it was another ritual. The paper and cloth in the grate went up fast and fierce, *whoosh,* smelling like a chemical burn-off. He took a swig and toasted the fire, then passed me back the bottle.

So, in the heat—and unpleasant smell—of the fire we knelt on the floor to count the loot. We made Paul's Gita Fund target of $6,000 with plenty to spare. He'd collected $7,465 in cash. That was on top of the electronic money the Moulin Rouge had taken. Matt Dixon was doing very well indeed.

I wanted us to split the extra money, but Paul said Gita had earned it, it was owed to her and she needed it. She should get all of it. Once he got to that sort of talk, I had to admit that this was so. Then he thought. He said he was starting to feel emotional about Gita, and he liked spending time with her, he fancied her, and it was important to him that she succeeded. None of that really applied to me. So, I could have the spare $465. I weighed up pride versus the sheer convenience of having $465, and I took it. It was a good hourly rate.

It was getting light outside. I called a taxi. It was late to be joining Jane, but I needed sleep. "See you later, Paul."

"See you, Spike."

TWO NIGHTS LATER I was lying on Jane's bed. We had the house to ourselves. The tension between Jane and Paul had dropped to the level where they could be polite, but it still tended to create an atmosphere if the two of them were in the same house. So, Gita was at Paul's. They usually slept at his place.

I was surprised at Gita. I don't mind Jane paying some of my bills, the bigger ones mostly, because it's mutually flattering for me to be, and her to have, a sort of gigolo. But I thought Gita had found the idea of accepting money from Paul, even stolen money, offensive. It'd make her a mistress, and she wasn't the type to find that amusing.

Jane was talking about Gita too. She'd paid her university fees, and the rent. Jane said, "I just can't believe Paul, though. I never thought he'd be able to pull something like that."

I was surprised she knew about it, but I said, "Yeah, just goes to show you never know someone. He's a bit of a crim, is Paul."

"Yeah. I never thought he was all that quick, but he must have talked long and hard. And he really ripped someone off."

I lost the plot there. "What?"

"The Mackiewicz, that thing I gave Gita, Paul got some idiot to pay seven grand for it. I wouldn't have given it away if I'd thought there were suckers like that around."

"Oh. Oh yeah. Right."

"I hope Mackiewicz never finds out he's still got a market. He'd be absolutely impossible."

It seemed Paul had told Gita he had a buyer. For her property, the painting. And the fire, the chemical blaze in Paul's grate had been Mackiewicz's daub, the city and the dream woman incandescent for a second and then returning to their composite atoms. A little sacrifice, a little knot of lies, for Gita's pride. I hope Mackiewicz never finds out too. Among others.

I craned up and kissed Jane, then pulled her down to me. Bodies mostly don't tell lies. Ah, bodies.

# Stuck on a Stranded Dog

Howard Isaac Williams

In the midnight hour
Of a June night
On a mountain pass
Between the River
And the Sea
The dog died.
A ship passing
Through the Night,
Carrying a cargo full
Of Masked Pilgrims
Each
On a separate Peregrination
All
To a common destination:
City of Angels.
But a belt snaps
On the alternator,
Disabling tons of steel
Stranding 4 score and 7
Leaving them all
Stuck on a stranded Greyhound.
Our Captain, our Driver
Says words muffled by his mask
"Wait for the relief bus
coming from San Francisco"
And

"Espera el bus
que va para San Francisco"
Four . . . hours . . . away.
The lucky fall asleep,
Leaving the awake but unlucky
To wonder
What more can go wrong
In this Year of the Rat
That's not even half over?
3 restless passengers—
Not wanting to snap—
Step out to wander
Into the night,
Gaze at the stars,
Wary for speeding semis
And silent pumas,
Smell fragrances
Of sage
And coyote bush.
Finally we return and wait
Hoping no one
Catches the Virus.

# Lost and Found

Arthur M. Doweyko

IT WAS DARK AND GETTING DARKER. THE WIPERS GROANED AS they skittered across the windshield over a relentless barrage of snow and ice. Their streaks burst into a blinding radiance as cars trundled by. Soon I would see nothing ahead. The engine coughed up a death rattle. So, I steered the car to the curb.

The snow left few landmarks uncovered, clinging to everything, including street signs. The funny thing was that I was both lost and sure that somehow I knew the neighborhood—that it would all come back to me any moment now.

I turned the key with fingers nearly numb. The click of a starter solenoid did little to lift my spirits—could be the battery. I tried the ignition a few more times. The fine layer of frost on the window made it hard to see much. I ran a wrist over it. My gut tightened when I saw the row of three-story apartments across the street. A tall chain-link fence on the passenger side sealed the deal—a park. I knew where I was.

An illuminated slit of light from a first-floor window ran a few hackles up my back. The apartment was the one I grew up in—so many years ago when both my parents were still alive—so many years ago.

That light peeked out from between drawn curtains. That was my spot. I used to watch the street, count the cars and people passing by. Heavy snow in the city was rare. I remember a night like this, excited about the blizzard, hoping that the next day school would be called off. My mother finished preparing supper, and she called me and my dad to the kitchen.

The curtains moved.

My hand shook, not from the cold, but from the grim feeling that something peculiar was happening. I reached for the door handle just as a car came by, splashing up a translucent smear of ice and snow. I rolled down the window.

A wooden porch circled the front of the apartment house—a style nearly a century old—painted a pale shade of green, faded, even when I lived there. The streetlamp from the intersection a half block away did little more than deepen the shadows. A living room window overhung the side of the porch. The curtains moved again, and the narrow band of light winked out.

I needed to get a tow. At least that's what I was thinking when I got out of the car and ran across the street toward the house, half skating to the curb. Icy water seeped into my shoes.

The virgin snow blanketing the porch steps made me feel like an uninvited intruder, which I was. Did it beg me to take a few steps closer, or did its pristine indifference tell me something else?

Tall Victorian-era front doors boasted oversized windows through which I saw a dim hallway light outlining a stairway inside. Every month my father sent me up those stairs to bring our landlord his monthly rent. The smell of damp wood was exactly as I remembered it, like the paint, like the curtains. I stepped to the door and inhaled the sweet scent of cooking, maybe chicken soup—my favorite dish. Mama used to make it from scratch.

Set into the wall to the side, three bronze mailboxes sported nameplates and buttons. We had the first one. Not enough light to read it.

Although the living room curtains were drawn, a fold remained slightly parted. Maybe I could see inside.

"ARTHUR, SUPPER IS READY. Hurry up, don't let it get cold."

"I'm coming, Mama." I tugged the curtain closed and walked back toward the kitchen. On the way I tapped my papa on the back as he bent over in his desk chair fiddling with some papers. "Dinner, Papa."

Chicken soup with noodles.

Mama and I waited for Papa to sit before starting in.

"Papa, do you think school will be called off tomorrow?"

"Hard to say."

"But it's a blizzard out there."

Papa continued to sip his soup. Mama sat across from us, grinned, and said, "We'll call in the morning."

"There's a car parked across the street."

Papa said, "Everybody parks there."

"But this one . . . I mean, the guy came out and he was coming this way."

I looked along the narrow corridor leading back to the living room. "I think he's right outside."

THE WIND STUNG MY eyes. My heart pounded in my ears. Despite the bitter cold, I swear I felt heat rushing up my cheeks. I backed away and grabbed the entry doorknob to keep from sliding down the porch steps.

I didn't see the whole kitchen table, only the end—the end where I used to sit. A boy about twelve years old hunched over like he was eating. He raised his head to talk to someone. When he turned, he stared directly at me—like he knew I was at the window.

That boy looked like me.

After a minute I regained my balance and bent down to see if I could read the nameplate. A car sloshed by and headlight beams flashed across the porch. My last name was handprinted in block lettering just the way my father used to do it.

Maybe the whole thing was just a weird coincidence. Maybe the kid just sort of looked like me and I was in the middle of some crazy nostalgic mind trip. The thought made me look back at my car, worried I might see myself still sitting there.

A light flooded the landing inside. Someone had opened the apartment door. A figure approached and spoke loudly enough for me to hear.

"Can I help you?"

My papa was speaking to me. There was no doubt.

"Sir, are you all right?"

The boy appeared alongside. I mean to say it was me who appeared. I don't know what I mean.

"Is it your car? Do you need help?"

I nodded.

My mama leaned out of the apartment's door. She said, "Ludwik, who is it?"

"This fellow seems to be in trouble, dear. His car—"

"Don't let him stand there in the cold."

The door swung wide.

"Please come in."

The boy led us through the hall and into the apartment. Warmth wrapped itself around me like a woolen blanket. They were using the new electric heater in my papa's study—the landlord had it installed just last week. What am I saying?

"Please sit."

My mama headed to the kitchen and said, "Would you like some coffee?"

I wanted to run up to her, to hug her, to let her know how much I missed her, but what would that look like?

"Y-yes. Thanks."

My papa said, "My name's Louis," and extended a hand.

Louis, the anglicized version of Ludwik. As I took his hand, I also took in his features—short, dark brown hair graying at the temples, rosy cheeks and a full nose. Everything was the way I remembered it. My papa, alive, sat in his desk chair like he always did.

"Oh . . . I'm Ar— Arnold."

The boy dragged a chair from the living room. "Here, mister."

I slumped into the chair. My legs were about to give way. "Thanks. My car . . . my car conked out. I'd appreciate it if I could use your phone to call for a tow."

My father said, "Is it a local call?"

My mother yelled from the kitchen. "Don't mind my husband. Go ahead and make your call, Arnold."

Mama's hearing was one of her powers. The black Bakelite phone threw me. I hadn't seen one in ages. "Do you have a directory?

"Yellow pages? Sure."

While my papa walked over to a wall shelf, the boy brought a hand to his mouth and whispered to me. "Who are you, really?"

HIS EYES SPRUNG OPEN, and I swear his face got even whiter than when he came in. I don't know why, but he looked really familiar.

"What do you mean?"

"Are you from around here?"

"Next town over."

"Arnold doesn't sound right. What's your last name?"

My papa returned with the yellow pages. "Here you go."

The man fumbled with the big book like he wasn't sure how to use it.

I said, "Just look under 'towing.'"

"Arthur, I'm sure Arnold knows what to do."

The man gave me a long look—the kind the nun at school gave me when she was ticked off, which was most of the time.

I said, "So, what do you do, Arnold?" emphasizing his name, which I was pretty sure was made up.

Papa said, "Arthur, that's none of your business. Get back to the kitchen and finish your soup."

I got up and smiled at the guy. I think he got even paler.

THAT KID, ME—HE'S some smart aleck. Was I really such a pain?

I made a call and a towing service promised to come. They were a bit unclear about when.

My papa led me back to the kitchen. "I think your coffee's ready. Why don't you sit with us while you wait?"

Mama said, "Milk and sugar?"

"Just sugar, ma'am."

"You can call me Helga."

Of course. She sat down opposite the kid. Papa stayed back in his den. I chucked in a few spoonfuls of sugar and stirred the coffee, taking my time, prolonging the moment. I couldn't keep my eyes off her.

Mama said, "You like sugar almost as much as my son, Arthur."

I said, "Is that right?"

The boy spoke up. "Any chance you like chocolate too?"

"Eh, yeah, sure I do."

"What's your favorite show on TV?"

Now I had to be careful. What was on TV in the '60s? "Oh, I just about like everything."

"Mine is *Twilight Zone*."

"Yeah, I liked that one too."

"Liked? You mean like, right?"

Damn smart aleck. "Yeah, yeah."

The boy slurped up the last of his soup. "Mama, I'm done."

"Did you do your homework?"

"Almost."

"No TV until you finish it, and your father checks it."

The boy went to his room next to the kitchen. When the door closed I looked to my mama. She was busy with the dishes. I forgot how young she was then. Light brown hair danced along her shoulders.

I couldn't hold back any longer. "Helga, I have to tell you something. It's going to sound awfully strange. I don't want you to be frightened."

She settled her dishtowel onto the rim of the sink. "Ludwik, could you come in here?"

"Now, now. You have nothing to fear from me."

Papa appeared at the entry to the kitchen. "What is it, honey?"

"Arnold, here, has something to tell us."

The doorbell rang.

Papa said, "Hold on. I'll see who it is."

Mama said, "So, what was it you wanted to say?"

Papa yelled from the hallway. "Honey, I think it's the tow truck."

Arthur barged out the door of his room and ran out to join his father.

I stood up from the kitchen chair. "I guess it's time for me to go. Thanks for everything." The whole thing was tearing a hole in my gut.

THE TOW TRUCK GUY was dressed in a raggedy coat and smelled like oil.

He said, "Is there an Arnold here? He called to get his car towed. Is that it across the street?"

Arnold showed up and said, "That's me and that's it. You can start hooking her up. Need the keys?"

The man said, "No sweat. I'll have her ready in a minute," and jogged down the steps.

Arnold, looking more disappointed than glad, said, "I'll be right with you. Just want to say bye to these good folks."

I followed him back to the door of the apartment where he thanked Mama and Papa for their hospitality. He looked like he was about to cry. When my parents went inside, he leaned down to me.

"Arthur. You said I looked familiar?"

"Yeah. So?"

"There's a good reason for that. Are you ready for this? I am you . . . just a bit older."

I thought about yelling out to my parents. I took a step away, but Arnold caught my arm.

"Hold on, hold on. I know what this sounds like, but I can prove it."

I decided to give him five more seconds. "Go ahead."

"My real name is Arthur with the same last name as yours."

I just stared at the guy. So what if his name was the same as mine?

"And I have two middle names, Michael and Philip."

I couldn't move a muscle.

"And here's the final proof."

He pulled back the sleeve of his coat and showed me his left thumb. It had a scar on it. Without thinking, I offered up my thumb, which had the same scar. I mean exactly the same scar, stitch holes and all.

He said, "And you, I mean we, got that while cutting a Davy Crocket poster with a razor blade."

I just kept staring at his thumb, when he shook me and said, "Now I have something very important to tell you."

THE NEXT MORNING I was the first to wake up. I ran over to the front windows. The sun hadn't made it over the skyline yet. Everything was a sort of blue-white color. And it was still snowing. No school today for sure. And that car from across the street was gone. Maybe it was buried in the snow.

I got dressed and grabbed a shovel from the hall closet. The snow was at least two feet deep right up to the front door. It was a monster and heavy as hell. I had to work fast so my papa wouldn't try to do it himself. That's what my older self told me, and he was serious.

About fifteen minutes later, Papa showed up. He placed his hands at his hips and said, "Your mother has breakfast almost ready. I must say this is a nice surprise."

I couldn't tell him the truth. Besides, he wouldn't believe me. "Just thought I'd help out. Besides, I'm building a fort."

"I called the school. You're off today, and so am I."

"That's great, Papa. I'm almost done."

When I got back in, I went over to the kitchen and handed Mama a note.

"What's this?"

"That man yesterday. He said you have to get Papa to call this doctor. He's a cardiligist, or something like that."

"What a strange thing."

"Mama, he said do it right away. It's really important."

"You stay here and have your breakfast. I'll talk to your father."

A few minutes later she came back and said, "I don't know how Arnold knew, but your father has been having some pains, chest pains. He's been ignoring them, but this." She waved the note. "This is a sign."

I heard Papa call to her from their bedroom.

Mama said, "It took some doing. I've been telling him for weeks he needs to check with a doctor. Your papa can be very stubborn."

She turned to go see what Papa wanted. Just then, the note fell to the floor. I picked it up, folded it, and stuck it in my wallet.

A month later he had an operation to fix his heart—a bypass they called it.

I WAS ABOUT TO follow the tow truck guy out. I gave my parents a final, lingering look, and waved goodbye to my little self. Each step away from them was agony.

When I got to the street, I forced myself to look away. A plow must have come through while I was inside—hardly any snow on the ground—and no sign of the tow truck. I opened the car door and angled into my seat.

"What took you so long?"

The voice startled me. Sitting in the passenger seat was an old man. A bald pate and white mustache that peeked over his wide-lapelled coat.

"Papa. You scared me."

"Well, what did you find over there?"

The falling snow paused a moment as if on cue. I could see the front porch clearly. No lights in the windows. In fact, the place had a rundown feel I didn't notice before. And a sign was plastered on the front door.

"I went over to—"

"Like I told you, son. It's been years since anybody's lived there. Didn't you read the sign? The place is condemned."

"But . . . I was—"

"Don't know why you stopped and insisted on going over there. That place is ancient history. Get this car started up. You know how your mother is when supper gets cold."

I turned the key and the engine sprung to life. What was it I expected to see? Why in the world would I go over there? Then I remembered something—something in my wallet.

"What are you up to now?"

"Hold on a second, Papa."

I unfolded the wallet and pulled up a wrinkled piece of paper.

"Well, what is it?"

"Nothing, Papa. Just something I thought I lost."

# The Brown Bag

## Karen Gregory

IT WAS A BEAUTIFUL CHRISTMAS EVE IN TUCSON. THE SUNSET had been amazing: starting with gold, melding into orange, then finally into an intense red that almost hurt my eyes, eventually turning into purple as the sun slid farther away. The holiday lights were twinkling as I drove along the back streets, a pretty sight in the desert this time of year. The coming spring flowers would be beautiful: golden barrel cactus blooms, white saguaro flowers, intensely red and orange poppies, yellow green Palo Verde trees—but this would suffice during the desert's sleep. Residents had strung lights on their looming saguaros and short barrel cacti, mesquite trees, palm tree trunks—wherever they could think of in addition to their homes. They don't mess around when it comes to the holiday spirit.

As I drove my new convertible toward home with the top down—a bright yellow Spitfire, a gift from my dad—I smelled the scent of the recent rain. It brought out the earthy, musky odor of creosote, a perfume like nothing else in the world. I inhaled it deeply and savored it. Everyone knows when it rains in Tucson by the fragrance.

It was 1971. I was sixteen years old, almost seventeen. Tall. Smart. A good-looking guy, I thought. I had thick eyelashes that fluttered at the appropriate time, and straight thick brown hair halfway down my waist. The girls loved both.

So, here I was, out and about that Christmas Eve, enjoying the lights, the smells, and the music blasting out of the brand-new stereo system that Mom and Dad had given me as a Christmas gift.

I knew my mother had worked overtime to help buy it, but Dad was trying to help out too. Together, they'd given me the choice between an eight-track stereo system and a safety roll bar for my new Spitfire. Both chipped in for the gift—and guess what I picked.

My dad was a big-time Tucson car dealer, and he'd given me every car I'd ever driven, including the yellow Spitfire convertible. My dad looked like Clark Gable, pencil mustache and all. His problem? He liked to rove with other women too much, and hung out with a lot of Italian guys like the Bonano family, who were into a lot of businesses that were never truly described. Mom threw him out of the house when I was eight years old but would never grant him a divorce. That wasn't how Catholicism worked. They'd met when she worked at the Desert Sanatorium, now the Tucson Medical Center, at one of the weekly nurses' pool parties. She lived in the two-story nurses' dorm. They'd fallen madly in love and married young. She was a beautiful brunette, and at first a stay-at-home mom. Now she was an RN, and often did double shifts to help us kids have the latest or whatever else we asked for. We were both quite selfish since Dad was gone, and they were both trying to buy our love.

My sister and I had no problem with that. My sister was three years older, gorgeous, and knew it. Mickey and I had a love/hate relationship. She was treated like a princess before I was born, and after I came along, she tried to drown me in the pool at our Wrightstown ranch. She really never forgave me for arriving. But I had to hand it to her: she was the only one who understood me when I was little. It turned out I was born with something called "reverse swallow," and everyone thought I was mentally retarded until I was in second grade. I just couldn't form words correctly. She didn't think I was retarded and figured out how to translate what I was trying to say to my parents until the speech therapist sessions finally unlocked my tongue.

Mickey was always surrounded by friends, but often seemed lost. For a while, she was a model for different businesses in Tucson. One sticks out in my mind: a newspaper ad for a new apartment complex, showing a happy couple in bed. Mickey was not wearing a wedding ring. Oh, the flack that builder got from that! They retouched the photo and ran the ad again. They rented every unit.

So, back to Christmas Eve. I'd just dropped off my friend John so he could get ready to go to the mass together, as was our tradition. As I drove home to get dressed myself, I leaned down to switch the tape in my new stereo. I glanced up. There was a car directly in front of me. It wasn't supposed to be there—this was a "No Street Parking" area.

BOOOOOOOOOOM!!!

I smashed into the car. Then I flipped, up and over. Crunch. I hit the car one more time—upside down. Smash, crunch. The sound of the metal was wrenching and screeching. Then I started rolling. Crunch. And rolled. Crunch. And rolled. Crunch. And rolled a couple more times. Then, as suddenly as the rolling had started, my car jolted to a stop—landing on the wheels, right side up. Well, this is lucky, right? How bad could it be?

While it was all happening, I felt the air whoosh through my hair. I heard the smashes and pings and crunching and crashing as my car turned over and over, each time it hit the pavement. I felt the shooting pain as I held on to the gearshift knob for dear life—because back then there was no such thing as a seatbelt in a Spitfire and I had the top down, so I would have been tossed into the street and run over and smashed by my own car. So, I just held on and waited for the inevitable end. And during all of this, I thought to myself, I should've gotten the roll bar . . . well, a bit too late for that. No shit. I really did.

Now it seemed so quiet. It took me a moment or two to grasp it all after the car settled. As I sat in the driver's seat, I looked around and smelled gasoline and oil and crushed metal. I had to get out. The car might catch fire. Weirdly, I could hear music, and thought it was still playing on my stereo. But it was someone in a nearby house. The car was a mess—completely totaled. In fact, it had literally been shaved in half; the entire passenger side was completely gone. Thank God I'd dropped off John earlier. He would've been dead for sure.

Witnesses said it took a total fifteen seconds for the accident to end after I hit the parked car. I beg to differ. It was an eternity. I found out later from the police and emergency personnel that officially, my Spitfire had rolled five times.

I managed to get out of the shell of what it had been and walk across the street to the nearest house. Neighbors were spilling out of their homes, and some had already congregated in their front yards, as surprised as I that I survived. Mom is going to be so pissed off that I totaled my car with that brand-new stereo, was all I could think. I got across the street and asked the homeowner if I could call my mom for a ride home. Well, sure. Mom was immediately on her way, her RN training kicking in. But an already-summoned ambulance arrived first on the scene, so she followed us to the emergency room at Tucson Medical Center. When we got there, I told her, "I'm fine. I just feel like shit about my car." Mom had seen the car. She was just happy I was alive.

We were now stuck in emergency room procedures, and honestly, they haven't changed over the years. Fill out the paperwork. Who's responsible for paying the charges. Write down an emergency contact. By then I knew that really severe wounds and incidents would be treated first—it was a triage hospital—and there were actually a few of those ahead of me. So, my mom and I sat there . . . and sat . . . and sat.

I agonized over my choice to look down at the eight-track and change the tape. Should I have pulled over first? But NOBODY was supposed to be parking on that street. I wrestled with that while I waited, and thought about my totaled car, and damn it, it was Christmas Eve and John would be waiting for me, thinking what the hell had happened? No texting or cell phone calls back then.

Eventually, I noticed a peculiar sensation: no sensation. I couldn't feel anything. Complete numbness. In my legs, feet, arms, hands. What the hell? I finally told my mom. She freaked. Got the nearest doctor/nurse/PA/attendant. Whatever. She got someone to pay attention, and an X-ray technician came out and asked me to come with him. He took the X-ray and had me walk back to the waiting area.

A few minutes later, he came rushing out, freaked, and ran helter-skelter. I guess it was to get someone in authority, because soon a neck surgeon appeared in front of me and my mom in the waiting room, very agitated, and revealed that I had a broken neck. Broken clean through. Hmmm. Not good. I had been walking and sitting for almost four hours, but the bones hadn't shifted enough to sever my spinal cord, he said. Well, thank God for that, I thought.

After so much waiting, everything happened really fast. Top medical personnel swarmed around me, put me on a gurney, and strapped me down so tightly that I couldn't move a muscle from my shoulders up. I was hooked up to an IV and given a lot of great drugs for pain. I thought, this is odd, because I can't feel a thing anyway, but I wasn't going to tell them to stop. Then I was wheeled into the ICU, surrounded by glass so they could see me at all times.

So, there I was: flat on my back, surrounded by surgeons and specialists. They hauled forty to fifty oxygen tanks into the room—apparently I'd broken the one vertebra that controlled my breathing. (I never had to use one of those tanks, and they billed my mom for every last one of them. She paid it, but she wasn't pleased about it.) My mom was a rock star that night, and many times afterwards. I truly didn't understand how seriously I was injured, and I found out later just how much she really knew about how close I had come to death or permanent paralysis. She was horrified that the ambulance personnel, the admitting nurses, the X-ray technician—all of them—had not recognized the severity of my accident and didn't immobilize me immediately. One small turn of my head could have paralyzed me from the neck down or killed me. She was justified in making sure the X-ray tech who took me to the testing area was immediately fired for having me walk at all.

The doctors informed us that the only thing they could do to immobilize and heal me was something they called the "tongs," explaining how they would drill a hole into both sides of my skull, screw in an attachment on each side, and then attach some weights and pulleys to them. Then they'd string me up to a steel rod attached to my bed until my vertebrae healed. Okay. No problem. But when they walked in with shears and a buzz cutter, and explained that my hair was coming off completely, I really freaked. My hair was a huge part of my identity.

Right about then, my dad rushed in, and I could see he was very anxious and worried. Mom must have tracked him down at one of his favorite bars, I thought.

"Are you doing okay, kiddo?" he asked.

"Yeah, Dad, but they're going to cut off my hair." Then I quickly tried a lame joke to ease his mind. "I know you've wanted me to get my hair cut, but this is a pretty radical way to do it."

He tried to chuckle, but it came out flat. I finally realized then, shit, this is really serious.

They cut off my hair, in huge chunks, as close to the skull as they could muster, and proceeded to shave my head. It was a real bitch to feel it all fall away, especially with an audience. I felt like crying. They applied a local sedative to my shaved skull in preparation for the tongs to be installed. I waited for the high-tech equipment to arrive. No. The doc walked back in with a hand drill. A fucking HAND drill.

He began the procedure on the right side. The hand drill squeaked at every turn into my skull. I thought, you'd think the hospital could afford to at least oil that baby once in a while. Every turn sounded like fingernails slowly screeching across a chalkboard, over and over. Squeak . . . squeak . . . squeak. I was waiting for the inevitable breakthrough that happens when someone's drilling through a piece of wood and the drill really whirrs and then pushes through to nothing but air. But that didn't happen. The doc stopped. I didn't die. Then the drilling of the hole on the other side began. Finally, success. The doctor and nurses strung me up, tight. Now the waiting would begin.

During my ICU stay, my sister came and ran away screaming the first time she saw me with a shaved head and with the tongs. She did come back, eventually. My dad came daily. Mom was always there for me, if not in the room, just outside in the ICU waiting area.

It was the day after Christmas when I first noticed the brown bag on the shelf; I wondered what was in it. Maybe it was a

Christmas gift that Mom brought along, probably from one of my friends who stashed it in a bag. They were that cheap. That thought came and went with all the coming and going from the medical personnel.

I was only in the ICU a few weeks, but it seemed an eternity. The doctors and nurses were checking on me every three or four minutes. I was awake twenty-four hours a day. I couldn't rest, ever. At first I was numbed up with the medication, but once I was trussed up, they quickly pulled back on that. So, in a few days, when the feeling slowly started to come back into my body, it came with extremely sharp stabs of pain and with waves of nausea. Very intense, yet very much welcomed. I thought, I could have been paralyzed, but I wasn't. I could have been dead, but I wasn't. But it sure wasn't pretty watching me as all the sensations returned. I wished they'd give me more drugs. But now I had to heal.

To prevent bedsores and circulation problems, the doctors and nurses had strapped me securely and settled me into a Stryker bed, which rotated upside down occasionally. A real trip, I thought, the first time they did it. When I was flipped upright, in my down time, ha ha—which was always—I passed it by counting the holes in the suspended ceiling. Last count was 2,860 holes. But when I was turned over, I got to check out the ICU floor for hours. Extremely clean, but not interesting in any way. God, why didn't they have some book or artwork or *something* they could put below me so I could at least pass the time intelligently? I thought. Eventually, I would get fancy thick Prism glasses to watch TV when I was upright, so I didn't have to move my head.

Luckily, tons of great friends and classmates visited me in ICU, and that took my mind off the pain. My best friend Brad even tried to sneak me out for New Year's Eve. He and I had been thick as thieves for the previous three years. Brad was my man soulmate, I think. He and I believed in expanding our horizons (interpret that however you'd like), independent movies, and very deep talks about life and existence. He was tall and thin and always wore a long peacoat. I was so excited when I found my dad's Navy peacoat, and together we'd walk around in Tucson's hot sun, wearing our woolen overcoats that hung down past our knees. His parents were super rich, but also separated like mine, so we understood our strange home life without a dad. His mom's favorite family member was not Brad, but her small white terrier dog, Wolfgang, on which she lavished all of her love. Brad hated that dog, and I don't really blame him. I saw how his mother treated him, and because of that, I hated that dog too. Unfortunately, Brad and I would get in trouble quite often, doing stupid things teenagers do, so his reputation preceded him. That evening, he'd brought in a bag of clothing so I could change, and when my mom asked him whom it was meant for, he quickly said, "It might rain tonight, Mrs. Gregory, so I brought along a change of clothes." My mom knew Brad, was not amused, and quickly put the kibosh on that by removing said bag of clothing.

But that night, my main ICU nurse sprang into action. Margie was the mother of one of my high school friends and she knew our scene. Once my mom finally left, instead of leaving us hanging, Margie arranged to let Brad stay with me to ring in the New Year. She knew he was breaking the visitors rule by staying past midnight, so she just kept us both quiet and we just hung out, like best friends do. Margie was the best.

The next day, after Brad had gone and Margie had left to do her other rounds with ICU patients, I again noticed that brown bag on the shelf across the room. It sat along with the few possessions I had on me when I'd had the accident. I was curious, but I couldn't figure out where it had come from. No one had brought it over to my bed to look at. After a while, with the flurry of medical personnel coming in, I forgot about it again.

I was getting better. Friends brought me my homework and books from school so I could stay on course for graduation in a couple of years. Couldn't let that good old brain of mine atrophy. Everyone already knew I was on course to get a scholarship to MIT or some such university, with my crazy math and science knowledge. I wasn't going to let them down. Besides, school seemed so damn easy.

More time passed. Some friends visited less. Some friends were steady, as they always had been and always will be. Finally, the day arrived. Margie came in and bustled about, as only nurses can do. She announced I was being moved out of ICU. Thank God, I thought. Maybe I can get some fucking sleep.

Soon some generic hospital attendant came along with the official hospital orders and a seriously happy look. "You're going into a regular room," he said enthusiastically. "Aren't you excited?" Yeah, right. I knew I had another six months of being strung up, stuck in and rotated on a bed, looking at a floor or a ceiling for hours, using a urinal and a bedpan. No, not so excited. The hospital was making room for the next severe case. My mom had replaced the clothing I'd originally worn into the hospital because it had been cut off when I came in—not that I could wear anything new yet—and their hospital gowns were so fashionable!

Margie and the attendant gathered up my things: notebooks, schoolbooks, and some other miscellaneous stuff. And the brown bag. Margie put my things together in a cart, threw away the older flowers, and then she picked up the brown bag and tossed it into the trash.

As the attendant began to roll my bed out of the door to my new home for six months, I finally asked, "Margie?"

"Yes, Kent?"

"What was in that brown bag? I noticed it sitting there the whole time."

She thought for just a second, and then replied, quite matter-of-factly, "Kent, that was your hair. We kept it so the funeral home could paste it back on your head when you died."

I was floored. It really had been that bad. I really had been that lucky. I really had been that close to dying . . .

With that announcement, I entered a period of my life that appreciated everything: scents, sounds, touches, friends, family.

My hair would grow back.

I would never be the same person.

And it was good.

# Green in My Face

## Oak Morse

There is a drought inside Mama's pocketbook
& all I know of a Valentine's Day party
in second grade is to bring cards.

I'd be a rainbow, grab my loose-leaf paper,
bold color markers, zig-zag scissors & create a card
as beautiful as a butterfly resting on a rose.

Cupid is going to be run straight into retirement
& my classmates will unfold a glory so luxurious
I'd be tethered in their everlasting memory.

Party day, I am an emerald balloon floating to Uranus.
My classmates are gathered with goodie bags & teddy bears,
while I am the only one with homemade hallmarks of love.

I was green & there was a lot of green in my face.
I pass out my cards like they are diamonds I'd spent all night
chiseling down to their shiniest version of perfection.

One by one classmates look at me like a bloody bouquet
of tulips. I drop out of a dream, fall into a swamp, watch
chuckles bubble from the basement of their bellies.

Left & right like confetti, remarks swarm over me. Bridgett:
What! Eww, you said you love me? I'm putting this in the trash!
Chris: What's wrong with you? I don't want this thing!

I was green & there was a lot of green in my face. Green monsters
with arrows erect from their seats, prowl around me like a hunt—
my essence is strangled with a thick ribbon.

My head tilts as my homestyle hearts are clawed into pieces—little doves
fluttering into the trash can. They clawed me down to a food stamp.
I count the centuries until dismissal & pray that on the dollar bill

George Washington's face would turn into an angel; then perhaps
money somehow would be free for people like me who are made of
pennies & prayers. I wonder if Mama would even care to know about this.

I was green & there was a lot of green in my face. Living in a garden
of weeds, those weeds poisoned my pink purity that I had
before I learned what money was & learned what rotten things come with it.

# The Glass Blower

## R.C. Goodwin

EVER SINCE MY FATHER DIED WHEN I WAS SEVEN, I'VE TENDED to seize upon surrogates. Some sufficed, to a point, while others fell far short. Among the better ones were uncles, two in Cleveland and one in Minneapolis. Distances posed problems, though. My mother and I lived in central Illinois. To see them in those pre-jet days of the 1950s took longer than it takes to fly to Europe now.

But they tried. Especially Uncle Marvin, my father's younger brother. Marvin taught high school art and coached baseball. Both his art and baseball expertise impressed me, but, fatherless and impressionable as I was, I might as easily have developed a passion for curling or playing the piccolo.

With Marvin's encouragement I became an art teacher myself, in a large suburban high school near Chicago. I began to go out with the school librarian, a slender dark-haired woman named Susan Josephson. We married the summer after my first year there.

We moved to an apartment near the school, a five-minute walk from Lake Michigan. Despite our modest salaries we lived comfortably. There was money enough for movies, inexpensive ethnic restaurants, and an occasional Cubs game. In the summer we swam in the lake, and in the winter we skated on the school's rink.

Two days before our third anniversary, Susan gave birth to our son. David Gordon Singer, a round-faced, placid little boy, had his mother's luxuriant dark hair and dark eyes. My hopes for him were very simple. I wanted him to be the happiest child who ever lived.

During my fifth year teaching, one of those life-changing events occurred—which, as often happens, seemed unremarkable at the time. While strolling between classes I noticed a posting on a bulletin board for an introductory summer course in glassblowing, sponsored by the Arts Department of one of Chicago's universities. I'd always wanted to take a course on glass, and I'd stumbled upon the perfect opportunity.

Before they let us near the furnaces we had three days packed with introductory lectures on the history of glass, on its physics and chemistry. On the infinite variety of colors and textures made by adding silver, gold, and scores of other minerals and metals. On the hardware used in this most technical of arts and crafts, and on the furnaces that heat to 2,000 degrees.

They showed us slides of glass in all its glory. Verzelini goblets and Birmingham decanters. Beakers from the Middle Ages and contemporary flasks and paperweights. Some pieces looked too intricate and dazzling to be made by the hand of man. They looked like relics left by superior beings from another planet.

On the fourth and fifth days we watched veteran glass blowers at work. It was broiling, a hot June day to begin with, and gas-fired furnaces brought the temperature to over a hundred. Fans as big as airplane propellers failed to cool us.

The glass blowers handled the molten globs of glass, called the gather, with nonchalance—blowing, bending, twisting, twirling, shaping. They lectured informally and answered questions while they worked, their hands in constant motion. I couldn't wait to try my hand at it.

The following Monday I sat in front of a furnace, the sweat pouring off me, as I turned my gather in the tongues of flame. We weren't making any particular objects. The purpose was to grow comfortable with the material and tools. As I worked, an instructor stood beside me. Absorbed in the task, I scarcely noticed him approaching.

"Not bad," he said. "You have nice touch. Important to rotate smoothly, with a steady hand." He had an accent, rather pleasant. You haff nice touch.

I glanced up, and through my safety glasses saw a stocky middle-aged man, his silver hair framing a ruddy oval face. No more than five foot ten, he had the massive chest and arms befitting someone six inches taller.

He shook his head. "Don't look up! You work with molten glass, you keep eye on it!"

His scrutiny continued as I brought the gather from the furnace and began to experiment with it. Stretching it, rolling it back on itself. Playing with it, testing its possibilities. From the corner of my eye, I saw the stocky man approaching me. "I will show you something, yes?"

"Please."

He sat down, reheated the gather in the furnace, and took it out again. His fingers, twice as thick as mine but fast as a pickpocket's, worked with strong, confident movements. Then, with a single turn of the glassworker's shaping jacks, he spun the glass around and drew out an end of it. A few more twists and the molten glass became a snail, its shell coiled on itself in a perfect spiral. He'd even put two tiny antennae on its head. The whole action took him four or five seconds.

I stared at the glass snail, not quite believing what I'd seen. "How long have you worked with glass?" I asked him.

"Thirty-five years, on and off. Would have been more, but I lose a lot of time because of goddamn World War II." He held out a massive hand to me. "My name is Jan Siroki."

"Glad to meet you. I'm Darryl Singer."

He started to move to another student who had trouble controlling her gather. "I will be back to see how you make out, but now I will go to others. Meanwhile you work on your own. You have nice touch."

WE TOOK A BREAK at ten thirty. Students and instructors crowded around the water coolers. I heard Jan's voice behind me. "Glassblowing makes you thirsty, yes?"

I turned around. "I've never been so thirsty in my life."

"In Sweden, two hundred years ago, glass blowers got free beer, four gallons a day. Most workers they treat like dogs back then, but glass blowers they treated different."

"Are you Swedish?"

"Czechoslovakian. I grow up in Brno, in Moravia. I live a while in Sweden, though, before the war. The Swedes have always had a way with glass. Perhaps you have heard of Orrefors and Boda."

We brought our paper cups of water to a less crowded part of the room, by a window. "Do you blow glass full-time?"

"Just about. I teach, and I have a studio at home. Sometimes museums hire me as consultant, and sometimes I give private lessons."

"How long have you been in the United States?"

He tossed the paper cup into a wastebasket. "I come to Chicago in 1949. Before that I spend three years in Nova Scotia. I liked it. I was young, no money, almost no English, and they were good to me there. My wife is Canadian."

We paused to glance out the window. Not much scenery, mainly an expressway and warehouses. I turned to him. "I'd love to see your own work."

He looked pleased. "It's mostly at home. Sometime you will visit and I will give you the tour. Maybe I get lucky, sell you something."

THREE DAYS LATER JAN stood by me as I put the finishing touches on my first significant effort, a goblet. I worked the base against my graphite paddle, trying to make it even. Goblet, a bit of an exaggeration. It was little more than a thick-stemmed glass. It earned what I came to know as Jan's standard compliment. Not bad.

"With next one you experiment a little," he went on. I show you about twisting stem if you want. How to make facets."

"I'd like that." I stopped to wipe sweat from my forehead and take a swig from the thermos by my side. My parched throat made it hard to speak.

"In time you get used to thirst. Maybe we go out later, have a beer." I nodded.

He picked up my goblet, turning it this way and that, inspecting it. "There is Czech beer house, a pivnic, not far away, serves Pilsner Urquell. Best beer in world."

The next break I called Susan, telling her I'd be late. Two hours later we sat in a booth at Vltava, a long narrow place with amber-tinted windows and dark wood panels. On its walls, a hodgepodge of plaques with heraldic crests, travel posters of Bohemia, and two deer heads.

Jan lit his pipe and spoke in Czech to a waiter. The language sounded soft and fluid, heavy on the D's and V's and Z's.

"Vltava is a river, winds through Prague," he told me. "Seven hills make ring around the city, same as Rome. Ever go to Czechoslovakia?"

"I haven't been to Europe."

He tssked. "Anyone interested in art must go. Prague itself is work of art. Sometimes, the way light reflects off hills, Prague looks as beautiful as Paris. If Rembrandt had been Czech instead of Dutch, he would have done more landscapes."

"You must miss it."

He shook his head. "Prague is in the past. I prefer to leave the past behind me. I came to North America and did not look back. Too many wars, too heavy is burden of history . . ." His voice trailed off as the waiter brought us steins of Pilsner Urquell.

He threw down half the stein. "I talk too much, like always. Tell me more about yourself."

I fired off the standard facts. Where I came from, where I worked, where I'd gone to school. I told him about Susan and David.

"I have son and daughter. Both married, one in Oregon and one in Georgia." He finished off the stein and signaled for two more. "Your parents are alive?"

"My mother. My father died of kidney failure when I was young. No dialysis back then."

"Hard to lose parents young. I was older, about your age."

We switched to less somber topics: art, the weather, the Chicago Blackhawks (he followed hockey passionately). The waiter brought our second round. I wasn't drunk but I was drinking on an empty stomach, and the smoky-sweet Pilsner Urquell had cloaked the world in a pleasant haze. I enjoyed my new companion immensely. He showed promise of becoming the best surrogate of all of them.

Just before we left I asked, "How did you survive the war years?" I don't usually ask such personal questions shortly after meeting someone, but Jan's manner—his warmth, and the easy flow of his own inquiries—prompted openness.

He tapped his pipe against the ashtray and looked up at me with solemn eyes. "Forgive me, Darryl, but I prefer not to talk about the war. After all this time is still hard."

NO SUMMER OF MY life went by faster. Each weekday morning, I arrived at the school at nine, often staying until six or seven. In the evenings I read about glass. The weekends we spent mostly at the beach, but even then I took along my glass books.

I saw Jan every day at school. He seemed to take particular interest in me, perhaps because I was so obviously smitten with the subject. Often he stood quietly behind me while I worked, offering the occasional comment or piece of advice. At times he'd demonstrate a point. "I show you something, yes?" It was both inspiring and disheartening to watch him do in minutes what might take me an hour.

Most days we had lunch together on a patio outside the furnaces. Once or twice a week he took me to Vltava after classes. As we washed down pickled herring and hardboiled eggs with Pilsner Urquell he told stories of his summer apprenticeship in Sweden. Stories of life in Brno between the wars.

Despite his talent as a raconteur, he divulged rather little of himself. Halfway through the summer it dawned on me that he hadn't mentioned his parents, apart from telling me that they were dead. I didn't know if he had siblings. Only in passing did he speak of his wife and children. If he had grandchildren, he never talked about them. And discussion of the war remained off limits.

We agreed that he'd give me private lessons when the course was over.

One evening in Vltava, around mid-August, we chatted about the coming Labor Day weekend. He asked if I had any plans.

"Yes. My cousin's son is having a bar mitzvah in Minnesota."

He looked surprised. "You are Jewish?"

I nodded. The subject of religion, his or mine, had never surfaced.

He scrutinized me. "I don't think I have seen a Jew who looks like you. Red hair, blue eyes."

"My mother's people are from Romania. The red hair and blue eyes come from there, most likely the result of a Cossack rape occurring four or five hundred years ago." I shrugged. "Quite a few of us look more Irish than Jewish."

"Darryl Singer. It is not a Jewish name." He seemed to have trouble letting go of this.

"They named me Darryl after a family friend who died early in the war. Singer . . . it's common for Jews and non-Jews alike."

We moved on to something else. At the time I gave the conversation little thought.

A MONTH LATER, ON a Sunday afternoon, Susan and I stood at the door of Jan and Margot Siroki. It would be a day of firsts. I'd meet Jan's wife and he'd meet mine. Our first invitation to their house.

Jan let us in, shook my hand, and greeted Susan with a bow. Margot waited behind him in the foyer, a friendly woman in her fifties, her hair gathered up in a blonde-gray bun. "So happy to meet you. We don't have many visitors out here." The Canadian pronunciation, aowt.

They ushered us into the living room. We sat in overstuffed chairs with antimacassars at their backs, their wooden legs bent like a fat man's knees.

Chairs and couch and even the TV with family photos on top of it were rendered incidental by a display case filled with glass pieces. The case ran along an entire wall. Afternoon sunlight reached it through a picture window with dazzling effect, like sunlight coming through the stained-glass windows of a cathedral.

Susan and I walked to the case. Before us were more than a hundred objects in every style and hue. Vases, bowls, pitchers, goblets, decanters, paperweights, statuettes of birds and animals. Some of the statuettes weighed only ounces, and some of the bowls were more than a foot in diameter. A collection of inestimable value, perhaps the high six figures; a collection that would have the pride of most museums.

"They're stunning," Susan said. "I've never seen anything like them. She pointed to one. "May I touch it?"

"Of course. Glass is made to be touched."

The object was a pinkish-orange vase, four inches high, the rim not much thicker than an eggshell. A pattern of oval lozenges formed the surface. Susan picked it up and held it as though it were a month-old kitten.

Jan moved beside her. "Ah. You have good taste, is one of my favorites. The French call it verre de soie. Silk glass."

She ran a fingertip across it. "The way the design puffs out, like little pillows—how do they get it to do that?"

"Is made with two different layers. Between them we trap pockets of air."

She held the piece up to the sunlight. "And the color?"

"The pinkish-orange comes from manganese salts. The inner surface is white. For that we use oxide of tin."

She put the piece back in the display case. "So, it comes from France?"

He shook his head. "It comes from here. A few years ago I become interested in verre de soie style. I read about it, I teach myself. That one I make in my garage."

"You made that?"

"Except for maybe fifteen pieces I make all of these."

I rested a hand on Susan's shoulder. "I told you he was amazing."

We ambled back and forth in front of the display case, looking here and there, when Jan came between us, putting an arm around us both. "You will have plenty of time to see what I have done, I promise. But now we will have something to eat and drink."

He guided us back to the chairs while Margot headed for the kitchen. She emerged a few minutes later with a tray of scones. "The tea's steeping, it'll be ready in no time."

"Unless you prefer slivovice," Jan interrupted.

"What's that?" asked Susan.

"A kind of plum brandy. Is favorite Czech drink, except for beer."

"Thanks, but I'll have tea."

"You, Darryl?"

"Slivovice, please." I'd tried it a few times at Vltava.

The next two hours passed quickly as we chatted, ate Margot's homemade scones, and drank tea and brandy. The conversation skipped from glass to books to the virtues of Czech food and drink to current politics (of little interest to Jan, notwithstanding daily headlines about the lingering war in Vietnam, Watergate, and Nixon's possible impeachment). Despite Jan's slew of anecdotes, his gift as a raconteur, he let Margot do the talking about the family. She spoke of their children and their four grandchildren. From time to time Susan and I got up, wandered over to the display case, admired a particular piece and took it out.

Just before we left Susan picked up the pinkish-orange verre de soie vase again, turning it in her hands, caressing it. She glanced at Jan. "I suppose you wouldn't consider selling that to me?"

"No, is not for sale. But since you like it so much, perhaps I give to you."

She was stunned. "Oh, Jan, it's only right that you let me pay for it."

He shook his head. "You take it, please, and we will talk no more of this."

She held the vase in one hand, put the other around him, and kissed his cheek. "I don't know how to thank you. It's something I'll cherish for the rest of my life."

I MADE USE OF my school's blowpipe, working whenever I could find the time. I came to school early, stayed late, skipped lunches. And every Wednesday afternoon, when my last class ended, I drove to Jan's for lessons. I stayed all evening. Sometimes we kept at it until midnight.

Jan had me try all kinds of projects, but gradually I developed my own interests, even the rudiments of my own style. My favorite pieces were Millefiore paperweights, in which tiny lengths of colored rods, called canes, were embedded in the gather. At their best the finished pieces looked like miniature gardens trapped in glass, with geometric swirls of flowers curving outward. "You do well," said Jan. "What is English word, prodigy? I have never had a student who learns so fast."

Every month or two we'd do something as a foursome. Jan and Margot would invite us over for dinner, or we'd invite them, or we'd go to a restaurant or a Blackhawks game. I knew little about hockey, had never paid much attention to it, but Jan's enthusiasm became contagious. They warmed to David right away, and he to them. David saw his grandparents infrequently, and Jan and Margot did much to fill the breach.

Susan liked them, Margot in particular. She liked her easy hospitality, her willingness to listen without passing judgment, her placidity. Susan had a prickly relationship with her own mother. Mildred Josephson, a nervous dumpling of a woman, expressed love by fretting and giving unsolicited advice and homilies.

Her attitude to Jan was less straightforward. One night, after a hockey game, I felt her toss and turn as we lay in bed. Usually she fell asleep in seconds.

"What's the matter?"

"I don't know. Maybe I drank too much coffee."

"Are you sure it's nothing else?"

She shifted in the bed and rested her head in the crook of my arm. "There's something . . . I warn you, Darryl, this is going to sound stupid, but there's something about Jan that bothers me. I've tried to figure out what, but I can't put my finger on it. Do you ever feel that way?"

"Never."

"Maybe it's his eyes," she went on. "The way I'll catch him looking at me."

"It could be that he finds you attractive."

In the darkness I felt her shake her head. "It's not that." She picked the words carefully. "It's as though he looks at me but doesn't see me, sees through me. Past me. It's as though he's in a walled-off place where no one can reach him."

"Come now, aren't you being a trifle melodramatic?"

"I don't know, am I?"

We fell silent. I listened to the wind whip in from Lake Michigan, watched the numbers change on our digital bedside clock.

"Does he ever mention the war to you?" she asked a few minutes later. "Where he was, what he did?"

"He's made it clear he doesn't want to talk about it."

"Well, don't you wonder about those things?" She took a deep breath. "I mean, for all we know . . ." Susan, unfailingly well-spoken, was slightly tongue-tied. "For all we know, he could have been one of them."

I jerked up in the bed. "What a thing to say! He probably doesn't talk about the war because of what the Nazis did to his country and his family. It's not as if Jews were the only ones they killed!" I wasn't yelling, but I was speaking distinctly louder and faster than usual. "Besides, if he were, why the hell would he cultivate a friendship with a young Jewish couple of all people? Invite them to his home and come to theirs? Play with their son on his hands and knees?"

"So, because he plays with our son it means he doesn't have a past? Maybe I'm melodramatic, and maybe you're naïve!" She cut herself off and touched my hand. "I suppose you're right. I hope you are. I'm sorry, Darryl. I don't know, I think that book is getting to me, it's making me a little crazy. I'm preoccupied with Nazis." *Sophie's Choice* had just been published, and Susan bought it the first day it came out. Sometimes she read until two in the morning.

"It's okay. How about we try to get some sleep?"

But it wasn't okay. I slid back under the covers although I was the one who tossed and turned now. Because she'd hit a nerve, of course. Never, in my worst flight of imagination, did I think he was one of them. Even so, I'd have liked to know just what he had done in the war.

TWO YEARS LATER SUSAN became pregnant again. With David everything went without a hitch. This pregnancy was the opposite. She had intractable morning sickness and could barely keep down saltines and herbal tea. She had headaches, backaches, and a bladder infection. One day, halfway through the second trimester, she began to hemorrhage. At the hospital they couldn't stop the hemorrhaging, and she miscarried. It would have been a baby girl.

In the afternoon they brought her down from the recovery room. I stayed with her until ten that night, holding her hand as she glided in and out of sleep. At times, delirious, she asked to hold the baby.

Walking through the hospital lobby, en route to the canteen, I saw a pay phone. On an impulse I called Jan and Margot and told them what had happened. "Come over," Jan commanded.

"It's too late. Besides, I have to go home to David." But my voice lacked true resolve; I had no wish to be alone.

"Where is David now?"

"We left him with neighbors."

"Ask them to let him stay the night and come over. By now they have put him to bed anyway, yes?"

It was almost eleven when they greeted me at the door in bathrobes. Jan brought me a glass of slivovice, and Margot made me a sandwich, the first thing I'd eaten since lunch. I talked, I mainly rambled, and at times I cried. Finally, just before I fell asleep on the couch, Margot brought a blanket and laid it over me. I remember thinking, just before I fell asleep, that I couldn't have felt closer to them if they'd been my actual parents.

THE SUMMER OF DAVID'S sixth birthday we bought our first home, a raised ranch in one of Chicago's northern suburbs. With Jan's help I turned part of our basement into a glass studio. By now I worked with glass at least ten hours a week, some weeks closer to twenty. My pieces were starting to sell, most for several hundred dollars, the best ones for four figures. Some years I made more from glass than teaching, but I lacked the confidence to quit my job and devote myself to glass full-time. Besides, I liked my students and colleagues; I would have missed them.

The summer of our tenth anniversary Susan and I sent David off to camp and went to Europe. Making full use of our Eurail Passes, we crisscrossed the continent from Spain to Sweden. We stopped as we chose, in smaller towns like Segovia and Carcassonne as well as Madrid and Paris. We swam in Lake Lugano, hiked in the Pyrenees. Avoiding pricey hotels and restaurants, we stayed in pensions and bed-and-breakfast places, ate in cafes and tascas. Between Susan's fluent French and my limited German, we usually managed to communicate.

In Sweden I wanted to pay respects to Orrefors and Boda, but Susan vetoed it. "Darryl, it's our first time here, and I want to see as much as possible. You can come back on your own and do the glass."

One excursion wasn't covered by Eurail Pass. From Zurich we flew to Warsaw, and from there we went to Auschwitz. Since reading *Sophie's Choice* Susan had been obsessed with it. This was before Gorbachev, before the Berlin Wall came down, before the Warsaw Pact collapsed. Travel to Eastern Europe was still a tricky undertaking, rife with bureaucratic hurdles. We had to fight our way through a thicket of red tape just to get visas.

Nothing prepared us for Auschwitz, a place for which we had no frame of reference. Once inside, past the double rows of electrified barbed wire, we saw the main gate, and there it was: the sign. *Arbeit macht frei.* A disconcerting quietude hung in the air. The season and weather contributed to a jarring tranquility. It was warm but not hot, and birds sang, and summer light suffused the well-trimmed paths. The ambience, more benign than appropriate.

Images, impressions—photos of children with haunted eyes, a pile of eyeglasses eight feet high, a mountain of empty canisters of Zyklon-B. A bin of hair as long as a bowling alley, three times as wide. The gas chambers, plain and squat. Right next to them, the crematoria, now bedecked with sprays of flowers and rows of burning candles.

The image that summed it up best to us was a simple one, a broken doll, with a leg missing and a torn dress. We wondered about the owner. Who was she? What had she been like? Where did she come from? What did she look like? How had she done in school, or had she been too young to go? What was her family like? Was the rest of her family here with her, or had some of them escaped? Once she arrived at Auschwitz, had she managed to survive? If not, how long had she lasted? Perhaps at least she'd died quickly.

At one point, as we walked along the peaceful paths, I thought of Jan. Except for Austria, Czechoslovakia had been the first place occupied by the Nazis, and they'd stayed until the week of the surrender. Hundreds of thousands of Czechs had been arrested and deported. I wondered if Jan's friends and relatives had been among them.

ON A WINTER DAY, eighteen months after our trip to Europe, Margot had a grand mal seizure driving home from the supermarket. She careened across a yard and into a tree. The heavy snow served as a brake, but she still broke a wrist and dislocated a shoulder. Worse news came when they found what caused the seizure: a highly malignant, inoperable brain tumor. Within a few months she died, just after her sixty-fifth birthday.

Jan reacted to her death with disbelief and thundering indignation. "How could this be, how could this be?" he raged, again and again. We brought him food, sat with him, drank tea and slivovice with him. He rarely expressed gratitude directly, but clearly these gestures mattered to him. One evening he took both our hands as we said goodbye at his front door. "You have been good friends," he said, a barely perceptible quiver in his voice.

I THOUGHT HER DEATH might open him up a bit. Might prompt him to talk more of their early days together, or of their family life, or even of the wartime years. It didn't. The only thing he said was this: "Darryl, I have seen too much of death." But from there he went no further.

For the first time he began to look his age, seventy-four. Always ruddy, his complexion gave way to pallor. His excellent posture gave way to a bent back and slumping shoulders. He lost weight, and his face became drawn and angular.

He showed scant interest in glass or anything else. For the most part he stayed home and parked himself in front of the TV. I called him one afternoon, heard the TV blaring, and asked what he was watching. "I have no idea," he answered. We wondered how long he'd last without her.

But he fooled us. By the second anniversary of Margot's death, he'd become something like his former self again. He did a little glassblowing and teaching. He frequented Vltava, and he followed the Blackhawks with his former interest. And he started to go out with women, mainly widows a few years younger than him. It pleased me to see him emerging from his shell, but Susan had mixed feelings about his new companions. She'd grown to love Margot dearly, had taken her death harder than the miscarriage.

ONE SUNDAY MORNING SUSAN and I lingered over a second cup of coffee, reading the paper while David occupied himself outside. It was a sunny spring day with a light breeze and temperature in the sixties. The sky was clear except for jet trails leading to and from O'Hare. The shattering of Susan's coffee cup broke the silence.

When I looked at her, I saw a stranger, her eyes wide with horror, her face as pale as milk glass. Usually the picture of serenity, she seemed about to scream.

"Susan! What's the matter?"

Her hand shaking, she gave me her part of the paper. Then she bolted from the table. "Have to throw up—"

I skimmed the section. ALDERMEN FEUD OVER BUDGET . . . GOVERNOR APPOINTS CHICAGO WOMAN TO CIVIL RIGHTS PANEL . . . What the hell had set her off like that? Then I saw it, the words hitting me like a blow to the gut. LOCAL MAN ACCUSED OF WAR CRIMES, FACES DEATH PENALTY IF DEPORTED

> MAY 2, CHICAGO. Federal officials served deportation papers yesterday to Jan Tomas Siroki, of 24 Grainger Street in suburban Oakton. Siroki, a 76-year-old widower and local glass expert, is accused of crimes against humanity during the Nazi occupation of Czechoslovakia from 1939 through 1945. These allegedly occurred in his native city Brno and at a Czech concentration camp, Theriesenstadt . . .
>
> According to Immigration and Naturalization Service spokesman Stewart Brannigan, Siroki assumed the name of one of his victims and fled when German defeat appeared imminent. After spending two years in refugee camps he made his way to Canada, living in Nova Scotia before coming to Chicago. His true identity, states Brannigan, is Vaclav Raymanova, the target of a worldwide manhunt since the end of World War II. He stands accused of murder, torture and reprisals against civilian populations. During the Czech occupation he became known as "the Jackal of Theriesenstadt" . . .
>
> Israeli authorities involved in the investigation announced they would seek the death penalty. Israel prohibits capital punishment except for genocide and crimes against humanity . . .
>
> Siroki made no comment on the charges, but his attorney Paul Riegrovy dismissed them as "resulting from a tragic case of mistaken identity, in which an innocent man has

> become the victim of a witch hunt." He plans to appeal, expressing confidence that the facts will vindicate his client.

I couldn't go on reading. I could make no sense of it, no sense at all. Jan Siroki, my friend and mentor, by far the best of the surrogates—Jan Siroki, or was it Vaclav Raymanova? The Jackal of Theriesenstadt?

My mind drifted, and Jan appeared in a dreamy collage. Sitting at our dinner table, working at the furnace, cheering wildly at Blackhawks games, holding court at Vltava. Thinking of him at Vltava made me remember the conversation we'd had there, the summer we met, when I told him I was Jewish. I played the clip again and again, trying to read his eyes for guilt or shame or hate, or even garden-variety prejudice. None showed, no matter how often I played it, and the eyes registered nothing more than surprise. Nor did the conversation mark a change in our burgeoning friendship, a pulling back or awkwardness on his part. We went on precisely as before. Working together, chatting, having lunch and drinking beer together. Relishing each other's company, or so it seemed.

I wondered, did he think twice about that conversation? Does he remember it at all? And (I'd have given anything to know this) what had he been thinking at the time?

Susan came back to the kitchen, poured herself a glass of water. "You know the worst of it? The worst of it is, I'm not surprised."

"You sure gave a good imitation of it." Why was I lashing out at her, of all people?

"Tell me, Darryl, what is an appropriate reaction?"

"I don't know." Words failed me, and speech suddenly became an effort. We glanced outside, watching David kick around a soccer ball on a beautiful spring morning.

"I want to see him," I said finally.

"Oh, that's just dandy! On your way home, maybe you can catch a neo-Nazi rally!"

"Susan, have you considered, even for a second, the possibility that he didn't do it? People are still innocent till proven guilty here.

There've been cases of mistaken identity, especially when crimes took place a generation ago." Hearing myself, I knew I sounded flat and stilted, utterly unconvincing.

She took a final swig of water and set the glass down. "A joint investigation by Americans and Israelis, target of a worldwide manhunt since the war ended? Yessir, sounds like a frame-up to me, all right. Well, I guess anything's possible. But I don't think I'd bet the ranch on it."

IT TOOK SIX TRIES to reach him. The first five times his line was busy, and I wondered if he'd taken the phone off the hook. But no, the sixth time he picked up.

"Hello?" His voice was tired, wary.

"Jan. It's Darryl."

"Darryl! I hoped you'd call. I get so many calls today. Hateful calls, threats. You have seen the morning paper?"

"Yes."

"Darryl, you must not believe these things." He had no idea how badly I didn't want to.

"Can we meet?"

"I would like that. But is bad idea for you to come to house. People march outside with pickets; police are here too. We go someplace quieter, yes?"

"How about Vltava?"

"They prefer I take my business elsewhere." He sounded aggrieved. "Let me think. Someplace outside would be better. Downtown, near Buckingham Fountain?"

"I'll meet you in forty-five minutes. Lakefront side."

"I will be there."

HE SIGNALED ME AS I started to walk past him. A pair of mirrored sunglasses made him hard to recognize. He glanced around in all directions while I approached, scanning the crowd as if expecting a new set of picketers, or worse.

"Hello, Jan." Neither one of us extended a hand. It occurred to me that I had no clear notion of what to say to him.

"We take a walk, yes?"

"Okay."

We spoke no more until we were a good two hundred feet from the fountain, when he broke the leaden silence. "It must be hard to you to read these things about me."

"It must be harder for you to read them about yourself."

"You believe them?"

"I don't know what to believe, but I'd like to hear your version."

He sighed. "So long ago, nearly half a century, so hard to remember now. I think I have put the war behind me, made new life. Trouble with new life, you never get away from old one. Well, Darryl, I will tell you everything. When Occupation started, I was working for civil police in Brno. We deal with routine crime, the job police do everywhere. SS, Gestapo, they leave us pretty much alone at first. They are aware how much we hate them, and they only trust their own.

"You see," he went on, "I knew a lot about police work. My grandfather, father, older brother were all policemen, all honorable men. They always wanted me to join them, to forget this foolishness with glass. So, when the Nazis come, I see police work as something better than joining army or helping them round up Jews."

He paused, and we scanned Lake Michigan. Hundreds of boats passed before us while sunlight sparkled on the dark green water. Hard to imagine a more glorious spring day. I wanted to be at home, in my yard, kicking a soccer ball around with David. I wanted to be anywhere but here, doing anything but having this conversation with this man.

"But then the war turns bad for Germans," Jan resumed. "They cannot beat England the way they beat France; they begin to lose in North Africa. Millions are trapped inside Russia, millions more are tied up in Western Europe preparing for invasion. For them, there is great shortage of manpower. They have to use the locals. So, one day I receive orders to go to Theriesenstadt. They give me a simple choice. I can go as guard or I can go as prisoner. I decide to go as guard. Perhaps I make the coward's choice. Who can say what he would do in my shoes?"

He took his pipe from his pocket, started to light it, but gave up. Instead he chewed distractedly on the stem.

"What was it like at Theriesenstadt?"

"Impossible to describe. Whole families, whole communities herded together and shipped to Auschwitz or Dachau. Oh, once in while they try to make it look better, when the Red Cross comes. They try to make it, how do you say, a showcase? But in reality it was hell on earth. Death was everywhere, every hour of every day. All the time I feel I am trapped in a nightmare. Even now, sometimes, I have bad dreams about it. I tried to do what I could to ease suffering, to bring in food for some of the children, to bring in aspirin. Not much, but they would have killed me on the spot if they caught me."

"Who was Vaclav Raymanova?"

He shuddered. "A man who breaks children's bones in front of parents, one at a time, to make parents talk. They said he couldn't sleep at night unless he tortured someone. I only see him two or three times. We try to stay away from him as much as possible. Everyone fears him, not just Jews. He is Czech, but even some Germans fear him."

"Is Jan Siroki your real name?"

"No. After war I want to make a clean break with past. Anyone who works in place like Theriesenstadt must be guilty, so they think. Siroki is my mother's family name, and I decide to use it. Now, years later, is easy to say I made mistake. They assume I took new name to hide behind it."

All in all, we talked for nearly two hours. More correctly, I asked questions and he answered them. He remained the essence of plausibility. Never did he contradict himself, or evade awkward questions, or lack conviction. If, in fact, he was guilty of the accusations made against him, he bestowed on me the performance of a lifetime.

* * *

STEWART BRANNIGAN HAD NO wish to meet with me. He agreed to do so only after I'd badgered his secretary with repeated phone calls. The meeting, when he finally acquiesced to it, was to last no longer than ten minutes.

Glaring at me over his bifocals, his face knotted in annoyance, he tapped his fingers against the desk as we sat opposite each other. We met in his cubicle in the Federal Building, the Thursday after the story first appeared.

"So, Mr. Singer" (not one, he, to waste time on pleasantries), "I understand you want to talk about the Raymanova case."

"I do. You see . . . well, my wife and I have known Jan Siroki for almost twenty years, and I believe there's been a terrible mistake."

"Uh hum. And what do you base this on?"

Well prepared, I launched into my discourse. "First, in all that time I've never known him to be other than an utterly decent man, a dedicated artist and teacher, a warm and loyal friend. Second, it strikes me as unlikely that a former Nazi would go out of his way to befriend a Jewish couple. You'd think he'd do anything to avoid people like us. Third, this Sunday he gave me a full account of his activities during the Occupation, including an acknowledgment of the name change and his reasons for it."

"All right, let's hear his story."

I paused to collect my thoughts, in order to pass on Jan's story as concisely and effectively as possible. When I did, Brannigan's face remained the same stolid portrait of annoyance. Although he said nothing, his opinion came through plainly: you're the biggest dupe who ever lived.

I glanced at my watch when I finished. He'd let me go on for twenty minutes, twice the time allotted. Did it mean I told him things he hadn't heard before?

When he spoke his voice was milder than before, and he even sounded slightly sympathetic. He pointed to a large bookcase to his left. "Take a look, Mr. Singer. The top shelf is full of files connected with the Raymanova case. Briefs, affidavits, correspondence, reports of investigators in six countries. We know more about

Vaclav Raymanova than he knows about himself, from his secret SS file to his dental records. At last count we have more than thirty witnesses who corroborate identification."

He folded his hands almost prayerfully. "This has been a no-holds-barred investigation. You see, we're not dealing with a petty functionary who got drunk one night and slapped a few Jews around. He's more along the lines of Dr. Mengele or Klaus Barbie. He personally picked out prisoners for transports to Auschwitz and the other camps, most of them children and old people. He personally supervised much of the torture, devised some new techniques. I won't go into details; you wouldn't eat for days. He personally beat twenty-two prisoners to death. Those are just the ones we know about."

"But couldn't this be mistaken identification, especially after forty years? Isn't eyewitness identification the least reliable kind?"

"Let me show you something." Standing, he walked to the bookcase and searched for a particular folder. He took an eight-by-ten photo from it and handed it to me.

I saw a man in his late twenties, in a uniform with shiny buttons, each stamped with a swastika. He had the dark eyes and oval face that had grown so familiar to me over two decades. The eyes, lively but distancing. What Susan termed his walled-off look. The same look he'd had while selecting prisoners for Auschwitz? The same look he'd had while breaking children's bones, one at a time, in front of their parents?

It was young Jan Siroki, incontestably.

Brannigan said nothing while I stared at the photo. "If it's any consolation to you, Mr. Singer, he took in a lot of others, and that includes a lot of Jews. Artists, professors, museum personnel, all as incredulous as you are."

"But how—"

"How does he live with what he did? How did he carry off a completely different life for all those years? How did he charm so many people? I don't know. They're questions for the shrinks, I guess. But he had another interest you may not know about. He was quite the talented actor. Before the war he thought seriously about acting school." Brannigan rose to show me out. "Acting, glassblowing . . . he even wrote some poetry from time to time. It's pretty good, I'm told. Yeah, he's a talented guy, all right. Brilliant, even. Too bad he happens to be a monster."

I ONLY SAW HIM once more, ten days after meeting Brannigan. Ten days in which I polished off a liter and a half of gin, considerably more than my yearly quota. Ten days in which I slept no more than five hours a night, in which I taught my classes in a sullen fugue and didn't speak to anyone I didn't have to, including my wife and son.

I called first, to make sure he was home. When I arrived the scene was quieter than I expected. There were only a dozen picketers, just one cop and no TV cameras. TV coverage had been nonstop the first three days or so, but even news like this grows old fast.

Parking a block away, I circled around to the back door. He smiled and let me in. "Ah, Darryl, I'm glad you come. Times like this, a person finds out who real friends are. Slivovice?" I shook my head no.

We stood by the kitchen table. "I bring you up to date a little, yes? My lawyer is optimistic. A good man, Riegrovy, a Czech. I have known him thirty years."

"I know everything, Jan."

"I beg your pardon?"

Unable to look at him directly, I glanced out the kitchen window. A nice enough day but overcast, hinting of a shower. "I know everything. I went downtown to INS and met with Brannigan. It was hard to wangle an appointment, but I insisted. I wanted to tell him the things you told me that Sunday, by the fountain. To plead your case. Then he showed me the documentation, about two shelves' worth. He also showed me a photograph of Vaclav Raymanova taken in 1942. It was you."

I turned to him. He drew himself up and assumed his military bearing, chest high, shoulders back. When he spoke, there was a steely edge in his voice, an edge I'd never heard before. "Why did you come here, Darryl?"

Perhaps he thought I came to kill him. It would have been easy. I could have brought a knife or gun along. No one had seen me, much less frisked me, when I'd entered. Or, perhaps he thought of killing me. It would have been equally easy. He could have snatched a weapon from a drawer, dispatched me in an instant. One last Jew for old time's sake, one for the road.

"Why did you come?" he asked again.

"I came to tell you, face to face, that I knew about you." I talked slowly and a bit robotically. "I came to look upon evil. It's an opportunity I never had before, to look at it from such close range. And I suppose I came to say goodbye."

He stood as still as anyone can stand, without a twitch or flicker, without the blinking of an eye, breathing in breaths so shallow they could barely be discerned. It seemed an eternity before he spoke. "Well, Darryl," he said finally, "I am afraid we have nothing more to say to each other." Then he stood in silence, shoulders back and arms akimbo, neither bidding me to stay nor asking me to leave. He scrutinized me, looking at me from a dark continent I'd never set foot on. He stood in silence, the silence of the Nuremberg defendants in their boxes, the silence of Iago, the silence of a guilt too broad and deep for words.

BY THE AUTUMN THINGS had pretty much returned to normal. I drank no more than my usual beer or two a week. Susan and I chatted with our customary ease. We worked, ran errands, paid bills, kept up the house, took turns driving David home from soccer practice. Sometimes, when not with his classmates, he'd join us for a pizza or a movie. We made the rounds of favored ethnic restaurants with our friends. Life proceeded in a calm and ordered fashion, and in the balance it was more than satisfactory.

After taking the summer off I started to blow glass again, at Susan's urging. "Don't give him that much power, Darryl, to make you stop doing something you love."

One night, while we watched TV, an announcer broke in. "We interrupt this program to bring you a special bulletin. Alleged Nazi war criminal Vaclav Raymanova, also known as Jan Siroki, died tonight, apparently a suicide. Raymanova faced deportation to Israel, to stand trial for crimes against humanity, and his last appeal was just denied."

The late news gave more details. He'd slit his wrists in the bathtub, leaving no note. His attorney, Paul Riegrovy, expressed sadness at the loss of a friend of many years, still claiming that this had been a tragic case of mistaken identity.

WE LAY IN BED on our backs, barely touching. "How do you feel?" asked Susan.

"Not much of anything. As far as I'm concerned, he died long ago. The day I went to INS, to be exact." I shifted my weight between the sheets, tried unsuccessfully to get more comfortable. "How do you feel?"

"Angry! It's so unfair. He killed so many people, caused so much suffering, and his own death sounds practically idyllic! He falls asleep in his bathtub, probably drunk on that awful plum brandy. He didn't deserve a death like that!"

I twisted in the sheets, saying nothing.

"Do you think he was ever remorseful?" she asked me, calmer.

"I doubt it, especially after seeing him that last time. Who knows, maybe he was, to a point. I remember something he said when Margot died, that he had seen too much of death. That might have been as close to remorse as he could come."

"You know what bothers me the most? I kissed him. Every time we met I kissed him on the cheek, and he kissed me. When I think of that, I want to wash my face for hours, the way Lady Macbeth washed her hands."

"What bothers me most is how hard I tried to believe him. Hell, I did believe him. Until that meeting I had with Brannigan, I really thought it was all a big mistake." I sat up in the bed. "Well, at least we weren't alone. Brannigan said he took in a lot of others."

"Somehow that doesn't make me feel much better."

* * *

THE YEARS FLEW BY in a dizzying blur. Susan and I passed our twentieth anniversary, and our thirtieth. I retired from teaching, devoting myself full-time to glassblowing. Susan retired too, but she kept busy doing volunteer work with literacy projects. We live unassumingly in the first and only home we've owned. Our main luxury has been travel, and we've been lucky enough to do a fair bit of it. Alaska and Hawaii, Australia and New Zealand, Israel and Egypt. David graduated from Vanderbilt, majoring in economics, returning to Chicago for a master's in healthcare management. Married now, with twin daughters, he works in Indianapolis as a hospital administrator.

Susan and I no longer talk about Jan Siroki or Vaclav Raymanova or whoever he was, but random thoughts of him still ambush me. When they do, I try to banish them, with varying degrees of success.

One Sunday afternoon last April, Susan and I were dividing up the spring cleaning. I worked in the kitchen doing windows while she busied herself in the dining room. One of her projects was to take out the contents of our breakfront, to rearrange and dust and polish them. We had the CD player on, but it didn't drown out her crying, a strange kind of crying, somewhere between a moan and a wail. I've never heard anyone keening, but I think that must be what it's like.

I ran into the dining room. She sat at the table, holding the pinkish-orange verre de soie vase that Jan gave her the day they met.

I sat next to her, tried to comfort her and wipe away her tears with the edge of my sweatshirt. It was three or four minutes before she stopped.

She put the vase down. "It's so beautiful. Perfect. How could he make a thing like this and do those other things? How?"

The same question, tantalizing and unanswerable, that I'd put to Stewart Brannigan at the conclusion of our meeting. I looked at the vase, its rim no thicker than an eggshell, the pillows of air trapped between its layers, as frail as decency itself, and lay a hand on Susan's shoulder.

# Required Debauchery

## Thomas Darlington

MY UNCLE GENE WAS VERY GOOD AT SELLING INSURANCE, GOOD enough that he became a millionaire and retired before he turned fifty. He lived in a huge apartment building near Cheesman Park. We both lived in Denver, and I took special pleasure in riding the elevator to the thirteenth floor to visit him. Later, he bought a cozy A-frame up in the mountains near Denver. He spent most weekends there, and when he retired, he gave up the apartment and moved to the mountains full-time.

I visited him at his mountain retreat four or five times a year. I'd drive up from Denver, and we'd have wonderful, marathon conversations.

He drank a lot, he gambled, and he was a dedicated philanderer. He became a card counter and did pretty well at blackjack. He liked Las Vegas, and he took advantage of the activities there—the drinking, the hookers, and the games. He was good-looking, and he was generous with women.

He needed women. He loved their attention. Men do, but this was more. I suspected that it had to do with his mother dying giving birth to him, giving birth to him and his fraternal twin brother. She lived for a day or two after his birth, long enough to write John and Gene a letter, which Gene kept and read. Women were an obsession with Gene. He needed to be wanted and loved by women, and he was.

He was seventy-eight years old when he acquired a disease that he knew would kill him in a year or two, multiple systems atrophy. He had difficulty swallowing. A therapist taught him a new swallowing technique. Later, even the special technique wasn't enough, and a surgeon installed a feeding tube.

We didn't avoid the subject of his death in our marathon conversations. He wasn't morbid at all, but it was one of the topics we talked about. He was afraid. I don't remember what he said; the gist was that he wanted me to assure him that there would be an afterlife. I appreciated his confidence in my philosophical reasoning, but it was a tough task, giving him a good reason to believe in an afterlife—tough because I wasn't convinced. I'm just short of being an atheist. What could I say that might reassure Gene?

I knew him well. In that moment, him stretched out on his recliner, a plastic tube bringing oxygen to his nose, and me sitting on the couch in his living room, a place I'd been a dozen times, gazing out at the forest. A squirrel and a blue jay were hopping over pine cones, attending to life's business just beyond the sliding glass doors. We seemed suspended in our short silence. I wanted to say something believable. I buzzed through everything I knew, frantically searching for a way to reassure him. He trusted me. He'd read my writings; he had encouraged me more than anyone else in my life. He thought I was a smart guy. I wanted desperately to say something convincing.

Inspired, I peered into his eyes and said, "Gene, do you think the God who created pussy would leave us without an afterlife?" I marveled at how my question was tailored perfectly for his psyche. I had delivered it with confidence too. One doesn't always say the right thing on short notice, but I had done it. Given who Gene was, my assurance was perfect.

On the next visit Gene said he would leave me something in his will. "Not enough to make you rich," he said, "but enough to notice."

I said, "Thanks, and I promise to spend it on debauchery." I said it to keep the conversation light. I also thought he would appreciate that, my taking pleasure in the sort of activity that would have given him pleasure. Maybe he gained a little sense of immortality from the knowledge that raw, sensual joys would continue after his demise and that he would be a kind of participant in those happenings.

Gene said, "Good. I'm glad."

He had lost weight. He was weak. He would probably be dead in a few months, but his voice was strong; he still laughed; his eyes twinkled. I understood his death in an abstract way, but the idea didn't have the heft of a solid fact for me right then.

Later, his wife called to tell me he had died. I had moved away from Colorado, so I hadn't visited in a while. The weight of my deathbed promise grabbed me hard as the call ended. The mood had been light; we had smiled at the notion of the promise. Right then, putting down the phone, it became a solemn obligation.

If I had promised on Gene's deathbed to make sure Little Nel got a college education, the promise would have been equally compelling. The fact that I might have fun with the debauchery made the promise no less binding. There was no little Nel, though, just a burning obligation.

As a child my mother read poetry to me. "The Spell of the Yukon" was my favorite. The protagonist of "The Cremation of Sam McGee" said, "A pal's last need is a thing to heed." However light the mood was when I promised Gene, I took my vow seriously.

The check came in a few months—five grand. Five thousand dollars. The notion was so frivolous sitting in Gene's mountain house, and it still was in a way. Debauchery, debauchery—I couldn't buy a new bed; I couldn't use it for my grandson's college fund.

There was no hurry. I could think for a long time about my obligation. I took up the habit of asking friends, "What would you do if you had five thousand dollars you had to spend on debauchery?"

Three people said, "Spend it on whatever you want. Your uncle won't know."

I thought, But I would know.

What is debauchery? I asked myself. Gambling, prostitutes, drugs, and alcohol. Later it occurred to me that food could constitute debauchery too.

For the next few months I kept asking, and at stoplights or waiting in line at the post office, I would imagine different occasions of debauchery.

Years ago I saw myself as the question man. I asked a question of half a dozen friends, then six months later I asked a different question: When did you stop being afraid of the dark? What is your first memory? If you had a foolproof truth serum, who would you use it on, and what would you ask? What is the weirdest thing you believe? I like the mini-max quality of that last one. Is there anything you cannot imagine ever receiving enough of? I asked people, "If you had five thousand dollars to spend on pleasure, what would you buy?" My friends had a hard time with that. The only solid answer I got was a cigar humidor along with the cigars to fill it.

My present chore was different, though. This was debauchery rather than just pleasure.

The concept of debauchery began slowly to congeal for me. It could include dinner at an upscale restaurant with good friends. In order to qualify, though, it seemed that it should feature money-is-no-object champaign or maybe a rare wine. Gambling can be a part of debauchery, but that activity didn't appeal to me. I like a friendly game of poker with folks I know, a game in which losing costs a little more than a movie with popcorn, but serious gambling doesn't thrill me. Debauchery would certainly include enjoying the services of a prostitute, and I'm glad some folks can absorb that pleasure, but it doesn't work for me.

On my thirty-fifth birthday I had sex with two women, two friends. That was exciting. It is one of those events that is great fun, but that one stops fantasizing about once one has done it. After the three-way I wondered what I would do for my fortieth birthday—maybe have a hooker. But the more I thought about it the less appealing it became.

Maybe my view of prostitution will soften in time. What would a ridiculously priced hooker be like? How would she go about her craft? She would certainly see herself as desirable. Would that confidence inform her technique? The idea didn't seem likely, but she might teach me something new; she might give me ideas I could pass on to future lovers.

Why do guys like hookers? Is their pleasure in romantic sex dampened by an overwhelming obligation to please their lovers? I wasn't cursed with that obsession. I like satisfying my lover, and have been told that I do, but it comes naturally, and I see each of us as having most of the responsibility for our own pleasure.

I've known guys who seemed to want to avoid revealing their most compelling desires to someone they might see again. They appreciate hookers for their discretion and their anonymity. But my capacity for shame is pretty low.

I had had a wonderful wife who died in a car accident. I eventually learned with her how sex and love can melt into unimaginable joy. I don't think I could be thrilled by someone whose job it was to make my penis feel good. With my wife I couldn't locate the boundary between my sensations and hers. I seemed to be experiencing both her pleasure and mine, and it was amazing.

No matter how much skill a prostitute brought to her work, no matter what was happening mechanically, it would lack the magic that I knew was possible, and I suspect I would miss it.

My ethics is more deontological than utilitarian, which means I believe in telling the truth and keeping promises. So, it was as if the debauchery, whatever it turned out to be, was already planted out there in the future. Somehow, I would settle on a delightful act of debauchery. I would assemble the necessary accoutrements and make it happen. The future could not be otherwise.

I was becoming very fond of a beautiful woman. Maybe we would fall in love. We could devote a whole evening to sipping champagne and exploring each other's bodies. With pricey enough champagne that would count as debauchery. Burning logs in the fireplace, flowers in a vase on the table—lovers enjoying everything human bodies and creative minds can offer. One could run through five hundred dollars for such an evening. Ten of those would deplete the inheritance, fulfill the obligation.

A few years ago some starlet's boyfriend bought her a pair of flip flops that cost $20,000. I thought, how does a person spend that much on footwear that one can buy from Walmart for two or three dollars? But I realized that the whole economic game is running backward in this kind of purchase. The idea is not to get the most satisfaction for one's money, the idea is to blow twenty grand. There is a kind of liberation that comes from that calculation. I was working with five grand instead of twenty, but the principle was the same.

I would blow five grand on something that brought me extreme pleasure. I had years to figure out what that would be. I had two good ideas. I might find better ideas, but it was there, perching at some unknown time in the future—I would celebrate debauchery. I would feel some exotic pleasure and not regret the expenditure, not regret because it was already gone. The oath implied that there would be nothing left once the deathbed promise was closed.

At first, at the moment of the phone call from Gene's widow, the obligation seemed onerous. As time passed, as I imagined the debauchery in more detail, as friends answered my question, as my definition of debauchery sharpened, the notion became liberating. My perception of debauchery acquired a crisp outline.

I saw myself at a restaurant with some good friends. I would have explained to them that I was fulfilling a sacred promise made to a quirky uncle. They would enjoy the meal without any feeling that they needed to reciprocate or owe me anything. Oysters Rockefeller, lobster thermidor, money-is-no-object champagne, flaming crepes suzettes or cherries jubilee for dessert.

I couldn't escape the debauchery obligation, but the definition could stretch a lot. The extravagant dinner would only cost a grand or so—I could do it five times.

Whatever the instance of debauchery would be, it had been installed as an inevitable event in my future. Pleasure and mystery and enlightenment from that future event seeped back to the present and sent a shiver though me a couple of times during every week.

When you are not religious, when you don't have a sacred story about how life, death, and the Universe operate, you can play with different ideas. I sometimes like reincarnation scenarios.

Between lives I want to meet my father, my wife, my cat, and some friends. In this version my cat was a wise being who just happened to be a cat in the piece of life he shared with me before he got eaten by a coyote.

In the place between lives a special spirit helper, someone who knew the recently deceased in his life, guides him through the inter-life rituals, someone who predeceased him. We review my life, talk about what I could have done better. We select deep propensities for my next life, attractions like the ones I have in this life toward watching flames and ocean waves and taking pleasure in washing dishes. And when all the important work is complete my guide says, "Would you like to have a sprinkling of debaucheries?" He hands me a huge silk-bound menu for me to choose from.

Now, I have indulged. I felt I had to make one debauchery real. A friend who has lived in the city for decades has a favorite restaurant. He said that every time he goes anywhere else, he is slightly disappointed that he and his wife strayed from their favorite. So, I invited him, his wife, and my new love to this place. We had service that was attentive but not obnoxious—no napkin folding every time you get up. The food was superb. I ordered a good brut rose champagne, and when we poured the last of it, I remembered to poke the bottle top-down into the ice bucket.

"Another one of these?"

"Of course."

I told my guests the night was on Uncle Gene. We all raised a glass. "To Uncle Gene."

So, I dipped a toe, ever so gently, into the wide river of debauchery.

In the fantasy there is no time. I rest my hands on the menu that says Debaucheries in gold letters on the front. The tingle of anticipation flows from the menu through my palms. The debaucheries are out there waiting, little islands of pleasure in a life filled with satisfaction and grief and mystery. Life would be fine without them, but they are extra, like icing on a cake—no, the icing is already there. They are more like the colored sprinkles on the icing on the cake.

# A Midsummer 2020 Night's Dream

Laura Holman

*Lights up on the lobby of an apartment building in the West Village.*

*An evening in July. Puck sits at a concierge desk, wearing a facemask. The elevator door opens and Fairy walks toward him, also masked, carrying a reusable grocery bag.*

**PUCK**
How now, good spirit! Whither wander you?

**FAIRY**
From sheet, from quilt; from pillow, from bed,
Through endless attempting a sourdough bread,
To thousand-piece puzzle, to meeting on Zoom,
On cleaning each inch of my tiny bathroom.
I must go seek toilet roll, hand soap, and yeast,
Or get the hell out of this building, at least.
Farewell, dear Puck; and with haste I'll be gone;
For Helena comes now, without a mask on.

*Exit Fairy. Enter Helena looking at her phone screen.*

**HELENA**
How happy some lifestyle bloggers can be!
On TikTok I surely am followed as she.
I move like Shakira at the halftime show,
But what of that? Demetrius thinks it not so.
I, after three weeks, that fuckboy did ghost.
And that day on Hermia's Instagram post,
Demetrius left hearts and emojis of fire,
When I was the littest in those three weeks prior.
And even though she says Lysander is bae,
Demetrius stans for her harder each day.

*Helena looks up and walks toward the concierge desk and holds out her phone.*

Puck, what say you; Should I filter or no?
I'm like "hashtag natural!" but still want that glow.

**PUCK**
From subway to sidewalk a score of germs teemed,
But hither I sit, for essential I'm deemed.
O Helena, do heed our distance with care.
I politely request that you filter elsewhere.

*Helena goes back to looking at her phone screen. The elevator door opens, and Hermia and Lysander enter the lobby, unmasked.*

**LYSANDER**
Hermia, hie, I do pray thee take flight
Before the store closes its doors for the night.
I told you to hurry, I did so beseech,
I hope they are still fully stocked up on bleach.

**HERMIA**
Anon, good Lysander, I'm rushing in heels.
And virtual therapy gave me the feels.
My shrink doth protest that I'm Mindful "Ay Eff,"
As quarantine model, as life coach, as chef.

**LYSANDER**
Dost not your therapist know what is up—
There's chardonnay hidden in your coffee cup?
You shell out one hundred and eighty a week
For one random stranger to keep you on fleek.

**HERMIA**
The flooding of sponsorship deals does draw nigh.
The one hundred eighty is worth it, boy bye.
Now ere the mood light of evening is gone,
To show that we're goals, a quick selfie anon.

*They pose.*

**LYSANDER**
Hast thou took care that the angle is right?
A few selfies more and then let us alight.
Anon on and on, pray your post keepest brief.
We must procure bleach per Commander in Chief.

**HERMIA**
Is it so told; does it come from on high?
For men of great power wouldst ne'er tell a lie.
Mine eyes the press briefing did not see; alack!
That bespectacled doctor's an absolute snack.

**LYSANDER**
I tire of hearing your lustings toward him.
And others that fill your DMs to the brim.
Your inbox obsession, the shit that it stirs!
Here's Helena now, should I slide into hers?

**HERMIA**
Don't say so, Lysander, oh say it not so.
Would that she want you, like, eight years ago.
Do what you will, though her bones surely creak.
The wear of her years dost my tongue truly speak.

**HELENA**
I seek not Lysander but let it be said
That more than one time I have left him on read.
Fie, puppet, fie, truest form of Gen-Z.
When you're out of the nursery, pray then talk to me.

**HERMIA**
What, though, is wrong with a fewer seen day?
Doth not Demetrius seek me that way?
Hark, I am little but fierce to be sure.
Fie to you, boomer, and fie to you more.

**HELENA**
Oh spite and oh hell and oh cruel enterprise!
Your tongue I do loathe and your youth I despise.
When that I was but of your years the same,
Late twenty-somethings were winning the game.
Prithee don't at me, as I know you do,
Must you be ageist in mocking me too?
If you were friend, as friend you are in show,
You would not mock a millennial so.

*A short, double-pulsed buzz sounds. Lysander pulls out his cellphone and reads the screen.*

**HERMIA**
A text for Lysander, but who is it from?
Tell me in good faith; pray whence did it come?
I bet it's Hippolyta shooting her shot.
For marry, her Theseus interests her not.

**HELENA**
Hast thou some gossip, pray do spill the tea!
He hasn't of late shown up on her story!
What news of the pair in their joint quarantine?
A living arrangement with rifts unforeseen?

**LYSANDER**
Helena, Hermia, breath do not waste.
Demetrius texted, let's go now with haste.
He didst go rallying with each Karen,
Heroically mansplained his way to a win.
He yelled our demands and he held up his sign,
And now you can spin, get your nails done, and dine.
Make merry in barbershops, prosper in bars,
Wave so victorious our stripes and our stars.

**HERMIA**
Good news to mine ears; ay, this country is free;
These dull roots and split ends have been woe to me.
Ho bottomless brunches, hie vodka and clubs,
Hark spa pedicures with the sea salty scrubs.

**HELENA**
Lo, I am shooketh, I'm actually dead.
It's time to get balayage back on this head.
Demetrius, love, I do come thy way swift.
Hasten, friends, hasten; I didst now call a Lyft.

*Helena, Hermia, and Lysander exit.*

*The lobby is empty except for Puck. He sits silently. After a few moments, the sound of pots and pans gradually crescendos from the outside. Two women wearing scrubs and face masks enter the lobby, nod toward Puck, and disappear into the elevator.*

*Puck breaks the fourth wall and speaks.*

**PUCK**
If these visions did offend,
Know thou canst rewrite the end.
Many have but slumbered here,
Till the springtime of this year.

And this weak and idle theme,
Might us summon from a dream.
Mortals who when pricked will bleed,
Voices who must take the lead.

*He stands.*

Give me your hands now, if they be clean,
Let us all meet when we enter phase green.
I hope not sweet slumber, nor wish a good night,
But bid you awaken to midsummer light.

*He walks outside.*

# Bolsonaro Eats Too Much Cheese

Andrew W. Jones

THE FIRST TIME WE RODE OUR BIKES INTO ONE OF JAIR BOLSONARO'S antidemocracy, coronavirus-denying rallies, it was an accident.

And this accident wasn't so easy to explain to a six-year-old wearing a pink unicorn helmet. I could see my daughter mouthing astonished words at me, but I didn't stand a chance at hearing her. The blaring of car horns and loudspeakers overwhelmed everything.

"Dad, why is it so loud?" I finally interpreted, putting my ear close to her mouth. "I don't like this."

It was a Sunday in mid-March, and Brasilia had just entered a version of Covid-19 quarantine. Schools, businesses, and restaurants were all closed, large gatherings prohibited, social distancing and mask wearing were encouraged, but since bike riding didn't violate any rules, my daughter Eliza had seen her opportunity.

"Dad, I really want to see where the president lives," she'd pleaded. "You promised we could ride our bikes to his house."

Seeing that life in Brazil's capital had essentially ground to a scary standstill, this seemed like a good time to give it a try. There was next to no traffic anywhere, and the presidential palace—right in the heart of the funky, airplane-designed city—was destined to be empty.

At least that's what I told Eliza and her mother.

So, when we arrived at the Eixo Monumental, expecting it to be apocalyptically empty and were met by the bludgeoning of car horns and bullhorn protests, Eliza quickly had second thoughts about her pleading.

"This is scary," she yelled ineffectually. "I wanna go home."

Though large gatherings had been banned, Bolsonaro's supporters had converged on the governmental center of Brasilia, some laying on their horns in cars, some yelling out their sunroofs, and some on foot, unmasked and angry. Their demands were clear: abolish the Supreme Court, disband Congress, and give all the power to their messiah, Jair Messias Bolsonaro.

"I don't get it," Eliza said once we rode a safe distance away. "Don't these people know about the coronavirus?"

At six, and a mere two days into having her physical, in-person kindergarten school year end, Eliza already understood plenty about the coronavirus—mostly because it had canceled the school field trip she'd been looking forward to for a month.

"I mean, there's all those people yelling without masks—and they're so close to each other. I mean, why would they do that?"

This is how our coronavirus world began—and in many ways, how it's continued for more than four months now. How do you explain a pandemic? How do you explain an antidemocracy, coronavirus-denying rally in the middle of a pandemic? How do you explain that the president whose "house" we were going to visit was a huge supporter of this rally? And how do you explain it all to a six-year-old?

By the time we got home, Eliza was stammering out her disbelief at all the commotion she'd just witnessed—and I worried I was going to receive the brunt of the criticism for our misguided jaunt into the coronavirus twilight zone. Why in the world would you take her biking there? was the question I was prepared for—and I felt equally unprepared to spit out a coherent answer. But instead of focusing on our bike ride, my wife's eyes were glued to the TV, where she could see Bolsonaro wading his way into the gleeful crowd of revelers who were waxing nostalgically about the days of Brazil's military dictatorship. Fittingly, Bolsonaro was saluting them, and then shaking hands and taking selfies.

The whole episode—even without tossing a six-year-old with a unicorn helmet into the mix—was surreal. And though my wife, children, and I are outsiders—gringos who can't claim to understand Brazil like natives—this was our fourth year living in Brazil. We liked to think we were used to the surreal, but this all still felt stunning.

That night, we found out we weren't the only ones.

The cacophony started at 8:30 p.m. sharp. Our neighborhood filled with rat-a-tat-tat-tatting mixed in with clang-a-clang-clanging. It was loud—seriously loud. It was the kind of loud that would rattle anyone except, of course, our three-year-old son Clark, who revels in all things rat-a-tat and clang-a-clang.

The *panelaço* is a Latin American tradition that involves banging pots and pans outside your window to express burgeoning political displeasure. Only a year and a half earlier, the air outside our apartment was filled with fireworks celebrating Bolsonaro's election victory. But now the pots and pans told a different story.

"FORA BOLSONARO!" filled the air.

"OUT WITH BOLSONARO!" the people were chanting amidst the clatter, and for my wife and me, this was a surprising turn of fate for the president. Brasilia and the Federal District had been Bolsonaro strongholds, as many supported his campaign messages based on rooting out corruption combined with religious conservatism. But since he'd returned from the United States a week earlier, numerous members of his traveling party tested positive for the coronavirus, he downplayed the seriousness of the pandemic, he opposed quarantine measures all over the country—and now he'd just spent his afternoon reveling in the adoration of protesters who wanted to upend democracy in Brazil.

All Clark cared about was the pots and pans, though. Bolsonaro didn't mean anything to him, but chaotic banging and clanging was his dream come true.

Perched on top of our living room couch, he was whacking away with a spatula on one of our kitchen pots. Though it was impossible to hear anything amidst the clamor, the look on Clark's bemused three-year-old face was unmistakable:

THIS. IS. AWESOME.

Eliza, who on her good days is six going on sixteen, was a little more reflective.

First you took me bike riding into the middle of one loud protest, and now we're banging on pots and pans as part of another protest. What in the world is going on, Dad?

Once again, there were no easy answers, so my wife did the most sensible thing of all. She rushed into the bathroom to grab cotton balls to stuff in all of our ears. The banging went on for nearly twenty minutes.

And this pattern—pro-Bolsonaro, antidemocracy rallies out in public every Sunday followed by their rebuttal, anti-Bolsonaro, stand-at-your-window-and-raise-hell *panelaços*—has continued unabated since March. Way back when it all started in March, the coronavirus had barely reached Brazil, and this aided Bolsonaro's contention that the virus wasn't that big of a deal. He called it a *gripezinho*, or "little flu." He bragged that, as an athlete, he would never be impacted by something as measly as this virus. But even at this point in March, plenty of Brazilians were watching what had happened in China, and what was happening in places like Italy and New York. Brazilians knew exactly what was destined to barrel its way below the equator.

As we checked the daily statistics of coronavirus cases all over the world, Eliza would ask a pertinent question:

"Dad, if the coronavirus is bad, but it's still not everywhere, why don't we just move to a country that doesn't have the coronavirus?"

Ah, yes, six-year-old logic.

"Like, hey!" she said as she pointed to my computer, fingering a blank space on the map, finding a country with no cases. "Let's move there!"

She was pointing at South Sudan.

"Um," I stammered—and realized that my stammer was now becoming a staple of our conversations—"there are other things in that country that are a little more dangerous than the coronavirus."

"Really?" She was incredulous. "I mean, the coronavirus can kill people. Are there other things in South Sudan that kill people?"

I called an audible.

"Should we give our bike ride to the president's house another try this Sunday?" I offered up.

"Yes! Yes!" she said excitedly. "And I hope all those noisy people won't be there this time."

Of course, the noisy people were there—but we left earlier in the hopes of getting our parliamentary bike tour in before the pro-dictatorship, coronavirus-isn't-real chaos ensued. Armed with her unicorn helmet, Eliza was determined to outrun the crowds, and when we arrived in the heart of town around nine o'clock, the crowd wasn't that big. But it was already plenty loud. In true Brazilian spirit, the rally felt like the blending of a political movement and Carnaval, with some people shouting on microphones while others danced to Brazilian hip-hop music. Most people were wearing yellow and green Brazilian soccer jerseys, Havaiana flip-flops—and very few were wearing masks.

"Let's go, Dad!" Eliza shouted. "We can out-bike them!"

As her unicorn sped off into the distance, I couldn't tell if the protesters found the sight of a masked gringo dad and his six-year-old daughter to be a rebuttal to their movement—or if, in child-friendly Brazil, they were hoping we'd join the party. Several minutes later, we stopped in front of the presidential palace and Eliza was exceedingly happy. She'd completed her biking mission, and we now had the pictures to prove it.

I was aware, though, that we shouldn't linger, as the protest was now gaining steam—and noise—and heading our way. Their chants were echoing off the rigid rectangular parliamentary buildings, and Eliza had started tuning in to their messages.

"Dad," she proceeded cautiously, "who are the communists?"

Oh, boy.

"Dad, you have to answer me," Eliza continued. "I mean, they keep yelling about the communists. They say they want to kill them. Who are the communists? And why do they want to kill them?"

If this were the 1950s when my parents were growing up in the States, I imagined this might have been a relatively normal question. Even in the 1980s, I could envision asking something like this to my parents. But in 2020? And in Brazil? Once again trying to explain any of this to Eliza, I was at a loss.

"Eliza, I think it's time we start biking home."

When Bolsonaro unexpectedly swept to power in 2018, some were attracted to his anticorruption stance and felt, like Donald Trump, that he'd "drain the swamp." Some liked his alignment with the three Bs in Brazil: Beef (agricultural lobby), the Bible (religious conservatives), and the Bullet (pro-gun lobby). But then there were others—many of whom were now gathered for this rally—who were passionately drawn to Bolsonaro's rhetoric about where all of Brazil's problems were coming from: communists who were trying to take over the country.

In four years in the country, I'd yet to meet a communist, but now a crowd of nearly a thousand people was headed my way ready to tell me a different story about the country I was trying to understand.

"Dad, I'm worried," Eliza told me as we biked our way out of the crowd and stopped for water a little while later. "I mean, what if those people give each other the coronavirus?"

I stammered out yet another unconvincing explanation, and Eliza waited a moment before changing her tune.

"Can we bike somewhere else next weekend?"

That ended our flirtation with the antidemocracy rallies—which, of course, still continued every Sunday. Bolsonaro appeared at many of them, basking in the adulation, one time arriving in a military helicopter, one time riding a horse through the crowd, and never wearing a mask.

In the meantime, though, we were firmly immersed in the 8:30 *panelaços* in our neighborhood. Clark looked forward to them more and more, as they offered him the opportunity to push his bedtime later and later. Running out of cotton balls, we put an end to his banging on pots and pans, so he resorted to using his voice to howl, FORA BOLSONARO! out his bedroom window.

Of course, none of this made any sense to Clark—though this didn't seem to bother him at all. While his six-year-old sister was asking all sorts of tough questions—If you're a president, isn't it your job to listen to the people?—Clark couldn't have cared less about democracy and protest. He hadn't even bothered to ask who Bolsonaro was; he was just addicted to the noise.

And based on what was happening in Brazil, there was plenty of noise.

On one April weekday afternoon, Eliza and I were biking through our neighborhood when the pots and pans started rattling away much earlier than their normal 8:30. If we weren't living in bizarro Brazil, you could've interpreted the noise as coming from the end of an exciting road race. This is exactly what was on Eliza's mind.

"Dad," she asked excitedly, "are they cheering for us?"

I didn't have to answer, though, as the chants started pouring out windows.

"FORA BOLSONARO! FOOOORRRA BOLSONARRROOO!"

"Oh," Eliza offered all too knowingly, "something happened, didn't it? It's Bolsonaro again, right?"

Right.

Now a month into the pandemic, Bolsonaro had finally got one of his most ardent wishes, the ouster of Luis Henrique Mandetta, his popular and well-respected health minister. While Mandetta strongly advocated quarantine measures like social distancing and mask wearing, this wasn't going to fly in Bolsonaro's administration. The *panelaços* made for an electric finish to our bike ride, and once we were home, it was back to local TV news again to find out the illogical details of the health minister's firing.

"Why would he fire someone who was trying to keep us safe?" Eliza asked dejectedly, in a tone similar to when she discovered earlier in the week that South Sudan now had cases of the coronavirus as well.

When Sergio Moro, Bolsonaro's minister of justice—the guy the country was counting on to root out corruption—quit and alleged that Bolsonaro himself was corrupt, the pots and pans rang out all afternoon and evening, starting at 2 p.m. and coming back for more and more.

Every once in a while, a counterprotest would spring up—either vocal support for Bolsonaro, or, as he encouraged, caravans of cars driving through the neighborhood honking their horns in a blaring display of support. Each time, this would lead to even louder FORA BOLSONARO! outbursts, along with more pain inflicted on kitchenware. Clark, whose accent makes him sound more Brazilian than the rest of the family, would start getting creative, howling out, "FORA THIAGO!" which befuddled his entire family along with the rest of the neighborhood that was getting used to his ever-booming voice.

Who's Thiago? we'd ask him, wondering if this was a playground bully who'd tormented him way back in life before quarantine.

In response, he'd just shrug his shoulders and keep on yelling.

"None of this makes any sense," Eliza would say, shaking her head.

When Moro released a tape implicating Bolsonaro in corruption—one that included the president swearing twenty-nine different times, creatively using eight different swear words—Clark's beloved *panelaços* began early again. Once again, he wanted both Bolsonaro and Thiago out.

As the case numbers and death tolls predictably mounted in Brazil, Bolsonaro came under more pressure to defend his opposition of quarantine measures. He showed no signs of backing down, though, answering a question about the accelerating catastrophe by snapping, "So what? I'm sorry. What do you want me to do?"

Then, in a nod to how his supporters glorify him, he continued with, "My name's Messiah, but I can't work miracles."

With this, Clark's bedtime continued to get pushed later and later.

"Dad, I understand it's going to take a while to find a vaccine for the coronavirus," Eliza mused one night after a particularly rowdy *panelaço*. "But is it possible for them to make a vaccine that makes presidents nicer?"

Once again, I had no answer.

Bolsonaro followed President Trump's logic that hydroxychloroquine, usually used to treat malaria, would be the cure-all for coronavirus, and when his new health minister refused to publicly support the use of hydroxychloroquine, they butted heads. Less than a month into the job, the new health minister resigned. For those keeping score at home—and trust me, we weren't going anywhere—that was two health ministers and one justice minister in less than two months. Bolsonaro's third health minister of the pandemic would be a military general with no medical background whatsoever, and he was just fine with promoting hydroxychloroquine as a miracle drug.

"Dad, I just don't get it," Eliza would tell me as we biked in our neighborhood. "I mean, can't someone just talk to Bolsonaro? Couldn't someone just teach him about science?"

I sighed.

"Well, sometimes it's just not that easy," I told her.

"But why? Why? It shouldn't be that hard. We don't want people to die. Someone has to be able to make him listen."

Again, I sighed.

"Sometimes when people get things in their mind," I explained, and felt this was the best explanation I'd given Eliza in months, "it doesn't matter what anyone else says. They're going to do what they want no matter what you say."

"You mean, kind of like Clark and how he does whatever he wants?"

She hit the nail on the head. There's nothing like the politics of a pandemic to bring together the leader of a country of 200 million and an out-of-control three-year-old.

That night, the neighborhood was rattling away again. Bolsonaro shut down the health ministry's website that was tracking coronavirus cases and deaths. Defying logic and science, he argued that cases and deaths were being overreported. After all, this was just a "little flu." This began a forty-eight-hour period where miraculously no one in Brazil got the coronavirus—at least according to the government. (It took two days for a judge to mandate that the website be reinstated.) In the meantime, our neighborhood's pots and pans weren't so sure. Clark sprung out of bed to his window and unleashed his fury in the direction of Bolsonaro and Thiago once again. Eliza, ever sage and eager to save her vocal cords, just grinned in the background.

In between Clark's shouts, I saw her lean in to him and whisper, "Say it, Clark, just say it."

Clark looked back at me to gauge whether or not this was a good idea. Like just about everything during the pandemic, I had no idea what was going on, so I didn't offer a protest.

"BOLSONARO EATS TOO MUCH CHEESE!" he belted out the window in perfect Portuguese.

What?

Eliza rolled over on the bed giggling. Clark beamed.

"BOLSONARO EATS TOO MUCH CHEESE!"

I could've sworn the neighborhood paused for a moment with this second declaration. The pots, the pans, the car horns, Bolsonaro, Thiago—it was all part of the routine. But too much cheese? In this craziest of crazy times, no one was exactly sure what to make of this.

But still, it was only a moment's pause. In this craziest of crazy times, we can say with a fair amount of certainty that anything goes. Even too much cheese.

"What are you saying, Clark?" I asked quizzically.

He howled it out again.

"Sometimes people just get things in their mind." Eliza smiled knowingly.

Probably because it was on our bikes where this all began, conversations on my daily bike rides with Eliza always seemed to find their way to the coronavirus and Bolsonaro. So, it was only fitting that we were on a bike ride and stopping for water when my phone blew up with news about Bolsonaro's testing positive for the coronavirus. The man who'd derided the "little flu" for so long had finally gotten it.

It didn't take long for Eliza to share her thoughts.

"I know the coronavirus is bad, and I feel bad for anyone who gets it," she said through her mask. "But I don't feel bad that he got it."

She paused to gauge my reaction.

"I know that's probably not right, but is it okay that I don't feel bad for him?"

I'd lost track of how many quarantine questions she'd asked me that I couldn't answer, so I just smiled and told her to put her unicorn helmet back on. We biked off into the distance—far from the president's house.

# Learning to Count

Elizabeth Argelia Leonard

Some of us learned to count toilet paper rolls and paper towel sheets and paper bags stacked high from deliveries. Some of us learned to count days past. Some of us learned to count moments. Some of us learned to count money, to count fewer things we needed, to count fewer paychecks, to count fewer ways to count.

Some of us learned to count breaths held, the distance between each a crucial kind of ruler.

Some of us learned to count blessings. And loved ones. And past loves and lovers and love lost and love missed.

Some of us learned to count memories, dipping back to count past adventures, and back again to count paths here. Some of us learned to count regrets. Some of us learned to count piles of sadness, divided into smaller piles.

Some of us learned to count rage. To count the broken ribs and broken limbs of broken systems. To count the ways we have been broken.

Some of us learned to count bodies.

Some of us learned to count joy in its tiniest forms
7:00 p.m. pot-banging
a clinking of across-balcony glassware
sidewalk chalk rainbows
the feel of a pen between the fingers
tropical bird's song outside someone else's window
the sponge of dough against the palms
the remembrance of touch

Some of us learned to count joy and hope and faith and joy and faith
and hope and hope and faith and joy

the only kind of counting that could ever count again.

# Blue Boy

Theo Johnston

UNCLE TILLMAN GOT HIS LEGS BLOWED OFF IN THE KOREAN WAR and never failed to remind us at least once every time we paid him a visit.

He sat next to the table: his scrawny carcass perched on the edge of his wheelchair and shrouded in a tobacco haze that never lifted, the gray caterpillars of his eyebrows rippling above the cigarette burns of his eyes. He hadn't shaved in days. He was staring down his vulture beak at me (just one month before my fourteenth birthday) and my four-year-old brother, like he was about to swoop us off to hell. Usually a chatterbox, Freddy just sat there fidgeting. I squeezed his knee to assure him that everything would be okay.

A couple of years earlier, Uncle Tillman had entered the holy state of matrimony with my Aunt Bessie, a petite, leather-skinned woman in her late sixties who had graduated from the School of Spousal Abuse with honors. She was Uncle Tillman's first wife, and Uncle Tillman was her third husband, so you'd have thought she'd have known what she was getting into. It sure wasn't a Doris Day and Rock Hudson movie. My dad's older sister (by almost twenty years!) didn't talk much because she had few teeth and breath that would gag a skunk. When she did talk, she would purse her thin lips to create a barricade for her breath, like she was about to start whistling Dixie.

Uncle Tillman didn't like to cover up the stubs where his legs used to be, so I was always looking up at the picture above the kitchen table of some stupid dogs playing poker. Momma said the picture was a wedding gift from his GI buddies. Uncle Tillman said it was "real man's art, not like that swishy Blue Boy your Aunt Bessie used to have up there." In a rare effort to be cordial, I asked him what he had done with the Blue Boy. "I burned that blue-assed little sissy. Why, Tommy, did you want it?"

"But Aunt Bessie loved that picture, Uncle Tillman, and I kinda liked it too."

"So, you liked that prissy fruitcake with the blue pedal pushers, hose, and frilly bows on his shoes? If you was to put that pitcher up at your house, everybody would think you was a fruitcake too. Good thing I destroyed it." I was afraid to ask what it meant for a person to be a fruitcake. One year for Christmas, we received a fruitcake as a present, which Momma promptly threw in the trash and then wrote a thank-you note to her great-aunt telling her how delicious it was.

"Tommy, if you ever tried to fit into that Blue Boy suit, them buttons would start shootin' off like shrapnel ever'wheres." That was about as close as Uncle Tillman ever got to wit. His spasms—first of laughter followed by coughing and then back and forth—took several minutes to subside.

Aunt Bessie came to my defense. "Tommy's not pudgy, Tillman, he's just big-boned. Leave the boy alone."

"More like big-assed," he insisted, and the alternating spasms started up again.

Sister Rosella had also told me I had a "bay window" I needed to work on. I asked Momma what a bay window was, and when she told me, I knew Sister thought it was cute, but "fat" by any other name is still "fat." Sometimes it's better not to know what something means, like "fruitcake," "bay window," or "fuck." But sooner or later, you always learn, and if you think it's not good, it usually isn't.

Momma finally spoke up, thank God. "Tillman, if you don't stop insulting my son, we won't come back anymore. Better a fat ass than your old snake hips any day."

The kitchen got quiet for a minute until Tillman started hacking up greenish gobs of phlegm. He kept a big IGA grocery sack on the floor where he tossed his wadded-up Kleenexes, often missing the target. Every time we paid our weekly social visit, Momma volunteered me to carry that overflowing bag to the trash. Then I had to come back and pick up (and in some cases, pry loose) any stray gooey tissues from the buckled linoleum with my bare hands. Sister Rosella said we should perform such humble tasks of service with a cheerful heart and offer them up for the Poor Souls in Purgatory, but my heart wasn't there yet. Not by a long shot.

Momma and Aunt Bessie were drinking coffee over by the sink, which was full of several days' worth of dirty dishes. They stood in stark contrast: Momma in a polka-dot red skirt with a white blouse and a loose red scarf around the collar, sporting fashionable black pumps, her hair stylishly short and curled, and Aunt Bessie in a faded yellow duster covered with little Valentine hearts, sporting pink bunny slippers, her frizzy gray hair sticking out everywhere. Her unsuccessful effort to tie her wiry mop back with a pink ribbon and bow looked ridiculous, but—in the spirit of Christian charity—I will say that at least it matched her shoes. Meanwhile, Freddy and I just sat there at the wobbly kitchen table drinking somewhat bitter Kool-Aid the color of cat piss and munching on stale saltine crackers. "Take me, oh Lord." I sighed.

"Well if it ain't Ellie Mae and Granny Clampett!" Uncle Tillman teased. "Yessir, your top reminds me of Ellie Mae, Marlene. All you need is a pair of them tight little jean shorts. If I'd of knowed you was coming over so gussied up, I'da shaved, but when you wake up every morning next to that Wreck of the Hesperus standing next to you, why the hell bother?"

I mused to myself, "What about when Aunt Bessie wakes up every morning to the Frankenstein monster? That probably doesn't make you want to get dolled up like Mae West either."

Momma just rolled her eyes, shook her head, and chided, "Shame on you, Tillman, for talking like that in front of your wife and my boys," and went back to blabbing with Aunt Bessie about planting their gardens now that spring was finally here. I knew that Momma was going to volunteer me to come over here and help Aunt Bessie with her tomato plants. "Jump for joy!" I thought as I downed another swig of the Kool-Aid. Where did Uncle Tillman keep the whiskey?

The reason Momma said we had to visit every week was to give Aunt Bessie support because "her home life was no bed of roses." But she'd gotten herself into this mess in the first place. When Tillman asked her to marry him, she should've just said, "Not in a million years, you old pucker hole!"

Aunt Bessie gave Freddy a picture book about the zoo so he could at least distract himself. It occurred to me that he didn't need a book about the zoo since we were already in one, although actually, it was more like a carnival freak show. Finally, my morbid curiosity won out and made me stare at that legless man in boxer shorts, his lap only half covered by a ratty old army blanket. I could have reached out and touched him, but I shuddered instead.

Uncle Tillman lit up another Camel and started puffing away, dropping ashes everywhere, and occasionally coughing up a big wad of sputum into yet another Kleenex. He knew I was staring, and then he turned in such a way that the blanket fell completely off his lap, causing him to partially expose himself.

My eyes were drawn first to the stumps crisscrossed with scars and then to the dark outlines of whatever grotesque organ lurked in the underbrush. He winked at me, covered his bulge with a brown-spotted hand, and then massaged his crotch like he was kneading dough. I was the kid at the horror show who wanted to look away from the scene but couldn't, no matter how hard I tried. I was going to take it all in and hoped to live to tell about it.

Then Aunt Bessie came rushing over. "Tillman, Tillman! There are children here. We don't want to scare them away." She tried to cover him back up, but he was having none of it.

Uncle Tillman threw the blanket on the floor and launched into his usual spiel: "Goddamn it, Bessie, how many times do I have to tell you that I'm proud of these fuckin' stumps. I lost these legs fightin' for America and for your freedom. Let them kids know the price I paid. Let them see that war ain't no Hollywood movie." His voice faltered and he turned away. And then he added, "Goddamn it, Bessie, where's my fuckin' whiskey?" Momma winced whenever he said "fuck," but "goddamn" really set her off. She probably figured she could only work on one bad word at a time, and this was the one that was worse.

Then Momma spoke her piece: "Tillman, I've told you a hundred times I don't want my boys hearing that kind of talk. I'm trying to raise them right. Haven't you ever heard of the Third Commandment or are you a Godless atheist? And could you please treat Bessie with some respect? You couldn't survive without her loving care." After a ten-second pause, she added, "And one more thing, you don't need to be drinking whiskey this early in the day."

Uncle Tillman always had the last word in this discussion: "Well I'll be god-fucking-damned, Marlene, them boys need to learn how real men talk, especially Tommy, who's going to high school next year. I ain't changing who I am for your druthers. I paid the price to talk any way I want and to drink whiskey any time I feel like it. Loving care? Look around this pigsty, for God's sake. And I ate better food in the trenches of Korea than the slop Bessie serves me."

Aunt Bessie rushed over with the half-full whiskey bottle. "Okay, but just one swig for now, Tillman. Remember what the doctor told you."

"Fuck that lily-livered quack. He never was in Korea, and he don't know what I been through," he added.

As for me, I didn't have the good sense to shut up. "Uncle Tillman, you say you fought for our freedom, but what freedom does Aunt Bessie have anyway?" I personally didn't see how her life could be any less free taking care of this repulsive old geezer and living in a shack that still had an outdoor toilet in the back, even though a porcelain commode had been installed inside the house as a wedding gift from my folks.

"She's living in America, ain't she? We got freedom here. If you'da seen what I seen over in Korea, you'da knowed what I mean. But now that we're married, it's her job as my wife to take care of her lawfully wedded husband. That's how it works, saith the Lord."

"What about the Emancipation Proclamation?" Momma asked.

"Well I don't know if you noticed, but Bessie ain't no nigger, although sometimes it's hard to tell with her kinky hair," he chuckled. Momma's face turned to stone, and my brother and I looked at one another like we wanted to crawl under the table, although Lord knows what kind of crud and creepy crawlers were lurking down there.

The only black person we knew was the garbage man. Once Momma had us go out and ask him if he'd like some of our old clothes. He forced a smile and said, "Well, ain't that nice. But no thanks! Ask the milkman instead." As he drove his trash truck off without saying another word, I wondered why we'd ask the milkman if he wanted our old clothes. After all, white people didn't take kindly to other people's hand-me-downs, so why would he say such a thing?

Clueless, Uncle Tillman continued his harangue: "She's free, white, and twenty-one. In fact, she's beyond twenty-one by forty-some years. She was lucky she found a young veteran like me [he was about ten years younger than her but you couldn't tell it]. No one else woulda married a wrinkled-up old hag like Bessie. And I wish I'da realized sooner that she ain't nothin' but white trash. She didn't even have a pot to pee in when I first moved into this little shithole, against my better judgment. I was a fool to think she would change for the better."

"Oh, so now we're directly descended from Queen Victoria, are we?" Momma quipped. "And, Tillman, how many times do I have to tell you to say 'colored,' not 'nigger'? I'm trying to teach my boys not to be prejudiced against people who are different. Also, I haven't exactly seen you change for the better either. If anything, you've gotten more and more irascible."

"I'm tired of you always trying to make me feel stupid, Marlene. What the hell does that fancy word mean?" he asked.

"You're a bigger pain in the . . . neck . . . now than you ever were."

"Well you try living with Bessie in this crap box day in and day out, Marlene."

"It's not paradise for her either, Tillman. Just try to be a little nicer, that's all I'm asking, and the both of you need to make an effort to communicate. And Bessie, while we're at it, I'm going to get you a new broom and some cleaning supplies. And maybe you could start watching one less soap opera so you'd have time to actually use them. It's a two-way street, you know."

"Oh, Marlene, thank you so much," Aunt Bessie said. Yeah, like she was going to make any changes, and I knew he wouldn't either. The only solution was to end this so-called marriage. But in my opinion, she was still more sinned against than sinning.

I also thought about coming back at Uncle Tillman with a follow-up refutation about how lucky Aunt Bessie was to be married to him, but figured it would ruin the "Kumbaya" moment.

I asked Momma once why Aunt Bessie married Tillman in the first place. Her only answer was that someday I would understand the ins and outs of love and marriage.

Love? Really? But even if things had been peachy keen in the beginning, which I found hard to believe, that didn't mean Aunt Bessie had to be stuck with that monster forever just because of a piece of paper that wasn't even from a church. Uncle Tillman always said his religion was "in his heart, not like you papists who worship statues in your gaudy-ass temples just like them pagans do." Momma always told him he was hopelessly ignorant and that she wasn't going to debate a moron on the topic of Catholic statues.

So, all my aunt and uncle had was a marriage certificate from the courthouse. Legal, but worthless in God's eyes. From my limited point of view, accordingly, Aunt Bessie could up and leave anytime she chose without God giving a goddamn—although there were probably legal issues I didn't know about. Practically speaking, however, Uncle Tillman was in a wheelchair, so it wasn't like he could chase her down. But where would my aunt go? I sure didn't want her to come live with us. I had enough problems as it was, but she was also too old to start over.

If I was Aunt Bessie, I would consider sneaking up behind Uncle Tillman and whacking him upside the head with a frying pan, and if at first that didn't get the job done, I would keep at it because he wouldn't be able to defend himself. Of course, it would be better to get rid of him without getting caught. Maybe she could push him out into the street at night when a fast car was approaching, and when the police came, just say he had gone out to have a smoke. Then she could get all hysterical and start screaming, "Now what will I do without the love of my life? I can't live without my precious Tillman." Then she could sniff some chopped onions hidden in a handkerchief and cry her ass off so the police wouldn't suspect her of anything.

But maybe she wasn't willing to commit murder even if she could get away with it. I got that. Sure, she didn't go to church, but even lapsed Protestants probably had some morals. I felt the same way when I thought about suicide a couple of times back in the sixth grade, when a bunch of little dipshits kept calling me "faggit." I tried to pretend like it didn't bother me one bit, and I never let on to anyone about what I was thinking of doing. But I couldn't bring myself to follow through with the deed. It's just not right to do some things, no matter how desperate you feel. Besides, Sister Rosella once told the class, "Remember that if you kill yourself, you won't go to heaven, and you can't be buried in a Catholic cemetery either. When things get bad, just pray harder. And of course, boys and girls, you can always come talk to me." I knew she meant well, but I couldn't see myself saying, "Sister Rosella, I think I might be a queer, and I feel like taking a whole bottle of Mom's sleeping pills because I'm an abomination. What's your advice?" Asking Sister for help would just make things worse.

Nothing was as easy as it seemed at first, but at least I was working on strategies. I would eventually figure it all out.

Anyway, everything got quiet again, and then out of the blue, Uncle Tillman said, "Well I'll be goddamned—sorry, Marlene—if I'm not out of Camels again. Tommy, here's some money. You and your baby brother mosey on down to the Mobil station and buy me two more packs, and with the change buy youselfs some candy bars."

"No, Tillman, no," Momma protested. She was against the candy, not the cigarettes, because back then kids could say they were buying cigarettes for adults and get them easy, especially at that sleazy filling station run by a bunch of redneck grease monkeys, as my dad called them.

"Oh, Marlene, if I can't buy my nephews some candy once-t in a while, what's wrong with this goddamn world—I mean gall-derned world? See, I'm trying, Marlene! I really am."

Uncle Tillman did have this one redeeming quality that took a while to surface: deep down he loved his nephews even if he had a hard time showing it. Maybe I needed to forgive him for the small stuff and try to see him from a new perspective like Momma did every now and then.

As I took the bills from between his tobacco-stained fingers, he broke into yet another coughing fit, spewing tiny brown globules all over the place, including on me. I shoved the money into my pocket and said, "Thank you, Uncle Tillman." And then I wiped my face off with my sweater sleeve.

"Why don't you switch to Kools, Tillman? I'll give you some of mine," Momma asked. "They're better for you, and you won't cough so much."

"Marlene, a man needs a man's cigarette. It'll be a cold day in hell before I switch to those faggitty smokes. Kools are nothing but sissified menthol sticks."

Uncle Tillman saw us still standing there and scolded us, "Why are you two still here? Get a move on. I needed them Camels five minutes ago. And Tommy, don't sashay when you walk. I got a reputation to maintain in this neighborhood."

Freddy and I ducked out the back way and headed off down the road. I tried to walk without sashaying, but I wasn't quite sure what was bad about that or what it meant to sashay in the first place. I tried to swagger like John Wayne in those westerns that Dad sometimes made me watch with him after the weather and sports. What I wouldn't have given for Audrey Hepburn or Fred Astaire over John Wayne any day.

"Why you walkin' funny?" Freddy asked.

"This is how a real man walks, Freddy."

"Dad don't walk like that." I just ignored him. What does a four-year-old know anyway?

I was hoping Logan was working at the Mobil station today. I couldn't help but gawk at that handsome high school dropout in his snug T-shirt and tight jeans. He sure didn't have a bay window like me. He was rippling with muscles where I was pudgy. My only athletic endeavor was badminton, and that was considered a girls' game, not even up there with tennis. In fact, liking badminton would be a mark against me, even though I could beat everyone I played. Of course, all I ever played was girls.

Dad thought being a dropout was awful, but I didn't get why. After all, Logan was working and not going to school, with nobody picking on him, and then, after four o'clock, lots of pretty girls would be hanging all over him. He might have been a dropout, but to me Logan was coolness made flesh. He was a younger, more accessible version of my TV heartthrob, Little Joe on *Bonanza.* All Logan was lacking was the horse. In fact, I sometimes thought about him riding that Pegasus sign out front wearing nothing but a jock strap. It was an impure thought I couldn't seem to get rid of. And even an impure thought was a mortal sin. There was no winning.

I kept doing my best at not sashaying, but I still attracted a few stares from the neighbors. I guess they saw the resemblance to John Wayne, who knows.

When we entered the office, I stared at Logan rubbing the crotch of his tight denims. He'd been looking at one of those peek-a-boo calendars covered with a transparent page that had a skimpy blouse on it so the woman underneath looked like she was wearing it. But surprise! When you lifted the sheet up, she was busting out all over. I couldn't help but notice the impressive effect it was having on Logan.

"Well I'll be goddamned," he said. "What are you looking at, kid? You're not on the peculiar side, are you? Sometimes you come in here like you was the Queen of Sheba, but today you're walkin' all weird-like. You wanna take a gander at this calendar? Maybe that will straighten you out." He laughed as if he had said something funny. The truth is that I wished I had a calendar like that, but with Logan wearing underwear on the see-through plastic and nothing on underneath. I was glad I was wearing loose jeans today. More impure thoughts.

"Maybe some other time. My brother is too little to look at sexy ladies," I said, planting my left hand firmly on my hip to make a point. "I just want to buy some Camels for my uncle and some candy for me and my brother. What's so peculiar about that? Can I buy them here or do we need to go somewhere else where they'll take my American money?"

"Sorry about that, kid. You're a little weird, but I gotta hand it to you: you got balls. Of course you can buy that stuff here, kiddo."

I really wanted to impress him today, so in my deepest, most forceful voice, I demanded, "Listen up, Logan. We want two goddamn packs of Camels, two fuckin' Butterfingers, and two cock-suckin' [yeah, I know, but it was the only other swear word I could come up with on a moment's notice] Snickers. You got that?" I slapped the money down on the counter.

It must have worked because his honey-brown eyes under those fluttering lashes got super big, and he muttered, "Whoa, pardner. Where'd a kiddo like you learn to talk like that? You been hangin' out with that pathetic old fuck in the wheelchair from down the street, the one who rants and raves about the war whenever he comes in here?"

"That's my uncle, and he's not pathetic. He had both of his legs blowed off in the Korean War. He paid the price for your freedom, and you need to show him some fuckin' respect. And while you're at it, stop calling me 'kiddo.' After all, I'm going to be fourteen in a couple of weeks." It felt good to show Logan that I could be a tough guy too.

On the way back from the filling station, me and my brother were cramming the candy bars down our gullets because if we didn't eat them on the way, Mom would be sure to snatch them away from us once we returned. Uncle Tillman was probably also timing us. The Mobil station was only three blocks away, so we had to wolf down our treats without delay.

When I looked back, I saw Freddy still chomping on his first bar while I was on my second. But I had to grin because Dad was right: with his curly red hair, freckles, and goofy little face, my little sidekick really did look like Howdy Doody. Dad was probably also right about me looking like Spanky from *The Little Rascals*, but in an older and taller version. As a little kid, I was on the chubby side and had a round face, except now I was even chubbier—but I liked to think I hadn't reached "fat" yet. When I was small, Dad said all I needed was a beanie like Spanky's, so he got me one. Much to my horror, he made me wear that cap whenever guests came over. Dad said it was cute for a little kid to be chubby with big round pinchable cheeks and that I shouldn't be so sensitive, but it sure didn't feel cute, then or now. He said I'd eventually grow out of the baby fat, but I was almost fourteen and still waiting.

I yelled at Freddy to hurry it up or Momma would make our lives a living hell for the rest of the day. "Are you done yet, Freddy?" I asked without turning around. "Yes, candy all gone." "Good," I said, and in we went.

Momma's line of reasoning was always the same: "You'll get more cavities from eating all that candy, and how are we gonna pay for that? You just got two fillings last month. That mercury that goes in your teeth doesn't come cheap. Furthermore, you need to lose some weight before you start high school. Give me those candy bars." Then she would grab them away from me, put them in her purse, and add with a voice that could melt butter, "Of course, I'll let the boys eat the candy later, Tillman, but I'll parcel them out gradually." But she and Dad always finished them off on their own. I knew that because I always saw the wrappers in the trash, which they didn't even bother to hide.

This time I reassured her, "Momma, you don't have to worry about our teeth. There wasn't enough change to buy any candy this time. Uncle Tillman, you must have done your math wrong, but it's okay. We shouldn't expect candy just for helping a patriotic war veteran of your renown." I had prepared more noble remarks, but Mom stuffed a plug into that bullshit before it could get any deeper.

"Then how come Freddy has chocolate all over his face and his hands and shirt?"

"Well I'll be goddamned," I thought, but I said, "Oh, Momma, he must have eaten those candy bars when I wasn't looking."

Freddy was standing next to me, so I pinched his arm to keep him quiet.

"Yeah, candy bars you supposedly had no money for," she smirked.

"Well I certainly didn't eat any candy," I lied. "Maybe he stole the candy bars when I was getting the cigarettes, Momma!" I pinched Freddy a little harder.

Tillman chimed in, "Maybe I really didn't give them enough money, Marlene. My eyes ain't what they used to be."

"Tommy, you know you can go to hell for lying as well as for stealing," she warned, shaking her finger at me. "Now you're accusing your own brother of stealing, and as for you, Tillman, you're in cahoots. You gave Tommy more than enough money for the cigarettes and candy. I'm not as stupid as you think."

Well, it was pretty cool for Uncle Tillman to buy us candy bars in the first place and then to back me up about not having enough change. On the days he didn't send us to get him more Camels, he even slipped me a dollar or two when Momma wasn't looking. In fact, I had already socked away over ten bucks. I was starting to think maybe Uncle Tillman had a soft side after all, and maybe I really was too judgmental. I mean, it had to be pretty awful to have your legs blowed off. Sister Rosella was always talking about compassion, and again, I wasn't there yet, but at least I had reached the feeling-sorry-for-him stage. That was progress.

Momma finally said, "I hate to cut all the witty repartee short [Momma had a master's degree in English and was always coming up with zingers like that], but I gotta get dinner started before Tom gets home or there'll be hell to pay. Of course, now the boys' appetites are ruined from gulping down all that candy. Tommy, don't you even try to tell me you didn't eat any. You all have a lovely [as if] evening, and don't forget Red Skelton comes on at eight." We bid adieu (but I could have done without having to kiss Aunt Bessie goodbye) and headed home.

After that visit, I regularly started spouting "Well I'll be goddamned" anytime I was surprised or angry, of course only when my parents weren't around and certainly not at school. I considered it part of my training regimen to become a tough guy who could finally get some respect. After all, Logan cussed, and he was a tough guy who had respect in spades. And Uncle Tillman was the cussing king, and you couldn't get any more manly than a brave soldier who got his legs blowed off in Korea to protect the freedoms we have here in the good old US of A.

Speaking of surprises, I got the highest grade on a math quiz the following week in school. That had never happened before. Math was my weakest subject, so I was in shock. After Sister Rosella gave me back my paper, I muttered under my breath, "Well I'll be goddamned, how the fuck did that happen?" Unfortunately, Sister heard what I said and ripped me out of that desk by the arm, pulling me into the hall where she tried to shake some sense into me, her veil flapping about like she was about to take flight. I didn't think she heard me say "fuck," but she did tell me I couldn't go to communion until I went to confession, because taking the Lord's name in vain was a mortal sin. I told her how truly sorry I was, and for a moment her tone softened. What with all the impure thoughts and taking the Lord's name in vain, I was on the express train to hell.

She asked me who I learned that kind of language from, and I confessed it was my Uncle Tillman. "Instead of imitating him, Tommy, you need to pray for him. Your uncle's getting himself a one-way ticket to hell if he doesn't stop teaching kids to cuss like a sailor." We'd be riding the same train.

"But, Sister, he buys me and my brother candy bars. Besides, he was in the army and his legs were blowed off—I mean, blown off—in Korea. He's a hero, Sister. He paid for our freedom as Americans, you know."

Her change in tone proved short-lived, and she started shaking me again. "Don't you talk back to me, young man, or I'll slap you silly right here in the hallway and won't care who sees me. Your uncle isn't the one who paid for your freedom. It was Jesus Christ who paid for it by dying on the cross for you. Jesus is the only hero you need to imitate. Do you think even a million candy bars are worth spending all eternity in hell for? How free does that sound? Answer me now or I'm calling your mother and telling her to get down here!"

"No, Sister, please, please! A million candy bars aren't worth going to hell for." Sure, I was scared of going to hell, but right now I was more concerned about how my folks would punish me if they found out. "Sister Rosella, please don't tell my mom and dad what I said about my test score."

"Tommy, I know you've had your problems from time to time with some of the other kids and that you're nervous about going to Jesuit Prep next year. Like all kids, you want to be cool. I get that, and so maybe you think it's cool to take the Lord's name in vain. But there's nothing cool about blasphemy. In fact, it's the most uncool thing because you could end up burning in those flames that can never be extinguished. Every time you abuse the Lord's name, Tommy, it's like you're spitting on Jesus as he's dying for you up there on that cross."

Sister teared up as she looked up at the crucifix above the exit. She reached into her sleeve, where nuns hid all sorts of things, to pull out a tissue. She dabbed her eyes and then asked me, "Don't you want to go to heaven, Tommy?" She put her hand on my shoulder and searched my face with glistening, inquisitive eyes.

"'Course I do, Sister, I'm a Catholic boy going to a Catholic school, and I get A's in religion." I felt like the most awful person in the world. I had actually made a nun cry! Holy fuck!

"Well that's not going to get you into heaven if you don't keep God's commandments. Every time you feel the urge to curse like that, say 'mercy!' instead. It's a prayer instead of a curse, and no sin is involved. In fact, saying 'mercy' is an avenue of grace. I won't tell your parents this time, Tommy, but I'd better not hear you blaspheme again or I'll tell them—and there won't be any changing my mind."

I thought about Sister's words for the rest of the day. I knew I'd have nightmares about spitting on Jesus while he was in agony on the cross if I didn't change. Why had I convinced myself it was cool to take the Lord's name in vain? Because of Uncle Tillman and

Logan? That was the devil messing with my mind, like Jesus when he was tempted by Satan.

But I was glad Sister didn't mention anything about me using the F-word. I was pretty sure that "fuck" couldn't be as bad as "goddamn" because it didn't involve taking the Lord's name in vain. In fact, some dimwit had once etched "FUK" into the plaster wall in the upper grades' boys' room, but instead of going ballistic, as she usually did when some kid did something asinine, Sister Rosella seemed to think it was kind of funny and announced in class that "Whoever did this might think it was cool to write that awful word, but he couldn't even spell it right! It's D-U-C-K, not D-U-K and L-U-C-K, not L-U-K. Do you get my drift? He's not only a little pervert but a stupid one to boot, and woe betide him when we finally catch him. And don't worry, we will. Like God, we nuns work in mysterious ways." The whole class had a good laugh, including Sister, but she never said anything about that kid going to hell. That was my one ray of hope! (And by the way, within a week, the good Sisters did indeed catch the little fart, who was then promptly punished and thoroughly humiliated by the monsignor.)

I knew "fuck" was a bad word that described people having sex, especially the kind for making babies, but the word wasn't nearly as bad as "goddamn," so I figured I could keep using it from time to time to bolster my tough-guy image. There would be plenty of time later to clean up my act. I could keep a few cuss words in my arsenal that were venial sins and wouldn't merit hell, but just add more time to my stay in purgatory. It seemed like a good trade-off for now. But "goddamn" was permanently off my swear-word list.

So, the next time we went to Aunt Bessie and Uncle Tillman's, it wasn't but five minutes into the visit when Uncle Tillman knocked over his ashtray and all the butts spilled onto the grimy kitchen floor that had crumbs everywhere.

"Well I'll be goddamned," he said.

I immediately spoke up. "Uncle Tillman, instead of taking the Lord's name in vain, try saying 'mercy!' for a change. It'll make you feel a lot better. You don't want to burn in hell for all eternity, do you?" Sister Rosella would have been so proud of me.

For twenty seconds he just stared at me with glassy eyes like I was from Timbuktu instead of Kansas. It was obvious he had already had several snorts. The whiskey on his breath was so strong, I thought this must be what a cheap bar smelled like. Then he launched his attack: "I never heard of anything more faggitty in my whole goddamn life, Tommy. 'Mercy,' my fuckin' ass. Speaking of asses, get your lazy ass over here, Bessie, and clean up this goddamn mess before I give you a taste of my mercy." Then in a high falsetto voice he said, "Murcee! Murcee!" and started laughing like a fiend from hell. "All you need is to wear some blue pedal pushers and sashay around with a limp wrist saying 'Murcee this and murceee that!' [He made some swishy hand movements.] You ain't nothing but a goddamn sissy little Blue Boy. Besides, there ain't no goddamn mercy. If there was, Tommy, I'd still have my legs and not be married to this old bitch."

My original frying pan idea for permanently dealing with this creepy old gargoyle flashed into my mind, becoming more and more appealing by the second.

He lit up another Camel and blew the smoke in my direction. "How's this for mercy, Tommy!" he snorted. I had stolen a couple of his Camels last time and had felt bad about that, but not anymore. Now I would smoke them guilt-free. In fact, they were hidden in my underwear drawer for later. I'd seen Logan down at the filling station smoking a Camel a couple of times. I never considered stealing any of Momma's Kools (she probably counted them anyway) because Kools should be renamed Unkools. Kools are for ladies and fags, not real men.

I finally looked over at Momma because she hadn't said a word. She was ready to blow. Her face had turned hard and red, her lips quivering like she was about to let loose a stream of profanities. But she resisted, getting up instead and grabbing me and my brother by the hand. Without uttering a single word, not even taking proper leave of Aunt Bessie, who was crawling around on the floor like an alley dog, she yanked us out of the house and over to our '55 Ford. In a matter of seconds, she had opened the driver's door, pulled the driver's seat back forward, and thrown us into the back seat like two burlap bags of potatoes. Freddy and I were terrified.

I'd never seen Momma strip the gears before, but she floored it, peeling out of the driveway, leaving rubber on the pavement, barely looking to see if any cars were coming. "Mercy!" I thought to myself. "Save us, oh Lord! Please don't let us have an accident! I haven't been to confession yet, and I don't want to go to hell." But I also felt that Momma had proven she could be cool too. I had no idea she could drive like that, but I also knew better than to tell her that she had balls.

After ten minutes, I finally got up the courage to ask, "Momma, I guess I'm a faggot after all, right?"

"Oh, mercy, Tommy, oh mercy, mercy me. No, you're not a faggot, sweetie. We've already put that business behind us about you getting caught in the same sleeping bag on a fishing trip with Justin [the buddy that I lost after his dad forbad him from seeing me anymore, even though we were just trying to stay warm in an ice-cold tent because I was the only one smart enough to bring a bag while his stupid dad only gave him a couple of light blankets: so there!]. You're just more sensitive than other boys, that's all, and not every boy has to like baseball, but you do need to stop saying 'mercy.' You'll be going to an all-boys high school next year, but if you don't stop acting so weird, you're going to be teased even worse than at Good Shepherd." I knew I was more than just sensitive (I mean, I actually liked cuddling in the same sleeping bag with Justin, and he seemed to too). But I still didn't really know if I was a "sodomite," which Monsignor said was the technical word for "queer." I sure didn't want to shove my dingus up any guy's butt or have any guy do that to me. That was just plain gross and nasty!

After a few seconds, she added an afterthought: "And another thing: You need to stop putting your hands on your hips when you're talking with other boys, you know, like that Blue Boy in the picture Aunt Bessie used to have. It just doesn't look right."

"I'll work harder on the hip thing, but, Momma, Sister Rosella told me to say 'mercy' instead of taking the Lord's name in vain, and you yourself just said 'mercy,' but now you're saying I shouldn't use it? I don't see what's wrong with me saying 'mercy' if it'll keep me out of hell." Then, a minute after I didn't get a response, I added, "Momma, why did we leave all of a sudden, without even saying goodbye to Aunt Bessie? She didn't do anything wrong."

Momma just kept driving like she was possessed, and I didn't say anything else. But she finally answered my last question. "I didn't say goodbye because if we had stayed a moment longer, I would have knocked your Uncle Tillman out of that goddamned fuckin' wheelchair, that's why. Your Aunt Bessie might have to put up with that drunken old excuse for a human being, but I sure as hell don't," she insisted as we pulled into our driveway going too fast and slamming on the brakes just a few inches away from the garage door. "Mercy, mercy! Here I am a lifelong Catholic talking like a heathen. I can't believe I just used that kind of language!" She was even trembling and was looking furiously in her purse for her Kools, but she couldn't find them. "I left my goddamned Kools over at Tillman's."

My little brother Freddy shouted, "Bad Momma! Murphy, murphy! Bad Momma!"

"Oh, dear Lord, there I go again. Boys, I'm sorry for what I said and how fast I was driving. I wasn't thinking of your safety. I should never let myself get that upset. I'll make us all our favorite lunch, some grilled cheese sandwiches and tomato soup. That'll calm us down. This has been a bad afternoon for all of us." She got out of the car and rushed into the house, slamming the screen door behind her so hard that I thought it had been ripped off the hinges.

As I got out of the car, I whispered under my breath, "Now Momma has to go to confession too," while Freddy kept squealing, "Murphy, murphy!"

"It's 'mercy,' Freddy, mer-CEE, as in 'Lord, have mercy,' just like in the 'Kyrie Eleison' we say at mass."

Freddy was upset and started to bawl, and I asked him, "Why are you crying?"

"Cuz I didn't get my . . . gawdam candy . . . don't want no tomato soup, Tommy . . . Gawdam it . . . I want . . . my gawdam CANDY!" He was stammering between sobs.

"It's okay to say 'murphy' if you can't say 'mercy,' Freddy. But you can't say 'gawdam,' which is a very bad word that can send you to hell if you're still saying it when you reach seven, which Sister says is the age of reason. Even though you're still four, you need to break that habit right now before it's too late to change."

"Okay, Lord have murphy, I want some fuggin' candy. I bet hell is like being at Uncle Tillman's but without no candy."

"You shouldn't say 'fuggin'' either, although it's not as bad as 'gawdam.' Hell's a place where you burn forever in a lake of raging fire, worse than being at Uncle Tillman's house any day. Hell is full of faggots and other bad sinners like Uncle Tillman."

"What's a fagurt?"

"I don't know. I think I might be a faggot, Freddy." I got sad because I knew that being a faggot was much worse than taking the Lord's name in vain, and as Monsignor told me last summer in a counseling session, was right up there with being a murderer, according to the catechism of St. Pius X. It was, after all, one of the sins that "cried out to heaven for vengeance."

"You ain't no fagurt, Tommy. But if you go to hell, I'll go with you cuz you my brother and my best buddy, and I wuv you!" He started crying again, and I grabbed him and held him tight, trying to calm him down before Momma could hear and come back outside and make a scene. It was a couple of years too early to tell him not to be so sensitive. I sure wasn't going to make him feel worse, or like Dad, call him a crybaby.

"I love you too, Freddy, and I ain't no fagurt. I was just making a bad joke. It wasn't funny, and I'm sorry. I'm also sorry for accusing you of stealing candy from the gas station the other day. Now we're going to follow God's rules and eat our tomato soup and grilled cheese sandwiches to prove what good boys we are. We're both going to heaven. No hell for us! No sirree! And later we'll sneak out and grab some candy from my private stash."

Freddy grinned and stopped crying. "Oh murphy, Tommy. I already forgived you." I wiped the tears from his red little freckled face and gave him a big hug.

The rich aroma of tomato soup wafting through the screen door made me hope it would still feel like home inside. Momma was even singing our favorite Frank Sinatra and Dean Martin hit song from a few years back that went, "Love and marriage go together like a horse and carriage." I was starting to feel that everything was well with the world after all, especially as she chirped, "You can't have one without the a-a-other!"

Later that evening after dinner, Freddy and I gobbled down some candy in the garage while Momma and Dad were watching *Gunsmoke*, and this time I made sure Freddy didn't get his face or hands dirty. In no uncertain terms, I told him not to say anything to Momma: "Cross your heart and hope to die, stick a thousand needles in your eye." Then I actually made him cross his heart. Even though it was awful of me to do so, I needed a guarantee. I didn't want to complicate matters any more than they already were.

Once everyone had hit the sack, I was ready to head outside and light up my first Camel. I heard that if you smoked, you would eat less candy and lose weight as a result. That sounded like a better way to lose my bay window than playing baseball (which I was lousy at) or lifting weights (unless Logan himself gave me some one-on-one instruction). And smoking was also manly if you smoked the right brand and did it the right way.

After all, I was going to the high school with the big boys next year, "where boys had to learn to act like men in order to survive in a man's world" (which Dad said), "where Christ prepared his soldiers to fight against the devil who was lurking around every corner" (which Sister said), and "where chubby Blue Boys need not apply" (which I said). I was aiming to become a silent, lanky cowboy type that no one would pick on, and smoking couldn't help but give me a leg up. Even Father O'Casey, who came all the way to our parish from County Cork to (as he put it) "save wayward American souls," smoked. I just hoped he smoked Camels rather than Kools. Momma said she also hoped he wasn't a secret drinker like a lot of Irish priests were.

After everyone had gone to bed, I snuck out of the house to begin my personal transfiguration. I tried to walk like John

Wayne and not sashay as I headed toward the garden to light up. It was the perfect spring night: honeysuckle thick in the air, a lone owl hooting off and on in a tree, and the sky spangled with shimmering stars just like the flag. And thank God the night was moonless, so no one could see me from the house once I got to my special spot.

I wanted to find that freedom Uncle Tillman was always going on about, but I knew I had to make some changes to get there. I was resolved not to place my hand on my hip while I smoked. Instead, I would put my thumb in my left pocket and lean my butt up against a tree with my feet crossed at the ankles. That's how Logan did it when he smoked, and I liked thinking about Logan. A lot. Probably too much. All right, too much.

Fuck both fat-assed Spanky and that mincing Blue Boy, from now on it was John Wayne or nothing. Finally, I decided it was time for my first smoke. I thought of that billboard out on the highway. It was for a different brand of cigarettes, but I liked it: "Take a puff. It's springtime." I hoped my first smoke would be a new beginning, just like springtime.

Just at that moment, I heard that wise old owl hooting in the background. I took it as a signal to get started and lit the cigarette eagerly, feeling sure this experience would turn my life around.

It did all right.

All of a sudden, I doubled over coughing and gagging like Uncle Tillman, and then I puked up the Baby Ruth. Holy fuck and Lord have mercy! What godawful shit had I just sucked in? This wasn't fucking springtime: it was a Satanic blast from hell. Maybe I should have started with Kools (incognito, of course) and worked my way up to Camels, but it was too late now.

Then it really hit me as the smoke and a stench worse than Aunt Bessie's breath started making me dizzy with nausea. Maybe this was what the monsignor meant when he told me that faggots made God sick to his stomach, and this was God's way of giving me a "little" taste of what was to come.

I couldn't stop coughing or puking. Even bits of the grilled cheese sandwich came up.

The next thing I knew I was screaming "God damn it!" while looking up to the heavens. "God fucking damn it!" A couple of dogs started barking, but thank God no lights came on.

I slammed my fist into the tree and fell to the ground. And now my hand was bleeding. To make things worse, I was crying too. "Where's the mercy when you need it?" I muttered.

Inside my head, I could hear Uncle Tillman whisper, "Come on, you goddamn sissy little Blue Boy," and then in an eerie falsetto, "say 'Murceeee,' Tommy. 'Muurceeeee!'"

His demonic laughter trailed off into nothingness, and then I could hear the sad hoot of the owl again, only it was closer now: "Who, who, who?"

# Test Flight

## Emily Nichol

I CAN SEE THE REJECTION HEADING TOWARD ME AS SOON AS JESSIE opens his mouth. It is not the first time he looks at me, right in my eyes, and grinds my emotions into the floor. But I know, I feel so certain, that this time will be the last.

"Look, I just don't think it's a good idea," Jessie says, even and unblinking.

I twitch my wings and try to hide my discomfort by looking away. I really cannot believe this is happening right now. Again. What I'm asking for is fair.

I take a breath and the bass thumps loudly, reminding me of time. The lights drop and then flash up red, and then green. For once this party is actually good, and there is no place I would rather be less. The adrenaline, making my heart pump fast, drains out of me, muting me like the light flickering out of a dying bulb.

I see my role right away. I can't let him win. I lean into the part, letting the personality wash over me. I feel my mouth curl into a wicked little smile. I hold in the tears heating up in my eyes by imagining Cynthia's voice in my ear: You're better than him, you don't need him, he is a nerd, and isn't good enough for you. I tense my face to keep it neutral and fluff my antennae up higher.

"Should we . . . join the group?" Jessie asks awkwardly, gesturing to the mass of our friends clustered around the radiator.

"Of course! Let's go!" I grin, maybe a little too fast. I'm going for warm, understanding, resilient, sexy, unforgettable. Like me, on my best, most confident day.

My smile drops the second I swish away into the crowd. I move too fast for Jessie to keep up on purpose; I want to give him the chance to drop away, and he does. He stops next to Shira, leans over, and makes her laugh. I walk over to the bar and pour myself a whiskey neat. I wish I had thought of a smarter line to sting him with. I wish I had spun around faster.

I spread and then close my wings to reset. I can tell they are sticking out below their covers and I pull them back in, straighten them out. It feels better. I light a cigarette and peruse the party. I feel bleak, but the party is warm. The humans who own this house are in town—rare—and cranked the heat up, which means that everyone is in a wild mood. We never get heat like this at night, but we are deep into the coldest night of winter. The thermostat is up so high that the piles of snow, pressed thick and tight against the brick walls of the house, start to slick over with ice. The heat makes us feel rich, spoiled, and stupid. Ready to get stupid. I can feel my bad mood starting to thaw like butter left out on the kitchen counter. I can feel myself starting to relax. I take another drink. I decide to wait it out for a few hours. Jessie will get over himself. He'll come back.

EVERYONE THINKS JESSIE IS so charming and charismatic. An unbeatable conversationalist. Interesting. I know all these things people think about him, and I know why.

It is because of his eyes. His eyes are unexpectedly light. And he uses them to look right into yours. It's hard to explain, but Jessie makes really good eye contact. He makes it unmistakably and he makes it often. But more than that: him, looking into your eyes, it carries this weight. It makes you shiver. He looks at you and he holds it, actively. He cradles it. It's like looking at you, into you, is something that is precious to him.

When Jessie looks into your eyes, his whole body stays relaxed and slouching. He tucks his chin slightly under, so his forehead is level with yours. He gives you a real gaze, right into your guts: strong, sustained, penetrating, piercing, probing. It feels like he knows you so well. Like there is nothing inside you he cannot see or tell—like you do not have to do any of the work of showing him who you are, of even knowing who you are all the way in your core because he can already see it and know it maybe better than you can. Even if he does know you well, it physically manifests an intimacy so deep that it could only be imaginary.

But it feels real to me.

It is easy to believe, every time he looks into my eyes, that he knows what is going on in my mind even if I know, with certainty, that he is thinking about something completely different. Even if I know, with certainty, that I'm not even thinking anything.

Plus, he is cute. He looks a bit nerdy, with a light orange body and exactly twenty-one spots, which is a lot for us.

But the point is that he isn't actually that smart. He isn't that probing. Everyone is always saying he is so damn intellectual, so damn charming. He is just quiet when he needs to be. He has the emotional intelligence of a fruit fly.

But the main thing is that when you talk, Jessie really does listen. He really hears me. I think. He's the only one who's tried to hear me. I think.

And now Jessie might be gone.

I TAKE A DRAG OF my cigarette and lean back. I was born not far from this spot by the radiator on the wall. Thirteen months ago—a Pisces. My mom liked to talk about the day I was born all the time, every time we flew past here. She liked remembering all her little larvae, telling all their stories in her favorite little hiding spot, a safe crack in the wall in a closet upstairs. No one could find us there.

She was my age when she accidentally flew too close to the exposed bulb on the patio: close to home, within range, but it was just too hot that day. Her aim had never been very good. Wings touched glass and it zapped her like a slice of bacon, right at middle age. She only delivered my 236 brothers and sisters. Almost every mother gets to at least 500—it's what is expected.

Now it is March. Again.

I stretch out an antenna, letting it spring back. Flying. Time is flying. That's what I say to Jessie, all the time.

THE THING ABOUT JESSIE is, when he knows what he wants, he gets it. No question. He can actually be pretty brave when it comes down to it.

Once, when he was really young, Jessie flew all the way down the mountain we live on and flew back with the nectar of flowers no one had ever seen before grazing his legs. Just because he wanted to see what was down there.

I was pretty impressed when I learned about that. I was curious, and I was terrified. I had never even thought you could do that kind of thing before, not even in a dream.

WE MET LAST MONTH. For us, that was a pretty long time ago. We met in front of the TV.

It was another Friday night, another party. The warmest spot behind the radiator knob was already packed when I arrived. I felt the buoyancy of possibility fill me up, lifting me a few inches off the floor. I took a drink—champagne, my usual—and the bubbles lifted me up a few inches even higher, percolating my insides, egging me on from the core of my chest. I always strived to be the life of the party. I felt like it was my job. My instincts were to be loud, to entertain. I never knew exactly who I would be until I got here: shy and coy, loud and rambunctious, dramatic and mysterious? I leaned against the metal pipe and considered the party unfolding in front of me, regarding my potential options.

I heard it before I saw it. That staticky, deep boom. People don't really talk that loud.

The humans had left the TV on.

The color and light captivated me. The flash between the seams of each show, each commercial. I flew in a daze from the party down to the shallow living room coffee table, wooden and topped with a thin crumble of some sort of cake. The humans were always leaving treats around: a raisin dropped on the floor; popcorn kernels, half popped; new houseplants, untreated and rife with greenflies. But no treat was more delectable, to me at least, than when they left the TV on.

No one loved the TV more than I did. Sometimes, my friends and I would jump on the red rubber button at the top of the remote control, all at the same time, to try to turn it on. It would take about fifteen of us. One out of every ten or so tries the TV would actually click to life. But it was hard exercise, and my friends were, for the most part, pretty lazy. No one cared as much as I did about seeing what movies were on. I could change the channel by myself sometimes if I really focused, but the power button was big—it was hard, and it was risky to be out there in the living room for too long. We really weren't supposed to. So, it didn't happen often. The best was when a human fell asleep on the couch, or even better, walked away with the TV playing at full volume.

That night, it was left on a channel I hadn't seen before. I was immediately absorbed by a talking yellow square and pink star. I had never seen anything like it.

It was a while before I realized someone was standing next to me. I wasn't sure how long Jessie had been there—it seemed like more than a few minutes had passed. He looked at me and smiled, mouth closed, and then looked back at the TV, chewing something.

It wasn't my first time seeing him: we met at a birthday party last summer. I know we did, but I couldn't remember talking to him. I could barely remember seeing him. It occurred to me that he had been standing next to the person that had been standing next to Isaac, and I had thought Isaac was cute. I had gone home with Isaac.

But now as I was looking at him, I wondered if Jessie might be cute too. He looked serious, a bit angular. He looked like he had been really skinny previously but recently started working out. Maybe a personal trainer or something. He looked a little nerdy, but also seemed very calm. He walked over even closer, stood next to me, smiled, and did not say a single word.

I looked at him. Okay, I thought. Is he . . . are you . . .

The silence was nothing at first. Truly nothing. I tried to focus back on the bright moving image in front of me. But I knew he was there, and I couldn't stop thinking about that fact. As his silence persisted, it grew. And as it grew, it became electric. It grew until I was vibrating. I could smell it. I could feel it pulse under my nails. I started jiggling my joints to release some of it, but then I needed to release some more.

I went for drama.

"So. I heard you had a crush on me."

Jessie laughed, his clear eyes twinkling. He looked straight into my soul and said, "Who'd you hear that from? Because it's not true. Gross." The smallest hint of a smile.

"Oh, I think it is. I only heard it from," I thought quickly of some of Jessie's closest friends, who had mentioned to me that Jessie had been single for far too long and indicated that he thought I was pretty. I said each name as it popped into my head: "Just from Patty. And Gibson. And Jules. And Sammy."

Jessie smiled softly. I was impressed by his composure. If it had been me, well. I tended to wear my heart on my sleeve. My face would have been bright red, my heart racing. Jessie was placid and relaxed and confident.

"Well Patty. And Gibson. And Jules. Must have lied. Because I never said that."

He leaned back. We were quiet again. My thoughts started to expand and wander, racing to fill the silence. "But I did see you over here and think you needed this," Jessie said, handing me an aphid cocktail. I took it with one hand and pressed two legs onto the remote. I got the channel to change without spilling.

"Oh my god. Have you ever seen this?" The camera panned across a scene of skiers and a piano plonked out a jazzy vamp. I recognized it immediately.

Jessie's face was a question mark. He sipped his cosmo.

"You have to see this, it's my favorite," I said. A hand holding a pistol—I knew it wasn't real—stretched out, pointing right at Audrey Hepburn's oversized sunglasses. I took Jessie's hand and explained the plot too quickly, laughing and doubling back to point out Audrey's perfectly pursed lips, the pause before surprise registers on her face, what she knows but isn't telling. Jessie didn't look back at the TV for another hour.

I HEAR THE CLOCK ticking on the wall, tick tick tick, louder than our music. I can't tell what time it is, because it has Roman numerals. But it's so dark outside. I know it won't be morning for a long time.

The walls of this house are blue, and the floors are made of wood with wide gaps in between each slat. Some of us like to live down there. The hairline cracks at the junctures where the wall meets the ceiling: some of those are really comfortable. My spot is in the closet, though. They say this house is cozy—the humans say that. It is small and old and far from any other houses that we can see. I heard the humans say once that we are three hours north of New York City by car, and I did the calculation: four years by flight. Impossible for insects our size.

The humans can come and go as they please. We never really know when they are leaving, or if they leave, how long they will be gone for. They forget food on the counter, food in the pantry, food in hanging wire baskets over oak cabinets. They flick the lights on, and they flick them off. They forget to turn the lights off, and it's a big problem. The warmth, the glare pulls us up. We want to be in it. It's not something we can control. We have to play in it, to soak it up, to flutter near it, to expose ourselves to the brilliance. It makes us visible. Vulnerable.

There is no sound outside the house. The lack of sound around us is complete and muffling. It's like a giant glass jar had been set down over us, blocking out any reverberation. I think about the frothy pink glass behind the wood, keeping us in—safe. There is a velvety layer of dust coating the fine leather furniture that is too fancy for anyone to sit on. We all like the old fabric couch in the living room, or even better, the antique lace curtains on the windows upstairs, the shining southern windows every morning that are bathed in the fresh, early sunshine and stay warm all day long. A puzzle is unfinished on the coffee table, and there are books no one had ever opened on the shelves. The family who owns the house is here, in bed. In the morning, they will wake up and begin with their incessant noise. Banging pots and buzzing phones.

There are hundreds of us here. We stay mostly in the walls, where it's safe and damp. There is so much space in between the walls, but we tend to stay close together in groups, crawling over and around each other in giant roundabouts, all day and all night. We whisper secretly to each other. But it's an open secret. There are so many of us, we spill out onto the baseboards, the lampshades. We march behind the window shades, along the crown molding. The humans know about us, but not the extent. The smallest human has a bedroom upstairs and lies on the floor and counts us. I heard the older humans say they think we complement the vibe.

I LOOK OUT THE window. Snow is falling outside, dropping thick and wet. I catch my reflection in the dark window, winking from the strobe lights behind me.

Seven spots, clearly defined and all of equal size, perfectly scattered across my body in an even, consistent symmetry. My body: red and shiny as a gem, a high-peaked dome like a sphere cut in half, now shuddering and jiggling with the deep tones of the party music. My eyes: naturally dark, set off by my electric scarlet coat, so bright it's startling. The way I swing my abdomen when I fly.

I'm used to people telling me I'm beautiful. I am, empirically, sexy. It is not a secret. It isn't like there is much competition. Everyone agrees. I look good, I am young. People still think I look young.

I USED TO SPEND hours in front of any mirrored surfaces I could find. There wasn't much to work with. The back window at sunset. The TV screen was reliable when it was off, and I was by the TV a lot. Sometimes, if I looked really, really hard into the thick metal butcher knives hanging on the wall, by a force like magic, I could almost make out my reflection. Moving in the same way I moved, a fuzzy, blurry mime. I would arch my back to try to see my contorted appearance in the brass door knobs. The angle was important. I learned young that I couldn't stand directly on the surface, craning my head down, unless I only wanted to see my belly, my legs—all six of them. But if I lay flat, perpendicular, I could admire the thin jacket of spots resting on my back. I could practice my expressions, the exact faces I would make in any given moment. Be my own audience.

I am always looking for an audience, and Jessie knows that.

JESSIE AND I LOOKED for Agatha. We watched TV for hours. We would jump when any ads came on with our favorite flowers. Once, we watched a French movie where the lead actress wore black and white stripes and a red beret and red lipstick. She looked sad, but she cried with her actions; her eyes remained dry. When she got mad, she screamed with her whole body.

We were inseparable. We never saw Agatha.

WE TALKED ABOUT ALL the wackiest, most far-fetched thoughts we could muster, challenging each other to go further. When he guesses my dream, I surprise myself and actually admit it. I hadn't said it out loud to anyone, not since my mom.

"You seem like a natural performer," he said. He said he could see me under a spotlight on stage.

"It's stupid," I said, unable to look up from the ground. I could feel his eyes on me.

"It's real," he said.

He daydreamed with me about finding an agent, getting my own show one day. His confidence in me radiated out, and I was starving for it. His energy propelled me. Every story I told, every word I said was the exact right word at the exact right time. With Jessie, my timing became perfect. My embellishments sparkled with a clear purity; they became truth. I believed it all. The others did too. Everything I said landed harder: my jokes were funnier, my critiques were smarter, more scathing. My expressions became better, sharper, attuned to my stories. I was rehearsing, and he knew it, and he helped me.

He held my hand when I couldn't sleep at night.

AFTER THREE WEEKS, JESSIE proposed the trip. On a date one night, he showed me the place in the kitchen where the window wasn't flush with its sill below. At the very corner edge, the screen lifted up. If we tugged at it a bit more, we could just walk out. The snow was heavy on the ground and the wind whipped lashes across the walls. It would be dangerous—

The excitement moved so quickly through me. It started at the tip of each leg and throttled up through my abdomen, landing in my center and glowing, pulsating. The warmth filled me up whole. I could see the future crystallize before my eyes. I could see it; for the first time I could see it so clearly and tangibly. The things I wanted to do, to be, the things I was never brave enough to even name, matured from my imagination into real options, messy and loud and possible and true. I could see time unfurl in front of me like a red carpet, rolling all the way to my dreams. I could see a suitcase packed with time, overflowing with days and hours we could use however we wanted. The space of a whole world I hadn't seen, folded up and stuffed inside, zipped up and ready to go. Ready for me to take.

NO ONE WOULD EVER understand why we would want to leave this house. We knew that.

We got here so long ago. I don't think we meant to stay here forever, but generations have passed and no one really knows for sure. The rumor I believe is the one where it was a total mistake: a couple flew in an open window one brilliant autumn day, then the house was closed up for winter and our numbers grew. We kept expanding. The sun was sunnier inside, concentrated through the windows and spilling long across the floor for us to bask in. There was plenty of food inside. It was warm and cozy, filled with blankets, pillows, crevices to shelter in. "We are indoor ladybugs!" was the refrain repeated throughout our colony. We eat, stay hidden, lay eggs, repeat. The comfortable and quiet life.

It's different from outside. It's not the birds' claws or frogs' tongues we hide from in the house; the threats are less constant, but more gruesome when they do occur. An unseen shoe falling from the sky. A newspaper carelessly tossed toward the bin that hits the wall instead. A hastily drawn curtain. A body, dropping down too fast. A heavy grocery bag plopped on the floor, on top of Raoul. Marianne—that one was sad. She was really young. She liked the TV too, and had crawled onto the couch one day when a movie was left playing. It was an action film, with lots of flashes and fighting and swords and backflips. I think someone even flew. She was perfectly hidden along the edge of a thick shag rug, even though no humans had been around for hours. It was a formality to be so well hidden; she had followed every precaution perfectly. But then the human man ran in, laughing and faster than any of us could have seen, the thrust of his whole weight burying Marianne so far into the looped fabric, we never found her.

Then there was the day when the bee flew in the house. I think about that a lot. It was summer, and the humans left the door open. They were running around outside. A lot of us had gone outside foraging too, but we knew all the bottom entrances from the gaps in the foundation and holes in the floor. We never used the door. The door was risky. But through the door, on a warm swell of wind, flew a large, humming black sphere, jetting inside with a loop-de-loop. It was fuzzy, round, and as heavy as a raindrop.

Jessie and I had been on the floor, sharing a snack in a poorly swept corner, but we were transfixed: we dropped our mites and stared. We didn't know what it was at first. It was louder than a saw. It twirled and rose and fell, effervescent. It was thrilling to watch—the others all stopped what they were doing to see. It zoomed and dived, the buzzing intensifying with each turn around the room, every so often thumping into the ceiling it didn't expect.

It happened quickly after it landed on the glass. The bee paused for a second on the glass, and then slid down fast. We could see what it was thinking so clearly; we could see it wedge itself down in between the panes, overlapping in the open window, thinking it was an exit.

We hadn't been able to see its wings before. Before, it was just a shooting sphere, a dizzying fat blob. Trapped between the glass, its wings were pinned to its back: they were freckled with black and brown dots in all sorts of shades and sizes, tortoiseshell. Wings closed, it was a piece of bark, a fallen leaf. Close up, the dots were mesmerizing, rich and intricate. If you looked too long, which we did, your eyes crossed.

There were about fifteen seconds of intense buzzing, the whole body shivering violently. Then quiet. Then again. It tried so hard to fly, with wings so thick and strong, twice the size of its bouncy body. You could tell they'd always worked before. It twitched its wings slower and slower, and then would start back up. Then it would pause its wings but run its legs, scrambling with such force, all six of them working at once, so, so fast. Another round of fierce tremors, trying to fly. But its wings couldn't open. It couldn't gain traction, the glass slippery as ice, as it tried to climb up. Not that it would have mattered: even if it had been able to ascend the two vertical inches, we could see the helplessness of the next step. It would never have been able to squeeze itself straight up between the overlapping sills again.

It tried unwedging one wing, but then the other went down lower. It turned around, then turned onto its back, then went parallel with the floor, moving as it could. It fought for hours, trying to climb out. It moved all the way to the left wall, and then all the way to the right. Then we saw it was just the first two pairs of legs scrambling and fighting. We can't turn our heads. We just wait. It shimmied in deeper and deeper. It tried to fly out again.

It was so loud. The buzzing.

It was a shock when it stopped moving.

Jessie and I stood trembling, holding each other. We couldn't do anything. Even the humans wouldn't have been able to do anything, if they had noticed.

IT WAS HARD TO leave, even if you wanted to. Dense layers of pink fiberglass packed the walls, impossible to penetrate, tangled and sharp as barbed wire. The windows were mostly sealed shut, and we couldn't turn the doorknobs. We were enclosed in solid insulation and wood. It was even harder this time of year. The cold would freeze you solid if you were accidentally blown out. Stupider bugs had wandered out in the winter for the thrill of it, for the quickening of the heartbeat, only to scurry back before passing the icicles hanging from the roof. Some flowers were frozen; others buried under new hills of frost. Best not to leave, to stay hidden and alive. Best to cling to the dusty corners, hover behind overlooked ledges in the bookshelf and gaps behind electrical outlets. Best to stick to the mites in the wood and in the upholstery. Best not to risk it. We were indoor ladybugs.

But. There was something out there waiting for me and Jessie. And we were going to get it.

I HAD NEVER SEEN Agatha Martin on TV. I don't think my mom ever did either. But I heard her shrieking with delight one day when she was listening to the radio. The interview with Agatha, she said, had ended just seconds before I crawled into the room.

It had happened before, she said. Agatha Martin, the first ladybug actress, discovered in LA. She told me Agatha had starred in commercials at first. TV ads for things like detergent and toothpaste. She was cast in a soap opera as a sexy cleaning lady. But she had worked hard, honed her craft. She became known for her comic timing. She got bigger roles, played more powerful women. She was on *Inside the Actor's Studio* after her run as Lady Macbeth, after she starred in a feature-length film, after she starred on Broadway. This was all a long time ago, she said. But it meant it could happen. For me, she said. If I got to New York, if I got to audition. I could do it too, she said.

My mom had stars in her eyes.

THE NEXT DAY, I flew over to the kitchen sink, the secret spot Jessie and I had agreed upon to start our journey. I had eaten a large meal, fuel for the flight, heat to burn. We were going to start the flight to New York City. Together.

But Jessie was not there.

I waited.

Jessie did not come.

I sat alone in my silence. I wondered what could have possibly gone wrong, what I could have done wrong, what I missed. Had I come on the wrong day? I went over and over our conversations, scouring them for my misunderstanding. For the part of the plan I had gotten wrong. I started wondering if I had made up the whole plan inside my head, one epic daydream. I became very warm and uncomfortable.

Eventually, who did come was Mark, an elderly insect with an unnecessary country twang—no one else had one. After absentmindedly nodding at my rushed and nervous excuse for being out so late, he spotted the hole and jammed it up with a wad of cotton he was carrying.

"There," he said, wiping sweat from his brow and heaving from the effort, "finally fixed that window. Won't be so drafty in here anymore."

THE NEXT TIME I saw him, Jessie looked different to me. I couldn't really tell you what it was. Sometimes his eyes looked closer together than normal. Sometimes his body seemed taller, broader, like I was looking at him through a warped piece of glass.

I was nervous to ask him what happened. Someone else had needed him, he said. One of his sisters needed him to babysit. She had a brood of 700 and growing, sequestered together behind a dusty old oil painting of a regal-looking dog—a banquet of mites—all the way in the study. He was so sorry to have missed our meeting, he said, finally meeting my gaze. Piercing me. There wasn't really anything for me to say.

I went back to my closet.

I was overcome with exhaustion. I was cold and stiff. The walls around me were unbearable, rigid. Way too close to me. My view floated up to the ceiling, watching my body below. My breath caught and I forced it out; I wanted to cry but I couldn't. Trapped and lonely and camped in my own shell. My eyes barely opened. I didn't want to see anyone; I didn't want to fly anywhere.

At first, my mind was completely blank. My brain was quiet, and in the silence my dreams drained out of me, dripping off of me, these things I had carried—that I had been prepared to carry so far. The future dissolved from my brain: the future, a delusion. I deflated into right now. There had only ever been right now, this moment, this day, the same as all the other days. All those months that had passed, identical to the dwindling number of months I had left. Of course we were really just stuck here. Of course we were like everyone else.

All those possibilities. Dreams. I couldn't stand it.

I needed more than that. And I needed it fast. And I wanted it to be exciting.

So, eventually I got it, with Travis. And Calvin. And Elijah.

When I told him, Jessie didn't see my rationale that it was just a stage in my life. Hormones! Who could control them? Plus, our life span! Already half gone! So, we might as well do as we pleased. He didn't buy any of my attempts at explaining. He said it wasn't an open relationship if I had decided that on my own.

So, he had ended it, breaking my heart.

MY MOM USED TO tell me not to think too much about my looks. She said I should focus on my talent. My craft. She said I had talent. She used to laugh and laugh: I would mimic every single person in our family, larva to pupa to oldie. Every mannerism, every vocal tic. I could do anyone, perfectly. Her favorite was when I imitated my uncle Frank, who could never really walk in a straight line because he was always a bit drunk off wood resin. She told me to chase it.

Chase it where, I think, taking another sip of my drink. Can't chase anything if you're stuck upstate, a lifetime away from Broadway, at a shitty party with the boyfriend who is becoming more of an ex-boyfriend every passing minute.

The music changes. A crowd emits a squall of laughter. I think about how many more drinks I can have before I lose my capacity to fly. I drink again.

Talent? Who knows. But I know I have looks. And, tonight, I know I want attention. Attention, I can get. Now. I down a shot of whiskey for courage, to get my juices flowing. I can feel myself heating up just thinking about it. The winter had been so long, the week had been so long, this night would be so, so long. I might be good at acting, but I know I am good at one other thing. So, tonight, I decide, I will be really, really good at that.

"HEY, MIRANDA, YOU GOOD?" Phillip waddles over to me at the bar. One of the wider ladybugs of the group, Phillip doesn't get out much. He counters his social insecurity with boisterous jokes he releases at inopportune moments and without true aim, often laughing at his own work loudly and alone.

I raise an eyebrow. "I could be better." I glance at him from the side of my eyes. "Want to sit with me for a while?" Phillip starts laughing to himself self-consciously and snuggles in close.

After Phillip, there is Ross, Claude, Karl, Noah, and Federico. Then I take a break. I clean myself up and walk through the carpet for a snack, aching. The possibilities, I groan to myself with sarcasm. The possibilities are endless.

I close my eyes and focus on my favorite fantasy. I am starring in a Godard film, dolled up like Anna Karina, lipstick and bangs and everything, but with dots instead of stripes. I ride to the top of the Empire State Building, and the camera zooms in on my face, flushed with cold and laughing at the exhilaration of seeing the view for the first time. A handsome stranger kisses me. God, I want to be kissed by a handsome stranger. To even encounter a stranger.

"I HAVE GOT TO get out of here," I say quietly. My voice is an echo across the room; it comes from my face but sounds far away. I hear myself, and I agree. The heat of the room has entered inside me, and I'm finding it hard to breathe. Think. My legs prickle. Maybe I would try walking in front of Jessie again. The thought alone makes me feel desperate to disappear. It's getting harder for me to exhale without focusing very, very hard on the practice.

And then—lights flash!

The sun is rising. The light switch flips on. The male human brings a suitcase on wheels down the stairs. The female human, yawning, brings down three more bags, hoisted over her shoulders, and opens the front door. The sharp relief of frozen air washes over me.

The female goes back up and carries down the small human, who is floppy with sleep and sucking her thumb. She walks to the car again, straps the small human into the car seat in the back, and leaves the car doors open. She runs back into the house, into the kitchen. She grabs a mug of coffee and an armful of coats.

The party has gone silent. Our group shrugs down lower on the wood slat wall, making ourselves less obvious, though we're still crawling all over each other.

"Miranda, you comin'? Ha, ha," Phillip shouts. The ladybugs around him groan.

I barely hear the crude joke, my mind filled with quick math and calculations. I am staring at the front door, inching closer and closer. The window of time will be short . . .

The door opens. I shoot out of the open front door, stars in my eyes. I fly across the icy steps and over the short stone wall, into the car's waiting back door.

"What the hell was that?" the mother says, trying to wave her hands, which are weighed down with more canvas bags. She ducks her head around the corner. "Jesus Christ, Paul. We need to spray for these."

Strapped into the car seat still is the little human. "Oh, how pretty! How pretty, little buggy. One, two, free, four, five, six, seven. Seven dots, seven dots. Will you be my friend? Stay here, little buggy, stay here and come back to the big city with us."

# The Dog in the Desert

## Stephanie Anderson

THERE ARE 1,000 VILLAGES IN AFGHANISTAN'S KANDAHAR province, which means there are 999 villages in which Matteen Sahar might have been born besides Nawala. But a birth anywhere but Nawala was impossible.

Matteen's great-great-great-grandfather fled Kabul for that rural village in the Arghandab River Valley when British soldiers arrived in 1838. It will be so green, he told his wife, Meena. Much better than dusty Kabul. There will be grapes and apricots, fresh goat milk, and a garden. You can learn to grow eggplants, yes? Meena did not want to leave her family, and the moment her feet crossed the border into Kandahar province she curdled like old cream. She told everyone how shameful it was for her husband to have fled Kabul. Well after Meena died, the story lived, planted its roots in the family memory, its message as unquestioned as the call to prayer. Generations of Sahars grew up hearing about the family exodus, which grew more dishonorable with each retelling.

So, when the Soviets came in 1979, the Sahar family did not think of fleeing; they stayed in Nawala. The civil war continued after the Russians withdrew, and Taliban recruits began knocking on doors, but still the Sahars stayed. In 2001, when Matteen was five, his parents saw photos of burning towers in a newspaper carried from Kandahar, and a year later they watched American tanks roll down the valley, right through their precious Arghandab River. They will not be here long, his parents said. They talked about buying more sheep with the money stored behind a faded drawing of Meena and her husband, sketched before the couple left Kabul. Even then, Meena had looked sour.

In truth, Matteen was not born in Nawala exactly, but a mile outside the village on the floor of his family's house near the wide, crawling Arghandab. Here was home: this valley oasis in the desert, where on terraced hillsides farmers grew grapes and okra and pondered the hazy beige mountains in the distance. Home meant walls of dried mud, a hard-packed dirt floor, an orchard of pomegranates and apricots irrigated by centuries-old ditches. It meant a flock of sheep that drank from a spring gushing out of a gray cluster of rocks above the river. To Matteen's parents, home was their son, with his close-cut black hair and voice that had not yet dropped low. He was an only child; a fever his mother caught days after he was born damaged her womb, or so everyone believed. At nine, Matteen conceived of home much as his parents did, with one important addition: Rasa.

"Little one-ear," he had cooed to her when she was a puppy mouthing his fingers and waddling like a duck between the rows of onions. "Too good for two ears, right? You don't need the other one." When she was just a few days old, a rat bit off most of Rasa's right ear; it healed but was reduced to a nub that swiveled. Rasa's mother must have found this deformity unforgivable because she abandoned the puppy shortly after. Matteen found Rasa curled in a ball along the road as he and his father were pulling a cart of wool to the market. Her tan coat blended so perfectly with the grass that Matteen would have passed her by if not for the white circle of hair on her ribcage. Matteen thought the white marking made her different from the street dogs that lurked in the market stalls and sometimes chased him. Three years later, when she would run ahead of him and suddenly stop and look back as if to say "hurry up," he loved how the white circle stood out against the dun landscape like the moon against the night sky.

Most days he and Rasa followed the sheep as they grazed the rocky hillsides. School had stopped when the Americans arrived. Matteen wore an ankle-length wool wrap the color of unwashed potato skins, and he carried a stick in case of snakes. Rasa followed suit, carrying some stick or bone in her mouth that she soon dropped in favor of newer, more interesting sticks and bones. Matteen sat against boulders, looking for coyotes and American troops. If he saw Americans, his mother warned, he was to run home and not look back. Matteen had seen soldiers in the village—they gave away candy, but his father said he couldn't have any—and what he remembered most was their loudness: their shouts echoing down the alley, their Humvees roaring through the square, their boots stomping the road.

Matteen wasn't worried about the soldiers, despite the way his mother's face went white when they marched through the orchard one afternoon. They did not seem to be doing much, just driving and walking. He mostly watched the lambs that scampered up and down the hillsides. Rasa slept nearby, or went sniffing, or chewed on the carcasses of rabbits or hedgehogs. Occasionally Matteen whipped a stick into the air and Rasa scrambled after it. If a ewe wandered too far from the flock, Matteen pointed and said, "Go get her!" Rasa's one ear pricked forward and her brown eyes roved until she spotted the ewe, and then she bounded over rocks and washouts to steer the lost sheep back to safety, her white circle of hair bobbing through the brush.

THE ARGHANDAB RIVER VALLEY was indeed the oasis Matteen's great-great-great-grandfather had imagined. In Kabul he had been a cloth trader, but within a generation the Sahars became shepherds and farmers. Matteen's father inherited a mature pomegranate orchard and wheat seeds that represented a hundred years of selective breeding for taste and suitability to the valley soil. Here the land was green, and the Sahars forgot the dust of Kabul. When Matteen was seven, he had asked his father for a corner of the garden plot. *I want to practice farming*, he said. This year the corner was mostly carrots. Matteen loved the smell of wet soil and sweet carrots together; he would pull up a carrot, hold it against his nose, and breathe in. To him it seemed like anything would grow by the shores of the Arghandab, and he was right.

For danger had sprouted in the valley. Men with guns came to the Sahars' house. They did not ask for tea. They asked for money, food, and sons.

Start teaching your boy, they advised Matteen's mother. Tell him what he will enjoy in the afterlife. At night she begged Allah: either rid Nawala of these people, or make Matteen stay a child forever. When rumors spread that the Americans planned to kill every boy in Afghanistan so there would be no more jihadis, Matteen's mother slid a knife into her drawer of saris. She would rather kill Matteen herself than let the Americans or the Taliban do it.

Day after day Humvees muddied the Arghandab River. So much back and forth, the farmers complained. The Taliban fighters burrowed like field mice into underground dens. By day, American soldiers patrolled the villages. By night, Taliban fighters dug holes along the road and laid bombs inside. Life on the Arghandab moved both slowly and quickly. Peasants toiled on among the grape vines. Boys followed flocks to the spring; girls helped their mothers make yogurt from cows' milk. But underneath these slow movements was fast-moving fear, which made even the smallest task—getting a bucket of water from the well, buying a pomegranate in the market—feel dramatic, because occasionally someone died while undertaking such things.

WHEN TALIBAN FIGHTERS CAME to the Sahars' door one night, Matteen barely heard them crack the copper lock with a gun butt and glide into the living area. The yellow curtain separating Matteen's room from the main room parted. He saw the silhouette of a turban, a long robe falling from broad shoulders, and an arm holding an upright machine gun. The man swept through the room, looking up and down, pulling Matteen by one arm from his mat, patting the thin wool mattress with the gun barrel, then shoving him back down again.

Rasa leapt up and bared her teeth, but the man raised his gun as if to strike her and she backed away, silent but staring. The man called out, and soon another man led his mother in and sat her next to Matteen. "Cover your head," he said, and she pulled Matteen's blanket over her hair. The man kneeled next to his mother, cuffing her forearm with the most enormous hand Matteen had ever seen, the three of them sharing Matteen's mattress, so close their shoulders touched. While the man conversed with the other strangers, his mother turned her head and, disguising her words as a sigh, said, "Do not speak a word."

Now everyone was in his bedroom, his parents and six turbaned men. Two were teenagers, their legs like sticks poking from their robes. The older men spoke a language Matteen did not recognize, and he realized his father was speaking back to them. He never knew his father spoke anything except Pashto and some Dari. With one finger he stroked Rasa's head and felt her trembling. He saw his mother's hand purpling under the man's grip. Matteen thought his father seemed to be pleading. There was silence, and then a slow, single nod of his father's head. He sank to the floor and set his face like stone.

The men stayed the night. The teenagers dozed, but the man next to his mother sat cross-legged and awake. Matteen and his mother lay on their backs, moving to and from sleep like sheep move to and from a stream on a hot day. Eyes dutifully closed, Matteen wondered what would happen in the morning. Would his mother make them tea? Would they let his father milk the cow? Or would they lurk in the house all day like cockroaches under a bed? Surely someone would ask why Mr. Sahar was not in his orchard, why little Matteen had not turned the sheep out on the hillside. Maybe the men would leave, or maybe they would take him away as they had taken Abed, an older boy from school. Abed's family, it was rumored, had spoken against the Taliban.

Matteen felt an irresistible sleep coming, the kind he felt when sitting against a sun-warmed rock in the afternoon. He was sleeping when the house door opened near dawn, this time flying off its hinges and crashing to the floor as men wearing helmets rushed inside. Americans! Matteen could see only their boots under the curtain. The turbaned strangers yelled in their odd language and pinned their bodies against the walls. One of the teenagers lunged for a gun and was immediately shot in the forehead, the bullet passing through his head and right through the curtain. Rasa leaped in the air at the sound and screeched like a wounded pig. She jumped over the dead teenager and tore through the yellow curtain and out the door, triggering a shout of alarm from the Americans and screams from Matteen, who jumped after her but was held back by his father.

The house rang with gunfire. Matteen and his parents crawled to the wooden trunk on the far wall and cowered behind it, the same trunk Meena had packed with her embroidered dresses and scarves all those years ago. Matteen felt like his head was being hammered again and again with stones. On his belly with his parents covering him, he watched one turbaned man fall, then another, and another, each leaking blood. He didn't know blood was as much black and purple as it was red, or that human blood had the same cold smell as that of butchered chickens. Then the Americans strode in, guns against their faces. It took less than a second for the heads of the last two turbaned men to explode against the mud wall.

In the same instant, Matteen felt what he thought were flames on his leg. "I'm on fire!" he wailed. The faces of the turbaned men were a mush of red, black, and white—and so was his leg. There was so much noise—his mother's shrieks, his father bellowing about a doctor. The Americans were silent except for the one speaking calmly into a black radio. A booted man stooped to look at his leg, and the moment he touched the wound Matteen thought this man, too, had burst into flames, so bright was the orange-red color that framed the man's body. The red and orange of a desert sunrise hot in his eyes—that was the last Matteen remembered.

THERE WAS A BOY in the house we raided last night. He got shot; I'm not sure who did it, but it was an accident. Just a little feller, had a dog with him. John read the words and knew he shouldn't have written them. Shouldn't have even thought them, because thinking about shit doesn't change it so why go there, his platoon leader would say. Because Rangers do the things other people don't have the guts to. John used to think he had guts, back when the only living thing at the end of the barrel was a steer that needed butchering. He thought he was tough because he could saw off the head, open the ribs like a stiff book, and pull out the intestines. The lessons of his South Dakota farm were not enough for Afghanistan. Neither was Ranger School. Perhaps there was no way to prepare for the guilt of killing a human being, even an enemy, only a way to train the eyes and hands to carry out the motions. To train the face to remain stoic.

The strange thing was, when John looked at the letter a few days later, he didn't remember including the boy. He did recall writing to his wife as the sun boiled over the horizon, hot like the magma of Kilauea he'd stared at on their honeymoon. He'd been mesmerized by the fact that death could slide by in slow motion. In Afghanistan death was fast. You couldn't see it coming. Even as he sat against the beige tent and wrote, the notebook against his thigh, he kept one ear pricked for death. He remembered writing about the spices in the markets, how the women kept them in barrels with the tops open, scoops resting on the yellow, red, and brown powders. He would send salt, he promised his wife. She collected exotic salts: black lava salt from Hawaii, citrus flake salt from Cyprus, coarse pink salt from the Himalayas. Somehow the boy from a few hours earlier had made it onto the blue lines of the wide-ruled paper, not long after his promise of salt.

Of course John could not send the letter. All mail was censored; sometimes whole sentences and paragraphs disappeared under a strip of black ink, and his wife would have to imagine what unsuitable words lay beneath. John wished they had developed a secret code before he left. Something silly: shoe stands for boy, run means shot, tree means I. Then he could tell her that the boy (had he shot the boy?) would likely be an amputee, if his parents could afford to take him to a hospital. If not, the boy would probably die. The medic had whooshed in with his camouflage backpack, shoving

John aside, who was crouching over the boy's leg and touching the purple flesh (this touching disturbed John later). There was a family dog, too, that had blasted out of the bedroom during the firefight, yowling and scaring the whole platoon. And there were men withered like dead leaves on the floor, so many they took up most of that small room. He felt guilty about the boy, but only a little guilty about the men, and that difference was like a nettle endlessly poking him.

The medic had gotten as far as a tourniquet when the call came to move, move. The boy's mother had grabbed John's leg as he walked by and held on with wolf-like strength. No one had ever clung to him like that before. You shot him and now you're leaving him to die, she screamed. That's what John figured she'd said, as he wrote his wife. He thought of his wife on their ranch. It was winter there, and she would bring hay bales to the cows with the old Farmall 560 and use an ax to chop the ice in the water tanks. She would wear her stocking cap in the house when a three-day blizzard came and cut the power. He thought of her muscled arms and her confidence and wondered if she might be better at being a soldier than him.

This is the first time our squad's hit a kid. It happens to everybody, so I guess tonight was the night. In the letter he had tried to make it all right. His training, he realized. But how could a man write something and not remember it? He tore the paper from the notebook and wadded it into a ball. He wondered whether the rules had anything to do with security—maybe everyone was working together, from his platoon leader on up, so that no one would remember anything about this war, especially not a boy's wails that could follow you down the valley on the long, silent march back to base.

A DOCTOR AMPUTATED MATTEEN'S leg just above the knee. In his morphine dreams, Rasa flew out of his arms and into the living room, the curtain flowing behind her and her white spot flashing. Then the room went red-orange and the curtain caught fire like a fuse. When the flames reached her head, it detonated like a roadside bomb, just like his leg and the heads of the Taliban men. She could never have escaped, he thought from his bed in the Kandahar hospital, with its green apple walls, traffic honking several stories below, and beds filled with patients. When he was awake, which was only a few hours a day, Matteen looked at his mummified stump and thought that part of his heart must have been blown off too.

Something about food—maybe its gelatinous feel, or perhaps its color in some cases—reminded Matteen of dreaming about Rasa's exploded head. When a nurse placed a bowl of soup or a plate of rice and vegetables before him, bile rose in his throat. Beets were the worst. His mother begged him to eat the boiled potatoes that she held to his lips, and out of pity he sometimes swallowed. Matteen knew Allah wanted him to obey her, but pleasing Allah suddenly felt useless. Matteen had always been an obedient son, mostly to avoid punishment but also because he liked making his mother happy, but now he had a stump. Obedience did not matter. He grew thin as a lamb. The doctor warned that if he did not eat then he would never go home, but Matteen thought it would be nice to stay at the hospital forever, where night nurses kept watch and bars over the windows protected him while he slept. There were even armed guards at the entrance.

A volunteer medical team from the United Kingdom arrived to fit him with a prosthesis, to his parents' relief and his utter disinterest. Allah be praised, you will walk again, his parents said. Hopelessness covered like him a wool blanket. A British therapist came daily, wearing white T-shirts and khaki pants and pushing her blonde hair out of her face. She was always fanning herself and sweating. She put her hands under his armpits while he stood. He stared at the stump dressed up with the fake leg and commanded it to move. Nothing. After two days he stopped trying, whined that he was doing his best, but the leg was stubborn. Inside he felt like a newborn kitten: blind, helpless, most interested in sleeping.

His father asked the doctor every day: When can Matteen-jan go home? An uncle was tending the sheep, orchard, and fields, but a farmer troubles over his crops as if they are his children.

Matteen's mother worried they would run out of relatives and friends in Kandahar to stay with. Matteen thought his parents were different people outside the valley. At home his father knew the precise day to cut the wheat with the scythe, and his mother could make Kabuli pulao from memory. Here they fretted over whether to ask the nurse for fresh sheets and how to locate the next friend-of-a-friend's house and whether to bring a gift they could not afford. They quarreled, something they rarely did at home. Nothing was the same.

After two months the doctor said go home, maybe the boy will do better there. He is wasting away here. The British therapist handed Matteen's parents a list of exercises to strengthen the muscles and help with coordination. He should be walking better by now, she said, but there is still hope. She took Matteen's hand and said in her broken Farsi, "You must not give up. You are a special boy." On the dusty ride in the packed bus, his parents asked if he was excited to see Rasa. He nodded but said nothing. They were pretending, something he'd come to realize adults often did.

When the Sahars returned home and his uncle said he had not seen Rasa, Matteen did not cry or even search for her. He did not go to the garden to tend his carrots or follow the path to the river to watch the minnows play among the rocks. He stayed inside on the mat, fingering the place where flesh ended and hard plastic began and looking at the maroon and black stains that his mother could not remove from the rug.

JOHN'S WIFE ONCE ASKED him what a mission was like, and he said it was like a pack of wolves hunting caribou on the Discovery Channel. Well, not exactly, he acknowledged. The Rangers weren't preying on the weakest members of the herd, so to speak. Still, John thought the comparison worked because of the platoon's pack-like mentality and the way he felt when stalking through valleys and alleyways: powerful, homed in, senses jumping, eyes glowing through night vision goggles. They killed for survival, not sport. They took fire almost every time they left the base. For missions lasting longer than a day, they dug foxholes to sleep in. Sometimes they slipped into a house and flex-cuffed half a dozen Taliban fighters before the captives realized what was happening. Other times they hunkered down on a hillside for a daylong firefight. "Small unit tactics" was the official description of their work, but to John it was the effort of a pack: a decisive leader, members who understood their roles, a clear objective.

But once, just once, they had relished the kill, caught in the relief of being alive after an especially brutal ambush with hand-to-hand combat. They were wading through chest-high grass in the irrigation ditches along the Arghandab. John's foot touched something that was not mud. He felt with the toe of his boot, trying to figure out what it was, and then a Taliban solider shot out of the water, a dripping knife raised. Five more men sprang up like fountains. The Rangers tackled several of them to the ditch bank, and after some punching and choking managed to shoot them with side arms. Two others they drowned. When the last fighter slumped under the water, the Rangers experienced two minutes of madness: howling with M4s pumping the air, feeling the urge to rip apart a dead man. The feeling later embarrassed John, haunted him even, but no one spoke of it.

Today's hump to a weapons cache ten miles upriver from Nawala would be nothing like the irrigation ditch night, John hoped as he trudged up the valley, though lately he felt little certainty about anything, especially himself. He tried to find the wolf-like state. A hot wind whooshed down the valley, so loud it muffled the crunch of pebbles underfoot. It sucked the strength out of him. John thought his muscles must've shrunk, like Popeye without his spinach. As a test he held his arm out in front of him, and it felt like holding a gate against an angry cow. A few minutes later, he stumbled over a rock and landed hard on one knee.

"You all right, man?" asked the soldier behind him.

"Yeah," John said, wincing as he stood up. "I'm good." He stepped off the narrow footpath. "Gotta fix my boots." His boots were already laced tight, but he needed a way to hide the tears. When John was prepared for pain, he could bear almost any amount—he fractured an ankle on day forty-nine of Ranger School and the next morning marched twelve miles with a 115-pound pack—but surprise pain almost always brought tears. He bent over and slowly retied the boots. As John stood up he saw something white move against the dun hillside above. He squinted, unsure if the white thing was real, then he saw it clearly, this time under the brush. He jerked his gun to shoulder and shouted, "Movement three o'clock!"

The men drew into a circle like magnets around a pole, facing outward with weapons poised. "Fido, northwest, one hundred yards," someone called.

"Hold," the platoon leader said.

John looked for the dog, but he saw only the blotch of white slip between two large rocks. A turban? Then he realized the patch was attached to something beige, and suddenly a dog's body materialized, like Waldo from the children's books. He had always been terrible at Where's Waldo. John cursed and lowered his gun. "Stay alert, boys," the platoon leader barked. John cursed again—his stupidity was alarming—and retrained his gun on the animal, which was trotting toward them.

The dog had one good ear. The other was a stub of white cartilage and pink skin. It reminded him of the baby calves in South Dakota whose ears froze during blizzards and fell off a month later. Every year it happened to a few unlucky ones. The dog's other oddity was a white patch of hair on its ribcage—the flash on the hillside. Like a piebald horse, John thought. Most of the street dogs were brown or black, rarely with distinguishing features. The dog stopped twenty feet away. It didn't move, just gazed at the platoon, panting open-mouthed as if smiling. John wasn't sure what to do; the platoon leader held a radio next to his mouth but said nothing into it. "Kinda weird for it to be this far out," someone said after a minute. "Looks mangy."

John studied the dog. It had the long snout, pointed ears, and height of a German shepherd, but the shape and hair of a Labrador retriever. Its mutt look reminded him of a childhood dog, a yellow Lab/golden retriever/Australian shepherd mix named Sparky.

Sparky could jump into the back of a pickup truck without lowering the tailgate. Once he hitched Sparky to a red Flyer wagon and pretended he was farming with a horse-drawn plow. John had seen probably hundreds of stray dogs in the province, and this was the first time he'd thought of Sparky. Suddenly he felt like a jerk for leaving his wife alone on the ranch. He should have bought her a dog.

"It's just a fucking dog," the platoon leader said finally. "Let's go."

WEEKS AFTER RETURNING TO Nawala, the Sahars were still putting their house back in order. They found bullet holes in their clothes, shards of glass in the walls, shell casings in a shoe. Almost every item suffered damage save for one: Meena's picture. It hung straight from its nail, her face as stern as ever.

It would have been understandable for Matteen to blame the Americans for murdering Rasa. But after turning ten and feeling quite grown up for having been shot, he took a more nuanced view. Maybe the problem was not the Americans or the Taliban, but Nawala. Lately the valley seemed hot and dusty and the sheep smelly and mean. His father had missed the pomegranate harvest while in Kandahar, so the fruit rotted under the trees, beckoning rats and flies. To Matteen the Arghandab was a long, muddy slug. The village people stared at his prosthesis and talked to him as if he were a toddler. His mother fussed over his food (which he still wasn't eating), how the shoe fit on the fake foot, and whether he would like to sit under the banyan tree instead of in the house. Rasa's death was the worst. No matter where he was, he felt like someone had kicked him.

Matteen missed the hospital: the lull of carts rolling in the hallway, the guard at the door, the clean bleach smell. In Nawala he felt exposed, like a baby bird fallen from the nest, but in the city buildings rose up and protected him. Traffic, television, and shouts in the street drowned out the silence that made him remember exploded heads. He wanted to live in one of the grand high-rises he'd seen from the bus window and walk on streets bustling with people who did not know him or generations of his family before. He could be just another boy with a prosthetic leg, not worth a second glance, and Meena would be a picture on a wall, nothing more.

How to get to the city? For months he considered this. The family had no mule, and Matteen had no money of his own to buy one. He thought about jumping on the bus that shuttled people over the mountains every morning. Older boys did that; he'd seen them clinging like spiders to the back of buses and trucks. But how could he leap onto a moving bus? While running he felt out of control, as if his severed leg answered the brain commands of someone else. Usually he fell after a dozen strides. One day he tried jumping over the narrowest canal in the orchard, a test for jumping on the bus, and fell in. He scrambled out, embarrassed though no one was there. He and Rasa used to sail over the canals, but now his body was as useless as the rotting pomegranates.

"I am going to leave Nawala," Matteen announced that night, though he had no idea how. He could still smell the canal water on his skin. "I want to live in Kandahar."

"What are you saying, Matteen-jan?" his mother asked, stroking his forehead. "Are you ill?"

But Matteen suddenly couldn't explain all the thinking he had been doing about leaving. He knew his family would never consider leaving Nawala, that it was shameful to even mention it. Matteen's vision blurred with tears, and he hated the boyish weakness of having to wipe them off his cheek.

THE RANGERS DID NOT return to the Arghandab River for several weeks, and John forgot about the dog. So, when they found it lying under a eucalyptus tree along the bank, they were surprised that it was still in the same place. At first it looked dead. John knelt by it—a she, he discovered—and saw the white patch moving up and down, but slowly. Her ribs lay in neat, visible rows under her skin. She opened her eyes, but she did not seem to see John and the other men looming above.

John wasn't the only one to feel sorry for the dog, and it was a group decision to set her on the medic's snap-together stretcher and carry her back to base. But it was John who organized the smuggling of MREs from the chow hall and petitioned his platoon leader for an industrial-sized bag of cream of wheat, which he thought was gentle but nutritious enough to help her gain weight. It was John who bartered for an extra blanket to make a dog bed and fashioned a collar and leash from the straps of his backpack. He took a bucket from the shower station to serve as a water bowl and located a soldier who had done a brief stint in veterinary school back home. He wrote to his wife to send dog food and demanded that everyone else do the same. And it was John who named her Rosa.

At first Rosa did nothing but sleep on the blanket, only waking when John carried her outside to pee. He knew it could never be true, but she seemed housetrained; she never relieved herself on the blanket or, when she healed, in his tent. She seemed to know not to chew on his things or jump on him or bark at people, but John figured she was grateful for being rescued. She learned her name almost instantly and how to fetch on the first try, so he thought she possessed exceptional intelligence. It never occurred to him that Rosa might have had an owner, because in Afghanistan no one owns dogs. They are dark figures in alleyways, silhouettes against the sunrise at garbage dumps, pairs of eyes reflected in a spotlight.

John began taking Rosa on simple missions in the Humvee, delivering a load of dehydrated meals to a school or riding backup for a resupply of ammunition and water to a mountain outpost. Then she went on foot missions, jogging alongside like his shadow. She went with him to the latrine, the football games played at sunset, and the mess hall. John and his ugly one-eared bitch, the men joked. We won't tell your wife you're fucking a dog, they snickered. John laughed along as he always did. It was something he'd never gotten used to in the military, how people could say words like cunt, nigger, and ass-fuck with the same nonchalance as coffee, lightbulb, or pencil. In South Dakota conversations were kind. Even if you hated the person, you still wished him or her a good day.

In five months with the platoon, Rosa misbehaved only once, when they were marching through a pomegranate orchard along the river. Up that path is the house where we shot the boy, John realized. Suddenly Rosa froze with her good ear pointed and sniffed the air, then darted out of the trees, baying like a hound after a fox. The platoon leader gave the "Stop" signal, then shaded his eyes to say "Look" and touched his ear to say "Listen." Ripe red pomegranates hung like Christmas ornaments. In the cool shade, John listened to Rosa's howling turn to sharp, angry barks. The smell of rotten fruit wafted up and made him think of oversweet communion wine. He assumed Rosa had spotted a rabbit, and he hoped she had cornered it because the dog food he was expecting hadn't arrived.

"That dog is gonna get us killed," the platoon leader whispered. "Go get that fucking thing before—"

A bullet whooshed over the platoon leader's head and struck a pomegranate, detonating a bomb of red juice, seeds, and peel. The men fell to the ground and belly-crawled to the nearest tree. John scuttled so furiously that his nose, lips, and chin dozed the dirt, and he flopped against a trunk looking like he had dipped his face in an Oreo pie. More bullets. He realized exactly how slim the trunks of pomegranate trees are, barely the width of a person.

The platoon leader mimed a plan, and the men advanced from tree to tree. Rosa's barks diminished, and when they reached the orchard's edge John could see her thin tail waving from behind a stone wall. She had something. One by one the men hopped over the wall. John could see imprints in the dirt where four people had lain on their stomachs roughly ten feet apart. In front of each shape, a stone had been removed to make a small embrasure. Shell casings littered the ground. Rosa paced back and forth, sniffing the imprints and barking, pausing now and then to stare north, her ear swiveling.

MATTEEN PLANNED FOR KANDAHAR in secret. In a hillside cavern he cached travel supplies: a cup and bowl stolen from a restaurant in Nawala, a map of Afghanistan he'd been given at school, a knife that folded into itself that he found in a gutter, and a burlap sack that once held onions. He resolved to steal more along the way.

Matteen had never stolen anything before the cup and bowl, and it had felt horrible, but he could see no other way.

He figured out how to get to Kandahar: a wool truck. They came to Nawala once a week to gather wool for the Kandahar cloth makers, chugging empty through the square and leaving filled to the top with layers of gray-white wool. Sometimes Matteen and his father brought a cartload to these trucks idling in the alley and his father haggled with the driver over the price. Matteen remembered the ladders on the sides and how the trucks sat for half a day or more until they were full. Matteen figured he could climb in when no one was looking and settle in under the wool. Once in Kandahar, he would find the hospital—this might be difficult, but he would ask a friendly looking person for directions—and tell the doctor his leg hurt. He would say his parents had sent him alone because they could not afford to come. He would pretend very well, crying if needed, and would "heal" very slowly. When his parents did not come for him, he would be allowed to stay in Kandahar. Where and with whom he did not know, but an opportunity would present itself, he reasoned.

Matteen knew he would miss his parents, and he prepared for this by telling himself that it would feel like missing Rasa or his amputated leg. Every day there was an emptiness, a not-the-sameness, an overwhelming loneliness, but no matter how severe these feelings were he remained alive. Missing something could not kill him, he had discovered. He worried more about his mother, who would think her only son was dead or kidnapped. Matteen comforted himself with thoughts of returning to Nawala when the war ended. He would explain everything and there would be no more fear, no more sadness. He would adopt a new dog and farm alongside his father when he was a man and no longer afraid.

The day before he planned to leave, Matteen hobbled up the hillside and packed his supplies in the burlap sack. He added four shirts and a pair of pants—all the clothes he owned—and looked over the valley for the last time. The sheep drank from the river and the breeze rustled the apricot trees. The little house stood with its mud walls and grapevines and garden. He understood the valley much as Meena had: an isolated place where unknown dangers lurked, where the safety of the city and its throngs of people were far away over the mountains.

JOHN BEGAN TO THINK Rosa went after the guerrillas in the orchard because she knew they were dangerous. Maybe something about their smell or voices. She never chased or barked at anyone—not the children in the villages, not the farmers in the fields, not the local tribal leaders who came to the base for talks. She had to have known something about these men . . .

For John had become consumed with knowing. Knowing who was an enemy and who was a friend, who was wearing a bomb, who meant well when waving at the Humvee. Because knowing these things was impossible, he was in a constant state of anxiety—nervous to the point of tears when riding through a village, paranoid to the point of pulling the trigger when he saw families on the path by the river. In a two-week stretch, the platoon lost five men to an IED and then accidentally shot two Afghan children that their targets used as shields. After an especially frightening day—the platoon had provided security in a larger town while a government leader visited, an event ripe for suicide bombing—John played fetch with Rosa in the orange glow of the desert evening. Rosa's one ear flopped as she ran after the stick that he threw over and over without thinking. In his mind he was in the orchard for the hundredth time, seeing Rosa tear through the low-hanging branches laden with bright ruby pomegranates. He remembered how she had looked after the vanished men, growling.

Rosa dropped the stick at his feet and looked up at him, her mouth open in what John took as a smile, her tongue dripping saliva. She knew, he decided. Somehow she knew. What that meant John wasn't sure, but it made him feel better.

"KANDAHAR: 50 KILOMETERS" READ the sign that flashed by as Matteen peered between the truck's wooden slats. Finally the truck was on the road after two extra hours in Nawala while the driver fixed something under the hood. Those two hours felt like two days to Matteen, who had scrambled into the truck box when the driver went for a plate of rice and shaved lamb. He'd huddled under the wool, the sheep-shaped blankets stacked like naan, and played his plan over in his mind: hospital, leg pain, promise parents will come, parents never show up, someone will offer a place to live.

The engine bogged down as the truck entered the mountains that Matteen had gazed at all his life, the exhaust pipe shooting out black smoke that made him cough. Under the wool it was unimaginably hot, a contingency he had not prepared for. He was forced to sit against the slats for air. At least he could see where he was going. He rationed sips of water from his father's canteen (stolen early that morning) and watched the valley below shrink, then disappear. A few miles out of Kandahar, traffic clogged the road. Teenagers wove through the cars on motorbikes, and street vendors sold Coca-Cola from coolers strapped to their chests. Matteen burrowed into the wool to avoid detection and listened to their calls. Cold beverage, refresh yourself, drink up. They sounded like songs.

At dusk the truck lumbered into the city and parked next to dozens of other trucks behind a warehouse. Matteen would wait for the driver to leave, then hop out. Just like in Nawala, only in reverse. Instead the driver flung open the truck's end gate and a flurry of hands grabbed at the wool. What was this? Matteen scrambled backward until there was nowhere else to go. The workers pulled out the last stack of wool, and Matteen put on his most defiant stare as they uncovered him.

"A stowaway," a worker cried. Matteen did his best to look tough, though he had the newborn kitten feeling. "Who dares take a free ride from me?" the driver said, jumping into the truck with clenched fists. Matteen glared up at him, this man he encountered in the market almost weekly, a frequent buyer of his father's wool. It had been stupid to pick this truck, he saw now. Even in Kandahar, a city of almost half a million, he could not avoid people who knew him and his family. "I know you," the man said, squatting down. "You're from Nawala."

The man said he would bring Matteen home. Matteen wasn't sure whether to tell his parents the truth or to lie, say he had climbed on the truck for fun and had fallen in accidentally. Either way it did not matter, he realized. He understood now that when he grew up he would be a farmer and care for his parents until they died, and by then he would have a wife, also from Nawala, who would not want to leave her family. His children would be born in Nawala. He would die in Nawala. The hopelessness he had felt in the hospital returned and he started to cry. It wasn't the Kandahar high-rises he cried for, or even the fear that awaited him at home, but the thought of Meena's portrait.

I CONTACTED GUARDIANS OF Rescue, John wrote his wife. It's an organization that brings dogs back from war. I learned about them the other day. They can't guarantee they'll get Rosa home, but they said they'd try. All we can hope for, I guess.

John was going home in two months. For good. He was not signing another contract, though the platoon leader had said (off the record) that not signing was dishonorable. John had walked away. He could go down as the most dishonorable Ranger in history for all he cared. He looked at Rosa, lying upside down with all four feet in the air, sleeping with her mouth open. One hundred thirty-nine missions, he had calculated a few days ago. That's how many they had done together, and they were still alive. Why test Rosa's knowing more than he had to?

John, this man consumed with knowing—if only he could have known that he would, in fact, return to his farm in Sioux County, South Dakota. One day a van would pull up to his white two-story farmhouse. Snow would blanket the prairie. He and his wife would be riding in the pickup checking the cows, the heater blasting, country songs on the radio. The smell of hay would fill the cab, and he would be more in love with her than when he'd left for Afghanistan, and she with him. He would have nightmares, flashbacks, and a few unexplained disappearances, and he would be unable to butcher the steers, but after some years he would feel almost like the man he'd been before Afghanistan. They would have decided to stay in Sioux County forever, where generations of their families were buried in a hilltop cemetery along the highway. They would feel as if they never had a choice in the matter, but that would feel comforting.

From the pasture they would see the van coming down the gravel road and drive to meet it. They would hold hands in anticipation and say, today is the day, our family will be complete. By then they would know that children were biologically impossible. John would stand on his tiptoes, trying to see in. The van's sliding door would open and a tan dog with a white patch on her ribs would jump out into the snow, shaking off the long ride.

# Tarzan in Decline

## Richard D. Key

"DOCTOR LATE. TARZAN GO."

"You will do no such thing. We've come all this way to speak with Dr. Schumann and that's what we'll do."

Jane, dressed in a simple khaki dress, and Tarzan, attired in a little-used dark brown suit with a white shirt and slender black tie, sat in the Douala office of Dr. Gregory Schumann waiting for the internist to arrive from his rounds at the hospital. He had been kind enough to take on Tarzan as a patient in his thriving practice as a favor to Jane, who had once been an acquaintance of his parents back in London. After nearly an hour of fitful anticipation, the good doctor arrived. They stood to acknowledge his entrance.

"Good afternoon. So sorry to be running late, but the clock seems always to be my enemy. And you must be Mr. and Mrs. . . . uh."

"I'm Jane and this is my husband Tarzan. I'm afraid we haven't bothered with surnames, although mine was once Parker, of course. We live in the jungle where things are simple."

"I see. Please be seated. Yes, my parents were very fond of the Parkers, as I recall. So, I'll simply refer to you as Jane and Tarzan if that is preferable. What brings you into the city?"

"Lately, Tarzan hasn't quite been himself," said Jane. "Actually, for some time he hasn't been his usual vigorous self. And perhaps it's to be expected at his age. I just want to be sure it isn't something serious."

"And how old are you, Mr. . . . er . . . Tarzan?"

"Tarzan younger than sky, younger than mountain."

"Yes, of course. But, how many years since you were born?"

Jane jumped in. "I'm afraid we don't know his exact age, doctor, but I would estimate between sixty-five and seventy."

"I see, and what is your age, Jane?"

"Jane younger than sky, younger than mountain."

"I see. Yes. So, what would you say is your main problem, Tarzan?"

"Tarzan good. Tarzan strong."

The doctor looked at Jane for direction.

"Well, doctor, Tarzan's correct. He is strong. Very strong for a man of his age, but his vision doesn't seem to be quite as sharp as it once was, and his reflexes are definitely not as quick. Why, the other day we were gathering fruit when we were charged by a rhinoceros and barely escaped being trampled."

"Tarzan just trying to buzz Jane."

"Well, you certainly buzzed me all right. I hardly slept that night."

"Tarzan need thrill. Jane just want to gather food and look at sunset."

"Is that true?" the doctor inquired.

"Well, I suppose so. These are our twilight years. Ever since Boy left the escarpment it's been difficult to regain the feeling of freedom and excitement that we once had there."

"Boy?"

"Yes. Our son. He lived with us until he was about twenty-five and then took off to see if he could make it in civilization. He started out as a safari tour guide. Now he's selling cars at a Hyundai dealership in Capetown. We haven't heard from him in months."

"So, you have no one else to look after you if something should happen?"

Tarzan shot in, "Cheetah like friend."

"Cheetah?" Jane turned to her husband. "Cheetah couldn't care for a tsetse fly in his condition." She turned toward Dr. Schumann. "Cheetah is our faithful chimpanzee who has lost all his teeth. I have to spoon-feed him mashed bananas and coconut milk."

"Well, at least you have each other. You'd be surprised how many people are absolutely alone in this world. Now, Tarzan, I'd like to run some tests if that will be all right."

"Tests? No run tests. Tarzan go."

"It won't be painful in the least. And I can assure you that everyone loathes going to the doctor. That's one universal truth—humans and animals alike. But you have nothing to worry about." Dr. Schumann called on an intercom for his assistant to come in.

"Heidi is my assistant and will draw the labs. By the way, have either of you been to a physician in the last ten years or so?"

"We sometimes go to one of the witch doctors of the Nyongo tribe," said Jane, "but you couldn't really call them physicians. They have some ointments and teas and things of that nature, but it's not what you'd consider real medicine. It's closer to quackery, I suppose, but it's better than nothing at all."

"Well, Tarzan, we'll start by drawing some blood and sending it to the lab. Then we'll check your temperature, blood pressure, and I'll listen to your heart and chest."

"No. Tarzan not need test. Tarzan go."

"Tarzan, dear, you're being unreasonable. The doctor only wants to make sure that everything is all right. There's no reason to be frightened."

"Tarzan not frightened."

"We'll need you to remove your coat, if you don't mind, Tarzan," the doctor said once he began to sense a spirit of cooperation. "That's good, and your shirt as well. Very good."

"My," said the doctor. "You really have a dearth of body hair. And clean shaven too. I imagine the jungle is not the easiest place to get a close shave."

"I told Tarzan when we fell in love that I could not tolerate a hairy torso. Man of the apes, fine, but hairy as an ape, no. I make sure he has a sharp razor, and I pluck his chest and back hairs. I refuse to be married to an orangutan."

A few minutes later Heidi entered with a tourniquet, a syringe, and some tubes. Tarzan held out his tanned arm.

"May I look at your hands, Tarzan? You have perhaps the most calloused hands I believe I've ever seen."

"Yes," said Jane. "He swings through the trees hanging onto vines."

"That's remarkable. Truly fascinating. I say, would you mind terribly if I took some photographs of your hands? This may be the world's first documented case of vine-swinger's palm. I'll just wager we could get a case report in *Lancet* with those hands, Tarzan. What do you think?"

Dr. Schumann proceeded to photograph the jungle man's roughened palms, during which he asked Jane if she ever used this mode of transportation.

"Well, certainly. There's no better way to travel through dense jungle than hanging on to vines. Of course, it does take some getting used to."

"But if you fell, it could be catastrophic."

"I suppose that's so. I try not to think about it."

"I really think you need to have a bone density study done, Jane."

"A what?"

"It's to see if you have osteoporosis—thinning of the bones. I really think you could use calcium supplements to make your bones stronger. And a mammogram wouldn't be a bad idea either."

Jane became quiet and pensive as she looked at the tall building outside the window.

"And I think both of you should be tested for parasites with your constant exposure to the outdoors and unclean water."

Slightly flustered, Jane said, "Well, certainly, Doctor Schumann, if I needed a doctor for myself, I wouldn't hesitate to find one. But I'm in excellent health and haven't personally seen a medical doctor since I was a child."

"Well, there's no time like the present. Since you are here with Tarzan, we may as well look you over too, and draw some blood work."

"There will be no need for that," said Jane as she gathered her things and stood. "Darling, put your clothes back on. The doctor is very busy, and I think we've taken more than our fair share of his time."

"I'm sorry if I overstepped my bounds," said Dr. Schumann. "I just thought it might be more convenient than coming back in the future."

"I think we've found out enough for today. Thank you very much for your time."

"But—"

Looking back from the doorway, she said curtly, "Jane go. Tarzan go."

With that, the aging couple exited the office and made their way down the stairs to the lobby and out to the sidewalk.

"You know, Tarzan," said Jane, "I may have been too quick to dismiss those witch doctors. I'm sure a lot of what they do really does help people. They don't seem all that bad after all, the more I think about it."

"Witch doctor better for Tarzan."

"Yes. I think witch doctor better for Jane too."

# Short Synopsis of a Life

Marina Datthyn

When I was nine
My best friend's mother
Smoked cigarettes, flirted with the piano,
Devoured novels, and
Occasionally
Polished the silver.
My mother was older and
Did not do
Any
Of those things.

When I was nineteen
I departed for California
To nurse soldiers back to health.
Boys my own age,
Home from the war.

When I was twenty nine
I donned a champagne-hued
Satin dress
And married a pilot who
Refused
To wear sunglasses.
He wanted to take me up
In his turbo prop
But I said, No, thank you.
I knew he would do
A loop-de-loop.

When I was thirty nine
I gave birth for the third time—
A daughter (finally).
Our 35th president was inaugurated—
A Catholic (finally).

When I was forty nine
I did nothing
But smoke cigarettes, trifle with the piano,
Feast on novels, and
Occasionally
Polish the silver.
I was a marvelous mother.
It was in that year I announced
My decision
To quit drinking.
Previous to this
I glutted myself
On exactly two Brandy Alexanders per year.
I have not touched alcohol since.

When I was fifty nine
My nursing experience called me
To a methadone clinic
Where I handed out strong opiates
In paper cups
To people who were addicted
To stronger opiates.
The same faces daily—
They had become dreadfully dependent on
The substitute.
One morning
Another nurse brought in brownies.
She warned me
Not to try them.
I didn't.
But
I'm not stupid, you know.

When I was sixty nine,
The pilot
(My love)
Got sick.
He died.
He used to tell ridiculous jokes
Of the "If you don't pull the shades down,

I'll be seeing you" variety.
I would roll my eyes
And cluck my tongue at him.
He gave his body for research.
But there is,
In the Bristol Hills,
A memorial site.
He would have liked the view.

When I was seventy nine,
I became a great grandmother.
I wondered about
The life this child would live,
The wars she would endure.
She was one eighth me.
She had my nose.
I wondered if,
At least an eighth of the time,
She would think or act like me.
Would she read voraciously,
Or dabble in music, like me?
I wondered
Just how much of her life I would witness.

Now that I'm eighty nine (!)
I'm curious
About the difference between
Texting and tweeting.
I'm reading Fifty Shades of Grey
And I'm not a bit scandalized.
I like
Burnt toast with butter
And coffee, black,
Every morning.
I've become fabulous at cooking
For one.
But I don't enjoy it.
I still read and smoke cigarettes,
But I don't play the piano at all,
And I no longer own any tarnishing silver.
I concoct my pink Jell-O
For every family gathering,
Because it is always requested.
I adore white birch trees.
My home is perfumed perpetually with
Lavender, sandalwood, and patchouli.

I no longer attend church regularly,
But I think of God rather often.

When I am ninety nine
I may have to stop driving.
I will wear an awful lot of leopard print.
Cigarettes will still be killing me.
My doctor will not necessarily approve
Of how often I indulge
In apple crisp.
My granddaughters will receive an early inheritance—
My jewels.
I'll work up the nerve
To throw away
My old tax returns.
I will not play Bingo.
I will write down my Jell-O recipe.
I won't be old
Or sad
Or done.
I may fall deeply in love.
He would have to be at least
A hundred.
I won't bother
Finishing novels
I don't like.
Many stories will come out—
Some true.
But I won't tell them all.
That would feel too much like
The end.

# Yusuf's Wedding Celebration

## Rosie Cohan

TEARS OF JOY, TEARS OF SORROW

I called Yusuf on his twenty-ninth birthday in 2015 and he had a surprise for me. "My family has arranged a match for me. I can't wait for you to meet Fatma," proclaimed Yusuf. "You must come to our wedding celebration!"

Tears of joy streaked my cheeks. "I wouldn't miss it."

I HAD MET YUSUF in Sultanhamet Square in Istanbul, fifteen years before his wedding day. He approached me and softly asked, "Madame, do you speak English? Would you practice English with me?"

The fourteen-year-old had slicked-back hair, flashing hazel eyes and a somewhat oversized nose, which had been broken in a soccer game. He was all legs and had a bright smile. Something about him seemed different from the streetwise touts who offer you tea to get you to visit their rug shops. There was innocence in his voice and sweetness in his shy manner.

He told me he began studying English in school. "But we don't speak in class, I learn to speak from tourists." He then proceeded to say hello in English, Japanese, German, Italian, Spanish, and French. Having just received my certificate to teach English as a second language, I thought it would be good practice for me and for him. So, I said he could accompany me for a few minutes and we would speak English.

Just then the call to prayer sounded and his smile clouded over. "I am sorry; I must go pray. Can we meet again?" I was impressed he wanted to go to the mosque when the soulful call of the muezzin sounded. I told him I would be at the Hagia Sophia, the church built by Justinian in the sixth century, turned into a mosque by the Ottomans, and now a museum.

When I exited the museum, Yusuf was sitting on the steps below. We walked and talked using sign language to supplement his broken English. He would point to things and I would tell him the English word, and then he taught me the Turkish word. He was an excellent guide escorting me around the Old City. Most people around the square knew him and would smile, wave, and shout hello to him. I could tell he was well liked, and I could understand why. He had a quick wit and radiated a fun spirit.

My tour ended outside his brother's shop. He introduced me, and his brothers invited me to sit on a square embroidered tribal rug to share a delicious eggplant stew with them. They thanked me for helping their little brother. They had high hopes for him to go to university someday. As I left, I was surprised they didn't even try to sell me a rug.

For the remainder of my time in Istanbul, I met Yusuf daily for tea and we practiced English. For over fifteen years of almost annual visits to Turkey, I continued these lessons with Yusuf. He grew into an intelligent and determined young man. I helped pay for more English lessons back in Van, his hometown in Eastern Turkey, and had him come visit me in California. Over the years, I became his "American mom" and he my "Kurdish son." Yusuf accomplished his goal of graduating university and became a National English Tour Guide. He also was getting a master's degree to teach English.

On one of my trips to Turkey, I stayed with his family in Van, a Turkish-Kurdish city forty kilometers from the Iranian border. Even though they spoke no English, his mother and sisters became my dear friends. We picked fruit from the trees in the orchard and vegetables from their garden. We cooked our meals together. On the hot afternoons, we sat in the garden drinking tea, while a peep of chickens paraded around us. We kept trying to communicate and laughed a lot. When my basic Turkish and our pantomime failed us, Yusuf's mother would summon him to translate for us. The three sisters took turns giving me handknit socks and scarves they had made. They lovingly dressed me in their traditional embroidered dresses, like a Kurdish Barbie Doll. I was showered with love and adopted as one of their own.

When I arrived in Van on a steamy day in July 2015 for the three-day wedding celebration, Mustafa, Yusuf's eldest brother, greeted me at the airport. We drove to the family compound, which had been in a rural area but now was filled with modest box-like cement houses. Yusuf's parents and brothers' families lived in separate houses on their property. The larger parents' house has a communal kitchen. There is a large cement courtyard closed off from the street by a high, sliding, solid metal gate. Behind the main house and the smaller dwellings was a large garden, abundant in vegetables, fruit trees, and chickens running freely.

Yusuf's mother and sisters hugged and kissed me. His father waved; his strict Islamic beliefs wouldn't allow physical contact with women other than his family. A gaggle of elf-like children wrapped themselves around my legs squealing, "Hala, Hala" (Auntie). I felt like a celebrity, but more than that, I felt I belonged.

Yusuf returned home after dark, exhausted from delivering wedding invitations to the neighborhood. Showing traditional respect for elders, he kneeled, kissed my hand, and then we hugged. Worry was etched on his face.

"I am so happy to see you. Unfortunately, our wedding celebration will now be two days, not three. Tomorrow is a day of mourning for Kurds killed and wounded by ISIS suicide bombers in the town of Suruc on the Syrian border. The Turkish government didn't stop ISIS from crossing into Turkey."

I understood why this tragedy would be felt by all Kurds. As a tribal nation without a designated country of their own, Kurds are connected to one another by blood and a culture that knows no geographic borders.

The next day, Mustafa drove me to the busy downtown to buy a gold coin, the traditional wedding present. At dusk, heavily armed policemen poured out of long white vans. Whistles blew. People scattered. Confused and frightened, I was paralyzed. Mustafa quickly led me to the car explaining the PKK (the Kurdish paramilitary organization) had killed two Turkish policemen who were complicit in the bombing of Suruc.

"Today, Prime Minister Erdogan ended the peace treaty between the PKK and the Turkish government." Mustafa suspected Erdogan used this incident as an excuse to punish Kurds whose political party won enough seats in Parliament to thwart Erdogan's party's majority and, therefore, Erdogan's unilateral control of the government. We retreated to the safety of the family compound, but I didn't sleep well that night.

Early Saturday morning preparations for the weekend were in full swing. Yusuf's father, a retired chef, directed the roasting of eighteen fleeced lambs rotating on spits suspended over crackling fires. Yusuf's uncles stirred cauldrons of rice with paddles resembling boat oars. The smell of chopped dill and mint permeated the kitchen as Yusuf's mother and sisters added them to pails of homemade yogurt. Yusuf's cousins hammered poles into the ground and attached a giant canopy to shield guests from the blaring sun.

Filling the patio, garden, and adjacent streets, approximately 600 relatives and tribal members began arriving for the Henna Night celebration from all over Turkey. Yusuf's sisters and cousins served hundreds of glasses of cay, Turkish tea. Despite the heat, women wore long-sleeved dresses decorated in beads and sequins that sparkled like amethysts, sapphires, rubies, and emeralds. Rows of gold bracelets spiraled up their arms, and gold necklaces and belts shimmered in the light. Some wore black velvet headdresses covered with mini black pom-poms. Colorful scarves edged in coins framed radiant faces. Long tresses hung low on slender backs. Dark eyes outlined in black kohl were in contrast to eyeshadows in shades of green, blue, and gold. Children in frilly party dresses and tiny three-piece suits followed me around begging me to take their picture with my telephone and show it to them.

Animated in conversation, men of all ages sat in small groups. Many wore Western suits, while others had on the traditional short khaki jackets, matching pants, white shirts, and black cummerbunds. Some had spent time in Turkish jails for demonstrating against Turkish repression, and looked older than their ages. One cousin arrived in camouflage battle garb directly from fighting ISIS in the Syrian mountains.

Midafternoon, the multitudes gravitated down the street to the open field and gathered under the large shade canopy. Soulful music began with the twang of a lute-like instrument called an oud, then other traditional instruments joined in. The crowd wrapped their pinkies around their neighbors' and danced grapevine steps. Everyone was connected as one community in a long, winding line. As the pace of the music increased, feet picked up speed. Stepping on forgiving toes, I awkwardly joined in.

Fatma and Yusuf arrived to lively music and clapping. They sat on red velvet throne-like chairs that matched Fatma's red crinoline-framed gown and thick lace veil, both adorned with sequins. Someone put a red, yellow, and green Kurdish flag over their shoulders. As is tradition, Yusuf gave Fatma a gift box, and then Fatma's sisters lifted her veil. The couple led more dancing.

Later, I joined the women escorting Fatma back to the house. Using a gold coin, Yusuf's mother dabbed dark green henna soaked in fermented tea onto the bride's palms. We then smeared a circle of henna on ours. Customarily, Fatma's relatives shrieked cries of mourning in this bittersweet ceremony. This was the last night Fatma would be living in their home, and marked her transition to married life within Yusuf's family.

Holding candles, we led Fatma back to the field in a procession. On stage, Yusuf's sisters sang and yelped in tribal calls as they presented their family's gifts of gold belts and jewelry to Fatma, welcoming her to their family.

The next day, the men ate first and then went alone to the wedding field. As a foreigner, I was allowed to attend the "gifting meeting." The tribal leaders, the couple's fathers and eldest brothers sat at a table in the center. As the heads of families offered their gifts of money and gold, an emcee announced the amount each family gave to the couple, calling the highest values first to raise the ante.

After the meeting, everyone joined the festivities. Most of the women were in the same jewel-colored dresses and gold jewelry as the day before. The men also seemed to just change their shirts. Fatma, in a white Cinderella gown and handcrafted lace veil, entered with Yusuf, who was wearing a white shirt, blue tie, and suit. His face reflected pride and exuded more than his usual joy. Applause, music, and dancing erupted. Relatives threw brightly wrapped candies at the couple and into the crowd, while screaming children dived for them. Turkish delight (squares of soft, fruit-flavored candy with nuts) and tea were served. At a table decorated in a colorful embroidered cloth, a red-robed judge presided over the signing of the wedding contract. Guests lined up to congratulate the newlyweds.

Tears started to pour down my face. It had been an emotional day, but that was not why I was crying. I was weeping from the clouds of tear gas burning my eyes, sneezing from the acrid smell in my nose, and coughing from the smoke burning my throat. The deafening clatter of a helicopter hovering overhead drowned out the band. I didn't understand an announcement made in Kurdish. But more tear gas and water cannons assaulted the neighborhood. Men yelled. Children cried as their mothers screamed out their names.

Sightless and frightened, I reached out. One of Yusuf's cousins led me to the family compound. I heard the solid metal gate slide shut and the steel bar slammed into the latch, locking out the chaos.

Someone gave me a damp cloth for my eyes. Yusuf was comforting Fatma. I approached. "Are you all right?"

"Yes. This is our life. Sometimes when police would see a Kurdish gathering at night, they attacked with tear gas, water cannons, and massive arrests to force us inside, even though we are Turkish citizens. Now that the ceasefire between the PKK and the government is over, this will happen more often."

"How long will this go on?"

"Only Allah knows."

Minutes later, we heard rapid gunfire, followed soon after with yelling and banging on the metal gate. Breathless, four cousins ran in. The helicopter had fired at them as they disassembled the canopy. Luckily, no one was hurt.

I sat in tears overcome by sadness for Yusuf, his family, his people. History has dealt cruelly with the Kurds, abandoned by allies, and oppressed throughout the Middle East.

The next morning, I visited Yusuf and Fatma at their hotel. We didn't mention the tear gas or bullets. I ordered ice cream sodas and toasted them. "May your life together be a new beginning filled with love and peace."

They both responded, "Inshallah." God willing.

SINCE THE ATTEMPTED COUP in 2016 against Erdogan, the oppression of Kurds in eastern Turkey has gotten worse. In a recent phone call Yusuf told me Turkish forces, looking for members of the PKK, bombed his uncle's home. Suat, his eighteen-year-old cousin, was arrested on a bus returning home from a wedding because he had attended a peaceful protest the week before. He was sentenced to six years in prison for just exercising his right to free speech. Yusuf had heard there was some ethnic cleansing happening in southeastern Turkey. He asked me why the world says nothing. I had no answer for him.

Yusuf is unemployed as tourism has died in eastern Turkey because of the coronavirus and the government's war with the PKK. His life is waiting: waiting to work, waiting to start a family, waiting and hoping to have a normal life someday.

During a call this past spring, I was both angry and ashamed speaking with him about the withdrawal of American troops from Syria and our abandonment of our Kurdish partners with no warning. I then heard loud on the other end of the call banging on the metal gate of the compound, and Fatma shouting for Yusuf.

"Stay safe. Don't lose hope," I said quickly.

He replied with a Kurdish proverb: "Patience is bitter but bears sweet fruit."

May the sweet fruit ripen, and Yusuf's harvest soon begin.

# On Sawyer Mountain

Erica G. Craig

IT HAD BEEN A WHILE SINCE I HAD THE KIDS ALL TO MYSELF. Andrew gets more alone time with them than I do. My traveling for work leaves me away a few nights most weeks. I'm jealous of the time Andrew gets with them. Doing whatever he wants. Being the sole influencer, keeping the house as tidy as he preferred, or in his case as unkept as he'd like. I used to appreciate that he scuttled about cleaning up and vacuuming before I got home, but I've grown to resent it. It's like everyone has to get things in tip-top shape for the Queen's arrival. It's me that he makes them clean for. Not because Andrew runs a tight and tidy ship, but because their mean mommy would eventually return, and she's the one who insists on a clean house. In other words, my appreciation for the clean house has morphed into resentment for the way in which he gets the job done.

Recently McClain wrote a persuasive essay about his unearthly desire for a Pomsky. A Pomsky is some undoubtedly yappy, mutant dog breed that's a cross between a Siberian husky and a Pomeranian. They're cute, but we already have Daisy, and Andrew and I agreed that a goofy golden retriever was enough for our family. McClain's teacher found the essay he wrote to be so hilarious that she emailed it to me. In it he writes, the only thing standing in the way of my dreams is my mom. Everyone had a good laugh, except me. Somehow everything is always my fault; I play the role of the bad guy, not because I want to, but because Andrew already took the good guy part. My bad guy status elevated to "dream crusher" that day, and Andrew was happy to let me take it on. Andrew led McClain on about the damn Pomsky. That's what he does, avoids conflict. He can't bear to tell his fourth-grade son that we aren't getting another dog, but he'll happily let me do it. The dream crusher, the bad guy, aka Mom.

Being the working parent leaves me little alone time with the kids. Of all my closest friends I'm the only one who works. The rest of them, every single one of them, are stay-at-home moms. Of course when they get free time they want nothing to do with their kids. It immediately becomes moms' night out, wine on the patio, or a weekend getaway. Those are good times, and I need some of that in my life too, but it's not as high on my priority list now as it once was. These days when I have free time I usually want to spend it with my little sweeties. I haven't seen my girlfriends, or my kids, as much since the move.

McClain is now ten, Atlas nine, and Violet six. I don't even remember them as babies. When I look back at pictures it's like I'm examining someone else's life. I know I was there, I'm certain they are my children, but I can't quite remember what the hell I was doing back then. I look both younger and older in pictures from a decade ago. Softer around the eyes, cheeks a little more plump, fewer lines creasing the corners of my mouth, yet tired looking, always so very tired. Sleep deprivation is hands down the worst part of parenthood. If it's not listed as an official form of human torture, it should be.

This afternoon's adventure is just what I've been craving: Time alone with the kids. No other adults to compromise with. Andrew is going to stay back and work on the house, and I'm going hiking with my sweeties. I'm taking them on an adventure to the top of Sawyer Mountain. We did it once last spring as a family, but the black flies were so bad and the trail too steep and rocky for Violet to manage. We turned back halfway, Andrew having to carry her on his shoulders the entire way down.

We moved to Maine a few years ago. Bought an old farmhouse in desperate need of restoration. We left the uptight, competitive lifestyle of Boston for a more laid-back existence in Maine. We had been talking about a simpler life for a long time. I wanted to spend my days reading and writing, and Andrew dreamt of a farmstead where he could make furniture and grow vegetables in his garden. Moving to Maine was Andrew's dream come true. As for me . . . I haven't written since we moved, it's been so long I can't recall the last novel I read, and now I travel weekly back and forth to Boston for work. All so Andrew and the kids can have the life they wanted. I guess the Dream Crusher has no mercy, in this case for herself.

This hike will be medicine for my soul. I love a physical challenge, something that makes you sweat. I used to run with Andrew when we lived in Boston. That was before I commuted over two hours each way to work. I love running, well, I used to love running. I ran in marathons, I ran for fun, I ran because it made me feel great. Andrew still runs; he says he feels great. I think about feeling great, but I only get to do great things on the weekends. I'm only alive on Saturdays and Sundays.

This hike will be challenging for the kids. The route I want to take is six miles, which is long for us, but the elevation is what will be the most exhausting. We'll be going straight up the mountainside, and that will put us all to the test. The kids and I stuffed my backpack with the essentials and plenty of nonessentials too. I let them throw in a few extra things. We had the room and I was determined not to be the bad guy today. We had plenty of water, snacks, tissues, paper towels, baby wipes for sticky hands, and dog treats for Daisy.

The kids said goodbye to their dad, their little arms wrapping around any available part of his body. Faces snuggled into his chest and thighs. He hugged them back and landed kisses on top of each one's head.

McClain asked one more time, "Are you sure you don't want to come, Dad?"

"No, I'm going to stay here and work on the house, buddy. You have fun with Mama, okay?" Andrew said.

I gave Andrew a big squeeze and a wet kiss on the mouth. Our family does hellos and goodbyes well. No matter how frustrated or annoyed with one another we are, we always manage a proper hello or goodbye. I like that about us.

"I'll text you when we get out of the woods," I said.

"Okay, honey," Andrew said. "If you give me a little notice, I will try and have dinner ready for when you guys get back."

"I'll do my best. I'm not sure how good my cell service will be, but I'll try," I said over my shoulder as the kids bounded out the door in front of me. Daisy charged ahead, knowing exactly what was about to happen and thrilled to be a part of it.

"Take care of my Daisy girl!" Andrew added.

Sometimes I think he loves that damn dog more than me.

"You know I will," I replied. My eyes were saying something entirely different than my words. "I love you," I added as I closed the door. And I meant it.

"I love you," Andrew said. And he meant it too.

SUMMER DAYS IN LATE August can be hot. I'm aware that hot for a New Englander might be laughable to those living in the South, but I've adapted to the cooler temperatures of Maine and if the thermometer passes seventy-five degrees, I feel hot. As we started out, I quickly regretted the timing of this adventure. I wished we had planned for a morning hike instead of an afternoon one. The heat might make the kids cranky, and I was not in the mood for cranky kids.

When we arrived the kids tumbled out of the car like a swarm of bees whose nest was hit with a rock. They scrambled this way and that all around the dirt parking lot. Daisy ran up and down several different paths, as if she were surveying which was best and reporting back to us. There were several trails splitting off from the parking lot. I was surprised to see that ours was the only car there. I began to wonder if everyone else realized it was too hot and too late in the day to be hiking up mountains, then I remembered that this network of trails had several entry points. I was certain we'd see other people once we got in the woods. Until then, Daisy would be lucky enough to run wild off her leash. Andrew normally takes control of Daisy on our hikes. She's a big dog and she has no manners on her leash. She pulls so hard, it becomes exhausting to control her. The more off the leash time the better.

We set out on the red trail. My little sweeties ran ahead with Daisy, and I marveled at how much energy kids and dogs had. I felt inspired by their carefree exuberance and decided maybe I should run too! I jogged about a hundred yards before giving up. My backpack was too heavy, it was too hot, and I was too out of practice. Maybe I'd try going for a run tomorrow, get myself back in shape.

Atlas came darting down the path toward me, followed by McClain and then Violet. Their faces were flush, hair already wet with sweat around the edges.

"Can we have some trail mix?" Atlas asked.

"Trail mix!" I said. "We've only been out here five minutes! You have to wait for trail mix, but you can have some water."

He ran off, not even bothering to reply. He knew damn well I wasn't going to let them eat trail mix yet. The kids prepared it, one little baggie for each of us, which upon my inspection, turned out to be mostly chocolate chips and mini marshmallows. I let it go; I wasn't going to be the bad guy today.

I whistled for Daisy and she came bursting through some bushes to my left.

"Good girl," I said as I patted her head.

She darted away as quickly as she came. She's never been one for staying on the trail, but I appreciated her responsiveness to my voice so it didn't bother me too much. She really was a good girl. We got her the same month we moved into the new house, because what makes more sense than getting a puppy when you have a complete mess of a house and a shit-ton of work ahead of you! Andrew always wanted a dog, but our landlord in Boston wouldn't allow pets. Andrew insisted we get a puppy as soon as we moved and so we did. I love Daisy. She's a clumsy, slobbering pain in the ass, but I love the way she is with the kids. A few nights ago, I overheard Violet telling Daisy that she was her best friend. Moments like that make the dog hair and muddy paw prints worth it.

We hiked for about an hour, stopping periodically for water breaks. I could tell the kids were tired. I was worried that they might not make it to the summit. I wanted to continue on; I was determined. I prodded them along and kept dangling the trail mix like a carrot on the end of a stick.

"As soon as we find a good place to stop we can eat the trail mix," I said. "Keep going, we'll eat the trail mix soon."

Eventually they grew tired of my promises.

"Are you ever going to let us have the trail mix?" McClain asked.

"Yes, Mac," I said. "Fine, let's stop now. We can have a rest and a snack."

"And the trail mix?" Violet asked.

"Yes, and the trail mix," I promised, and this time I came through.

We rested on a huge set of boulders covered in moss so green and lush it reminded me of a fairy tale. The cool rocks against my skin were a welcomed reprieve from the heat. I handed everyone their water bottles and little baggie of marshmallows and chocolate chips. Daisy lapped from a small brook that was trickling nearby, before lying down directly in the water. I looked at my babies, wondering where the time was going. McClain was getting older; I could see new muscles revealing themselves, his chin sharpening, a slight aging right before my eyes.

Atlas finished his bag of trail mix and started climbing around on the giant boulders.

"Be careful, Atlas, you don't want to break a leg this far away from the car," I said. "I'm not sure I could carry you back!"

"Mama, take my picture," he said as he scrambled to the top of a particularly dangerous section of rock.

I was both scared he would get hurt and proud that he was so brave. I reached in the backpack for my phone and snapped a shot of him, legs spread apart, arms open wide to the sky, making himself look as big as possible.

"Take one of me!" Violet shouted.

And I did. McClain too was on top of a boulder and wanted his picture taken. He was sitting cross-legged, hands resting on knees, fingers pinched in a meditative mudra. I liked his pose.

"Come on, guys, my battery is starting to die. I want to get a picture of all of you together," I said.

They squeezed together and locked arms around one another, smiling at the camera. Kids these days are so well trained at getting their picture taken. They've had cell phones in their faces since the moment they were born. I looked down at the photo I took; it was exactly how I wanted to remember this day. McClain looked like a handsome young man, Atlas with his enormous ear-to-ear smile, and Violet so innocent. I don't know if it's because she is the youngest of the three, but at six years old, I couldn't help but think she was still a baby. My baby.

IT WAS TAKING LONGER than I expected to get to the top. The trail was steeper than I anticipated, which was surely slowing us down, but I felt like we should have made it to the summit by now. Violet had been holding my hand for the past thirty minutes, and I felt like I was dragging her up the hill most of the time. She was asking when we'd get to the top every few minutes, and I wasn't sure she was going to hang in there for this whole adventure. I started to wonder if I'd made a mistake, she's only six after all, maybe a hike like this is too much for a six-year-old? The boys seemed to have the stamina to keep going, but I was seeing myself carrying a little girl down this mountain if we didn't get to the top soon.

"Mama, there's a dog!" Atlas shouted.

I whistled for Daisy and she came running to me as expected. I pulled her leash from around my neck and clipped it onto her collar. Good girl. I could see a man walking on the trail ahead. He was coming in our direction. We shuffled to the side of the trail to let him pass. He nodded in appreciation, and as he went by I asked, "Are we much farther from the top?"

"Almost there," he said. "About ten minutes."

"Thank you!" I said.

I was relieved at this news and found a burst of energy that would carry me the rest of the way. The kids felt it too.

"Just ten more minutes, guys!" I said. "We can do it!"

We all set off with a little more pep in our step and hope in our hearts that we were about to conquer this mountain after all.

A few minutes later Atlas shrieked with excitement. "Look!" he said, pointing.

"It's a porcupine!" said McClain.

McClain had just finished studying Maine's native animals in school. He liked it so much that we bought him a wilderness survival book that he had been looking at every day. He was becoming very knowledgeable about local wildlife.

I screamed for Daisy, maybe a little louder and more panicked than I should have, because the kids all turned back to look and see what was wrong. The last thing I wanted was to be on the top of a mountain dealing with a dog whose face and mouth were full of quills. She came and I clipped her leash on again. We inched a little closer to the porcupine. I wondered out loud if it could shoot its quills at us.

"No, Mama, they can't shoot their quills at people," said McClain.

His tone had an air of disdain, and I wasn't too thrilled with it. Not so fast, Mac, you are still my child and you must respect me, I thought, but said nothing.

We watched the porcupine walk away, the kids excited and bounding once again along the path. I followed them, listening to their recounting of the porcupine sighting. There was debate on who saw it first, who wanted to be the one to tell Andrew when we got home, and what would have happened if Daisy had tried to eat it. I let their little voices carry me along the trail. Listening to them chatter with one another was like listening to a symphony of the most beautiful songbirds in the world. Mothers love to see their children being friends, and however fleeting those tiny moments may be, they are the moments that we live and die for.

WE CRESTED UP OVER the edge of a rocky part of the trail, and I could see we had done it—we reached the summit! Daisy was near my side; I only had to gesture for her to come closer and she knew I wanted to leash her up. There weren't any other hikers in view, but everything all of a sudden seemed wide open and the cliffs looked too menacing for this clumsy golden retriever.

"Guys, be careful. Don't go near the edge," I shouted.

Violet turned back, skipping toward me, clutching my hand once again.

The view was spectacular. I found myself trying to inhale what my eyes could see. I was shocked at how far I could see and how clear the late afternoon sky looked. I took out my phone to snap a picture. I got one shot, then the battery went completely dead. Stupid phone, I thought. I had been hanging on to an older model for years because it still worked, and I was trying to be frugal, but the battery was shit. I suddenly wished Andrew was here with us. My earlier desire to be alone with the kids felt selfish now.

I wasn't sure what time it was, but I was certain it had taken us longer to hike to the top than I had calculated. I wanted to immediately turn back around and start heading out before it got too late, but I knew the kids needed a break, and how could I make them leave the beauty of this place after just discovering it?

I hooked Daisy's leash to a tree and set my pack down next to her. I opened it up and gathered the picnic blanket and snacks we brought. I laid the blanket out and arranged a neat little meal for the four of us. I wanted our mountain-top snack to be special. I poured some water in a dish for Daisy. She lapped it up, then lay down on the corner of our blanket.

The kids explored near the edge of the cliff, closer than made me comfortable. They urged me to come see. I came to take a look, but as I peered over the side, my stomach instantly flipped, and I had to step back quickly.

"Stay away from the edge," I said, confirming my initial thought that it was a long way down.

The last thing I wanted to see was one of my babies bouncing off a jagged rock face all the way to the bottom of a mountain. Kids were braver than adults. Maybe because they haven't had as many bad experiences to teach them what kind of hurt life can throw at a person.

"Come on, let's have our snack," I said.

Violet had stuffed her favorite teddy bear, Teeny, deep at the bottom of my pack. I didn't realize she had done it, but there she was, snuggling Teeny while she nibbled cheese, apple slices, and fists full of cashews. Teeny looked as if he wanted her to share, and I wished I could have taken a picture of my girl at that moment. Six was one of my favorite ages. Growing up and becoming independent, but still so much a baby who needs her mama.

McClain and Atlas ate like marooned sailors devouring the first fish they'd caught since being stranded on an island.

The kids finished, drank more water at my urging, and began to wander about the mountaintop again while I tidied up our picnic. Everything fit neatly in my pack, but thankfully it was a much lighter load now. We would be heading down soon, and the rest of the adventure would be smooth sailing from here. I had been feeling uneasy about how long it took us to get to the top and how exhausted the kids were, but everything seemed like it was going to be okay after all. We would be later for dinner than I originally planned; Andrew would have to adjust. He wasn't an awful cook, but I wished he was better at timing his meals. It was almost a given that something would be ready before something else, leaving a cold dish of food sitting on the table long before its comrades arrived.

I wondered if I complained too much? I would try to be kinder and more patient when I got home. I felt like I could manage things a little better now; fresh air has a way of doing that for me.

My feet and thighs were beginning to ache.

"Okay, guys, let's get going," I said, throwing the pack over my shoulders and grabbing Daisy's leash off the branch.

The kids were tumbling over one another on a mossy patch of land nearby, hardly acknowledging my existence.

"Guys, let's go." A little louder this time.

Kids don't listen. You have to say the same things at least two or three times, increasingly louder and louder to get their attention.

"Guys! Come on!" I shouted.

Finally they stood, still giggling, brushing little bits of moss and dried leaves from their clothes and hair.

I walked near the edge to take in the view one last time. I breathed the crisp summer air. I noticed a far-off lake shimmering in the sun. I had heard you could see all the way to the ocean from here, but I wasn't sure which way to look or how I would tell the horizon from the water.

As I turned toward the kids, I was startled by a large bird that flew up over the side of the cliff. It was huge, wings flapping so near my face, I could feel the air rushing over my cheeks and dancing through the tiny hairs on my forehead. Daisy saw it too. She leapt at it, yanking me violently toward the edge. She caught herself just before tumbling forward over the mountainside, planting her strong paws firmly down. But it was too late. I stumbled, tripping over the leash until I fell hard to the ground just at the very edge of the drop-off. I managed to cling for a split second, looking back at my three little sweeties, knowing that I was going over. I locked eyes with Atlas as I plummeted off the edge. I dragged Daisy down with me.

ANDREW LOOKED AT HIS watch. He wondered how we were doing. It was 5:15 p.m. I had told him we expected to be done by now. He missed the kids. It's strange how that works. I could see the happy look on his face when we left, how excited he was to be getting some time to himself. That's how most parents feel when they have had enough of their bratty kids. But only a few short hours have to pass before you start thinking of them and missing their smiling faces.

He wasn't worried, just annoyed that I hadn't texted him yet.

"Typical," he grumbled.

He had texted a couple times, asking if I'd send pictures and if everyone was managing okay. I never saw his messages. The service was so bad, and with the phone constantly searching for a signal the battery died quickly. I wished I could explain that to him now.

He made baked ziti for dinner, and it was warming in the oven. He was proud of himself. He had decided on something easy, that everyone would enjoy. He knew it could be hot and ready no matter what time we arrived home. Maybe I'll even get laid tonight, he thought. Vacuuming might seal the deal, so he decided to quickly run it around the house. The Queen's arrival would be soon.

ATLAS REALIZED WHAT WAS happening first and shrieked out loudly, "Mama!"

I heard him on the way down. I saw the look of terror in his eyes as he saw me fall from view. The look on his face hurt me worse than the blow I took to the shoulder. It shattered instantly as I smashed it upon the jagged rocks.

I heard Daisy welp in pain. The leash was still looped tightly around my wrist, and as Daisy and I careened down different rocky routes I heard a loud popping noise, immediately followed by a ripping feeling and searing pain coming from my other shoulder. I knew the leash had ripped my arm out of its socket. I could instantly tell it was bad. My head, my legs, everything was abused as we fell off the side of that mountain, Daisy and I linked together on a tortuous journey to the bottom. Then, finally, stillness.

I lay with my eyes closed. I was afraid to open them; I knew things would be bad and I didn't want to look. I heard nothing at first, just the wind blowing through distant treetops, a subtle faraway rustling. I heard birds chirping; a crow cawed. Maybe it's that fucking dinosaur bird that knocked me off this cliff, I thought.

I heard a wisp of raspy breathing coming from Daisy, then one final exhale. I could tell she was gone. I had to be sure. I slowly opened my eyes and was blinded momentarily by the sun, which was getting lower in the sky. As I blinked the white light from my eyes I saw Daisy's lifeless body only feet away from mine. I gasped. She looked as if her insides were removed, blended up, then stuffed back into a shell of her former body. Nothing was in the right place, her legs twisted and bent so unnaturally, they looked like one of Violet's pipe cleaner creations. Her head had a large gash on it, right above the eye; I could see white bone peeking out from between the matted tufts of golden fur. Blood pooled beneath her. I squeezed my eyes tightly closed and left them that way for a very long time.

* * *

THEY ALL SAW ME go down. I had locked eyes with Atlas, but they all understood the horror just the same. McClain came running up to the edge of the cliff, more cautious now than he had been before. Was this what life would be like for them now? A little more measured, more cautious, more fearful. A short time ago I had wished they had some sense in them, and now I would mourn for the loss of their innocence. Never again would my children dance freely on a mountaintop.

McClain looked over the edge; he couldn't see me or Daisy. We had fallen far, and the rock formations jetting out blocked his view of where we landed.

"Mama!" he shouted. "Mama! Mama!"

Those were the only words that came. Atlas stood frozen, silently staring at where he had last seen his mother; he hadn't moved an inch. It was as if he'd forgotten how to make his body go. Violet wet herself, pee dribbling out of her shorts, down her skinny legs, soaking the tops of her socks. She began to cry. Big heaves of air in and out, tears rolling heavy down her cheeks, dripping onto the front of her shirt.

"Mama," she whimpered over and over and over again.

THE FAR-OFF SOUND OF my son's voice roused me from my trance. I heard him calling for me. I thought it might be Mac, but it was difficult to tell. The wind was louder now, bouncing and echoing off the rocky face of the mountain. I lay there, eyes still closed tight. I was terrified to open them. If my body looked anything like Daisy's, I wouldn't be able to bear the sight of it. I heard the buzzing of a fly. Can that be right? How long have I been lying here? I thought. Are flies already coming to scavenge on my dead dog's body? This was a nightmare.

There was something odd about what was going on here. I couldn't quite put my finger on it but knew something was off. I felt a tingling sensation all throughout my body as I lay motionless, but I didn't feel any pain. I was buzzing all over, but comfortable.

Maybe that's what going into shock feels like, I wondered. I slowly opened my eyes and saw myself lying in a mangled heap next to Daisy. There was blood, so much blood. Limbs twisted this way and that. There were flies, the little fuckers. I was startled by the way I looked. Lifeless, stone still . . . dead.

ATLAS SHOOK HIS HEAD, like he was emerging from under the water of a pool; he looked over at Violet. He saw his baby sister whimpering, wet with piss, and more scared than he had ever seen anyone before in his life. He stepped toward her and wrapped his arm around her shoulder.

"It's okay, Vi," he said. "Everything's going to be okay."

Violet buried her face in his chest and heaved more tears. She was trembling, and Atlas wanted her to stop. He felt his own eyes stinging and becoming heavy with salty water, until the tears came billowing out, rolling down his face, and landing in tiny puddles on top of Violet's head.

McClain was screaming now, "Help! Help! Anyone, help!"

There was a frantic quality to his voice, and it scared Atlas; he wasn't sure what was worse, Violet's sobs or Mac's fearful screeching. He needed them both to stop. Atlas moved closer to the edge of the cliff where McClain was pacing back and forth alternating his screams for his mama and help from other hikers. Violet stepped along with Atlas, afraid to release her grasp from her big brother's side. Atlas gently pushed away from Violet and got down on his stomach; he wasn't going to take any chances. He inched himself closer to the edge of the mountainside and peered down below.

"Mama!" he called out. "Mama, can you hear me?"

No reply came.

McClain was crying now too. "She's gone," he shrieked. "She fell right off the side! Did you see? Did you see that? Daisy's gone too."

"Daisy!" McClain cried out for his dead dog.

There was a shrillness to his voice that could only be described as the pain of a ten-year-old boy who just realized he lost his mom and his dog in the very same moment.

"Maybe she's okay?" said Atlas. "She might be okay, maybe she can't hear us."

Violet lifted her face out of her hands at the thought of this and said, "Do you really think so?"

There was far too much hope in her tiny voice given the circumstances, but that little shred of hope that they all felt in that moment was enough to ease some of their pain. They each clung to it the way they used to cling to their mother's breast as infants. Lingering there, not wanting the sweetness of her milk, or the tenderness in her eyes, to ever go away.

"She could be," said Atlas. "I don't know, I can't see her, but she could be okay."

It was getting late now; they could feel the air cooling as the afternoon turned into evening.

"What should we do?" asked Violet.

The three of them gathered around each other and endured a painful pause as it became obvious they were on their own for now.

McClain finally spoke. "I think we should try heading back down the way we came. We can flag down help when we get to the road."

"We can't leave her!" said Violet.

"We don't even know where she is," McClain said. "She could already be walking out on her own. Maybe she isn't hurt too bad and she is making her way out right now."

"I don't think we should leave," said Atlas. "Mom and Dad always say we should stick together and stay on the trail. If we get lost, we should stay exactly where we are."

"We aren't lost!" said McClain.

He was getting frustrated. He wanted to move; he had to move. Staying there was making him feel more anxious by the second.

"I think we need to just start walking back," he said. "We know it's the red trail, we can find our way out."

McClain began to realize he was going to be outvoted, the way his younger brother and sister looked at him.

"Someone will come, Mac. We should stay here. Someone will walk by or come looking for us," pleaded Atlas.

"I don't want to walk back. I can't do it," whined Violet.

"Violet is tired and wet, we don't have water, we have nothing. We need to stay here for now," said Atlas.

"Fine," McClain said, realizing he was not going to win. "But I'm going to walk down some of these trails a little bit and call for help. Maybe someone will hear me. You stay here."

"Don't go, Mac!" said Violet.

"I'll be right back. I'm just going to shout out for help. Maybe someone will hear me. You stay here with Atlas. I'll be right back," he said.

At that Violet started to cry again. The heat of the summer day was fading, and she was quickly becoming cold, her clothes wet with the day's sweat, pee, and tears. The temperature swings from day to night could be pretty dramatic in Maine, especially in the mountains. It could easily drop down to forty degrees on a late summer's night in western Maine. Atlas snuggled his baby sister into his arms and told her over and over again that everything would be okay. They sat on the top of Sawyer Mountain crying together, both hoping that if Atlas said it would be okay enough times, it might be true.

IT WAS 6:30 P.M. and Andrew had begun to worry. He knew his family should have been back by now. He also knew that Kate could have decided to go out for ice cream after their hike, or do some other grand gesture to solidify her spot as favorite parent while she had the chance. He kept trying her cell phone; it went straight to voicemail. Maybe the battery died, he thought. He decided if he didn't hear from her by seven, he'd go looking for them.

Five minutes later, he couldn't stand it anymore. He shut the oven off, grabbed his keys, and jumped into the car. As he pulled out of the driveway he realized he wasn't exactly sure where to go. He knew they were heading to Sawyer Mountain, but there were several trailheads that led to the summit. They had only been there once before, and they were still relatively new to the area. He had to take a guess and start somewhere. He suspected Kate would want to try something different this time; she liked trying new things. She said it kept things interesting. Fuck, Kate, you should have told me where you were parking! He tried to think clearly as he drove.

ATLAS AND VIOLET HUDDLED together; they could hear McClain calling for help in the distance over and over again, his voice bouncing among the trees. If someone were out there, they would surely hear him. He returned a little while later, having walked up and down each of the four trails that emptied to the clearing on top of the mountain.

"There's no one," he said. "People must be heading home. It's getting late."

"What time do you think it is?" asked Atlas.

"I don't know, but it's getting cold and the sun is moving behind us now. I think it's going to get dark soon," said McClain. "I'm worried about coyotes," he added.

"Coyotes!" said Violet. Her eyes opened wide. "Do you think there are coyotes out here?" she asked, not wanting to know the answer.

"Of course there are!" said McClain. He was remembering what he learned about the Maine woods and the animals one might find in the night.

"Stop it, Mac!" said Atlas. "You don't have to scare her."

Atlas was not interested in being scared either. The thought of coyotes coming out at night made him shiver, and once he started he found his body could not stop.

"Besides, someone will come for us. Dad will be looking for us," he said.

"If Daisy were here coyotes wouldn't bother us. Daisy chases everything away," Violet said.

The tears kept coming, until she had nothing left, all that remained was her puffy face and the crystallized rivers of white that stuck to her rosy cheeks.

ANDREW DECIDED HE WOULD try the trailhead closest to Rickers Village first. There was a sweet little bakery there and he thought

Kate might have stopped for fresh cookies or croissants before setting out. That's the kind of thing Kate would do. She made everything special. Maybe she was overcompensating for how much she had to travel, or how little she saw the kids during the week, but she made the weekends magical for them. She planned adventures, she took them out to fancy dinners, she bought warm breads from local bakeries and let the kids tear off big hunks at a time, smothering the pieces in butter or olive oil as they wished.

"Fuck!" Andrew said as he slammed both hands down on the steering wheel.

The Rickers Village parking lot was empty. Kate's car wasn't there. He shifted into reverse, a little more aggressively than he should have, and whipped the car around the dirt parking lot in one quick move. He sped on to the next lot, dust flying up behind his tires. He looked down at his phone. No calls, no texts. It was 7:15 p.m.

I COULD SEE THEM, my little sweeties, sitting together on top of Sawyer Mountain as the sun was setting. I was watching from above. I was gone. I knew that for sure now. There was no pain, just a tingling, a warmth, a knowing. I knew I had died. Right there on that mountainside, I had tumbled to my death, and I knew that my children would never be the same again. I felt like a fool. Who falls off a mountain and plummets to their death, in front of their children, and takes the damn dog with them! I wanted to reach down and wrap my arms tightly around them, tell them everything would be fine, but I knew nothing would ever be fine again.

They were talking to each other, not like before, when they were chatting about the porcupine; now it was different. They were scared. I could feel their fear; it rippled through me. I could taste it like metal in my mouth, hear it like a flailing bug stuck in my ear. They were talking about coyotes coming in the night and what would happen if no one finds them. They agreed they would have to stay put for now; it was too late to try and go back, nearly dark. They were afraid to move about the woods in the dark. If no one came for them, they decided they would walk out as soon as the sun came up. They knew they could find their way easy enough. Mac wished that they had already gone, but it was too late, night was upon them, and now none of them wanted to leave this spot.

ATLAS LOOKED TOWARD THE horizon, deep into the inky black night. There were dots of light from houses scattered in the distance and stars twinkling above. The new moon was hardly visible. Darkness cloaked the mountaintop and the surrounding woods. They were cold. Violet was still damp. They all longed for a warm bath and dry clothes. When camping, Andrew would make them change into completely fresh clothes before bed, socks and all. He told them how even a little moisture left on your clothing from throughout the day would freeze you in the night. They understood now. Their sweaty shirts, shorts, and socks clung to them like icy blankets that they wished they could discard. They talked about building a fire, but none of them knew how.

"Didn't you learn about building fires in your dumb book?" Atlas said to McClain.

There was tension between the boys now.

"Yes, but we don't have the supplies to do it," said McClain.

"Isn't that the point of reading a survival book," said Atlas, "so that you can build fires when you don't have any supplies?"

McClain just rolled his eyes. Little brothers didn't understand these things.

Atlas wasn't that much younger than McClain, they were just twelve months and two days apart. Most of the time they were best friends, but occasionally McClain tried to play the big brother card. He was only one grade above Atlas in school but acted as if all the answers to life's important questions were learned in the fourth grade.

The boys sat silently for a while, Violet nestled in between them. Her head was bobbing forward periodically, as it became difficult for her to stay awake. She had been asking for Teeny. She didn't think she could sleep without Teeny. They looked out at the stars and listened to the noises of the woods. The wind was blowing, softly with occasional gusts that sent shivers down each of their backs.

After a while Atlas spoke quietly, almost in a whisper. "Mac," he asked, "do you know what kind of bird it was? The one that knocked Mom down."

McClain sat still; no words came. Stupid wilderness survival book is good for nothing, Atlas thought.

ANDREW PICKED UP HIS phone and dialed his friend Shawn as he raced down the road. He and Shawn had become close over the past year. Andrew and Kate had made a few friends since they moved, and Shawn and his wife Sarah were the best of them.

Shawn was an ex-Marine and had spent most of his life living in the area. He knew all the trails and hiking spots, the best places to fish, which old-timers allowed you to hunt on their property and which areas to avoid. He never passed up an opportunity to shoot guns or talk weaponry. Once, when Andrew and Kate discovered that there was a family of skunks living under one of their barns, Shawn showed up with a crossbow ready to slaughter the lot of them. Shawn was the only person Andrew could think of calling.

Andrew dialed, then almost hung up. Maybe I'm overreacting, calm yourself down, I might be overreacting, he thought. Just before he could end the call, Shawn picked up.

"Hey, what's up, man? No one ever calls me," he said.

"Shawn," Andrew said, trying not to seem upset.

He was starting to feel like he may be making a big mistake and acting dramatic about nothing. There had to be a good reason that Kate hadn't called.

"Hey, look, sorry to bother you, I don't even know why I called, but Kate and the kids went hiking this afternoon, and they were supposed to be back around five. I haven't heard from her all day, and she isn't answering my calls or texts," Andrew said.

It was like he was speaking each word individually with great care, playing the role of laid-back dad casually sharing mundane facts with a friend.

"Shit, man!" Shawn said. "Do you know where they went?"

"Sawyer Mountain," said Andrew. "But I don't know what lot she parked at. I was just at the Ricker's lot and her car wasn't there. I'm about to pull into the Limington lot now, gonna check here."

Shawn spoke next. "Oh, man, what do you think happened to—"

He was cut off before he could finish his thought.

"Fuck! Her car is here," said Andrew.

The call ended abruptly, leaving Shawn on the other end of the line realizing something may have gone terribly wrong on Sawyer Mountain today.

ANDREW FLUNG HIMSELF FROM the car nearly before it was in park.

He started shouting for his wife. "Kate! Kate! Kate!"

He heard nothing but silence. He looked frantically in the dusky night, almost completely dark now. He saw several trails leading into the woods. He felt a sourness rising from deep inside his gut; he felt like he was going to vomit. He planted his hands on his knees, his head hung loose between his legs, breathing, thinking. Maybe one of the kids got hurt? Maybe they're lost? Maybe they stopped because it was getting dark? Maybe someone took them from the parking lot? Thoughts flooded his mind; he could not think of one good reason that Kate's car was here and his family was not.

He sprung up, having tamped down the urge to puke, ready to find his family. He went to his car and rummaged around in the glove box, the center console, under the seats. He wasn't exactly sure what he was looking for. Maybe something to help him find his way? His hand seized something jammed in between the back seats. It was a small makeup box that Violet once carried with her everywhere. It had been sandwiched between two seats in Andrew's car for who knows how long. Andrew opened it; a set of lights on either side of a mirror illuminated the inside of the car. This will do, he thought. He slammed the door shut and started running down one of the trails, the makeup box just barely lighting his way.

"Kate! Mac! Atlas! Violet! Daisy!" he shouted their names and ran.

VIOLET WAS SLEEPING NOW. Her head lay on McClain's lap, Atlas draped over top of her, Mac's ten-year-old arms wrapping around them both. The boys were trying to keep her little body from shivering in the night. McClain was silently crying. Atlas felt the occasional jerking breath deep in his brother's chest and he knew. It made him cry too and soon they were both jerking and heaving as gently and quietly as they could manage, trying not to wake Violet. She stirred as her brothers' sobs and sniffles could no longer be contained, and before long, the three kids were huddled together bawling and crying out for their mother. Something had broken in each of them. They clung to one another, as if the tightness of their hugs could somehow make them whole again. There was a rustling in the leaves behind them. There was a distant howl in the night.

I WATCHED MY CHILDREN. Motherless and alone. The minutes turned to hours. I was coming and going now, wanting to stay with them forever, but unsure if I could. As I looked over them shivering helplessly in the cool night, I felt warmth and joy coming from some distant place. It was beckoning me. I didn't want to leave, but occasionally I couldn't resist the urge to turn toward the warm glow, and when I did I felt myself drifting a little further away. I'd turn back quickly, searching once again. I'd spot them and feel relieved that I was still here and they were still together, but each time I looked away I was a little more gone from the Earth and I knew it wouldn't be long until I never saw them again.

ANDREW RAN WILDLY THROUGH the woods. He mostly stayed on the trail, trying to use Violet's pathetic makeup box as a flashlight.

It was enough to see a few inches in front of him, not much more. He tripped on a root and fell hard to the ground, a rock cutting his knee open wide; he could feel the warmth of blood edging down the front of his shin. It's nothing, he thought. He didn't take the time to look, got to his feet and kept running.

Andrew came to a fork in the trail. He could faintly see that one trail looked like it was turning back down the slope and the other maintained its gradual incline. It was so hard to tell in the dark of night with nothing but a six-year-old's makeup mirror to light the way.

"Fuck!" he screamed. "Kate!"

He had been running up the green trail. He only just realized this now as he glanced over and saw a green marker nailed to a tree beside him. He had to make a choice. The green trail seemed to be looping back down. His current path was now intersecting with the red trail, which seemed to be headed up the mountain. He felt his chest tighten. A panic attack was coming on. He realized now, after running in the woods for—had it been over an hour? he had no idea—that he didn't know which way he should be going. He didn't know where his wife and kids were; he didn't know where Daisy was. The tightness in his chest twisted harder, pressing against his lungs, when he thought of Daisy. What was Daisy doing right now? he thought. Andrew imagined Daisy as the great protector; she would never allow something bad to happen to Kate or the kids. Daisy would figure it out; she would know what to do, how to save them, to fend off a criminal, or a wild animal.

"She's not fucking Lassie," Andrew said out loud.

Hearing his own voice snapped him back into action, and he started running up the red trail now. His breathing became rhythmic; he pumped his arms and moved his body like the athlete that he was. He stopped every few moments and called out for his family. He knew they were here, he felt it. "Kate! Mac! Atlas! Violet! Daisy!" he shouted. Then ran on, seeking, being drawn by instincts, a powerful knowing that they were near. A similar instinctual knowing to the one that revealed the whereabouts of Kate and Daisy's dead bodies to the flies.

* * *

"DID YOU HEAR THAT?" McClain said.

"No. What was it?" asked Atlas.

"Shhhh, listen," McClain was whispering now. "Do you hear it?" he asked again.

They sat motionless together, ears straining, reaching deep into the woods. They both held their breath for what seemed like minutes, but no sound came. They exhaled and were resettling themselves with Violet rolling over in their laps when Atlas put his hand up, a gesture indicating that they should be still and listen again. A faint call came from far in the distance.

"You heard that, right?" asked McClain.

"Yes, yes, I heard it," said Atlas eagerly.

They listened. They couldn't make out the words, but they could tell it was a person. Someone was calling for them.

"Violet, wake up!" said Atlas. He gently rolled her off his and Mac's legs. "Wake up, Vi, someone is coming!"

The boys were already on their feet, Violet shaking off the sleep, readjusting to where she was and what was going on.

"HELP! WE'RE HERE! HELP US!" shouted McClain. He had his hands cupped around his mouth and was yelling as loud as he could.

Atlas joined in. "HELP! HELP! SOMEONE, HELP!" He was turning in all directions, not sure which way to direct his plea.

They'd tried screaming for help earlier. Up and down the trails that led from the summit of the mountain, off over the edge into the open air. No one heard them; no one replied.

McClain raised his hand this time, silencing his brother and sister, all three listening to the night sounds. This time they were certain, it was someone calling their names. "Is it Mama?" asked Violet. The boys knew it wasn't their mother; they had each come to the conclusion that their mother was gone. She had died when she fell off the side of Sawyer Mountain, and she wasn't coming back. It would take Violet longer to understand. She saw her mother go over the edge, plain and clear, but how does a six-year-old make sense of that? How does a cartoonish blunder on her favorite show end in laughs, and a mother falling mean she's dead?

"I think it's Dad!" squealed Atlas.

They all started shouting now, as loudly as they could, their voices careening down the trail and stinging Andrew directly in the heart. He felt them, and now he could hear them! He ran faster than before, sprinting toward his family. He stumbled over rocks and logs but kept moving at a pace only a father seeking to find all he ever loved could move. He called for them while he ran, he screamed for them, he dropped the makeup box and ran and ran and ran.

Andrew burst into the clearing with a force so powerful that the energy of his body, his longing, could be felt immediately by his children despite the darkness. He ran to them, dropping to his knees, not even noticing the stones that were now grinding into his open wound. As he embraced his children he realized his entire body was soaked—his hair, his clothes, all soaked. Sweat, tears, blood. The kids collapsed in his arms. In all their short lives, they had never felt so happy and so sad at the same time.

"Where's Mama?" Andrew asked, extending his arms out to look in their eyes but not daring to let go. The children didn't speak; not one of them could manage to make words in their mouths.

"Where is Mama?" Andrew said. "Where's Daisy?"

Violet pointed to the edge of the mountain, to the spot she last saw her mother and her best friend. Andrew's eyes tracked to where her tiny finger indicated. In the darkness, in the confusion, it didn't make sense. He half expected to see Kate standing there, Daisy wagging her tail wildly at the sight of him. He was unclear . . . until he wasn't. He looked back at the boys this time.

"What happened? Where is she?" he asked.

He felt the tightening in his chest return; it was unbearable, he couldn't fight it, he was slipping away. He heard the sound of a helicopter, looked above to see a large light scanning the woods off in the distance. He collapsed hard to his bottom, legs splaying out front, chest and head hanging heavy. He saw the searchlight above, coming closer. His vision was closing in; he knew he would be out soon. He heard his oldest son speak.

"Dad, she fell off the edge. Daisy too. We think . . . we think they are . . ."

Those were the words Andrew heard as he fainted to the ground.

I STAYED ABOVE THAT mountain for as long as I could. I watched as help arrived. Shawn had called the police when he got to the parking lot and saw Andrew's and my cars both abandoned there. The Maine Forest Service search and rescue team was deployed, and within the hour they were hovering above Sawyer Mountain. The helicopter spotted Andrew and the kids shortly after the search began. People came next, bounding up the trails on machinery and with supplies. My family was evacuated on the backs of four-wheelers and taken to the Maine Medical Center for evaluation. Andrew and all three kids were deemed healthy and released the next morning.

The search and rescue became a search and recovery mission for me. Daisy and I were discovered late in the afternoon on the following day. It didn't take long; the kids were able to explain to the police exactly what had happened. The young man who came upon us first was only twenty-three years old. It had been his first search and recovery mission. They all knew we'd likely be dead when they found us. I watched him from above. He vomited when he discovered our bodies.

I waited for Andrew and the kids to return to the top of Sawyer Mountain. They never did. But other hikers and adventure seekers came and went. The parks committee installed a split rail fence along the edge of the cliff; Andrew demanded it and they were happy to oblige. I watched the hikers looking out over the horizon, marveling at the view, just like I once had. Some of them knew about my accident. Sometimes I'd hear them talking. How sad it was, how scared those poor children must have been, how their father was a hero, and how lucky they were to have a dad like him to raise them. Sometimes they talked about me. Some speculated that I committed suicide. Some acted like I was irresponsible for falling off a cliff in front of my kids, like I planned it. Others were more upset about Daisy than anything else. I guess that's just the way people are—no one really knows the truth unless they've lived that truth.

I don't know how long I stayed there, waiting for my family to return. It was difficult to understand time now. I suppose they may have come, to the place I last held my children and kissed the tops of their sun-soaked heads. If they had, I missed them. There were long stretches that I was there keeping an eye out, and even longer stretches when I was turned away, moving toward the warmth and joy that were calling me home. Eventually I had drifted so far away from the top of Sawyer Mountain that I decided maybe it was best to be gone from that place for good. So, I said goodbye, to whom I wasn't sure, and I went to find Daisy.

# The Whole Artichoke, Stem and All

## Sharon E. Svendsen

MY NEPHEW BILLY DIED IN CHILDBIRTH. HE WAS A GROWN MAN. He didn't like to be called Billy. He preferred to be called Bill or William, not Billy or—God forbid—Willy, but I started calling him Billy when he popped out of his mother's womb. I've been calling the boy Billy ever since. I'm not about to change things now.

Billy's mother is my sister Fern. My little sister. I always wanted to protect her, to keep her out of trouble, but you can't do everything. Fern was away at the time of Billy's death.

Billy's wife, Sue, was the manager of a health food store. A big one. Health nuts from all over the northwest used to shop at that store. At the time of Billy's death, Sue was home on maternity leave. Not many people worked at the store, but they were progressive as far as leave goes. I think they even gave leave if you cut your finger.

Maternity leave! When my boys were born, I wanted to leave home. Not really. Well, part of me did. The rest of me wanted to love my boys to death—preferably my death.

Billy was a long, lanky fellow. Until he got married. Health food or not, he developed a gut.

Sue was five foot six, blonde, with a kind of Meg Ryan hairstyle, which to me is no hair style at all.

Billy was six foot two, tall, dark hair, blue eyes. I always thought that combination made a man seem handsome and mysterious. Billy was handsome, but he was not mysterious. He was as obvious as a cow standing in your kitchen mooing at you. Much as I like cows, I wouldn't want one spitting its cud onto my tablecloth.

Anyway, Sue and Billy looked all right together—even if they did look like a bottle of catsup and a small jar of mustard. One of those skinny jars of mustard.

They got married after living together for six years. Seems pointless. They were common law as far as I'm concerned. I suppose they got married because of the child. Funny, people used to stay married, not get divorced, for the sake of the children. Now they get married—they don't stay single—for the sake of the children. It's a strange world.

On the day of Billy's death, Billy called me to say that Sue was dilated. He sounded as excited as swarming bees when you accidentally whack the nest with a stick.

"I'll be right there," I said.

"Well, I didn't mean—"

"I'll be right there." I hung up before he could tell me not to come. Then I ignored the insistent ringing of my phone.

When I walked into their house, the living room—off of the entry—looked like something from a magazine or from a furniture store's showcase. I would have admired Sue's expert housekeeping, but I knew they had a part-time maid. And my nose was attacked and tackled by an overpowering flowery scent.

In the kitchen and family room about a thousand candles were burning—on every flat surface. The scents were mixed up, like the ingredients of some great celestial pie made out of wax fruit. There were even a few sticks of incense burning. My late husband would have had a fit and left, but their potpourri didn't scare me.

Sue's mother and Billy were standing in the kitchen—one of those big modern kitchens with all the normal stuff plus a sink that sticks up above the counter, a faucet that looks like the horn on a trombone, granite countertops, stainless steel appliances, a pot rack on the ceiling that was decorated with dangling copper pans, and a half-size black-faced refrigerator just for wine. The kitchen was separated from the family room by only a stout few feet of island.

"Hi, Aunt Margie," Billy said without enthusiasm. "You didn't have to come."

"Sure I did. Hi. Smells like a florist's shop in here," I said. "I hope the little bugger ain't allergic." I don't say "ain't" very often. I said it then because I knew it would annoy Sue to no end. Sue could hear me perfectly well from her queen's perch in the family room.

"It's aroma therapy," said the mother's mother, hereafter to be known as Madame Grandmother-to-Be, make that MG2B. "The scent is meant to be relaxing and refreshing," she said. She was wearing a caftan or a muumuu or whatever. (Cows again!) Something loose with swirls of miscellaneous blues and reds connected by gold. Her blonde hair was wavy, but the style was stuck together as if held by the wax from all those candles.

"Seems like the candles would over-exercise your nose," I said. "My nose is already exhausted, and I've only been here five minutes. Won't these candles suck all the oxygen out of the air?"

MG2B's face hardened, but she tinkled out a laugh and said, "Certainly not. But aren't you witty."

"I guess I am. If you say so. Seems like someone here should have her wits about her."

MG2B fell further from pleasantness and turned away. Lord, that woman reeked of perfume, though it was amazing I could smell it over the aroma brigade. But who was I to stop her from attempting aroma suicide?

All the stink was enough to make the baby stay inside the womb.

MG2B wandered off into the other room to talk to her daughter, who had yet to speak to me.

Billy said to me, "You'd better behave yourself."

"Me?" I asked, touching my chest. "I will if you will."

Sue, of course, was into all the new age crap. She wanted to have natural childbirth. Makes me shudder just to think about it. I read someplace that natural childbirth is promoted by sadistic male doctors.

Not only did Sue want to have natural childbirth, but she wanted to sloosh the kid out into a pool full of warm water. And she wanted a doula or a duma or a cha cha, whatever you call it. It's just a fancy name for a midwife as far as I'm concerned.

Sue (short for Suzette, of all things) came into the kitchen, looking like she had just taken a shower. Her hair was wet. She was wearing a long blue T-shirt (and blue underpants, as I later found out). She put her hand on her abdomen. "Oooh," she said with a smile. "Another contraction."

Just wait, honey, I thought. You won't be saying oooh with such delight.

Billy and Sue strolled into the family room. Sue still hadn't spoken to me.

On the kitchen island between the candles were the makings for vegetarian sandwiches—brown bread so full of seeds it should have been in a bird feeder, bean sprouts, cucumber slices, sliced tomatoes, lettuce, other things that were unrecognizable. There was some sort of cheese that looked as if a goat had stepped on it—or sat on it. There was a tofu concoction that was supposed to taste like egg salad. "Why not just make egg salad?" I asked.

"This doesn't have meat in it," MG2B said.

"Eggs aren't meat," I said.

MG2B just rolled her eyes and walked away.

Tofu non-egg salad was not tempting. There was also no real mayonnaise to give this silage any taste.

I used their ultra-modern powder room. Along with a sink that looked like a salad bowl it had both a toilet and a bidet. Lord almighty.

When I came back to the kitchen I heard Billy and Sue arguing.

"I don't want her here," Sue said.

"My mother wants her here." He didn't really know that, but it was true.

"I don't think your jailbird mother has much of a say in the matter." This from a woman who had never even met Billy's mother—not even in the years before Fern was sentenced.

"Why doesn't my mother have a say? Because you won't condescend to meet her?" This from a man who had never visited his mother in prison.

"She's a horrible person," Sue said. They were both partly turned away from me so they didn't see me.

"My mother?" Billy loomed over her.

"No." She held her baby bulge as it contracted. "Your aunt."

"She's not horrible. She's my aunt." Stunning logic.

"I hate her," she said with gritted teeth.

Billy noticed me then. "Shh, she'll hear you."

"Let her hear me. I don't care."

It was all I could do not to say, I don't give a rip if you like me.

But Billy was sticking up for me—probably to agitate Sue. I didn't care. I wanted to give my sister a full report. "Sure are some interesting refreshments here," I said. "Too bad I didn't bring a hamster."

Sue made a kind of growl and walked toward the birthing pool.

So, the king and queen allowed me to stay, even though I knew I was as welcome as warm dog poop on a porch step. Poop from a very big dog—maybe a mastiff.

The heavily scented air was giving me a headache.

The dooloo headed out of the family room, which was covered with waterproof tarps. The woman's name was Glenda. She wore her partly gray braids pinned in circles around her head, and she was wearing a long gray dress. She looked to be time-warped from 1965.

Glenda came into the kitchen and drew herself a large glass of water. She slathered some birdseed bread with tofu egg salad. "Need to keep my strength up for what's ahead."

Seems to me like she'd have been better off with a T-bone steak.

Glenda finished her meager strength-building meal and went back into the family room where Sue was sitting on a wooden kitchen chair.

Every time Sue had a contraction, the dooloo held Sue's hand. Sue wasn't in the long-legged wading pool yet. That's what it looked like—a big blue inflatable wading pool with much higher sides

So, the dooloo kept holding Sue's hand while Billy paced back and forth.

"For God's sake, sit down," Sue said as a contraction nailed her.

Billy sat for about thirty seconds then got up and paced some more.

MG2B put something on the stereo that was supposed to be music. First it was clicking sticks, then running water, then birdsong. I would have played a Sousa march, but just to be ornery.

When the contractions got to the point where they meant business, the dooloo had Sue breathe out with a foo foo foo.

Phooey.

Sue had just foo foo fooed, but she wanted to walk around. She came into the kitchen and that's where her water broke. "Oh no," Sue said, and she dropped her pretty blue drawers.

"It's all right," MG2B said. MG2B wanted nothing to do with the mess. She simply escorted Sue to the bathroom, with the dooloo trailing behind.

I found a bucket and sponge and got down on my hands and knees, sopping up the mess, then I dumped it all out the back door—along with the blue underpants. Then I filled the bucket with hot water, a little detergent, and some Pine-Sol—my contribution to the aroma therapy. I washed the whole floor, drying it with a towel so that no one would slip and fall.

"Auntie Marge," Billy said softly, "you didn't have to do that."

He seemed admiring or grateful or something. It embarrassed me. "It wasn't going to clean itself," I said. "Besides, I'm wearing jeans, not silk." I didn't want to tell him I was bored to tears.

"Cecily isn't wearing silk."

"Who said anything about Cecily?" (MG2B)

"Oh."

An EMT arrived. They had hired him to stick around in case something went wrong.

"Susan is the name of the baby's mother," MG2B said to the EMT.

"That's good to know," the EMT said.

Good to know? My Lord. The house was full of idiots.

The EMT looked at the vegetarian buffet with a sigh.

"Crazy, ain't it?" Ha! Two ain'ts in one day.

Everyone but Billy and me went into the family room.

"You haven't been up to see her since she first got there," I said. "Four years. In four years you haven't visited your mother once."

"This isn't the time." His ice-blue eyes avoided mine.

"Excuse me? When would be a better time?"

He looked at me then. "My mother ruined my life."

"Yeah?" I looked around at his nice house, his leather furniture, his college-educated wife, his fancy unpleasant mother-in-law, the dooloo, and the EMT. "Looks like your life is sure in ruins now."

Billy was some sort of a computer guru. He brought the money from his paychecks home in gunny sacks.

"You know what I mean. Those reporters. TV. I couldn't look the other kids in the face."

"Sounds like cowardice to me."

Billy shook his head.

"You should visit her sometime. You might find out she's not a monster with eight sets of horns. She just got a little greedy."

"A little greedy?"

"Okay. A lot greedy. [$154,672.35 at a large car dealership.] But no one holds that against you."

"Against me? Why would—"

"Please, please," said the dooloo, "we need to create an atmosphere of peace and serenity."

Billy and I glared at each other. With peace and serenity.

The dooloo changed the CD to classical music—Mozart or something else I'm sure they never listened to.

Time wore on. Sue was not happy anymore. Billy ordered several pizzas. When they arrived I said, "That's my kind of buffet."

The EMT ate slices from the all-garlic pizza. They were paying him just to stand there doing nothing, and he ate the all-garlic pizza. If he was going to give mouth-to-mouth resuscitation, I hoped it wouldn't be to me.

So, we ate pizza—all except for the dooloo and Sue. One of the pizzas was vegetarian. Even MG2B avoided that one.

After we ate, we all sat around the "birthing pool" while Sue progressed through closer and closer and more powerful contractions. Sue finally got into the birthing pool. I was skeptical. I said, "I read about a woman in the *National Inquirer*. She had her baby in a pool and the baby came out with gills and fins."

"Get that woman out of here!" Sue bellowed.

I said, "I have a right to stay." Actually, though, I was feeling on shaky ground.

Fortunately, Sue screamed from a contraction. Then she started breathing foo foo foo again and everyone forgot about me.

We continued the long, soggy, noisy (screams) wait.

At one point I sang, "'Can she bake a cherry pie, Billy Boy, Billy Boy? Can she bake a cherry pie, charming Billy?'"

"What's that supposed to mean?" Billy asked.

"It's a song. It's an old song. Haven't you ever heard it?"

"Why are you singing it now?"

"It just popped into my head. My aunt Mary used to sing it to your mother and me."

"Are you implying that my wife can't bake a pie?"

"No. For goodness sake. Don't be so touchy."

Sue's fingers and toes must have been getting pretty pruney. I wondered if the baby would be pruney.

Breathing foo foo foo when she had her contractions, Sue was doing just fine, though she had that how-did-I-get-myself-into-this look on her face. I sure do know that one. Billy and MG2B traded off being her helper. Sort of. They held her non-dooloo hand. To me, they seemed pretty useless.

I had to give Sue credit, though, having natural childbirth. I wanted all the drugs I could get when I had my two boys. My doctors weren't sadistic men.

Billy asked if he could take a picture of me. "Knock yourself out," I said. Imagine my surprise when (later) he did.

"There should be quietness and soothing music now," the dooloo said. She put on some music that sounded like a dirge.

Everyone was paying attention to the dooloo and the mother and waiting for the baby. We heard a little thump but didn't think anything about it. The baby was coming. I looked over at Billy and there he was, unconscious with his head in the water. I said,

"Excuse me, but I believe that Billy is drowning." The dooloo looked from Sue to Billy and chose Billy.

The dooloo tried to resuscitate him, but the EMT pushed her aside and the dooloo went back to Sue. "Bill," Sue cried. "Bill! Bill!" Then she screamed in labor. So much for the foo foo foo.

I went directly to call 911.

"This excitement isn't good for you," MG2B said.

I turned around and said, "For crying out loud, her husband might be dead."

"Bill! Bill! AAAAAAAAAUUUGGGGHHH!"

The EMT breathed his garlic down Billy's throat, then he sat back. Billy spurted out water and came around. His hair was all wet and spiky, and the EMT was sitting by his side.

The dooloo said, "The baby's coming now. Push hard." Sue grunted, screamed, whimpered. The baby boy was born.

When the neighbors heard the sirens, they thought it was paramedics for Sue or the baby or both. But no, it was for Billy. He was, of course, alive again by the time the paramedics got there. I'm happy to say he's still alive today.

But Billy was technically dead for about a minute and a half, and dead is dead. He was fine afterward, but his personality was no more pleasant than before.

I said, "Billy, did you see a tunnel or a white light or God or dead relatives or anything when you were dead?"

"I've asked you a thousand times, please call me Bill, not Billy."

"Okay, Bill. Did you see angels or anything?"

He looked at me as if I had eaten a whole artichoke, stem and all. "No," he said. He said it in a very definite way, so I have to believe him, even though I find his answer disappointing.

They named the baby Phineas. Lord almighty.

Once the baby got cleaned up and everyone else had held him, I got to hold him. He was the cutest little guy. I said, "Doesn't a baby make you feel like peace on earth is possible? Doesn't it make you think of your own parents and how they loved you like you love this new little life?"

I looked up and they were all looking at each other with softened expressions. Well, Billy's frown was softened. Sue was looking at her mother with glowing happiness. It was as if they understood what I said. But this goodwill from them made me feel squishy. I looked down and cooed to little Phineas, "Pumpkin, I hope your mama never goes to prison."

The baby's mama, who had slithered out of the pool, hobbled over and gently snatched the baby from my arms. "Well I do hope that," I said. I do.

Billy was almost purple. "My wife is a wonderful woman."

"Of course she is. So is your mother. You ought to visit her once in a while. She got greedy and she got caught. But she's still your mama."

There was more stuff after that, but it doesn't really matter. That's how Billy died in childbirth.

Billy was kind enough to send me a set of pictures from that day—pictures that included about ten shots of Phineas. I took the pictures to the prison. They knew me there. They even joked with me as they searched me. I always pretended to be scandalized when they patted me down. It made them laugh.

When Fern saw the pictures of little Phineas, the tears streamed down her face. It broke my heart. I wanted to hit that doggoned Billy up the side of his head. Hard. I left Fern alone to have her moment of moments, and I stood and looked first at the bars on the window then out at the empty exercise yard where the wind was blowing a piece of white paper in circles. It was a sad, bleak place. I stood there for a long time just watching that paper going round and round.

And I never once mentioned the fact of Billy's death.

# The Bells of St. James

## Holly C. Tabor

PENNY SAYS THEY TALK. SAYS THEY TELL YOU WHEN IT'S TEN o'clock and when to go to church and don't forget your wallet. Tell you that old Mrs. So-and-So kicked the bucket or Billy and Susie tied the knot. Tell you you're bad bad bad and to say ten Hail Marys and you're good as new till next time. Says they tell you to feed the starving children, but only if they're Christian, and that Jesus died again. You know, she says. Things.

Only I don't know; I think they don't talk to me. All I know is the hollow hymnal gong that comes from somewhere far away, but Penny says no, it comes from there, and she cups the side of her hand to the temple and points up with the other to a dark room high in the steeple out of reach of everything, even the sun.

What else do they say? I ask, visions of altar boys in white robes and sneakers grabbing hold of a rope-knot the size of a dog's head and tugging it down to their knees and riding it straight off the floor and down and up and down again and trying not to laugh while Father shakes hands and greets and blesses.

Everybody knows they don't do that anymore, Penny says. And I start wondering since the altar boys don't ring the bell, who does? Just some sinner, Penny says, just presses a button and it's all gong gong gong. And I imagine being small enough to ride that gong, kicking and sparking and sticky with static straight up the spine of the spirit and into the hearts of believers. I look up into the dark tower and wonder is there even a bell in there anymore, and Penny says of course there is, silly, everybody knows that.

So, what else do they say? I whisper, bruises deepening in my knees from the wooden kneeler while the prayerful wait in line for a taste of Jesus.

They say to pray for all the mothers, she says, so we start naming all the mothers we can think of.

Mother of God.

Mother of Peace.

Mother of Thorns and Rose Garden Bathtubs.

Mother Hubbard.

Mother of Mothers.

Mother May I?

No, you may not.

Penny slaps my hand hard so my rosary beads clang against the pew in front of us and startle the deacon, who spills blood from the chalice onto the church carpet, and we try to hide our giggles. My own mother puts her chin on her shoulder, glances backward telling me next time it's the family pew with the rest of them, packed in uneven and tattered like an old box of crayons. I think maybe she'll forget like she does sometimes.

Mother of Thimbles and Thread and Blue Cotton Birthing Hips.

Mother of Late Nights and Early Mornings.

Mother of Perpetual Hope.

Mother of Sorrow.

Mother Fucker.

No, not that one!

Penny gasps and smacks a red palm on my leg and shrieks, her eyes the size of robin's eggs, and I sit there hot and quiet as nothing wondering why it's always she does and I don't and what everybody knows but me because I thought we were just playing a game.

Mother of Mercy, I say because maybe She's listening and maybe she'll wash away my sin so I'm pure as white again, like all the other white kids in white shirts and pressed pants praying to white Jesus.

Except one day at school our friend Nina says, nuh uh Jesus is black. I saw him one day in that other church, black as coal, black as a fly in a blue robe, she says.

Jesus isn't white or black, Penny says, he's African or something, there's a difference, but if you want to know what it is you'll have to ask somebody else.

After mass, it's pats on backs and clasped hands and talk about children and the president. And the bells gong and Penny and I sit on a stone wall like we do sometimes thinking how its sole purpose seems to be to keep the dirt from getting into the sanctuary and wondering who decided to put the church there in the first place. Our legs dangle like wind chimes, Sunday socks flutter back and forth like white butterflies playing hide and seek, and the stone wall digs dimples into the backs of our thighs unprotected by last year's dresses. Penny looks down a long time. Maybe at the ground. Maybe at the tiny suns on the tips of her black shoes penduluming back and forth.

He's dying, you know.

Only I don't know, of course.

Who's dying? I ask.

The Holy Ghost, she says.

But isn't he dead already?

A spirit never dies only once, she says. It's again and again and again, but this time, no one knows if he's coming back.

Where is he? I ask, and she says in the upstairs bedroom, pacing back and forth in a dingy white gown the same color as his skin and fingering rosary beads and not knowing today from Tuesday because that's how old age is sometimes. And he's talking to the bells.

Yes, James, he says, it was a lovely service today.

And yes, they are the voices of angels.

And love them? Of course, I love them. I love them all.

And yes, I'll pray. I'm always praying.

And then the Holy Ghost, he lies down in his bed beside the window and takes a nap because he's exhausted from all that praying, and the bells of Saint James shush him and rock him against their chin and swaddle him in love and so many blankets and the ghost says who'll ring in tomorrow, James, who? And how will I know when it's time—

And that's it. She shuts off like a spigot, like the story just dried up in her mouth.

What do the bells say then? I ask Penny, both of us still staring at our ankles and the earth so far below and wondering if it's worth the risk to forsake the wall for two seconds of sky.

Nothing, she says. Everybody knows bells don't talk.

And she jumps and lands hard on her feet first, then on her knees and hands. Then she stands and brushes the hair from her face and studies the raw pock marks in her hands. A trickle of blood lets loose from her knee. She looks up at me, smiles and turns, skips along the sidewalk and around the corner.

And I just sit waiting for Mother to remember she's missing one, and I listen and listen. Dogs bark. A mower kicks up. An old lady coughs and spits. A car thumps past, its windows open like angry mouths yelling. Leaves and cicadas rattle to one another and cherry blossoms plop plop plop in the fishpond. But the bells, they don't say anything, just gong and gong and gong.

# Fearful Child

## Kimberly A. Werner

Dear fearfully and wonderfully made child of Mine,

I want you to suffer.
I want to watch you be beaten, then beaten, then beaten again.
And watch you slowly rise and be beaten again.
I want you to hurt so deeply and excruciatingly that death would be merciful.
Death would be kind.
I want you to feel unbearable, crippling pain such that in a peculiar phenomenon you begin to hate yourself.
I want it to last and continue without hint of relief except for in the brief moments where you consider complete surrender.
I want you to be broken just to this point but not beyond, so that the abuse can endure.
In those moments, I want you to taste the tease of hope to ensure that your torment continues without pause.
I want the thought of being rid of this suffering to be so magically and unbelievably incredible that you envy everyone around you.
That your biggest dreams are of neutrality.
Then despise yourself for feeling jealousy.
I want you to be disgusted by yourself, physically, mentally, and emotionally.
I want you to begin to believe this is what you deserve, and feel unworthy of anything but cruelty.

I want it to eat your soul to the point of changing your personality into something disgusting that you nor anyone else can recognize nor love.

I want you to feel and be alone.

I want it to push away everyone that cared to love you so that you are offered no comfort.

I want it to create such havoc that it begins to insidiously destroy everything else you have built in your life with dedication, devotion, and love so that it slowly leaves you with nothing in its wake to offer you any brief comfort.

I want it to destroy everything you have created and were proud of in the life you once knew.

I want it to drown your every thought and consume every waking and non-waking moment.

I want others to forget about you while it drowns your every thought and consumes every waking and non-waking moment.

I want you to be bombarded with proof constantly that it is you and you alone I seek to crush, while I offer blessings to those around you only to elevate and magnify your torture.

I want those around you to accidentally trigger your deepest fears surrounding your torment.

I want them to unintentionally support your self blame.

I want you to scream and plead and barter to be saved and hear the silence of abandonment, in hopes that it furthers your loss.

I want you to have ill-conceived notions of sacrifices you can make in attempts to save yourself, in futility, only to deplete you of more but without solace.

I don't want you to question why I've forsaken you, because I want your acknowledgment of my active participation in your destruction.

I want it to be chaotic, without reason or understanding.

I want it to defy odds so that you are aware it is not random, but purposeful and directed.

I want pure physical pain to seem comparably blessed, though I also want physical pain to compound your suffering.

I want you to wonder if you will ever be without fear, without tears again.
I want you to wonder if you will ever laugh again.
But I want you to remember those memories vividly so you know exactly where you are.
So that the hole feels deeper.
I want you to cry until your body is physically withered and sucked empty.
I want this to be your identity.
And I want you to hate it.

I know you believed in the beauty in the world.
I know you believed it to the extent you dedicated your life to helping others see it too.
Such that you lived each day in conscious gratitude, radiating joy in moments of challenge to prove your constant and intentional thanks.
Such that you devoted yourself to helping others in both the trivial and monumental.
Such that you laughed every day.
I know you thought that life could be what you made it.
And that it was intrinsically innocent and beautiful and good.
I know you loved hard and generously.
I want this pain to make you burn all of it.
I want it to make you question everything.
I want it to make you wish for the peace of nothingness.
I want you to love nothing.
I want you to hate your life.
I want you to hate yourself.
I want you to fear.
I want you to suffer.

—Your heavenly Father

# Football with Leatherman

Ross Berger

HE WAS BALDING WITH GRAY SIDEBURNS AND HAD WHITE HAIR sprouts all across his ears. His belly protruded after years of unhealthy eating, particularly cinnamon krullers and Utz Original potato chips. He had prodigious forearms though: thick and fibrous, a gift of genetics, patrilineal. He was a man of unimpressive height, maybe five foot nine at most; nonetheless, he was formidable even at age eighty. Broad shoulders spoke of his days as a street fighter in various Brooklyn alleyways; they were nothing more than products of teenage mischief and hormonal showmanship. Once he turned twenty-five, he kept up the strength of his shoulders with a daily routine of push-ups that eased in his later years due to high blood pressure. The aforementioned belly followed. His left eye looked like it was in a constant squint. The squint scared people; made him look like a pirate without his patch on. There was lore around this eye. He told strangers that a piece of glass scraped his cornea during a bar brawl with a Polish anti-Semite in Greenpoint. The Pole suffered a broken nose and was unable to walk without a limp and never called a Jew a dirty kike again. Don't mess with me, said the eye. In truth, the man who shared this lore contracted acute retinal necrosis—herpes in the eye—after an encounter with a prostitute during his days in the Merchant Marines. The man's name was Gabriel Samsky, and he was my father.

I never knew Gabriel like Gabriel wanted to be known. It started with his gifts, which—I admit today—I never appreciated. He once made me a briefcase that he fashioned from full-grain leather, tanned to perfection. This was ideal for a lawyer or businessman. I wanted a knapsack. I was in third grade.

As a child of the 1980s, I made countless attempts to watch football with him every Sunday in the fall. He was a bleeding blue, diehard New York Giants fan. While I appreciated the brute force of Lawrence Taylor on the gridiron and the coarse charm of his coach Bill Parcells, I couldn't quite follow the rules of the game and bored of it routinely by the second quarter. Gabriel viewed me as either soft or spoiled and seldom listened when I had a reasonable gripe, as if children were too callow to have one. He was never interested in the things I was interested in. Theater, books—"girly stuff," he would say. When I acted in plays, he reddened at the sight of me in makeup or, while playing Peter Pan in seventh grade, in tights. "Just don't become one of them," he warned—that is, of gay people—and summarily bought me a subscription to *Playboy* magazine when I was thirteen. It was a welcome gesture for the first year, but when I started to read the magazine just for the articles, Gabriel canceled the subscription.

I was a skinny child, who surpassed my father in height at an early age. He was never threatened by me; I never had the bodily template of manhood. I was cursed with ectomorphic lankiness that befitted a permanent teenager or, in my case, a dutiful son. "Bean" is what he'd call me, short for "String Bean." Even when I won an academic scholarship to college, he called the local Jewish newspaper a proud father and asked that they write an acknowledgment of this milestone, "as achieved by David 'Bean' Samsky." The announcement was a surprise to me and my high school friends, who thereafter playfully jabbed me with the "Bean" moniker, first incessantly, then periodically, and to this day seldom but lovingly.

Gabriel and I didn't speak that often after I left for college. He wasn't much of a conversationalist over the phone, and, in the summers, I was too busy with various jobs—tutor, telemarketing agent, house painter, librarian assistant. Christmas breaks were the last time we saw each other on a consistent basis. But, even as a young adult, I engendered little, if any, curiosity from him about my studies. When I did on that rare occasion, we'd wind up fighting and vying for Loudest Voice in the Room. He backed down when he was no match for my wit. He knew then, quietly, that my station in life would surpass his one day. After all, when it came to a good education, he knew the score. Had he not dropped out of high school, it was likely he would have done more with his life than be a leather craftsman whose business was always in hock. We stopped trading barbs during my sophomore year in college. The days of manly one-upmanship were coming to an end. Asserting oneself in that department lost its sting and fatigued us both.

Oddly, in 2012, both my mother and father were diagnosed with lung cancer. My mother didn't make it very far after her diagnosis. The radiation did little to shrink her tumor. The chemo caused her hair to fall out and nauseated her. The disease first robbed her of her right to breathe and then it took away her Mediterranean beauty. She succumbed in her sleep in less than a year's time. My father, however, took to the treatments like a pro. Radiation shrunk his tumor significantly, and surgery gave him a new lease on life. He was alone for the first time in forty years and still made little effort to reach out to me. I was working as a financial journalist at the time, writing for *Bloomberg Magazine.* It was a thirty-five-minute subway ride from my apartment in Midtown Manhattan to his row house in Flatbush, Brooklyn, so, upon the six-month mark of my mother's death, I made it a habit to visit my father every Sunday. We'd frequent Edelman's Delicatessen on King's Highway. It had an all-you-can-eat salad bar. My father, whom I'd often call by his first name, never ate greens during the week. Sunday was his time to be healthy. So he thought. The pastrami sandwich he'd invariably inhale that day, with its savory fatty rims, nullified that effort. After a few months, he discouraged me from visiting him, often refusing to answer the door when I knocked. I was worried about his health, but he assured me over a rare phone call one day that he was fine.

"I just want some time alone," he told me.

I missed my mother too and yearned for her daily check-ins. They were annoying. But they were reassuring all the same. And without the reassurance, I—like my father—felt adrift and fragile. She was there for me during my divorce; she had the presence of an otherworldly force like the goddess Minerva, dispatching wisdom and guidance on topics of love and survival. I worried that, without my ex-wife in my life, I'd lose what little connection I had to the social world. Work was one thing, friends were another, and I was not very good at making those back then. My mother kept me whole and even introduced me to potential guy friends. She was my shadchan, a Jewish matchmaker sans romance. I met my poker buddy Neil Holzman that way. I survived my ordeal, but my father was a different story. He didn't have his Minerva when a tragic absence was forced upon him. He had Schnapps and television.

Gabriel made several attempts to date, but with his small nest egg and gruff personality, he was no longer a pot for which there was a lid. His drinking kept pace with his misery, which was frequent. I continued to make several pleas to see him, but he never budged. I had a book published during this time. It was on trading derivatives—a basic how-to, peppered with interviews with three Wall Street juggernauts. I was interviewed on CNBC and Fox Business, but I was criticized online for my lack of enthusiasm. I stated facts of the book as if I were drugged on lithium. Frankly, it was a boring book; I did it just for the credit. My father didn't tune in to see the interviews. "I don't understand that stuff," he said. I offered to deliver the book to him personally, but he admonished me for not respecting his privacy. "Just send it. I'll read it," he ordered. And so I did. I never heard from him. Then, nearly a year since my last visit, I wished him a happy Rosh Hashana and heard barking.

"Where are you? At a park?" I asked.

"No, I'm at home."

"You got the TV on?"

"Nope."

Again: not much of a conversationalist, my father. The barking continued.

"What is that, Pop?"

"That is Lulu."

"Who's Lulu?"

"My service dog," he said and then fed her a piece of boiled hot dog. I could hear her chewing when he kneeled down to feed her more bits of meat. Gabe struggled to get up and anguished some. "Oy," he uttered. This was said not because the effort was taxing, but because it's the reflex of the Jewish Old Man.

"Why do you need a service animal?" I was scared to hear the answer. He unleashed a drawn-out exhale with the tone of annoyance.

"I need a little help around the house. Okay?"

When I inquired further, his temper rapidly skyrocketed. I admit: my approach was journalistic, unkind even. I was interrogating him like I did with many a Wall Street executive. I thus didn't trust anything he said. I assumed the worst, and soon my questions were unvarnished and hostile. I was off my game. I worried that in a year's time he'd suffered from a serious ailment that kept him off his feet and he was too proud to tell me.

"I'm coming to see you," I said. "And you're letting me in this time."

I could hear another annoyed sigh.

"Okay, but on one condition," Gabriel said. "You bring over half a pound of pastrami from Edelman's."

THE WAX PAPER HUGGED the slices of beef tightly and preserved the aroma of coriander and garlic. The scent enticed me. While walking from the subway stop to Gabriel's house, my stomach growled and my salivary glands kicked into high gear. I unwrapped the packaging slightly and slinked a slice to keep my appetite at bay. I had laid off red meat for two years at the behest of my cardiologist, and despised him during those thirty seconds of gastronomic rapture. The taste was like discovering El Dorado. Good pastrami is sumptuous gold. The key is, as Gabriel once told me, it needs to be fatty and have the right proportions of allspice and mustard seed. "And don't over-smoke it," he'd say. "You want the slices to be moist, not dried out. You're eating beef, not a

Florsheim shoe." (Of leather and pastrami, my father was not to be second-guessed.) I ate another couple of slices before turning onto his street. And then a couple of slices more. I got startled when I saw his house. The small plot of grass out front was overgrown and browning. The bushes were shaggy, gray, and unloved. A series of newspapers piled up on and around the small stairway that led to the front door. There was dogshit in the alley between his house and his neighbor's. I knocked several times, but he didn't answer. His new friend Lulu barked repeatedly. Finally, I reached him on my cell phone. He had two voices for the same dialogue: one emanating from my phone and the other, uttered a half a second before, from the top floor, that was muffled but vibrating through the wood of the house. He yelled these days, even during benign conversations. "I have a twenty-fie-dollar copay when I see the urologist!" Onlookers might interpret this as righteous indignation against—in this case—an oppressive medical establishment, but it was nothing more than Gabriel's going deaf. He opened his window and waved.

"You brought the meat?" he asked.

I held up the package, ripped sticker and all. He gave me a thumbs-up.

He was wearing prescription sunglasses when he opened the door and told me he accidentally stepped on his regular pair three weeks before. "Cool look, right?" he said. "Like Don Johnson in *Miami Vice*." I nodded politely, didn't want to tell him he's thirty years too late, and peered around. As I expected, the place was in disarray. There were more piles of newspapers, opened this time. Dust caked every fixture, every knob, every inch of floor and wall. The family room was filled with various go-nowhere projects in medias res, including endless rows of leather shoes, styles dating back to the 1970s, that awaited restoration. Five years retired, and still a leatherman. The house smelled as such, of polish and sundry shoe lotions. It also smelled of mildew, mothballs, and wet dog. CNN was playing on a 1990s Magnavox, the one we still had when I was in high school. The closet door was open and housed even more shoes, mostly muddy galoshes, and ten different umbrellas, some open, some not. My mother's beige raincoat and rain bonnet were still there, untouched since her passing. I attempted to walk through but was stopped by the growls of a chocolate Labrador.

"Easy, Lulu," said Gabriel, but the Lab kept snarling. "She'll calm down if you feed her a slice of meat."

I wasn't scared, like Gabriel thought. Labs aren't known for being aggressive. This was my father's way of inserting his virility. He assumed everyone around him was weaker than he was and spoke for you to enforce that. I took out a slice and dangled it in front of the dog. She lapped it up in one bite, turned her head down, and chewed in staccato. Gabriel glanced at the deli package, which was now less prodigious than before. He was irate:

"I said half a pound."

The kitchen table had a transparent plastic covering over it; there was a tablecloth in between. The plastic covering was through edict of my mother. She forbade natural wear and tear from crumbs and spillage from damaging the tablecloth, even though she could easily wash it in the washing machine. This was her quirk, one of many. My father hadn't cleaned the plastic covering, likely ever. Dried tomato sauce and pepper seeds crusted the covering. Countless coffee stains spoke to his hourly addiction.

Gabriel manhandled the slices of pastrami and slapped them in between two pieces of seeded rye. He then schmeared Gulden's brown mustard on the bread and on the top layer of meat. He heaped some sauerkraut from a foggy Ba-Tampte jar that had an expiration date from three years beforehand. He devoured the sandwich unapologetically. Bits of kraut and mustard adorned the sides of his lips. Lulu looked at my father with great adoration, panting heavily.

"Don't beg," he told her. He tore off a fatty edge from the beef of his sandwich and offered it to her on his palm. She sponged it with her pink tongue, which didn't look too unlike a slice of corn beef. (That day, everything to me looked like cured meats.) My father and I ate in silence, that is, without conversation. The lip smacking, the yums, the mmmms—they spoke for us. When I went for my glass of Dr. Brown's Cel-Ray (which he kept in the fridge for likely many months; it was flat), I saw my father get up to wash his hands and mouth. The meal was over, even though I wasn't done.

I noticed, though, that there wasn't a limp or hip discomfort that would typically merit the help of a service animal.

"Where do you take the dog?" I asked.

"She just stays with me at home."

"How does she help you exactly?"

Gabriel felt the second coming of an inquisition. He folded his arms. "Why is that your business?"

"If your health is in decline, I need to know."

"It's not. So, relax."

"I have a feeling we have a different interpretation of the word 'decline.'"

He stared me down, his only weapon in a dwindling arsenal. If Gabriel were to lie, it would not be without precedent. He squandered family money on half-baked business ventures that nearly bankrupted us. He covered up his failures by blaming his business partners, of which—as my mother and I later discovered—there were none. After a while, we stopped paying attention to my father's manic excitement over new ideas. Whenever he got an audience, he'd bet the farm. We figured if we ignored him, we'd at least keep the roof over our heads.

"Lulu's an emotional support animal," said Gabriel.

"Emotional support?" I asked dubiously.

My father paused, darted a glance to the floor, and said plainly, "I'm sad."

A laugh hurled out of me, deep from my diaphragm. I stifled it once he perched his head down. He then pursed his lips awkwardly, as if he never learned properly the mechanics of crying. The muscles in his cheeks slackened. His face was still pudgy, but the eyes were innocent in their despair. This meekness was new to me; it rendered my father, the Brooklyn street fighter, the son of a Russian immigrant cement mason, unrecognizable. I laughed because I expected more out of him; I expected more out of people. You don't just say "I'm sad." You talk around it; you hide behind a metaphor. But these were the circles I traveled in. Not his.

"The dog has helped a little bit. But, boy, was that a tough sell," he said, lost in thought. "My psychologist finally wore me down five months ago."

"Since when have you been seeing a psychologist?"

"Since your mother died."

"Why didn't you tell me this?" I asked.

The none of your business refrain played again. But this was not an issue of privacy; it was one of strength. He thought, to be perceived as weak is to kill the soul. Thus, Gabriel was not giving up what little strength he had left. Still, I regretted laughing at him. I was guilty of cruelty, and as my ex-wife accused me of, I was no stranger to doling it out on occasion.

Lulu sidled up next to me and sat upright with her back facing me.

"She wants you to pet her," said my father.

I scratched her back with long, linear rubs with my nails embedded deep into her fur. The flourish of my wrist resembled the act of sharpening a straight edge razor on a narrow foot of cowhide. When I stopped to look at the time on my phone, Lulu moved her head straight up and raised her brow. Through her adoring eyes, she asked me why I stopped. I obliged her, picked up where I left off, and, after the fifth stroke, fell in love. My father looked on and smiled.

THE MAGNAVOX WAS LARGE enough to display MetLife Stadium in its full glory. The New York Giants were playing the Dallas Cowboys one Sunday in October, and a rookie named Odell Beckham Jr. was the Giants' only saving grace to what would be, yet, another miserable year. It had been three seasons since their last Super Bowl victory; how far they fell in such a short amount of time! Like so many men his age, Gabriel presided upon a throne that was a raggedy recliner from which he would seldom rise. His kingdom? The living room. He would get to his feet in front of guests only on rare occasions. If you were lucky enough to witness such a feat, you were likely sitting next to him on a leather sofa, maroon and rife with crumbs dating back to the days it was first bought twenty years beforehand. On this day, however, my father got up on his feet for every Odell catch—each one a masterstroke in athleticism. As one would discover in the games to come, OBJ was superhuman.

"We're gonna win it this year, I can feel it!" exclaimed my father, wearing his Don Johnson sunglasses again. He, of course, was talking about the Super Bowl. But, for a victory that day, the Giants' hopes were dashed in the third quarter. Their offensive line was too porous, unable to thwart Dallas aggression. Even the weakest of Cowboy linebackers dominated Eli Manning, the oft hapless Giants quarterback. The G-Men's defense was gassed and couldn't keep up with Tony Romo, Dez Bryant, and a series of other offensive arrows in the Cowboys' quiver. Final score: 31–21.

My father stewed. He kicked a pile of newspapers to the ground and threw his remote across the room. Lulu saw this as a sign of anxiety, circled his legs, and leaped up to console him. He then shot me a gaze of pure rage, as if I didn't share the same indignation.

"What, you a Cowboys fan?"

"Absolutely not," I said.

"Then why aren't you angry?"

"It's a game, Pop."

He threw a couple of cashews at me and told me to go to hell. When Terry Bradshaw and the other Fox broadcasters reviewed the highlights of the game, my father stood up and paced. He cursed out the Giants' head coach Tom Coughlin and kicked another pile of newspapers over.

"Pop, why don't we take a walk?"

He was too much in his head to reply. Then: "If you really want to spend some time with me, you gotta get into it. This game is the only thing that makes me happy these days."

"Happy? You nearly punched a hole in the wall!"

"David, you can just go home."

The tone of a stern father—hadn't heard that in two decades. It hit a nerve, a primal one. I was suddenly faced with two choices: to fight or to please.

"Sorry," I pleased. "It's been a while. I need a refresher course on the game."

"You got seven days." Gabriel sat down on his recliner and crossed his arms. Scolding complete. This was his victory for the day.

I was feeling petty at that moment and told him I'd oblige, but on one condition: that he read my book. He let out another annoyed gasp. He couldn't look at me; he hated compromise. My mother made so many concessions for this guy . . .

"Send it," he said.

"I already did, like five months ago. Don't tell me you threw it away." I then looked around his House of Piles and figured it was collecting cobwebs under a newspaper somewhere.

"Send it again," he said, "and I'll see you next week."

That was it. Dismissed. There was no need to say goodbye. Lulu followed me to the door. I kneeled beside her and petted her forehead. She wagged her tail and panted. She walked within a half an inch of my nose, unfurled her tongue, and licked upwards. She grazed the tip of my nose, leaving a spot of moisture that I left there to dry on its own. It was the first kiss I received from anyone in over a year.

THE BOOK—*THE DEFINITIVE Guide to Options Trading*—was a three-year effort that should've taken me just nine months. I lobbied for several extensions from the publisher, who was sympathetic to the hardships of my divorce. She endured two herself by the age of thirty-five. I dedicated the book to my mother ("In loving memory . . . Dolores Samsky 1940–2012") and took no solace, relief, or joy once I had a galley in my hands. I burned out long before the book's final phases, thanks to a demanding job at Bloomberg and to the permanent schism from my ex-wife. I took several sick days to recover from the fatigue after submitting my first draft; I couldn't get out of bed, except to use the bathroom. Then, when my mother died, I entered the final phase of copy-editing in zombie mode. The mechanics of grammar—this I could do without heart, without investment, without precision. I dared not read the book afterwards for fear of encountering a chapter or passage that was subpar. There were too many to count, I imagined. I had, simply, run out of steam.

I sent my father another copy the Monday after our cashew-laden spat. It had been two years since I wrote the book, so I flirted with skimming the pages and randomly spot-reading a passage or two. The book was foreign to me, as if it were written by someone else, someone who cared. This was more painful than burn-out.

My father called me in the middle of the night the following Thursday, complaining of chest pains. I told him I'm calling 911; he yelled at me and told me I must pick him up instead and drive him to King's County Hospital.

"I need to make sure Lulu is taken care of," Gabe said frantically.

"Of course she'll be! Just call 911 and I'll find my way into the house after!"

"No!" he screamed. "I don't want you breaking a window."

"Pop. Call 911 or I will!"

He was pale when I saw him in the ICU. A nasal cannula plugged his nostrils. Tufts of white hair from his chest sprung up above the collar of his hospital gown. He was playing Solitaire across his food tray. He didn't look my way when I ran in.

"Hey, boychik," he said. He was nonchalant, like the old days when I returned home from school. I kissed his forehead and he pushed me away. To Gabriel, affection was sappy, and sappy was intolerable.

"The doctor told me you're gonna be fine."

"Doctor schmoctor. What does he know?"

"He knows that it was just indigestion."

"And what—so I can pay twenty thousand dollars to fart in the emergency room? Thank God for Medicare!"

"They're still gonna run some tests," I assured him.

"Good. Make it a cool hundred grand. Why not, I'm worth it."

I gazed at his hands. He was ignoring the rules of Solitaire and just placing cards down willy-nilly.

"You want me to get you a magazine, Gabe?"

"Too tired to read."

He wasn't wearing his Don Johnson sunglasses. His eyes were bare and defenseless. Even the herpetic one was at rest. He made little effort to focus on anything more than a foot away.

I rested my hand upon his shoulder and lightly grappled the tough muscle. He was still mighty at eighty. He swatted my hand away and let out an old man's growl.

"I'm delicate," he joked.

I took a seat beside him and became mesmerized by his sleight of hand with the cards. It was like watching the same article of clothing bounce around inside a clothes dryer. It's rhythmic and predictable. My anxieties calmed.

"Got your book," he said.

"Oh good." I paused. "You gonna read it?"

"I'll try," he said, once again annoyed, as if he were placating a child who kept asking him questions over and over again. "Can you take me to the park later?" "Can you drive me to the toy store?" "Can you take me to the movies?" I'll try, I'll try, I'll try. It's lip service, really. Gabriel might make an attempt at reading it. He'll look for the pictures and study those and only those and call it a day. Good deed for the week? Check. The joke's on him: there are no pictures.

Gabriel shook me from my stare when he slammed the rest of the deck onto his tray. It was rage at its fullest for a man of eighty. His fits had frightened me and my mother; they usually happened at the dinner table. There was no fair warning; it was pent-up frustration from the day that boiled over randomly. The cause was typically about money; sometimes about a customer. Today, I wasn't sure why. He regained his breath and gathered the cards. He reshuffled and laid out the first seven cards for a game of Tableau. Upon placing the eighth, he stopped, shook his head, and said, "I miss your mother."

THE TESTS DIDN'T FIND anything unusual. A slight arrythmia—that, he knew for fourteen years. He was told to stay on his blood pressure meds and was warned about eating in the middle of the night. "Do not recline or sleep within three hours of eating," were the wise words of his ER doctor. I went to Gabriel's house in the early morning and called a locksmith to jimmy open up the front door. Lulu greeted me with a thousand licks and kisses. I grabbed a few items of clothing in his bedroom, as Lulu got in my way and tried to entice me to play with her. I noticed a puddle of urine in Gabe's bathroom next to his bedroom. I wondered if it was from him or the dog. It was in the shape of the Mid-Atlantic states. I sprayed Fantastic over it and wiped the urine away. Lulu stared at me, plunged her front paws forward, and pulled her ass and hind legs in tow to signal her need to defecate. Suiting her up with her collar, I noticed a leather key chain strap on the mahogany table next to the front door. The chain strap had been lacquered with a finishing wax. It was liberally polished and gleaming. Lulu tugged and forced her way to the door; I managed to pocket the key strap before we left. Streaks of black polish hash-marked the palm of my hand.

We had a nice meal after I brought my father home. Bagels and lox. No onions, no tomatoes. Capers were the only pungent food he could handle. I wanted to ask him about the key strap, to see if it was a gift for me, but I changed my mind at the last minute for fear that it wasn't. I walked Lulu one last time before saying goodbye and heading to my apartment. That evening, when I emptied the contents of my pockets onto my nightstand, I examined the key strap thoroughly. There was no label on it, no brand name inked onto or imprinted in the leather. My father didn't just lacquer this; he made it entirely himself from scratch. It was a modest creation but stitched and cut to perfection. It carried the signs of a craftsman's love. No shortcuts. No cheap paint or polish; no thin stitching. No imbalanced proportions of its cut; the shape: a coat of arms. A loose chain went through its leveled top. The leather was ample and turgid. Regular scissors couldn't penetrate it. You needed the hefty shears of a tailor to do so. It was small cowhide, gussied up, made usable; the bits and pieces, the leftovers of unwanted bovine flesh reinterpreted, repurposed. Its beauty was found in the impossible odds of its functionality. It was elegant. These were the fruits of my father's labor.

The Giants were playing on Monday night against the Indianapolis Colts. My father and I dreaded what was to come. Quarterback Andrew Luck had the makings of a legend in just his third year. He was considered a worthy successor to Peyton Manning, an offensive juggernaut who, after being traded from Indianapolis because of a neck injury, was now breaking records in Denver. Peyton Manning was also the older brother of another high-profile quarterback: the Giants' own Eli Manning. Eli, despite his two Super Bowl MVPs, was mediocre (and, at times, pathetic) in his default state and was, unsurprisingly, no match for Luck that day. Gabe and I gritted our teeth from the opening kickoff. My father sipped hot consommé from a coffee cup and surrendered to the bloodbath that was to come. I brought a half a pound of pastrami from Edelman's again. I shared some with Lulu. My father asked just for a nibble of half a slice; I said no and reminded him of his recent visit to the ICU. He bum-rushed me and invaded my personal space. Here comes the third degree, I thought. But no. Instead, he sniffed my sandwich. Off the bewitching aroma, Gabriel patted his belly and proclaimed: "That's it. I'm full."

When the game was over, Luck had thrown for 354 yards with four touchdowns and led his team to a 40–24 drubbing of the G-Men. When I turned my head to Gabe to say, "That's that," he was deep asleep on his recliner, his sunglasses collapsed on his chest, his mouth wide open. The sounds of choking apnea blared from the back of his throat. I put a blanket over him and cleaned up around him. I stowed dishes in the sink, and then felt guilty about the enormous pile that I left for him. I spent the next thirty minutes soaping and scrubbing them and putting them in the dishwasher. I predicted they'd stay there until next Sunday, whereupon the responsibility of unloading them would fall squarely upon me.

Lulu followed me around like a loyal friend. Her eyes were wide open, eager to play. Her nose was moist from self-preening and shined like two contiguous nubs of black licorice. I planned to take her outside for one last pee, but morbid curiosity struck me suddenly. I entered my father's bathroom and there, once again, was a new puddle of urine. I soaked it up with a dusting of baking soda before wiping the floor clean. When I threw away the refuse of the paper towels, I noticed a book lying upon the rim of the garbage pail. It was my book.

I paid no attention to the location upon where it lay. A normal author might be offended that it was next to the pot. But I took it as a compliment: Where else but the toilet does one do their best thinking?

The book was dog-eared in several places. There were smatterings of penciled underlines and notes in the margins. The notes were often in broken English and rife with misspellings. "Whut?" "Jim Simons = muney" et al. A bookmark lay upon page 63, the chapter on "Put Options." If he was confused before, this chapter was not going to make things any easier. Good luck, Pop. I refastened the bookmark to its original position and kept the dog ears firmly flattened. My impulse for anal retentiveness perked up; I wiped off any fingerprints on the cover with a hand cloth. I made sure no trace evidence was left in my wake.

I was returning home on the Q train when, at the Dekalb Avenue stop, an elderly Asian woman pushed her grocery cart over my foot. I clutched a metal handle near an exit door, covered my face with the orphaned sports pages of the *New York Post*, and sobbed uncontrollably. It was a slight graze upon the foot, nothing more. The elderly Asian woman stared at me and wondered what the fuss was about. When I flitted her away so as not to be looked at, she understood this was not about the cart, frowned out of empathy, and then descended her gaze to be courteous. The misery, she thought, was mine and was not to be shared or infringed upon. Indeed, it was mine. It was not to be shared or infringed upon. But it was not misery.

"ARE YOU HAPPY?" HE asked me on a Friday morning in early November. This was a rare occurrence, in that Gabe took the initiative to call me.

"I'm all right. How 'boutchu?"

"Eh."

There was a long pause. My father's conversational dexterity at its finest.

"You callin' to shoot the shit, Pop?"

"I just want you to be happy. You know that, right?"

"I do. Thank you."

"Your mother and I were happy."

"I know."

"You're smarter and more successful than I am. You should be happier too."

I rolled the leather key chain strap in between my fingers. I brought it close to my nose and took a whiff of its polish.

"I don't have much in my will," he continued, "so I don't want you to hold a grudge against me when I'm gone."

"I will," I said half jokingly, "but not because of money."

"It was never about money for you, was it? Life."

"No. Never."

"Yet you write about it."

"It's just a paycheck," I said.

"I think I did a good job raising you."

I raised my left eyebrow like a cynical owl. If anything, it was in spite of my father's profligate ways with money that turned me against it. He had no program about life to instill in me. Morality, you needed to find on your own. There was no wisdom. No guidance. You just ate what was in front of you. And you did it fast.

"Will you take Lulu when I'm gone?" he asked.

"Yes, Pop. I will."

"She likes you."

"Yeah, I like her too."

IT WAS AN UNUSUAL Sunday in late November because the Giants were winning that day. The Jacksonville Jaguars were lackluster that year, and pretty much every year up to then, so the victory—if it were to be—wasn't deserving of chest-thumping.

Gabriel said very little to me and was indifferent to the game. He removed his sunglasses in the middle of the second quarter and pinched the skin between his eyes and rubbed the muscles of his brow.

"What's wrong, Gabe?"

"These glasses . . . they're giving me a headache. I can't see the screen."

"It's about time we fix your real frames. Where are they?"

"Forget it."

"WHERE ARE THEY?" I didn't mean to raise my voice or to startle him. The issue with his glasses was nothing more than absurd neglect, and I accommodated it for far too long. He told me they were in the desk of his study. My old room.

He used my bed as a workspace. There were several tools laid out: a scratch awl, a punch hole, a mallet, several knives. Remnants of leather were ready to be remade into a cell phone belt holder or a pocketknife sheath—things no one needed; nonetheless, they were to become well-crafted nice-to-haves. I looked for another leather knickknack to steal, but Lulu scampered in and started barking.

"What are you doing in there?" Gabriel called out.

"Can't find it!"

"Look in the upper drawer on the right!"

My old desk from high school still housed my Ti-81 calculator along with several pens, pencils, and desiccated erasers. My gold chain, a bar mitzvah gift from my great-aunt Elisheva, was tangled in the clip of a Bic pen. My father's glasses were inside a gray soft leather eyeglass case. It carried the raw, synthetic smell of leather conditioner.

The glasses held two very thick plastic lenses. It was top-heavy, and the frames were made of a light rose-colored metal. The rupture was located where the left hinge met the left screw. The screw had been frayed after years of fixing and no longer offered a secure tightening of the frame's temple. It was too far worn to be restored and needed to be replaced by an optician. But Gabriel was a skinflint and thus a do-it-yourself kinda guy. Either he was too lazy to fix or replace it, and the sunglasses enabled that inertia. Or: he met his match with this Lilliputian, threadbare screw and could not offer it the same love that he gave his leather dregs.

I found a roll of narrow electrical tape in the lowest drawer of the desk. I remembered putting it there in ninth grade after I secured the wires for a video game console that I stored in our basement. I wonder where that is . . .

I cut two centimeters worth of tape and rolled it tightly around the vertex of the screw and the hinge. I added another layer to make sure the connection was as rigid as could be. I excised the excess tape and blew a couple of hearty breaths over it to clear away any scraps.

When I held up the frames to his eyes, Gabriel inspected my handiwork. His herpetic eye soured.

"The hell is this?!"

"What do you mean?"

"I can't wear these."

"Just try 'em on, Pop."

"No—"

I pushed the frames onto his face above the ridge of his nose. He squirmed like a baby rejecting a spoonful of rancid Gerber's. The glasses were imbalanced: the left temple tip was outside of his ear and hooked the ridge above the lobe. Gabriel's meaty hands throttled my chest; a swift shock sent me backward.

"You dunno whatchu doing!"

"Let me try again—"

"NO!" He slapped my hands away when I reached for the glasses. "You don't have good hands."

He frantically attempted to resettle his glasses upon his face, but when he failed:

"Jesus Christ—LOOK WHAT YOU DID!"

He grappled the frames and twisted them until the lenses popped out and its bridge snapped in half.

"NOTHING!" he screamed and threw the broken pieces at the window. After a deep breath, he slicked the temples of his hair with his palms and gingerly—ever so gingerly—placed his sunglasses upon his face. The muscles in his hands tensed. He could've easily ripped off the arm rests of his recliner and thrown them at me.

Instead, he repeated, "You don't have good hands."

And then: "You don't have my hands."

KICKOFF WAS JUST TWENTY minutes away. Last game of the season. Giants were facing the Eagles, a likely loss in the waiting. It was raining in Brooklyn, and I wasn't in the mood to see him that Sunday, but I made the effort perfunctorily. Once I entered the family room, Gabriel asked me to walk Lulu. I didn't even get a chance to take off my shoes.

"I'm too tired today," he said.

"Everything okay, Pop?"

"My back, no big deal," he said and then slapped my hand with a ten-dollar bill. "While you're out, get another half a pound at Edelman's."

I stared at the bill. It was a kind gesture. He knew I could pay, but he was being surprisingly generous. Maybe it was an attempt to make amends for the week before. I didn't want to tell him, though, that ten bucks didn't cut it for a half a pound of pastrami these days.

Before I headed out, he stopped me and paused and then garbled a few words; it was an awkward dress rehearsal for what he really wanted to tell me.

"David . . ." he said—his eyes like a fawn's, sympathetic and shy—"a quarter pound o' kraut too. Okay?"

"Okay, Pop."

I saddled Lulu up and headed to the door. There, on the table, was something out of the ordinary once again. This time, not a leather knickknack.

My book was dog-eared on more pages than beforehand. There were also more notes in the margins, more spelling mistakes. The underlines were intentional, focused on the mechanics of trading derivatives. He was paying attention this time; he was learning. And he had finished the book. He wrote some chicken scratch three centimeters below the final line of the last page. The penmanship was eroded cursive; I took a moment to piece the lines and curves together. I was second-guessing several letters too. Then it became clear: "Well dun, Bean."

Well dun. My father . . . Not much of a speller or grammarian. Dropped out of high school at seventeen. He was a craftsman, a physical laborer. He expressed love through what he made for you, even if you didn't need it. He'd never pay you a compliment through words. His idea of praise was having you by his side at his work bench. To see the craftsman ply his trade is to reveal his secrets, is to expose his heart. In the grand scheme of things, "Well done" is part of the stable of staid compliments like "Solid" or "Keep it up." They are tiny encouragements, but they're needed. Not every street is paved in gold. Asphalt gets the job done too, almost always.

Lulu scratched my leg before pawing the door. I couldn't keep up once we walked the sidewalk. The rain had let up, so I shoved in my side pocket one of my father's unused umbrellas that I had taken with me. I was lost in thought, trying to figure out if my father left the book there on purpose. Lulu didn't let me mull; she was too restless and needed to go faster.

Her cooped-up energy spawned a new curiosity for the neighborhood. Yet, she had walked these streets many times before—why is everything so new to her now? What had Gabriel done to this poor girl? Had he not taken her out even once this week? She defecated four times and sniffed every sprig that budded from the sidewalk. I reined her in when she attempted to chew on an ant trap that was turned upside down next to a city trash bin. She pushed forth several times, trying to make a fast break toward a cat or squirrel. Skateboards inspired her wrath. Lulu possessed a deep bark: formidable in breadth, unrelenting in repetition. She walked ahead of me often and, at times, looked back to check on me. She was less a service animal than she was a guardian—this, the true emotional support.

The manager at Edelman's was kind enough to have Lulu join me when I ordered. We stayed six feet back from the deli counter. I defied my father's request and asked for a full pound each of pastrami and sauerkraut. Whatever my father and I (and Lulu) could not finish that afternoon, I'd take home.

I ate a few slices on our walk back. I was gobbling shamelessly. When we got to Gabriel's house, I noticed the lawn had been mowed and the hedges had been clipped, likely earlier in the week. The newspapers though—the stacks and stacks, now soggy from the rain, tumbled over the stairwell. The collapse cleared a pathway for me. I hadn't noticed any of this when I first stopped by that day. Funny, the things that you see clearly when you're suddenly in a good mood . . .

Lulu trudged through and sat on her hind legs on the top stair. Her face was dopey: her deranged tongue exerted its independence, searching for different parts of her snout to lick; her eyes were wide, caffeinated. She looked at me lovingly as I foraged for my dad's keys.

"Pop?" I called out. Lulu headed straight to the kitchen with me and already started begging for food. Roaring from the TV, Howie Long was arguing with Jimmy Johnson and the other pregame analysts on Fox. Lulu barked as I made my father's sandwich. Light load of pastrami this time, but always—always, always—heavy on the mustard. A schmear on the top layer of meat and, of course, another schmear on the bread.

"What's the score?" I called out as I shoveled some 'kraut onto Gabriel's plate. I made sure the dollop wasn't too wet; leaked excess would dampen the bread irrevocably and turn it into mush.

I walked into the family room, balancing his plate on top of my palm like a brasserie waiter. "Dad—"

He was sitting in his recliner as usual, but his head was bobbed down slightly to the left. His sunglasses, outstretched, lay upon his lap. One of his eyes was closed; the other—the one of lore—was open, but defeated; it no longer bore the signs of fight. His mouth was ajar. A string of saliva dangled from the mid of his bottom lip down to his chin. He was frighteningly still. And he was pale.

"Gabe . . ."

I sat on the floor and grappled his legs and could feel the last bits of warmth leach out of him. Lulu caught the early scent of morbidity and started to whimper. She pawed his knees, not once but twice. She circled aimlessly and scuttled away, frantically, before returning. Her whimpers intensified until she bayed. It was long and human-like; she was finding the right note, the right key to fit her pain. Her daddy—our daddy—was gone.

I raised the bottom of his left pant until it got stuck halfway around his calf. I kissed his shin and dug my face into it. Gabriel's smell was drifting away. I dreaded this. This transformation. I dreaded what fresh death made of someone you knew: The body and face may be the same, but the signature quirks are gone once emptiness takes over. A corpse is a stranger.

No, Gabriel. No, Dad. No, Pop. It was you—always you—who deserved a pat on the back. You lived fearlessly, you loved unconditionally, you admired quietly. Of compliments large and small, saying little said the most. Well dun, indeed.

# Like the Sun in Winter

## Lesley Bannatyne

EVERYTHING IN AN INSTANT: THE SKY LIT UP HOT ELECTRIC WHITE. House, farm, horizon vanished, their outlines etched onto Sandy's retinas, orange, then yellow. A wall of furious summer-like heat. Then the sound of the meteor, siren sharp, a blast like cannon fire that shook the metal grate on the thresher. Hot liquid in her ears. The wet thuds of a mare throwing herself at the walls of her stall. The air, velvet and smothering, the sky, roiling like lava, the wild wind making tornadoes in the hay dust that covered the barn floor. Sandy was in the house, hunched and screaming for Alec, as the windows around her shattered, raining, raining glass. Alec was in the barn, his hands glued to either side of the door jamb, knees locked in a crouch. Neither of them could know that the skylight over Sandy's head would then splinter and fall, as if in slow motion.

She woke in the hospital. Sickly green light. Nurses. Boiled oats. Alec, sitting too close.

"Sandy."

She squinted toward his voice, throat parched, tongue huge, damp sheets twisted around her legs. "It was a meteor, Sandy. It exploded in the air over Chelyabinsk. Our windows shattered, the skylight—you were hurt."

The flowers he'd brought, already wilting.

Pain arced through Sandy's legs, chest, groin, and back, hot in her left arm. She reached up to touch Alec's hand, and he recoiled at the sight of her thick, padded stump. To save the rest of her, a surgeon had taken the four fingers of her left hand.

A doctor appeared, unsmiling. Tomas translated: the glass slit her tendons; the skylight crushed her bones. The hand would have become infected, there was no other choice. She would heal, she would learn to do all she needed to do with what remained, her thumb and her knuckles.

What did you do with my fingers?

Tomas dutifully translated what Sandy had said to the doctor. The doctor shook his head; he did not understand the question.

There was a garish red, heart-shaped box of chocolates decorated with Cyrillic script on her bedside table. It was the day after Valentine's.

SANDY DRIFTED IN THE hospital for seventy-two hours: valium, oxycodone. Most often she dreamt she was back in New York City, purple pansies full-out in every planter along Houston Street and on her way to the NYU Farm Lab, her mother so proud she'd finally found a science job, and there was Alec, the brilliant BioChem grad student with the beautiful, pale olive skin, the two of them drinking Moscow mules in the tiny basement bar near his apartment in Brooklyn, her leg flung over his thigh, her forehead against the side of his face so they could hear each other's every word.

She hallucinated her best friend Colleen.

Don't go. You don't know shit about real farming.

Any loud sound, a bang of trashcan outside the hospital, clatter of meal tray, and Sandy would bury her face in the crook of her right arm, wrap the left over her head to protect against jagged spikes of glass, and wake to an imposter's body twisting inside her own.

The hospital released her with pain pills that lasted two weeks. The itching kept her awake most nights, and she lay in bed hour after hour trying to shut out the dull litany that forced its way into her thoughts. Can't thread a needle or push earrings into their backs, clasp a necklace. Can't floss, drive a stick shift, wrap a present, open an oyster, unscrew an aspirin bottle, pick up anything over fifteen pounds: a car battery, a child. She'd have given anything for five more minutes with two beautiful, long-fingered hands; to cradle, fold, grab, clap, fondle, cup, gather, press, rub, wring. To revel in the miraculous balance of a perfect body: two of these, two of those. It was the pairing that made you human.

WEEK FOUR, NEARLY SPRING, and it was still hailing sharp, snapping ice chips. Sandy stared out at the weak, white light of dawn on the drifts. She felt the buzzing of the generator, heard the mare exhaling a deep, wet sound. At Magda's, a rooster crowed.

Alec came in from the barn stomping freeze from his boots.

"There's a wolf coming around nights," he said.

"How do you know?"

"Magda, next door. She told me her son spotted it, but it ran off before he could shoot it."

"Just one? I thought wolves came in packs."

Alec smiled at her.

"Don't patronize me." Sandy handed Alec a Tylenol bottle with a childproof cap. "Open this?" He twisted the top, shook out two capsules, poured water into a mug, and handed it to her.

"There were tracks."

"What?"

"That's how they knew," Alec said. "Gray wolf. They're everywhere. Kill horses, reindeer. People hunt them."

"Poor thing must have been desperate to come so close to people."

"There's six figures for whoever can bring in the most wolf skins this season."

"That's harsh." Sandy's gaze drifted to the coat rack, to her bright red parka, one arm knotted against the cold—her stump was always cold—and she thought how un-Russian she was, a flinty cardinal among crows. And they were dark, these Ural farmers, with their paranoia about the state and the way they drank.

With her good hand, Sandy lifted a cup from the dish drain and set it on the table. She picked up the coffee pot, poured. She rummaged in a drawer for a spoon, placed it on the counter, then lifted the top of the sugar bowl. She'd taught herself how to make fried eggs with her one good hand. She found new patience with every tiny pearl button she twisted through its buttonhole, every snap she pushed against her breastbone with her right hand. She kicked her lace-up boots under the bed and ordered loafers from Ozon, gave up bras altogether.

"It's like driving a new car," she told Alec. "It feels different, but you know what to do."

Sandy was learning, as the doctor had told her so coldly, to do what she needed with what remained. Alec looked unconvinced.

"I'm fine," she told him. I'm fine! she screamed silently at him.

SHE WAS NOT FINE.

Russia was ugly in winter. The snow was relentless, storm after storm, new snow as indistinguishable from the old as water in water. It shouldered shut the doors and windows and trapped her inside. The stink of the propane heater gave her headaches, and the town, what there was of it—Three Cigars bar, gas, hardware—shut down for weeks at a time. The snowdrifts alongside the road were black with diesel filth and cat piss.

She'd once spotted their neighbor Magda sitting on a lawn chair in the snow, wrapped in her thick coat and scarf, her wizened face tilted back to catch the faint rays of late winter sun. Sunbathing in Russia.

"For strength," Magda had called out to her. *Prochnost.*

"COME INTO THE SHOWER with me," Alec called. "Water's finally hot."

Sandy heard the desire in his voice. She shrugged off her T-shirt and sweatpants. Alec folded her into his arms, and they stood swaying slightly feeling the warm water run across their shoulders. He turned her around and soaped Sandy's back in light circles. He ran his hands across her shoulders, down both arms. She steadied herself against the shower stall, and for an instant the stub of her hand and thumb splayed out on the white tile. Alec hesitated, then ran his soapy hand over her stump. Sandy clenched her teeth together, willing him to stop. He turned her to face him, but she buried herself in his chest, reaching both her hands around his back, locking herself down. Alec pulled her hands to his chest, closed his eyes and kissed one hand, then the other. She tried to tug her hands away but he held tight. Sandy sunk her teeth into his shoulder and bit down hard. He dropped her hands in shock.

"Jesus, Sandy!"

SHE HADN'T TOLD ANYONE but her family what had happened to her.

"I miss you," she said to her brother's raggedy image on Skype.

"Sandy, come back. Seriously. It's been too long. Come soon, come for Easter. Bring him."

"He's got things here on the farm, Freddy. He couldn't come."

Sandy glanced out the window at Alec, who was lining up a log on a stump near the barn. She loved the steady rhythm of axe and log, the simple, sometimes pleasant task of splitting wood. Something she wouldn't do again.

"So, come yourself. We'll drive out and see Mom. She needs to see for herself that you're all right."

Sandy waved her fingerless hand at the screen. "You know it barely hurts. I'm getting used to things."

She saw the shock on her brother's face. "Sorry. I know it's creepy."

"No, it's not that," her brother said. "I just wasn't expecting you to wave it around."

Sandy tucked her arm tight against her side and pulled her sweater over the stump. "Honestly, Freddy? This really sucks."

Freddy nodded. "You know what it looks like? Like you're hitchhiking. Or, kind of like an armadillo with a long tail."

"Or a snail."

"No. Armadillo." He poured a shot of vodka into a glass. "In your honor," he said, hoisting the glass.

Sandy lifted her own glass in a toast. "Nostravya! It does make me wonder about how this is going to go. I mean, I'll have to talk about this for the rest of my life. It's kind of hijacked everything else I was doing, like it's more important than any other part of me, this missing part."

"Will you come home?"

"I don't know." Sandy picked up a pen between the thumb and first knuckle of her bad left hand. She made a few senseless marks on the notepad in front of her.

"But you'll think about it?"

"Yes."

Even Freddy had told her not to go; he said Russia was too far, too big, too different, too cold. It would only be a year or two, she argued, enough time to fix up Alec's family farm so they could sell it. And she'd loved the physicality of it, loved having a horse and working an axe and learning the orchestration of gas-choke-clutch-gear that started the tractor. Where was that person now? She'd become angry, silent, and mean. And Alec hadn't signed on for this. She could feel him willing her to grow back a proper left hand as a starfish would, as if she could do that if she just wanted it badly enough. They'd known each other less than a year. She wasn't sure they had enough love in the bank.

After Freddy's call, Sandy could still feel the vodka in her body; it was good. She wrapped herself in a quilt in the upstairs alcove and sat in the window listening; tiny sounds filtered in. A rush of water from the sink, the sharp chat of squirrels in the firs. From here Sandy could see fresh footprints ending at tiny excavations two or three feet deep. It was the children: they looked for small pits in the snow, then dug down to find the polished stones encased in ice. Children had plastic bags filled with these meteor fragments hidden in their homes. They were worth a lot of money now. Magda told her that a woman in the next town was offered more than 100,000 rubles for the chunk of meteor that had burned a hole in her coat. Magda had found one in her side yard. She was saving it for her grandson because, she'd told Sandy, "It came from space. Our scientists send rockets thousands of miles to find these, and here they are, dropped right in our yards. People sell them too quickly."

Sandy had smiled as if she agreed, but really, she thought, the kid will sell it on eBay.

"What do you remember most about it?" Sandy asked Alec after dinner. An icicle detached from the roof and shattered on fieldstone with a crash. She didn't flinch; she was used to it by now. "I mean, when you think of the blast, what comes into your mind?"

THERE WAS BEEF STEW left in the pan, and Sandy poked a spoon at an onion stuck to the side.

"You were hurt, you collapsed," he said, opening a beer and taking a drink. "Magda and I carried you to her truck and we drove you to the hospital. She wrapped your hand in a towel and kept the pressure on. I drove."

"That's what you remember most? I remember calling for you—that's what I remember. Why didn't you come?"

"It happened in a split second, Sandy. There wasn't time—"

Sandy slammed the beer on the counter and pulled on her jacket and boots.

"Where are you going?"

She walked to the barn. She climbed up into the seat of the tractor, started the engine, and jammed down the gas pedal until she heard an aggravated roar.

"Sandy, stop!" Alec hollered. "Damn it, you're flooding the engine." He sprinted through the yard. "Stop!"

Sandy gunned the gas, shoving the pedal down so hard that the tractor shimmied. Alec grabbed the key and shut off the ignition. "What's the matter with you, Sandy?"

Sandy turned her head away from Alec and pressed her cheek to the tractor's cold metal window frame.

"You ran here in three seconds," she said. "You could have reached me in three seconds!"

"Why is this my fault? What about you? Why didn't you run? Get under a table? Save yourself?" He stopped himself. "I didn't mean that. I don't know what I mean."

"Let me explain, then." Sandy was furious. "You don't really want to take care of me, but you don't know how to get rid of me."

"You know you should have gone back home after it happened," Alec said. "But you won't admit that. You want me to tell you to go. If you want an exit, you're going to have to make it yourself, Sandy. I won't do it."

"Of course you won't."

"You're goading me now. Pull yourself together."

Alec strode back to the house. Sandy counted his steps. Twelve. She turned her face to catch the last of the setting sun and rocked gently in the tractor seat, eyes closed, taking slow, deep breaths. She touched the hard, cold steel of the tractor's body with her stump; there was no feeling in it, never would be. Her right hand, her "good" hand, could define the edges of her world as she always had. But with her left, if she closed her eyes, her missing fingers felt—what? Table or paper cup? Peach skin or hairbrush? There was nothing to warn her: this is me and that is that. Drifting in a Valium haze those first nights in the hospital, she wondered why no one mentioned that her ghosted left hand could also reach out into the realm of gods, wrap itself around the hospital, town, farm; gather everything precious and hold it close. It was really no different than imagining the touch of spoon, bowl, counter. She could feel nothing; she could feel everything.

Through the tractor window she watched a dull gray state car motor slowly down the street, as if searching for something. Magda believed the government would try to take back all the rocks people were hoarding, for science, so Magda had stashed hers in an old Drano bottle. People in Russia have to hide everything, she'd said.

Four fingers. The height of a Russian shot glass.

LATER THAT NIGHT, WHEN she was in bed reading, Alec sat down next to her.

"I don't know what you want me to do," he said, rubbing his ears, head hung. "Do you want me to talk to you or leave you alone? What? I can't figure out what you want anymore. Just tell me."

Sandy watched him like she'd watch a stranger on a train platform. She saw the beginning of blotches on his cheeks, the deepening crow's feet. She breathed out slowly, waiting for patience.

"What would you do if I was gone?" she asked him. "Could you manage?"

"You mean, with the farm?"

"No."

"You mean, if you left?"

"If I went home."

"Is that what you want?"

"I asked you a question. Could you manage?"

"Yes. No. Yes, what do you mean?"

"For God's sake, you know what I mean."

She turned away from him and pulled the duvet over her shoulders. Alec shifted and pulled on a boot. He started talking, about the wolves, about how he'd refill the propane tank in the morning if the outpost opened early. Sandy closed her eyes. She pressed the index finger of her imagined hand down into the mattress, as if poking a hole for a radish seed. God, she was sick of pitying herself. She thought of Magda, the first time she'd come to visit after Sandy left the hospital. She'd taken Sandy's tender stump, turned it this way and that. "It's not so bad," she said. "Four fingers. Pah. You're still you." This, thought Sandy, coming from a woman who was terrified the government was going to steal her rock.

Alec stepped into his second boot and shoved his wallet into his pocket. "I'll be back early," he said, and closed the bedroom door behind him.

Hours later Sandy lay in the dark, facing the glow of the electric clock: ten thirty, and no sign of Alec. She got up, pulled a blanket around her shoulders, and went to sit in the alcove chair. It was freezing. A small movement caught her attention: Close to Magda's barn, a wolf—belly low to the ground, dirty white. It was sniffing its way along the boards, looking for a way in. Then it stopped and dug, claws tearing at the icy crust.

Sandy pulled on her red coat, her boots. She lifted Alec's rifle from the rack and cradled it in her armpit. She fingered three bullets from the silverware drawer, shivering, sat down, and balanced the rifle on her lap. She put one bullet in her mouth, pulled back the rifle's chamber latch with her good hand, and loaded each bullet by pressing it between her thumb and stump. She opened the kitchen door and eased outside. Millions of stars shone overhead, like a reflection of a vast phosphorescent sea. It was so clear she could see every blade of frozen, dead grass along the road. She raised the gun with her good hand and sighted the wolf.

The crack of rifle shot shattered the night. A lamp flicked on in Magda's house.

"It's only me," Sandy called out. "The wolf."

"Spasibo," Magda said hoarsely. "Thank you."

The body lay slumped in colorless snow. Dots of blood that should have been bright red on the drifts were gray in the night. Sandy couldn't look at it another second. She dragged the gun into the kitchen and emptied the two unused bullets, weeping angry tears. It wasn't in her nature to kill wolves. The sharp pain from the gun's recoil burned in her body.

ALEC GAVE HER A quick, sidewise glance when Sandy came downstairs the next morning. "Magda and I put the wolf in the truck," he said. "It was a good shot, Sandy. It didn't suffer. We can drop the body off at the outpost on the way to the party."

"You sure you still want to go?"

"Why not? Drinking and karaoke and darts. What could go wrong?"

The Three Cigars cafe was having an all-day spring equinox party, and the parking lot was already filled with trucks when Sandy and Alec pulled in. They squeezed into a small table next to the stage, where an Asian man with a runny nose was singing a folk song. The bar was packed with men who'd been drinking all afternoon. Sandy slouched down in her seat and kept her hands in her pockets.

"You want a whiskey shot?" Alec asked.

"Two. And a beer."

After a few minutes her eyes adjusted to the dark, and she was relieved to see a few other women in the crowd. The Asian man finished his song to half-hearted applause, and a few people chanted, "Mi-kail! Mi-kail! Mi-kail!" Sandy looked around to see who they were yelling for. A man in the back of the bar rose to his feet, swaying slightly in unlaced boots. "Mi-kail! Mi-kail!" the rest of the room took it up. Mikail walked to the stage, climbed up, and took the mic.

He was a classic fairytale oaf. His face was a patchy crimson, and his thick, straight hair stood up in tufts. His ears, enormous, tipped out from his head like tiny wings. Mikail fumbled with the karaoke console, then stood tall and rocked foot to foot as if he were giving an oral report in the fifth grade.

*In a bar in To-le-do across from the de-pot—*

The crowd erupted in cheers.

"Sounds like he's done this one before," Alec said, handing Sandy her shots and beer.

"You think?" Mikail's voice was a surprise to her: deep, with that Kenny Rogers smoke in it.

The big hands were calloused; he looked like a mountain—

Mikail crossed the stage to where Sandy was sitting and dropped to his knees. Sandy turned her face as far as she could away from the huge man, but the salt-stink of his jeans was only inches from her nose.

*But he started shaking, his big heart was breaking, and he turned to the woman and said—*

The crowd roared.

*You picked a fine time to leave me, Lucille, four hungry children and crops in the field—*

Sandy looked desperately at Alec.

He shouted into her ear: "Just ignore him; he'll go away."

*I've had some bad times, lived through some sad times, but this time your hurting won't heal—*

To her horror, Mikail took one huge arm and scooped Sandy up onto the stage with him. She went red-faced, her heart pounding.

*You picked a fine time to leave me, Lucille—*

Mikail shuffled his feet back and forth in a crude waltz, one arm around Sandy's waist, one holding the mic. The stage lights made her blind. She heard bodiless voices shouting encouragement in Russian, everyone clapping. She tried to look like a good sport and shuffled side to side in an awkward 1-2-3 with Mikail, her hands shoved into her pockets. The chorus came around again, and the whole crowd joined in.

*You picked a fine time to leave me, Lucille, four hungry children—*

Mikail grabbed Sandy's wrist to spin her, the grand finale. He lifted the stump—the red, itchy-looking knuckles, the slender thumb—into the glare of the cheap red and blue lights, and she saw the oaf's expression erupt into confusion, then surprise, then revulsion. The crowd clapped and cheered till the end of the song, unseeing, drunk.

A bleached blonde in enormous furry white boots immediately jumped on stage and blasted the first lyrics of an Adele song. *Hello, it's me—*

Sandy left the stage and squeezed through the crowd toward the bathroom, brushing past Alec. She could still feel the hot flush of mortification on her face. A horse-faced woman in overalls gave her the thumbs-up, and a set of dyed-red-haired twin girls opened a path for her so she could get through. Mikail lurched after her, his face twisted, mouth set in a tight line, eyes wide. Faster, bigger, taller than Sandy, he got in front of her and blocked her way. She looked past him, moved to the side. He countered. She gave him a withering look. Then, to her surprise, he wrapped her in his enormous arms and hugged her so tenderly she felt tears well up. She smelled the liquor on his breath, felt the humidity of his skin warming hers like sun in winter. His touch was gentle, not sexual, not even friendly. It was pure compassion, from this oaf of a man who in a split second had seen and understood everything. As did she—his horror at what he'd done, his sorrow for embarrassing her. It's okay, she whispered. Sandy reached her arms around him and hugged him back, and the two of them rocked slightly. She didn't let go, didn't ever want to let go, and even when she saw Alec coming toward her through the crowd she didn't let go.

# The Whole Story of the Girl Who Talked to Fish

Meli Broderick Eaton

HOME WAS WHEN SHE LET HERSELF FALL BELOW THE SURFACE, when her body was no longer hers but instead belonged to the water that carried her gently into its depths. Home turned to heaven when the liquid tension rejoined itself far above her head, the two sides suturing back together just like Moses in reverse.

When her lungs eventually betrayed her and she had to come up for air by pushing her feet deep into the pale silt of the creek bottom, and when the day turned traitor and nighttime forced her to the house for supper, she reluctantly gathered her vestigial appendages and dragged herself from the wet. On the slow walk up the yard, at the dinner table with her hair drying like still-damp wheat and quiet conversation between her parents passing over her, and later under her unpleasantly dry and crisp bedsheet, she invented the sound of water tumbling between her ears and flowing through the clever folds of her brain.

She liked that water only went one way. It ran from the faucet to swirl down the drain; it coursed between the steep banks of Seevers Creek, always running one way and never coming back. With it went discarded things, things that went into the water and got carried away into forever, never to be seen again.

In the water she felt complete. She was whole; she was something instead of being part of something that was no longer whole.

The fish seemed to believe she belonged there and let her join their drifting cadre. They came close to her cheeks that puffed so far out with breath that she could see fleshy fringes in her vision as she stared back at their piscine eyes peering curiously into hers. She never had to blink in the water, and the fish never blinked either. They just floated and watched each other until eventually someone had to rise through the gradually lighter teal layers to break the surface for a gulp of air.

People were much more difficult. When Mama tugged her hand to get her to look up for an introduction, people would gasp and step back, as if they'd seen a ghost. She knew this was because her eyes were a color that shouldn't exist, a color people said was Caribbean blue, but she didn't know what Caribbean was and she didn't think of her eyes as blue. When she looked in the mirror, she saw glassy marbles the same color as looking up through deep water right where the sun shatters itself into shards of light that might be silver and might be blue going green. The old ladies at church and the clerk at the market, when they stopped in their tracks, made her squirm to escape Mama's hand and flee to the restroom where the water running into a pool in the sink calmed the electricity that thrummed through her veins.

Mama said it was the fever, the high temperature when she was a baby, that turned her eyes into miracles, as if heating the fluids she saw the world through could change them into the color of impossible possibility.

Whatever it was, the color matched the creek, and those matched the watery insides of her bones that felt floated into place just right when she was no longer in the air. From before she could walk, the water called her into itself like a warm hen calling her chick to wing for protection. Where Seevers Creek ran deep and quiet along the end of their yard, she was pulled starting when she was just beginning to crawl and made it to the water for the first time when her parents moved their eyes away for a moment. They found her out of reach, under the current, visible only by the edge of her tiny shirt floating pink along the pooling surface. The way they told her, before they could reach her with their horrified hands, sure she was dead because even a second can be too long, she bobbed up to take a breath and gave a giggle of delight at seeing them there, then disappeared with a flip as though by being born into this world she'd been taken from the water first. They swore that day they checked her for gills because there was never a moment after that when she didn't find water or that they worried for her safety.

As she grew, she didn't have friends in the way other kids, kids who were creatures of the air, had friends. She preferred the unblinking attention of the fish and the filtered light, the muffled sounds, the tangible thickness of water. Maybe it was how other kids fell silent when she looked into their bovine faces, or maybe it was the whispers about the underbelly-pale smoothness of her skin if they could stop from staring at the silver-flecked cerulean oddities that were her eyes. She spent her days in school coloring whole pages green and blue, drawing the fish she knew one from another, though her teacher asked her why she drew the same fish over and over. The teacher couldn't see with his normal eyes the nuance of fin angle or the extra half spot just under the tail. She frequently fled to the hallway to lean into the drinking fountain's cold trickle and found the noise of the runoff burbling down the perforated metal drain comforting in a way that she was sure no person would ever be able to soothe her. She wished she could grow webs between her fingers to help her swim away from there, through the air if she had to. The other kids would watch her one last time as she paddled faster and faster into the sky until she could splash back into the creek and settle into the glinting shards of mica mixed in with the creamy silt at the bottom of the creek bed.

It was the people who all looked alike, not the fish. Every last one of them was rubbery with dry skin and had hair that rasped dryly against itself and their pink tongues made icky sounds as they chewed and laughed, and this is why they stared at her so, because they were leaves blown scratching across the asphalt on a hot day and she was made of hidden scales and dappled light and didn't need to chatter the way everyone else did.

The relief of seeing Mama outside the school each day, waiting to take her hand and walk to the house they shared, was about the closest to water feeling the air world could provide. The feel of her small white hand disappearing into the toughened grip of her mother's hand, and sometimes Daddy's big mitt when he started coming more often too because Mama was tired lately, the sure squeeze and tug from people who knew how she needed the water, made her racing electricity turn instead to stars that coursed through her veins. She could feel the softening of sharp edges and she knew she would be in her real home in the creek or the bath soon.

"How's my fishy?" was all the talking they needed, then they could pretend to blow bubbles at each other with cheeks ballooned out as the stars in her blood lost their points and turned instead into tiny balls of light that just might carry her above the ground and away from the school just as she had imagined.

By April, still stormy and cold, she could see the end of the school year on the paper calendar on the classroom wall, the one she hated being chosen to place the day's placard on because the paper made her skin stick like frog fingers and goosebumps rise under the tiny pale hairs of her arms from the unpleasantness, and she knew the months when she had all day to spend in the creek would tumble toward her soon. Mama's voice was hoarse this spring and they sometimes went in the car because Mama didn't feel like walking. The car was worse than the air, everything hard plastic surfaces and artificial comfort, but she did enjoy the way the heavy door swung shut and blocked out the sounds of laughter and shouting outside the school, much like water closing over her head after parting to let her in.

May slid from April like a slightly darker sister of the same pale green light. May was her favorite because it was the first month after the long winter when she could get back to the creek without freezing, even if it was still chilly. Following the cold months when she submerged herself in a warm bath for hours every afternoon, the May creek was crisp and startling enough to make her gasp the air she liked to think she didn't really need. August was also her favorite because the driving heat of the air vanished once she dropped away into the depths where the fish seemed to wait for her in the green shadow of the banks. But August was months away and all she could think about was how it would feel for the water to lower her gently, slowly, to the creek bottom where winter might have moved the stones or carved new channels between the hidden hills of silt.

The first day that cracked sixty degrees, she was allowed to run to the edge of the property like she had all winter, only this time she got to jump in instead of mourning the fingers of snow that had lingered in the shadows of the trees until just weeks ago. The first jump that broke the slippery surface with a satisfying crack made the air stop in her lungs for a moment as her chest seized from the shock. Feeling the weightless float made her newly alive again, as though she'd been occupying a temporary shell and had finally returned to her real body, and she slowly treaded water, sensing the heaviness of land and the demands of the air world leaving her body. In her mind this leaving looked like the shimmering waves that rise from the summer highway. She stayed breathless on the surface, a push against the gentle current and the quick return of her limbs when she relaxed, until her lungs agreed to work again. As soon as her breath came easily, she allowed the water to swallow her under. Her hair had grown long since October, and it swirled into a yellow halo around her, trailing her like a comet's tail all the way to the bottom.

There was so much to tell the fish. The swimming club down at the Y all winter, where the artificial lights bounced through the chlorinated pool, leaving her skin streaked turquoise under the water and her hair tinted green out of the water, and how the other kids didn't understand why she spent so much time hovering at the bottom instead of skimming across it with the rest and all their frantic splashing feet. Most of all, she wanted to consult with the fish about the coughing that had started in Mama's body and racked her all winter long. Fish never coughed, so they must know a secret to keeping their lungs clear. Maybe they would be okay with Mama joining them in the water where, in the silence and trickling, the fluids of their veins learned to flow gently in the rhythm of the creek and they didn't need to think about breathing.

She couldn't whisper underwater, so she whispered inside her head and took the fishes' bobbing as affirmation. When she whispered to them about the sickness in Mama's chest, the illness that grew like barnacles and hardened her lungs so she could scarcely move air from the outside of her to the inside of her anymore, the fish stared and bobbed their understanding as bubbles of light danced down the rhythmic waving of their slick dappled sides.

She thought thoughts about the treatments Mama went to during the school day, the ones that dripped medicines into her that were supposed to eat the bad and chase it down the stream of her blood and out of her body somehow.

Three speckled fish the color of mossed honey hovered in front of her face, listening to her think these thoughts, as if they understood the magic of a doctor's potion that ran in tiny rivulets through a needle into the body of a person whose lungs were turning into an open oyster shell, butterflied and unmoving.

The consultations with fish stopped just before she thought to them that instead of eating away the barnacles, the medicine just made Mama tired now. Fish never seemed to tire, and they wouldn't understand a person who lived in the air but couldn't breathe enough of it. Over the spring months, Mama's eyes sank deep into her face like a fish that had been pulled from the water and left on the shore for days, the water leaving the body a shrinking husk as it dried. The fish wouldn't want to hear about this part.

June was birthed breech from powerful thunderstorms overnight that sent water rushing on top of itself through the steady banks of Seevers Creek and pushed what was a generous stream into a raging river with unrecognizable curved waves that lashed the water faster and faster. The next morning, the creek ran deep and swift as it swept itself clean of the storm, sending the unwanted turmoil downstream for the ocean to swallow.

On the last day of school, she looked up from packing her backpack with what little she kept in the cubby taped with her name surrounded by blue and green and brown fish, to find a girl she had never noticed before staring at her. The other girl didn't react when their eyes locked together like branches from two different trees caught by the wind twisting them just right.

"I'm going to the beach this summer," she announced. "Your eyes look like the sea. They make me happy."

Before she could respond, the teacher hurried over and pointed to her father in the doorway to the classroom. Thoughts rushed into her head in fast bubbles that she couldn't organize. He was early. He never came into the school. Mama wasn't with him.

She zipped her backpack and said goodbye to the other girl, hoping the girl would be back when they started the next year.

They didn't go home.

Trapped in the hard surfaces of the car, she watched a long, slender piece of marsh grass trail in the wind from the outside mirror. It was wrapped around the arm that held the mirror onto the side of the car, this slice of green that grew along the edges of the driveway where Daddy must have turned too sharply and been driving as fast as he was now. The engine strained dryly. In the minutes between the building where they started and the one where they stopped, they hurtled through the air world from a known place to an unfamiliar, hard landscape.

Daddy parked and hurried around the car to scoop her into his arms so he could run. The jostling, the air, the pavement, the glass and metal doors scratching open as if by magic. Lights glared and sounds ricocheted and her eyes began to make water of their own.

They stopped at door 128. It was closed but before she could read the white board hung on the wall next to it, a nurse hurried through toward them. She just barely glimpsed Mama, tiny shrinking Mama looking foreign on a white-sheet bed with the head part tilted up so she was halfway sitting in a way she never did. Machines like attentive robots surrounded the bed with flickering lights and insistent beeps. She felt her eyes widen to try and take it all in like a gulp of too much.

"Oh, good, you're here in time—" The nurse stopped herself with a short intake of breath as she looked up and their eyes met.

She pulled away from the woman's gaze, pressing herself into Daddy's shirt. His heart pumped beneath her ear, and she thought about the blood that raced through him like his own river rushing between its banks. Letting her eyelids drop closed moved her away from the nurse's stare and the bright lights.

"Her eyes . . . goodness. I'm sorry, I forgot what I was saying."

The nurse scurried away down the hall as Daddy quietly opened the door. The room's curtains were pulled across the windows, casting the bed in a gentle twilight even as the coming summer's sun burned its best outside. Daddy took a few steps and relaxed his arms, letting her slide slowly to the tile floor so he could take Mama's hand.

She felt her lungs freeze as if she'd jumped into the May creek. There was no current to calm her systems so she stood behind Daddy in the way the fish hover behind an overhang in the creek when an osprey sweeps across the sky, standing where his Daddy-shaped shadow would be if light were allowed into the room. All she could see of Mama was her arm and the tubes that ran in all directions from just above her hand.

Daddy made noises that weren't words, but she understood them just like the fish must understand her thoughts when they nod back at her. Sometimes what is meant doesn't need rules in the sounds. She finally peered around his hip to see what else she could recognize of the person in the bed.

Mama lay pale, pale as the dry white sheets beneath her, gasping as though she had been pulled by a fisherman's line and tossed onto the unfamiliar shore where the air was an assault to a body that needed water. Her mouth gaped and her chest heaved up as tiny wheezes escaped her throat. Daddy must have felt the electricity spark up because his big arm came around behind him to pull her close to his leg.

The same nurse hurried back in and put a shot of something into a joint in the tubes and it flowed into Mama like the June creek. Mama's body relaxed and fell silently into the sheets.

For all the wonder of her marbled eyes, she was betrayed by them for they showed her what she didn't understand. She only knew that what she saw, she didn't want to see. She was running, scrabbling at the door handle and out into the hall before she realized she'd pulled away from Daddy's leg. Her insides were water with nowhere to go. She ran past door numbers that grew smaller and smaller until she spied the big metal belly of a water fountain along a wall. When she pushed the button a useless trickle of water slid from the opening and ran quietly down to the drain where it disappeared without a sound. The electricity flashed through her veins and made her watery insides begin to run again, now toward a red EXIT sign that hung from the ceiling in front of a door with a silver push handle. She poured herself down textured rubber stairs and through another door into the bright sunlight. A sprinkler shot rhythmic sprays of water across the air onto pink and orange flowers that lined the hospital wall, and she paused to listen to the drops land on the flowers' faces.

Water runs whichever way is downhill and joins more of itself until the drops form a rivulet that reaches the stream, reaches the creek, reaches a river, reaches the ocean and it can be all of itself at once. She thought about Mama gasping like a landed fish in a bed where she didn't belong, and suddenly the water inside her bones ran her legs down the street to another street and another and another. Her lungs were made of fire and the light was sliding from the sky when she saw the bent grasses at the end of her driveway. The water inside her bones kept running, past the house she shared with her parents, past the grasses and garden, until it met Seevers Creek and she was buoyed for a moment as air trapped in her clothing kept her on the surface. Then, as the sun pulled its light behind the edge of the planet, she dropped below the surface of the creek and was whole again.

The electricity went quiet and her body was no longer hers but was given over to the current as she dropped from the world of air. The water sewed itself back together above her head and she sank through darker and darker layers into the black quiet. She knew her marbled eyes were open, but there was nothing to see. Or hear. Or feel.

Grounded with her feet buried in the silt, she reached out in hopes of finding fish who could listen. She combed her fingers back and forth, finding the resistance unpleasant for the first time. The water was empty.

She wondered what it would be like to breathe the water, to let it inside her all the way, but she knew her body would never let her breathe like the fish.

Because the sun was gone, she had no way to judge the passing of time and did not know how long she'd been hovering in the silt, rising to break the surface for a breath, and sinking back into the black depths. At some point, a light flashed across the surface and caught her attention. Of course Daddy would be looking for her. But she didn't want anything to do with the air world anymore.

The yellow beam strobed back and forth, slicing the darkness and just barely entering the top layer of water.

She kept her toes buried in the soft silt, and part of her hoped he would just go away so she could live with the fish, but the fish weren't around and her body betrayed her like it always did when the burning in her lungs drove her up to the surface. He heard her breach like a tiny whale, and his long legs took him straight to her without even trying. He pulled her from the water, and she knew what a fish feels as it's reeled from its home in a way that changes everything. She clung to him, gasping in the foreign air, the soaked fabric of her dress pressed against them both, listening to the drips fall into a growing puddle at her daddy's knees on the ground.

Through his soaked plaid shirt his breath was ragged and uneven and more sounds that weren't words escaped him as his arms pulled her tight. Behind the sound of his laboring lungs was a rush through his chest that pumped a rhythm like waves. She listened to the river that pulsed through him in a slowing pace, she listened to the air moving cleanly in and out of his body, she listened to the trickling water that dripped from them both and ran and ran until it rejoined the creek to be carried away with all that was discarded.

# The Dog Days of College

Jacob Wratten

You have been here I can tell.
Your scent lingers in the air
again I have come downstairs
through that door too late.

You walked past the counter
dragged your fingers against the wall,
paused to stare and breathe.
Shifting your weight from one foot to the other
Still in your boots, in your jacket.

I walk on your footprints
I imagine you are still here
trying to see through your eyes.
Trying to reason why those boots stayed tied,
why that jacket stayed on
and not discarded on the back of some chair,
so that I may embrace you
so that we may be together.

You have been here I can tell
again I have come down those too late.
Left to follow your scent to the door
and long for you.

You have been here I can tell.

# Synchronicity

Geoffrey K. Graves

THERE WAS NO QUESTION WHO OWNED THE DANCE FLOOR; Antonio owned the dance floor. The Spaniard strode to its center, radiating the attitude of lead beast in Spain's running of the bulls. "I am now striding to the center of the dance floor!" he announced to one and all. "Notice how I stride, and learn! Boldly! Purposefully! Gracefully!" Antonio always spoke in exclamatory sentences. Every set of eyes, even Phoebe Fenwick's single eye (there had been that unhappy accident with the pool cue in the rec room), was on his lithe athletic figure.

"Would you just look at that man stride?" Phoebe said to her friend, Betty Espinoza. "Have you ever seen a man stride like that?"

"Carlos couldn't stride like that," Betty said, referring to her late husband. "There was no genetic problem. Even before he started using that walker, he just shuffled everywhere. He was a born shuffler. Wore out more shoes."

"Neither could Nigel," Phoebe said about her own dead husband. "Couldn't stride if you paid him. His left leg was two inches shorter than his right."

"That's not true," Betty said.

"It is," Phoebe insisted. "We had to dance in circles. You didn't have to dance with him. I'm telling you, circles."

Breaths rapid, hearts aflutter, the entire room was focused on the striding dance instructor—he of one name—standing tall like Michelangelo's David, bathed in a pool of soft amber light. Deliberately Antonio took his time pivoting on the ball of his right foot, carefully scanning the gathered crowd seated at tables along the margins of the room. All in attendance desperately awaited his patented signal indicating he was ready to choose his partner for the evening's premier dance. Who would be the lucky one? It was an honor all sought but few attained. Face-by-Botoxed-face, he examined the wishful hoofers, hopes high every time his electric blue eyes flicked their way. Had there been a percussionist at hand, they would have been rolling a rat-a-tat-tat anticipatory drum beat on their snare drum till just the right moment, when—cymbal crash!—Antonio would hop onto his toes, a ballet dancer on point. He would hold the pose in a remarkable display of balance and toe strength, eyebrow arched, razor-thin mustache waxed and twisted into wickedly sharp endpoints that defined his full upper lip. Stock still he would stand as onlooker breaths were held in unison while he zeroed in on the person who would be his partner for that first ceremonial dance that kicked off each Friday evening's festivities.

FOR WHATEVER REASON, THIS two-person first dance ritual had become the tradition of the weekly Donuts 'n' Dancin' Soiree at the Heavenly Hills senior community's culture center. To be selected by the professional dance instructor/choreographer/writer/actor/director/producer/singer reputedly famous for his way-off Broadway turn in his own musical, *Rowboats o'er the Mighty Mississippi* ("You'll wish you'd stayed home and done laundry. Don't go!" —Harold Pullman, *Showbiz Review*), was an honor desired by every ballroom dancer in attendance. Many would have given their left something-or-other if only Antonio chose them to join the very select group who could brag that they had been granted the honor of the first dance. And if afterward he agreed to a late evening drink at their personal residence in Heavenly Hills, well, that would be a heavenly bonus, for Antonio's rumored lovemaking exploits were the thing of legend around the community. Fearing legal issues, the homeowners' association board had tried to get rid of him several times, but he was the only dance instructor they could find who would work solely for tips. Plus, secret pressures by two dance enthusiasts who sat on the board and who were the only dancers in all Heavenly Hills to have been selected by Antonio multiple times for the coveted first dance, put a stop to those removal efforts. Beyond that, Antonio possessed a fearsome temper that erupted whenever things did not go his way, so the situation stood at a stalemate.

In his early fifties, Antonio was the youngest person in the room though a tad too young to permanently reside in Heavenly Hills, which was probably a good thing. You could attribute his popularity to his relative youth as well as handsome good looks and amazing dance floor moves not to mention his reputed romantic prowess. Many Saturday mornings Carlton Chesterfield, USMC, Ret., standing sentry at the gated community's entrance, found himself waving a wistful farewell to the lothario as Antonio sped out the exit in his half-restored 1970 green AMC Gremlin, neck scarf flapping out the window. Nobody got action in Heavenly Hills like Antonio, Carlton thought to himself. It wasn't fair.

"Have you ever seen anyone dance like Antonio can dance?" Phoebe asked of Betty. Phoebe was attired in a Calvin Klein Illusion-Trim Fit & Flare dancing dress she'd purchased at Macy's online store that thank goodness arrived just in time for the evening's soiree. Phoebe was hoping her new subtly sexy dress would be the added touch she'd need to catch Antonio's eye for that first special dance. He'd never selected her before, but she had a feeling this was her night. The FedExed dress came so late she barely had time to fashion a new eye patch that matched the dress's baby blue color. Her many patches had become fashion statements for which she'd achieved a level of respect among dance regulars, who gave her props for making the best of a bad situation. Betty wore a simple black cocktail dress.

"Indeed, I have seen people dance better than Antonio, Phoebe," answered Betty, who had recently moved into the community and was still coming to terms with the whole retirement thing, loath to think herself a senior citizen. "It was just last night on the TV dancing show. Now, those people can dance! Excepting Antonio, what you've got here in this geriatric crowd is a lot of floundering and stumbling. The hip and knee replacement doctors around here must be making serious bank off this crowd."

"That may be true, but I wouldn't miss these Friday nights for the world," Phoebe said. "If I wind up getting a hip or knee replaced, it will be worth it if I get a shot at Antonio. On the dance floor, I mean." She smiled. "It certainly beats staying home watching *Golden Girls* reruns or *Wheel* or *Jeopardy*. I'd much rather be here, feasting my eye on Antonio. He's better than any TV show."

"Oh, no," Betty groaned.

"What?"

"Here comes your D'Artagnan."

Phoebe's eye widened. "Doesn't have his pool cue, does he?"

"No. You're safe."

Before them stood a man attired in a pink tuxedo with matching baseball hat, the words "Pink Thunder" emblazoned in sparkly sequins on the front. The hat covered most of his bald spot and was inspired by his two-toned white and bubblegum pink 1957 Nash Metropolitan convertible. No one ever went on a second date after riding in the tiny car. The problem wasn't "that clown car," as every date had referred to it, it was "the clown driver" who was a never-ending fount of nutty stories full of self-aggrandizement. Worse was his dancing, for he was not just a flounderer and stumbler, his reputation as a dance floor klutz was beyond notorious. Many a previous partner's foot wound up in a bucket of ice before the evening was half done. Management made it policy to keep a standby ice bucket at the ready whenever he showed up.

"Beg pardon, dearies," interrupted the amply girthed and pinkly attired man. "Might I entice one or both of you lovies for a go 'round on the floor later this glorious evening?" he suavely purred.

"Not in five lifetimes," replied Phoebe.

He clapped his hands. "Maybe the sixth, then! You know me! Always positive! Persistence is my middle name!"

"It will never, ever, ever, happen."

"Sounds like a maybe to me! Not still holding a grudge, are we, Phoebe?"

"Ever."

"Hear me out," he forged on. "You may have noticed I haven't been around for a few months."

"No, but thank you for that," Phoebe said.

"We didn't miss you," Betty chimed.

"Dying to know where I've been, right?" The women were silent. "Knew it! I've been taking an intense series of dance lessons on the side. Shown great improvement according to my new teacher, who is not Mr. Antonio, you might be curious to know why."

"We're not and we don't believe you," said Betty, who'd opened her compact ostensibly to powder her nose but really to check out Antonio, who was behind her and had eased down from his position but quickly got back up on tiptoe when he caught her looking. He was still scanning the crowd.

"He has such nice buns," Betty side-mouthed to Phoebe.

"Why, thank you!" the pink guy said. "That's the nicest thing anybody's ever—"

"Not you, Double Bubble. Antonio."

"Oh."

The pink interrupter realized what she was doing with the compact and nodded in Antonio's direction. "What a showoff, huh? That tiptoe routine of his. Big deal."

"Let's see you do it," Phoebe challenged.

"Could if I wanted to. Don't feel like it. Haven't done my stretches. About those dances, I'll swing by later. All good?"

"All bad. Go away!" said Betty, snapping her compact shut. "I like my feet just the way they are, unmangled by those clodhoppers of yours."

"Nevertheless, I'll circle around in a while, just in case!"

"Wasting your time!" Phoebe called after him.

THEIR REFUSALS WERE UNDERSTANDABLE, for it was indeed he who had clumsily wielded the wicked pool cue responsible for Phoebe's unfortunate ocular accident. At the hospital after her surgery, he tried to cheer her up by enumerating a list of benefits he'd concocted that she could henceforth enjoy. "Look at the bright side," he said.

"Which side would that be?" Phoebe asked. "Because I've only got the left side, now. Hope the bright side's not the right side."

"Think about this: If you ever contract pink eye," he consulted his notes, "you'll only get it in the one eye. That's fifty percent better than most people would have to endure! Or, say you require vision correction, you'll only need to purchase a monocle! Start a fashion trend!"

"Fashion trend? Monocle on the left, eye patch on the right? Why, what's that sound?" she said, cupping her hand to her ear. "Do you hear it?"

"Hear what?" he said, cocking his head to listen.

"There! There it is! It's the Parisian runways, and they're calling me. It's the year of the eye patch in the fashion world. Calling all pirates!"

"Now you're getting the picture!" he said, referring back to his list. "And since you don't need a set of glasses, you could probably demand a discount from your optometrist in the neighborhood of fifty percent. I wouldn't settle for less if it were me. Plus, when you go to renew your license, you'll whip through that eye chart in half the time. The people behind you will thank you!"

After that one, the nurse turned to him and said, "If you don't leave this hospital right now, you're going to need your own room."

"HE'S TAKING FOREVER TO make up his mind," Betty said, jerking her thumb over her shoulder at Antonio.

"Antonio Anshmonio," the pink guy who hadn't left spat out the name. "That's all anybody around here ever talks about. You're both practically drooling. There are other fish in the tree, you know!"

"Sea," Betty said.

"Si," he responded, completely misunderstanding the Hispanic lady. "I tell you both, I've just about had it with Mr. Antonio Antonio or whatever his last name is. What is his last name? Who cares? Him and his skintight bun-hugging black unitard. He prances in like a panther in that getup with that schnookie mustache. What a peacock."

"I thought you said he was a panther. Now he's mutated into a peacock?" Betty asked.

"If he's a peacock, you're a big pink flamingo," Betty added.

"That hurt." He frowned, hand over heart.

"Good," Phoebe said.

"You know what?" he said. "I'm going to start an anti-Antonio movement. You both ought to be with me on this. He's never asked either of you to dance the first dance. I say it's time somebody else got a little attention around here, and I'm gonna do something about it. Right now! Watch me!"

He stuck his nose in the air, which was not any kind of statement, it was just the way he always walked, and headed for the center of the room to get in Antonio's face. Antonio was teasing the crowd, at one moment down on his feet, then up on point, then down again. The pink man a foot shorter, he found himself looking up the dance instructor's nostrils.

"And just what do you want, little man?" Antonio peered down at him, a biologist examining protozoa under a microscope.

"Now hear this, An-fonio!" he bellowed loudly so the entire room could hear. "Good one, huh everybody?" Silence. "I, uh, I challenge you to a dance-off!"

The entire room gasped, shocked at the temerity of the pink man. How dare he confront their hero, everyone's fantasy lover, and some not even fantasy. Before Antonio's renowned temper could show itself, the dance crowd began booing so loudly the challenger slunk off to a corner, on his way grabbing a pink, of course, glazed donut from the buffet table. Things settled down and all attention returned to the magnificent Antonio, who had a strange look on his face as he bounced up, again assuming the point position.

"Hey, Phoebe, take a look at Antonio." Betty had turned her chair toward the floor.

"Yeah, what's with him?" Phoebe asked. "That's a weird expression on his face. Like he's really mad about something, ready to blow."

It was true. Antonio's eyes were lit like the blazing fire under one of those large paella pans at the buffet table. Everyone noticed it and figured his temper had been ignited by the pink man, which it had. A slow burn had become a raging inferno with his jaw line twitching uncontrollably on both sides as he screamed, "I pick you!" All 191 eyes of the group turned to see at whom the dramatic dancer was pointing. Murmurings began immediately. Did he really mean it? Was this a joke?

STUFFING THE LAST BITE of pink glazed cake donut into his mouth, the bulldog-jowled and turkey-wattled pink fellow in the corner looked up to see Antonio's long finger aimed directly at his chest. The effect on him was palpable, like a cannon ball shot from a galleon in the Spanish Armada headed straight for his heart. Ouch, he thought. His mouth dropped agape, chunks of donut tumbling down the pink tuxedo jacket to the floor. This he did not expect. He turned to see if the finger was meant for someone behind him, but no one was there, just the wall he'd been leaning against. So, he was the chosen one for the sacred first dance of the evening. Well, he was not surprised given the lack of competition in the room as well as the obvious stares of approval his new stunning ballroom outfit had drawn. Oh, yes, he'd seen all those looks of jealous admiration.

To say others were disappointed would have been like the time Sir Cosmo Duff Gordon, who survived the sinking of the *Titanic*, had said, "It was rather a serious evening, you know."

"Well, it's not us again," Phoebe said to Betty, dropping her face into her hands, elbows propped on table.

"Yeah. But on the plus side it sure looks like someone's going to be taught a lesson," Betty said. "This could be good. I think Pink Zorro, there, just stepped in it."

"Hm. You might be right," Phoebe said, nodding with a grin. She was going to enjoy this.

The pink man looked at everyone glaring at him, threw his nose up, and took his time attempting to approximate the stride Antonio had earlier demonstrated. As he got closer, he noticed the dance instructor was wearing a worrisome expression. His teeth were gritted, nostrils flared, brow knitted into a tense set of tight lines. The chosen one started to panic as Antonio grabbed his hands and violently pulled him belly to belly. "Oof," the pink guy said.

Antonio, as always, assumed the Lead role, and the pink guy would be the Follow for this dance. Antonio yelled out "Foxtrot!" and snapped his head at the DJ, but before a note was heard the big pink fellow tripped on his own feet, face-planting to the floor. Antonio stared in disgust at the supine figure at his feet. He bent over with hands on hips and said, "Ha! Ha! Ha!" the crowd joining in with laughter.

As the hilarity subsided, the big guy surprised everyone by jumping up and dusting himself off. He grabbed Antonio, pulling him hard and close as he assumed the Lead, shocking Antonio, who had never been the Follow in his entire life. Next, in a blur, off the two sped, fox-trotting around the floor to Lady Antebellum's "Just a Kiss," a perfect tune for a foxtrot.

Everyone knew of Antonio's famous temper, and no one ever crossed him, so while at first it seemed his intention was to make a fool of the troublemaker, something unbelievable was happening that surprised not only onlookers but Antonio himself. No one had ever seen such precision, such well-timed movement on the Heavenly Hills culture center dance floor. The pink man started with his left foot, taking the dance's first two walking steps straight ahead with confidence, pulling Antonio around like a rag doll behind. Side-step left, went the pink man, drawing his right foot across with a pop of the heels to close against the left. Antonio looked confused as slow-slow, quick-quick together they went, fox-trotting across the room, but after a while he seemed to relax into his new role, mirroring his Lead partner's movements with the two steps backward, side-step right, then drawing his left foot across with a heel pop and closing. Slow-slow, quick-quick, slow-slow, quick-quick they glided like birds in flight, winging together from one end to the other.

The room stood stunned. To some, the dancers seemed to be floating in an enchanted fairytale-like dream, inches off the ground, their perfectly harmonized movements matching the song's 4/4 tempo. To others, it was a nightmare. How did such a thing happen?

"Tomorrow I'm sending this dress back to Macy's," Phoebe said.

"I need a drink," Betty said.

Then, remarkably, the pink guy pushed Antonio away and lightly skipped over to Phoebe and Betty's table. He held out his hand to Phoebe, then at second thought offered it to Betty.

"Oh, why not," said Betty.

"Betty!" Phoebe said.

"It's better than just sitting here, Phoebe. I mean, it is a dance."

"I'll tell them to get the ice buckets ready," Phoebe said, irked by her friend's betrayal. Everything changed again when, in the blink of her eye, Antonio bowed before Phoebe, proffering his hand. Without hesitation she stood, and he called out "Jitterbug! Saints!" Before you could say Fred Astaire and Ginger Rogers, both couples were jitterbugging to the New Orleans Jazz Band's version of "When the Saints Go Marching In." It was a battle to the finish between the two couples. The energy in the room was electric, as first one couple would do something that engendered applause, then the other would top it as back and forth they went. There were magical moments in the dance when both couples appeared to be mirroring each other in synchronicity, as though their movements had been choreographed. It was a wonder to behold till the dance finally concluded. The crowd went crazy, gleefully shouting and clapping with admiration for both couples, who were at first puzzled then gratified they had been part of such a moment. Nothing had ever been seen or heard like it in the dancing history of Heavenly Hills. Phoebe was elated she'd finally got her dance with Antonio, and Antonio had a look of pure adoration for his newest dance partner, who had completely impressed him. Betty was even rethinking her attitude toward the pink guy, who had treated her as respectfully and kindly as anyone could have wanted, and for once he was right—he really had become a heck of a good dancer. In short, sparks were flying.

The following morning, Carlton Chesterfield was once again at his assigned post at the guard gate. For the first time ever, Antonio was exiting the community in his half-restored AMC Gremlin with a lady beside him and a second couple in the backseat, all headed out to brunch that would be followed by a nice walk through the park and after that, who knew?

"Strange day," Carlton said to himself. "Strange day, indeed."